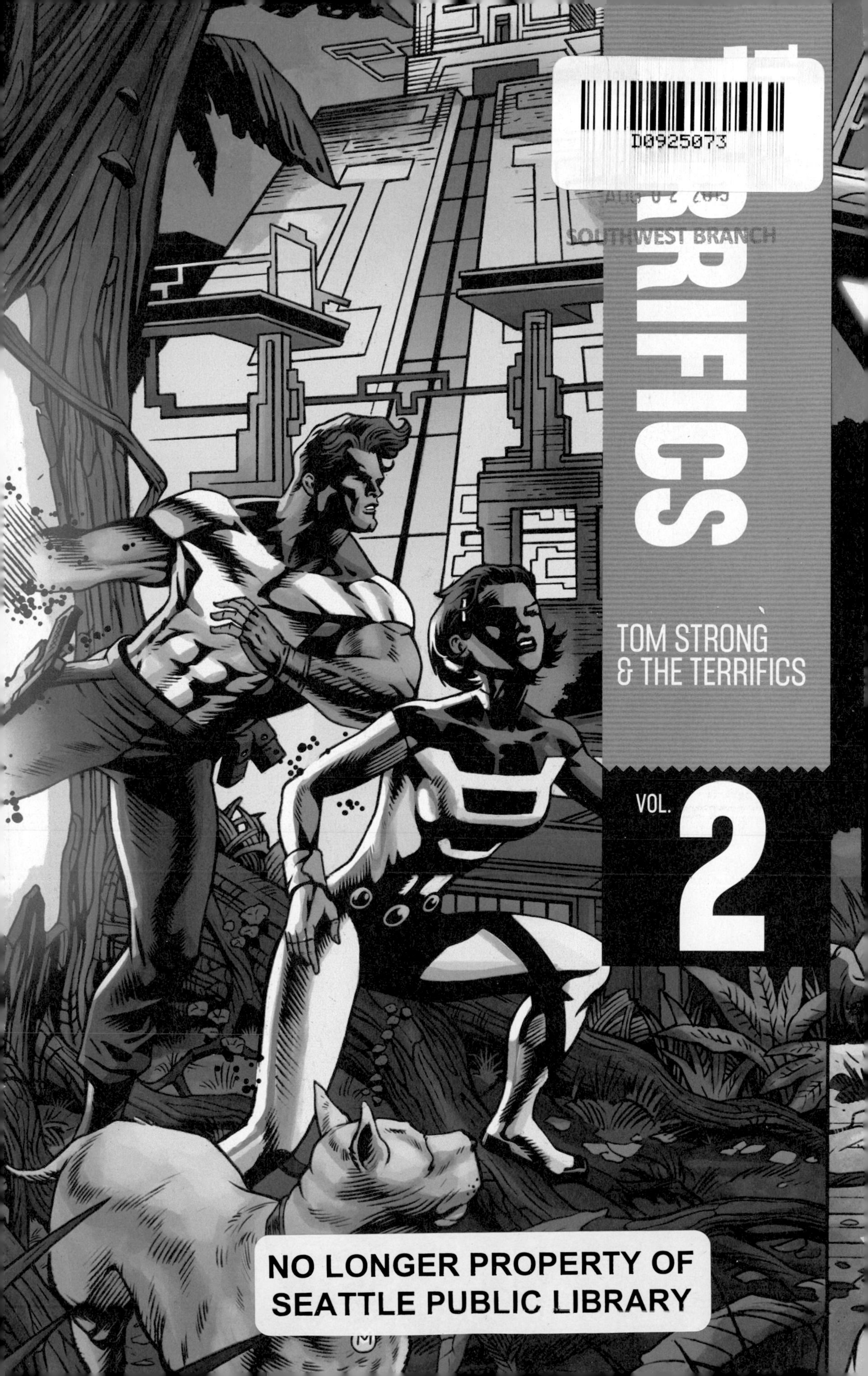
TOM STRONG
& THE TERRIFICS
VOL. 2

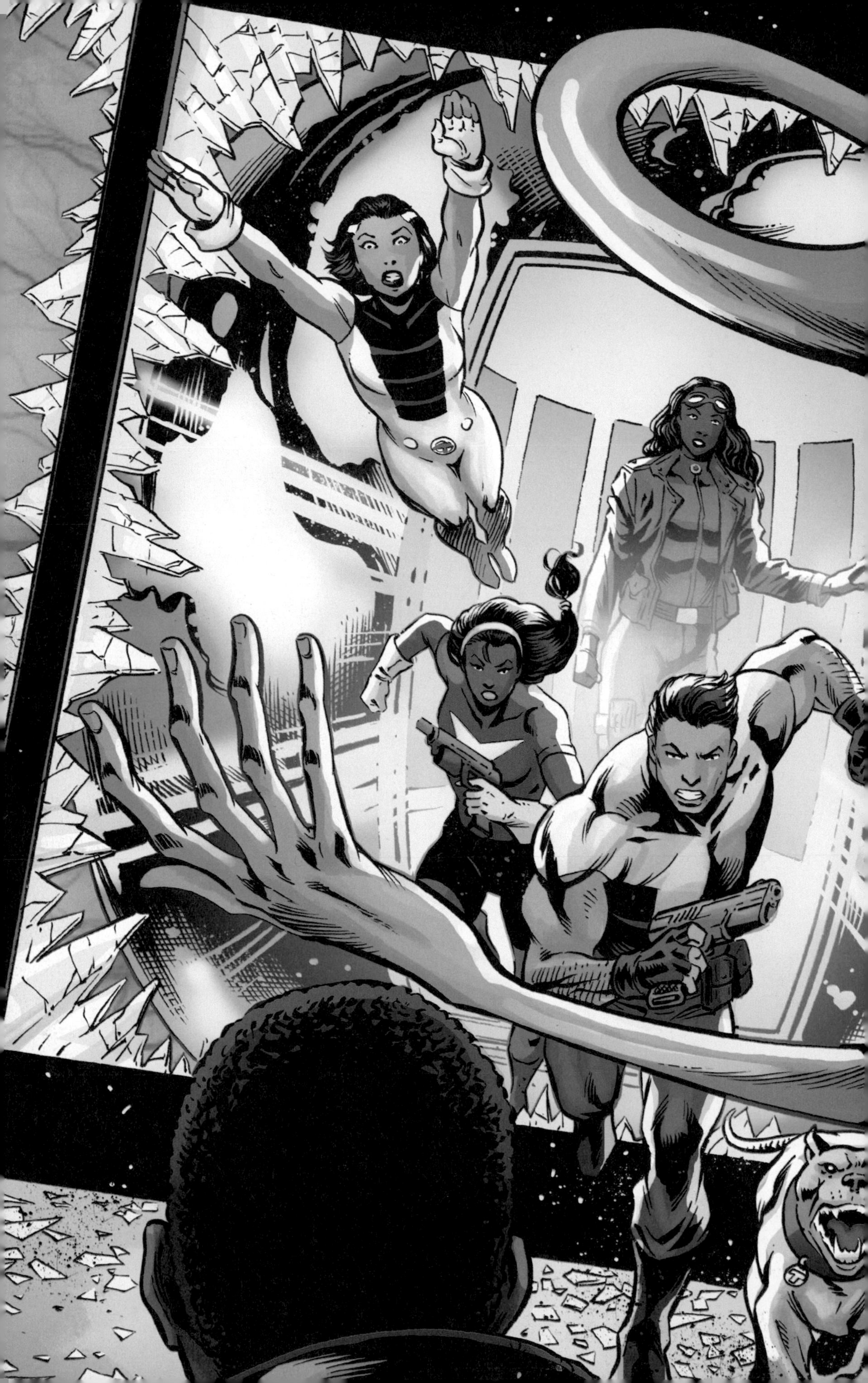

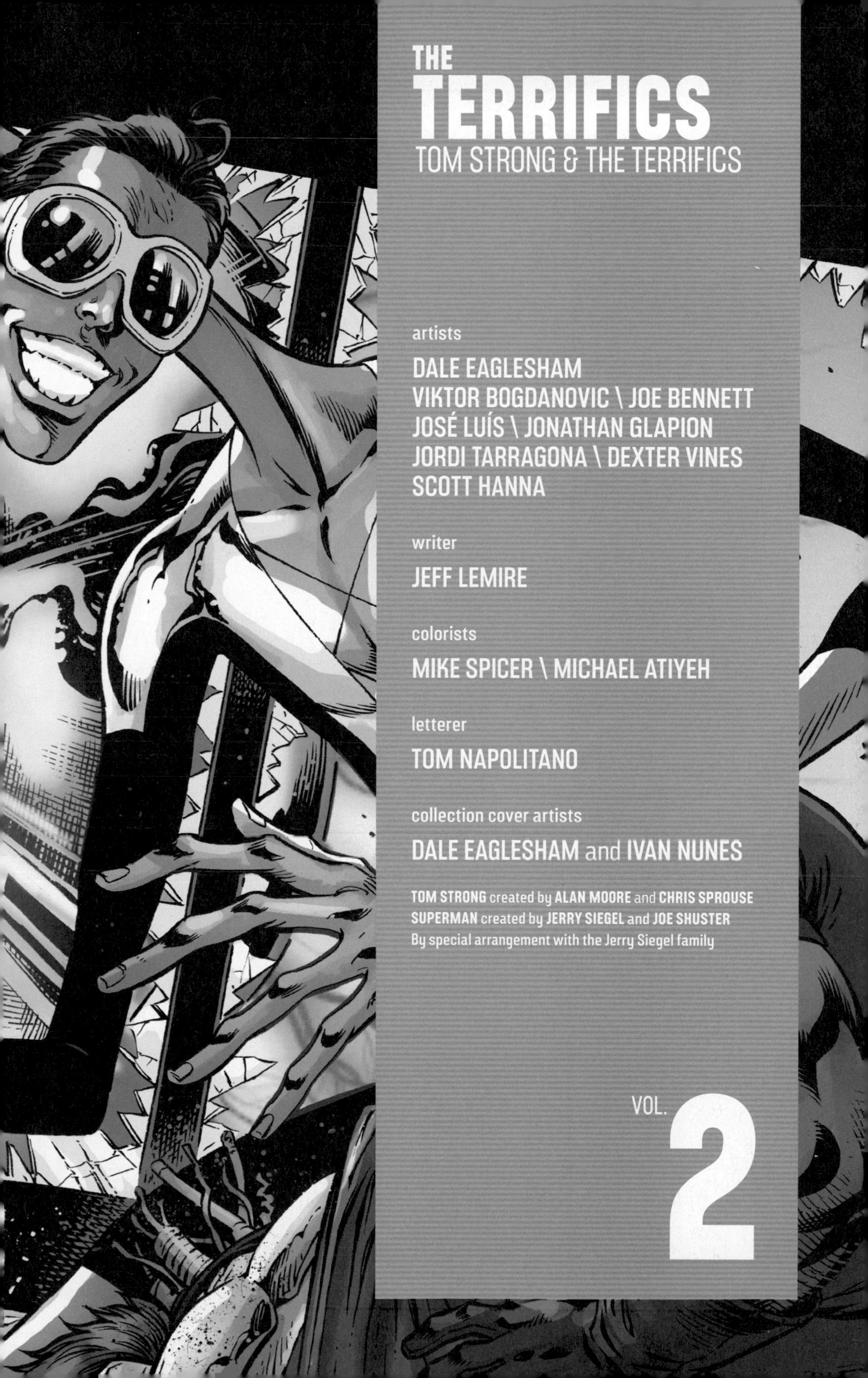

THE TERRIFICS

TOM STRONG & THE TERRIFICS

artists

DALE EAGLESHAM
VIKTOR BOGDANOVIC \ JOE BENNETT
JOSÉ LUÍS \ JONATHAN GLAPION
JORDI TARRAGONA \ DEXTER VINES
SCOTT HANNA

writer

JEFF LEMIRE

colorists

MIKE SPICER \ MICHAEL ATIYEH

letterer

TOM NAPOLITANO

collection cover artists

DALE EAGLESHAM and **IVAN NUNES**

TOM STRONG created by **ALAN MOORE** and **CHRIS SPROUSE**
SUPERMAN created by **JERRY SIEGEL** and **JOE SHUSTER**
By special arrangement with the Jerry Siegel family

VOL. **2**

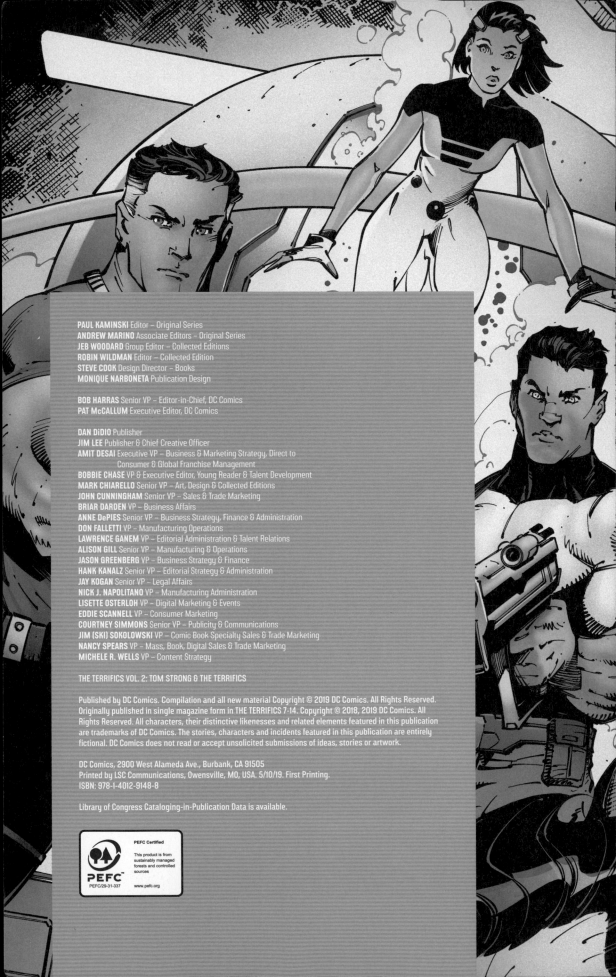

PAUL KAMINSKI Editor – Original Series
ANDREW MARINO Associate Editors – Original Series
JEB WOODARD Group Editor – Collected Editions
ROBIN WILDMAN Editor – Collected Edition
STEVE COOK Design Director – Books
MONIQUE NARBONETA Publication Design

BOB HARRAS Senior VP – Editor-in-Chief, DC Comics
PAT McCALLUM Executive Editor, DC Comics

DAN DiDIO Publisher
JIM LEE Publisher & Chief Creative Officer
AMIT DESAI Executive VP – Business & Marketing Strategy, Direct to Consumer & Global Franchise Management
BOBBIE CHASE VP & Executive Editor, Young Reader & Talent Development
MARK CHIARELLO Senior VP – Art, Design & Collected Editions
JOHN CUNNINGHAM Senior VP – Sales & Trade Marketing
BRIAR DARDEN VP – Business Affairs
ANNE DePIES Senior VP – Business Strategy, Finance & Administration
DON FALLETTI VP – Manufacturing Operations
LAWRENCE GANEM VP – Editorial Administration & Talent Relations
ALISON GILL Senior VP – Manufacturing & Operations
JASON GREENBERG VP – Business Strategy & Finance
HANK KANALZ Senior VP – Editorial Strategy & Administration
JAY KOGAN Senior VP – Legal Affairs
NICK J. NAPOLITANO VP – Manufacturing Administration
LISETTE OSTERLOH VP – Digital Marketing & Events
EDDIE SCANNELL VP – Consumer Marketing
COURTNEY SIMMONS Senior VP – Publicity & Communications
JIM (SKI) SOKOLOWSKI VP – Comic Book Specialty Sales & Trade Marketing
NANCY SPEARS VP – Mass, Book, Digital Sales & Trade Marketing
MICHELE R. WELLS VP – Content Strategy

THE TERRIFICS VOL. 2: TOM STRONG & THE TERRIFICS

DC Comics, 2900 West Alameda Ave., Burbank, CA 91505
Printed by LSC Communications, Owensville, MO, USA. 5/10/19. First Printing.
ISBN: 978-1-4012-9148-8

Library of Congress Cataloging-in-Publication Data is available.

PEFC Certified
This product is from sustainably managed forests and controlled sources
PEFC
PEFC/29-31-337
www.pefc.org

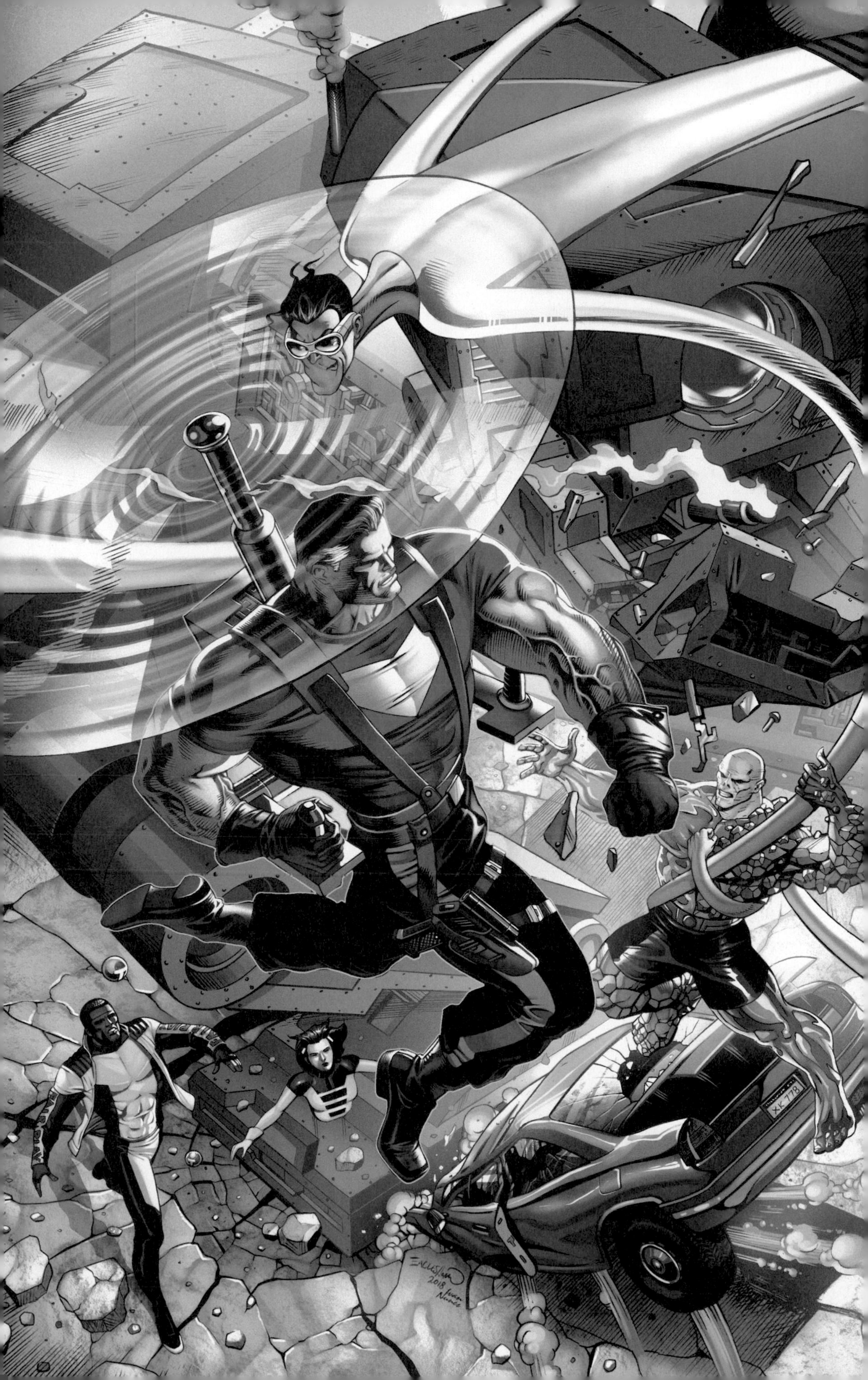
XK 778

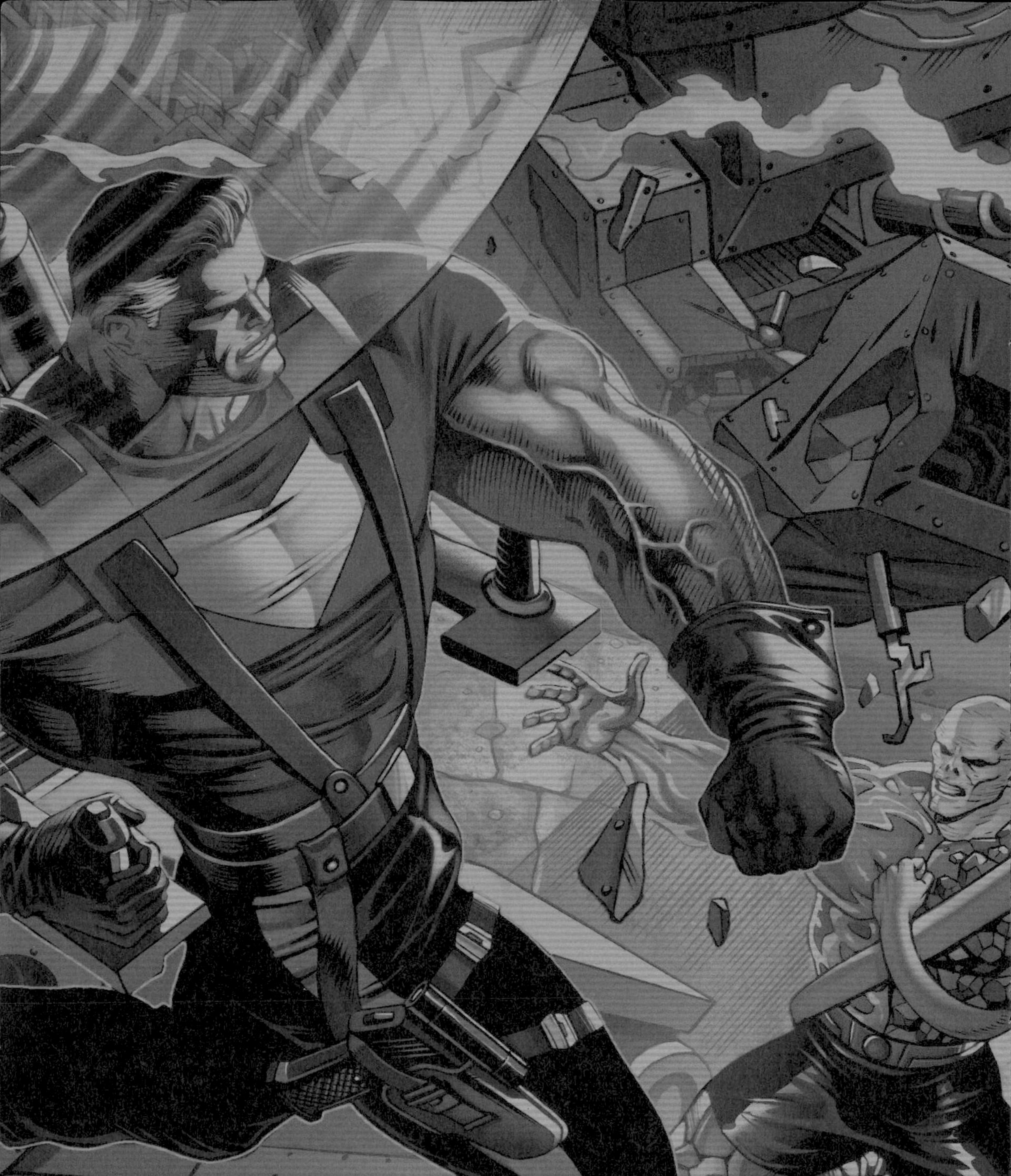

THE
TERRIFICS
#7

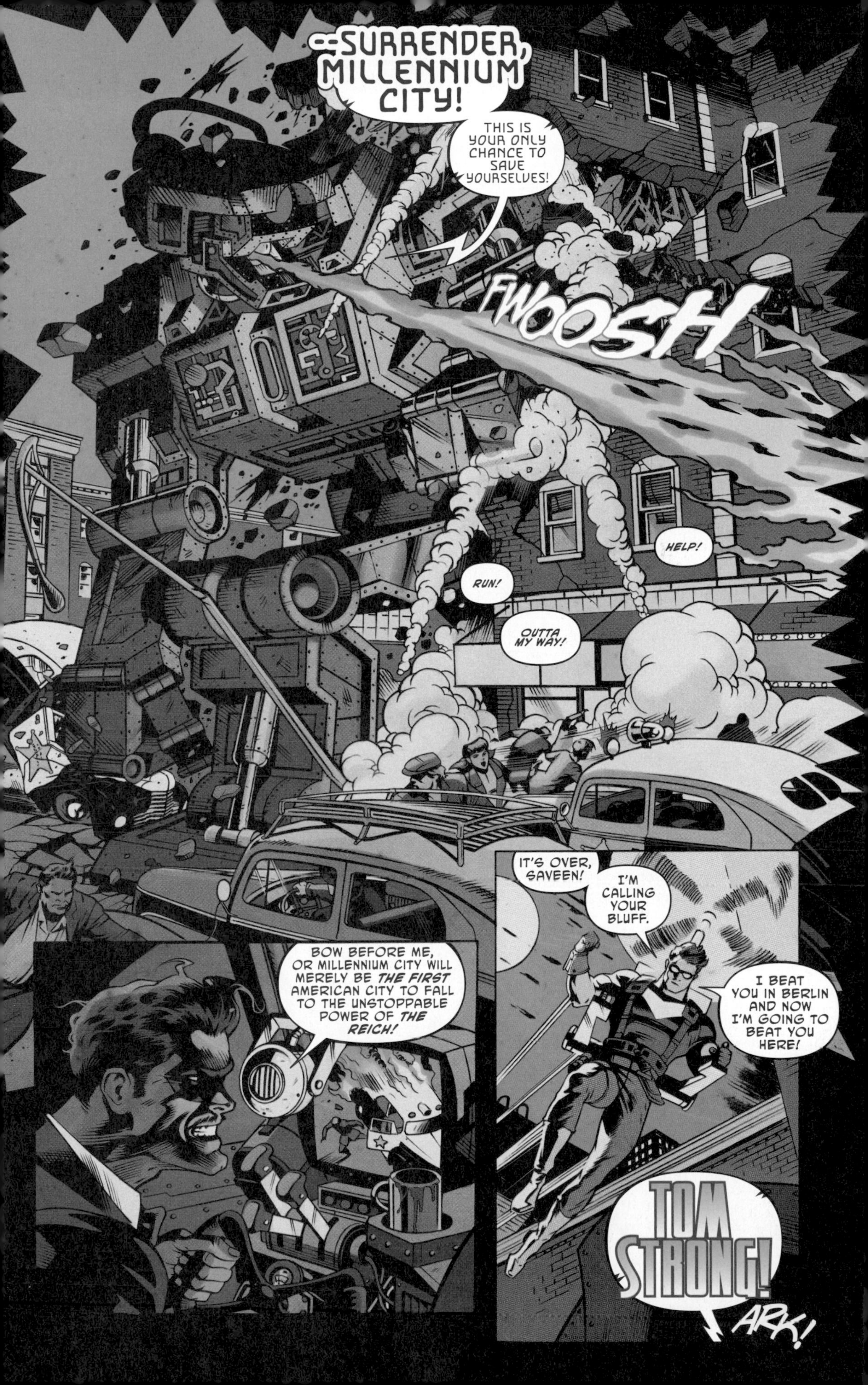

-SURRENDER, MILLENNIUM CITY!
THIS IS YOUR ONLY CHANCE TO SAVE YOURSELVES!
FWOOSH
HELP!
RUN!
OUTTA MY WAY!
BOW BEFORE ME, OR MILLENNIUM CITY WILL MERELY BE THE FIRST AMERICAN CITY TO FALL TO THE UNSTOPPABLE POWER OF THE REICH!
IT'S OVER, SAVEEN!
I'M CALLING YOUR BLUFF.
I BEAT YOU IN BERLIN AND NOW I'M GOING TO BEAT YOU HERE!
TOM STRONG!
ARK!

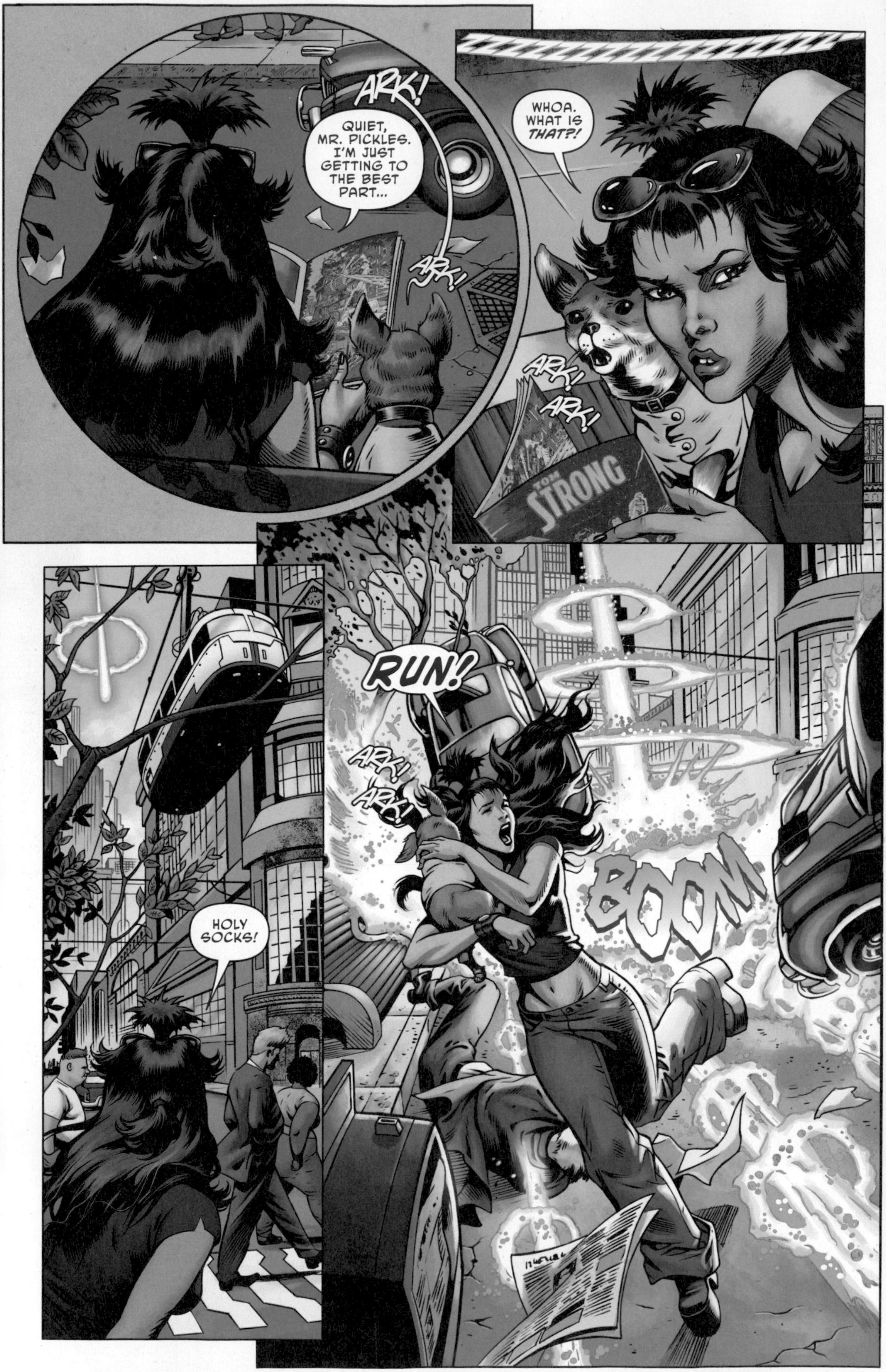
ARK!
QUIET, MR. PICKLES. I'M JUST GETTING TO THE BEST PART...
ARK!
ZZZZZZZZZZZZZZZZZZZZZ
WHOA. WHAT IS THAT?!
ARK!
ARK!
TOM STRONG
HOLY SOCKS!
RUN!
ARK!
ARK!
BOOM

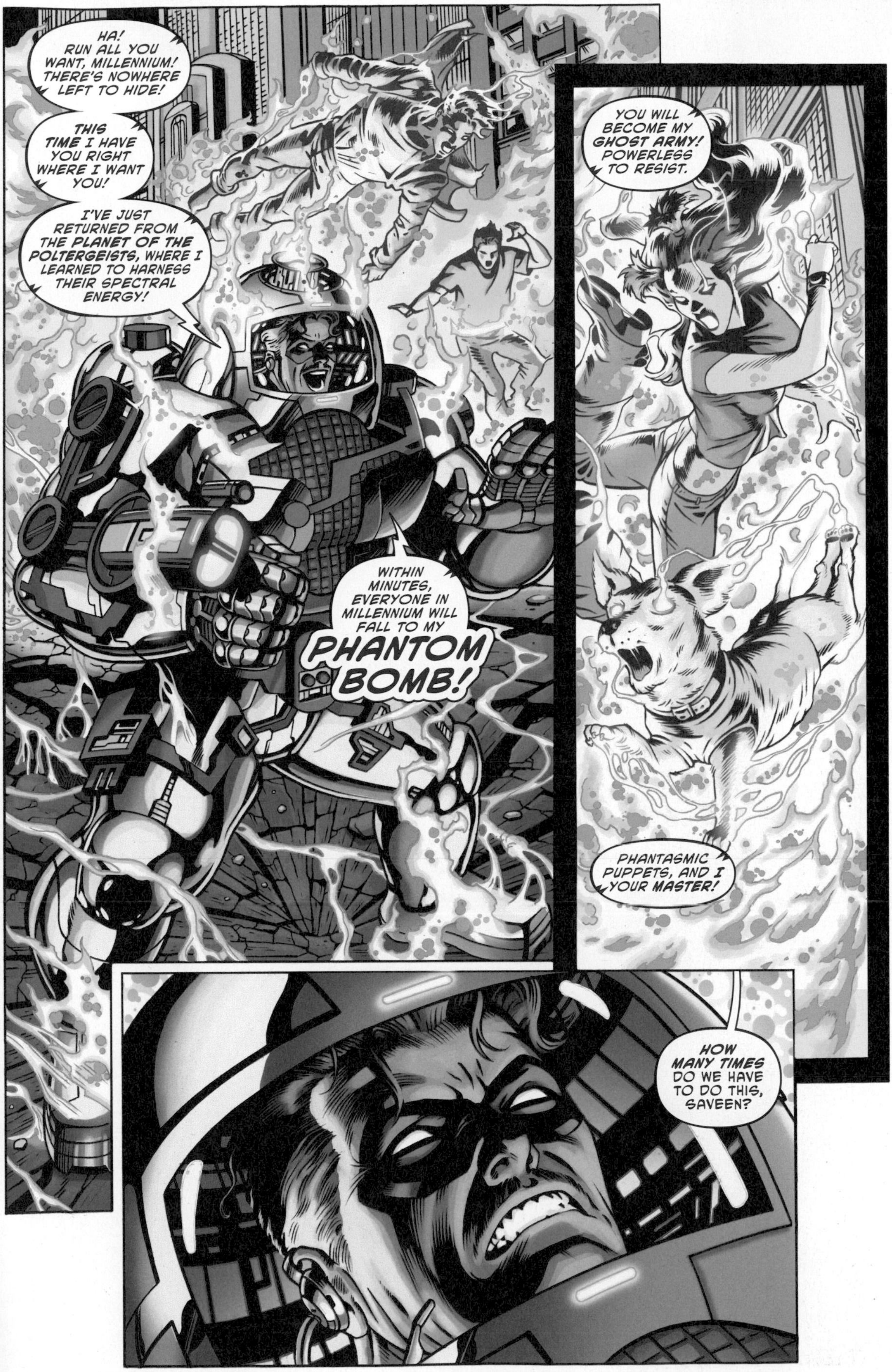
HA! RUN ALL YOU WANT, MILLENNIUM! THERE'S NOWHERE LEFT TO HIDE!
THIS TIME I HAVE YOU RIGHT WHERE I WANT YOU!
I'VE JUST RETURNED FROM THE PLANET OF THE POLTERGEISTS, WHERE I LEARNED TO HARNESS THEIR SPECTRAL ENERGY!
WITHIN MINUTES, EVERYONE IN MILLENNIUM WILL FALL TO MY PHANTOM BOMB!
YOU WILL BECOME MY GHOST ARMY! POWERLESS TO RESIST.
PHANTASMIC PUPPETS, AND I YOUR MASTER!
HOW MANY TIMES DO WE HAVE TO DO THIS, SAVEEN?

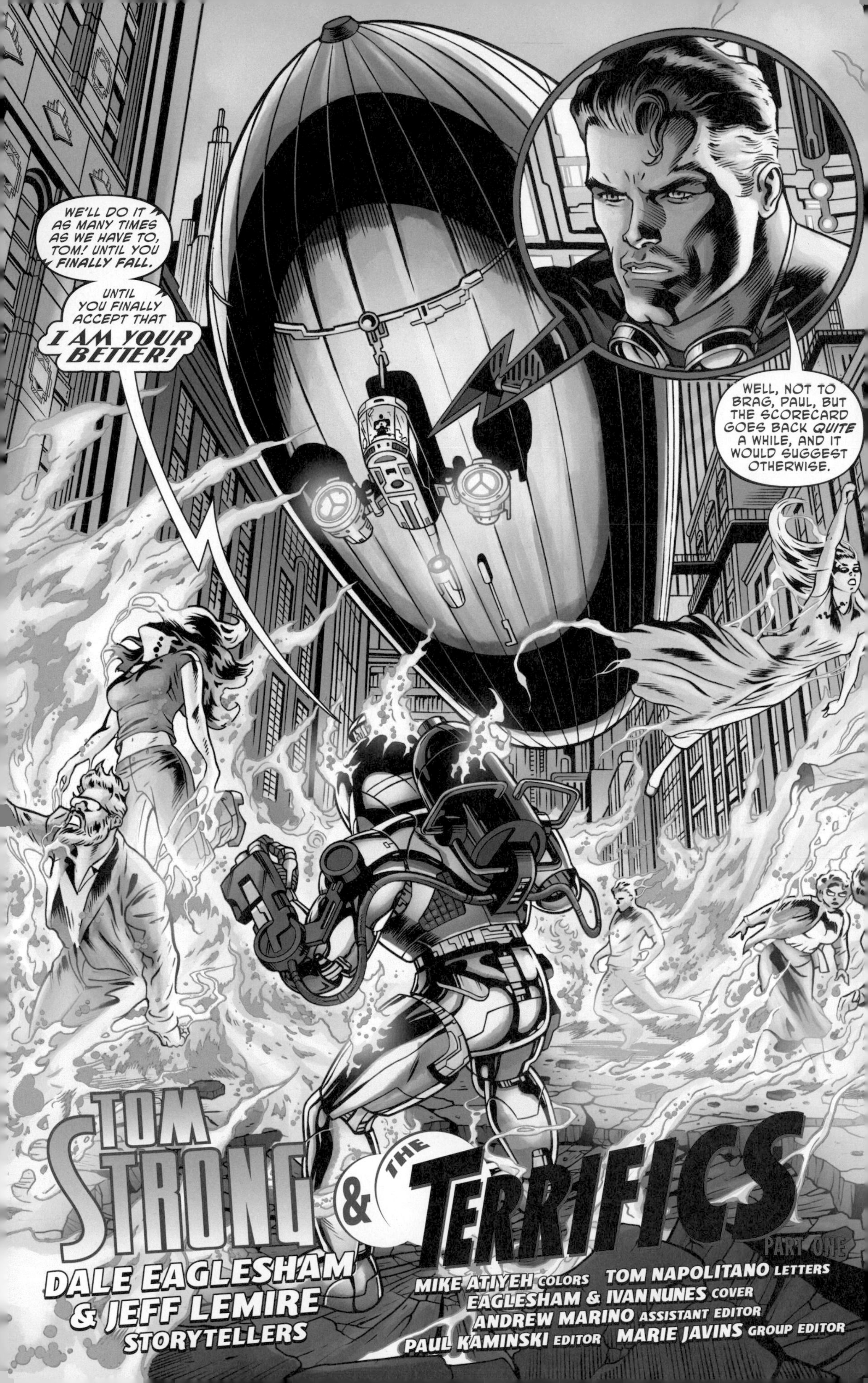
WE'LL DO IT AS MANY TIMES AS WE HAVE TO, TOM! UNTIL YOU FINALLY FALL.
UNTIL YOU FINALLY ACCEPT THAT I AM YOUR BETTER!
WELL, NOT TO BRAG, PAUL, BUT THE SCORECARD GOES BACK QUITE A WHILE, AND IT WOULD SUGGEST OTHERWISE.
TOM STRONG & THE TERRIFICS
PART ONE
DALE EAGLESHAM & JEFF LEMIRE STORYTELLERS
MIKE ATIYEH COLORS TOM NAPOLITANO LETTERS
EAGLESHAM & IVAN NUNES COVER
ANDREW MARINO ASSISTANT EDITOR
PAUL KAMINSKI EDITOR MARIE JAVINS GROUP EDITOR

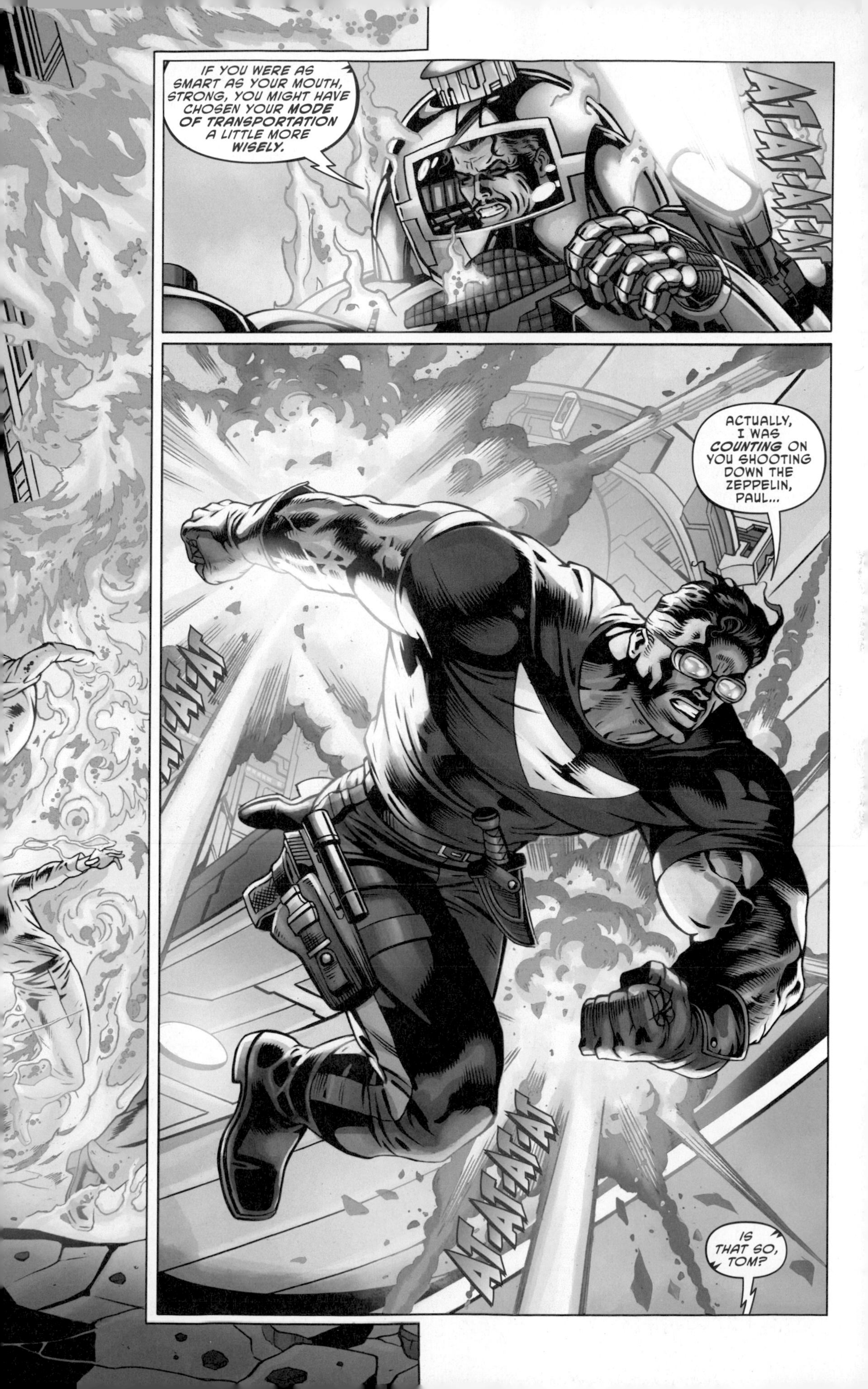
IF YOU WERE AS SMART AS YOUR MOUTH, STRONG, YOU MIGHT HAVE CHOSEN YOUR MODE OF TRANSPORTATION A LITTLE MORE WISELY.
AT-AT-AT-AT-AT
ACTUALLY, I WAS COUNTING ON YOU SHOOTING DOWN THE ZEPPELIN, PAUL...
AT-AT-AT
AT-AT-AT-AT
IS THAT SO, TOM?

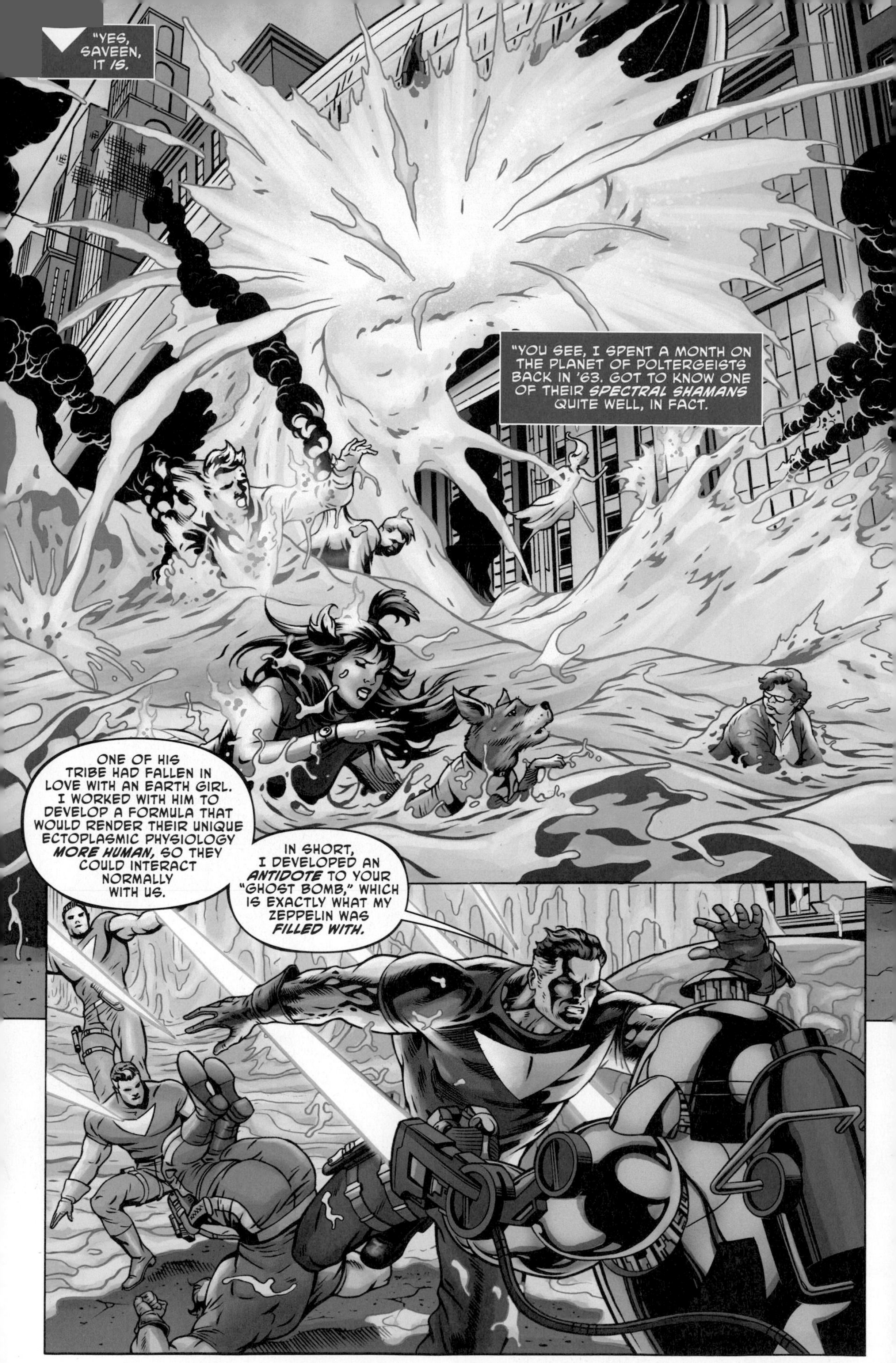
"YES, SAVEEN, IT *IS*.
"YOU SEE, I SPENT A MONTH ON THE PLANET OF POLTERGEISTS BACK IN '63. GOT TO KNOW ONE OF THEIR *SPECTRAL SHAMANS* QUITE WELL, IN FACT.
ONE OF HIS TRIBE HAD FALLEN IN LOVE WITH AN EARTH GIRL. I WORKED WITH HIM TO DEVELOP A FORMULA THAT WOULD RENDER THEIR UNIQUE ECTOPLASMIC PHYSIOLOGY *MORE HUMAN,* SO THEY COULD INTERACT NORMALLY WITH US.
IN SHORT, I DEVELOPED AN *ANTIDOTE* TO YOUR "GHOST BOMB," WHICH IS EXACTLY WHAT MY ZEPPELIN WAS *FILLED WITH.*

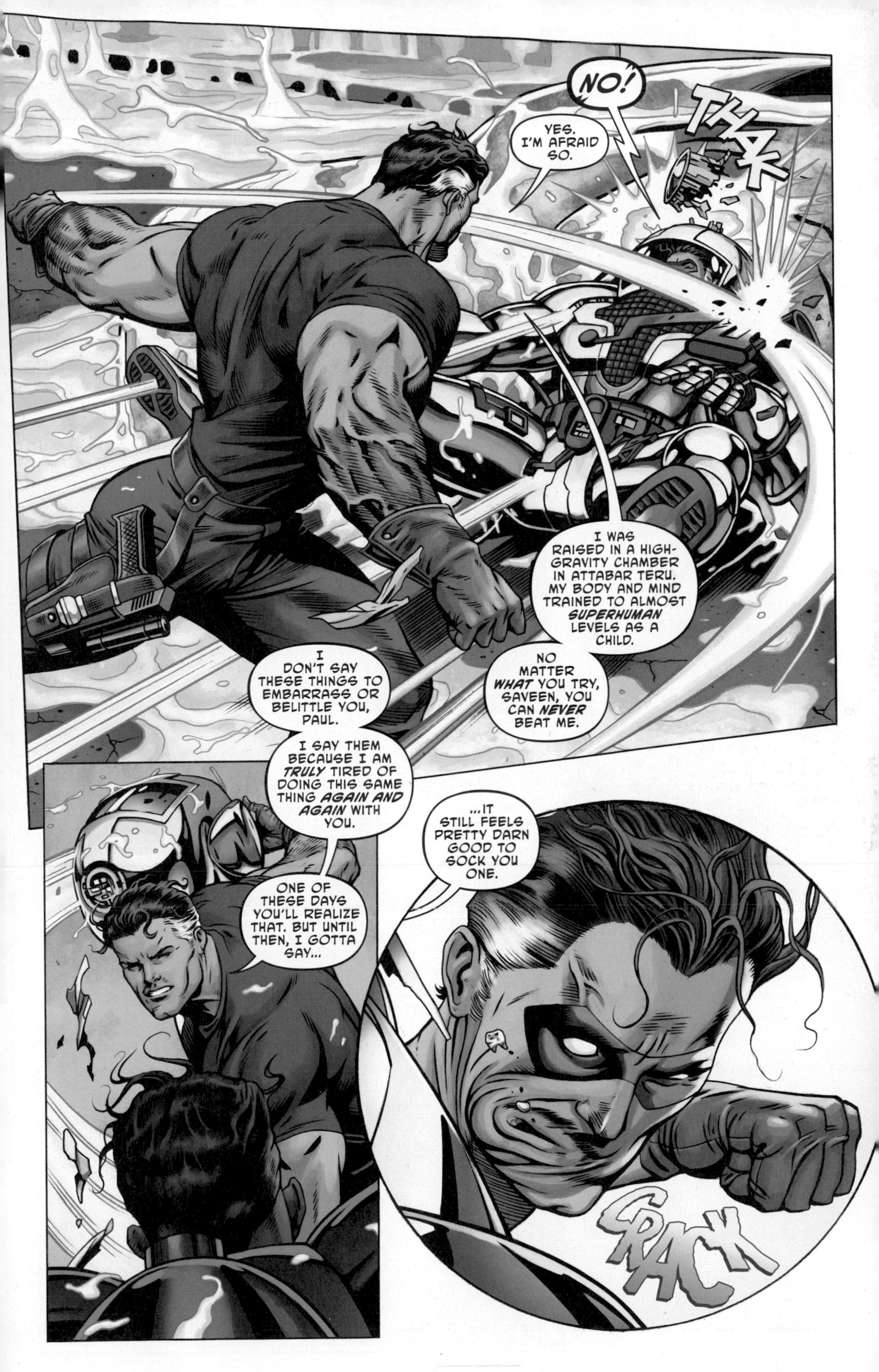
NO!
YES. I'M AFRAID SO.
THK
I WAS RAISED IN A HIGH-GRAVITY CHAMBER IN ATTABAR TERU. MY BODY AND MIND TRAINED TO ALMOST SUPERHUMAN LEVELS AS A CHILD.
NO MATTER WHAT YOU TRY, SAVEEN, YOU CAN NEVER BEAT ME.
I DON'T SAY THESE THINGS TO EMBARRASS OR BELITTLE YOU, PAUL.
I SAY THEM BECAUSE I AM TRULY TIRED OF DOING THIS SAME THING AGAIN AND AGAIN WITH YOU.
ONE OF THESE DAYS YOU'LL REALIZE THAT. BUT UNTIL THEN, I GOTTA SAY...
...IT STILL FEELS PRETTY DARN GOOD TO SOCK YOU ONE.
CRACK

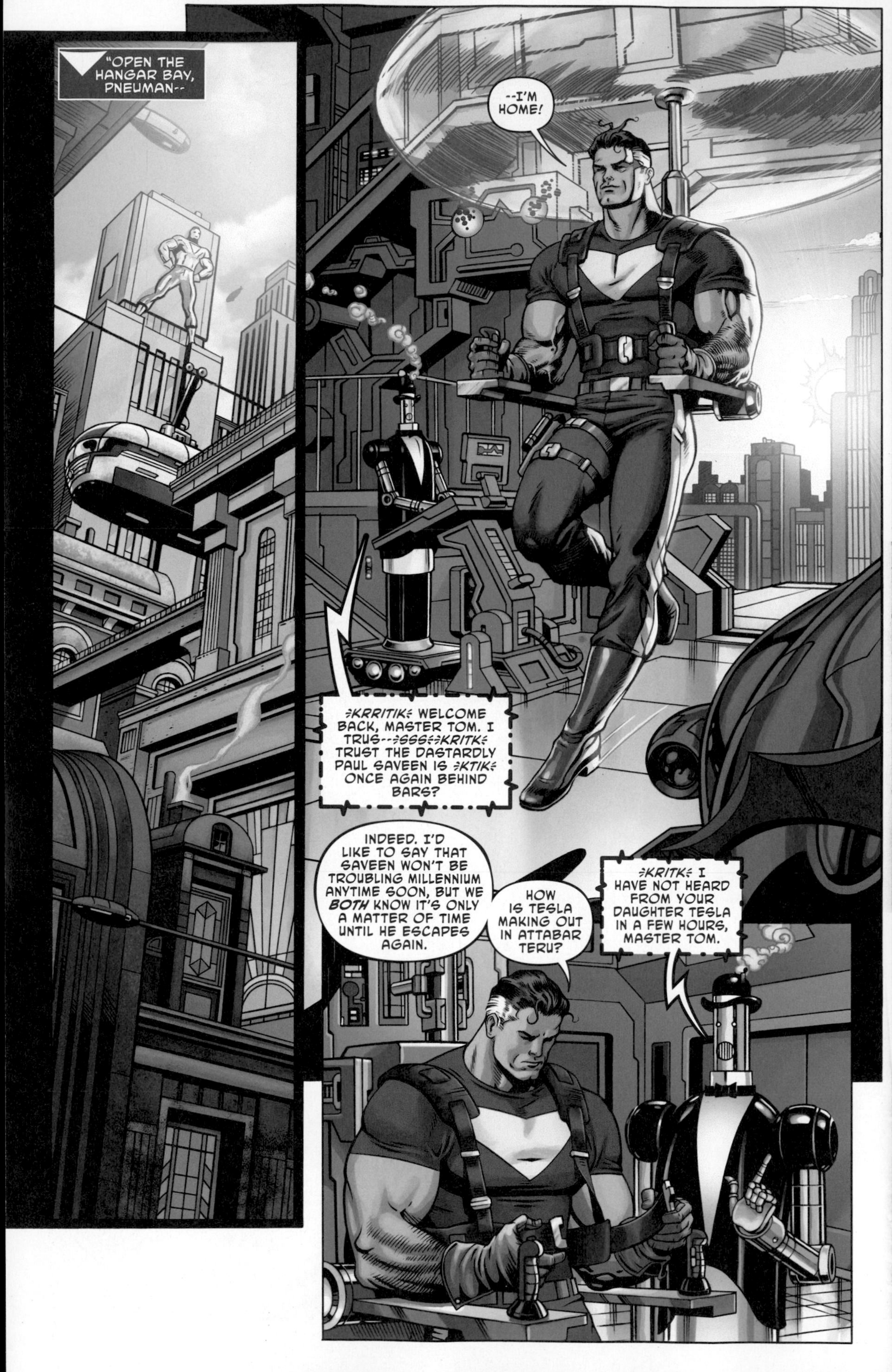
"OPEN THE HANGAR BAY, PNEUMAN--
--I'M HOME!
⚡KRRITIK⚡ WELCOME BACK, MASTER TOM. I TRUS--⚡SSS⚡⚡KRITK⚡ TRUST THE DASTARDLY PAUL SAVEEN IS ⚡KTIK⚡ ONCE AGAIN BEHIND BARS?
INDEED. I'D LIKE TO SAY THAT SAVEEN WON'T BE TROUBLING MILLENNIUM ANYTIME SOON, BUT WE BOTH KNOW IT'S ONLY A MATTER OF TIME UNTIL HE ESCAPES AGAIN.
HOW IS TESLA MAKING OUT IN ATTABAR TERU?
⚡KRITK⚡ I HAVE NOT HEARD FROM YOUR DAUGHTER TESLA IN A FEW HOURS, MASTER TOM.

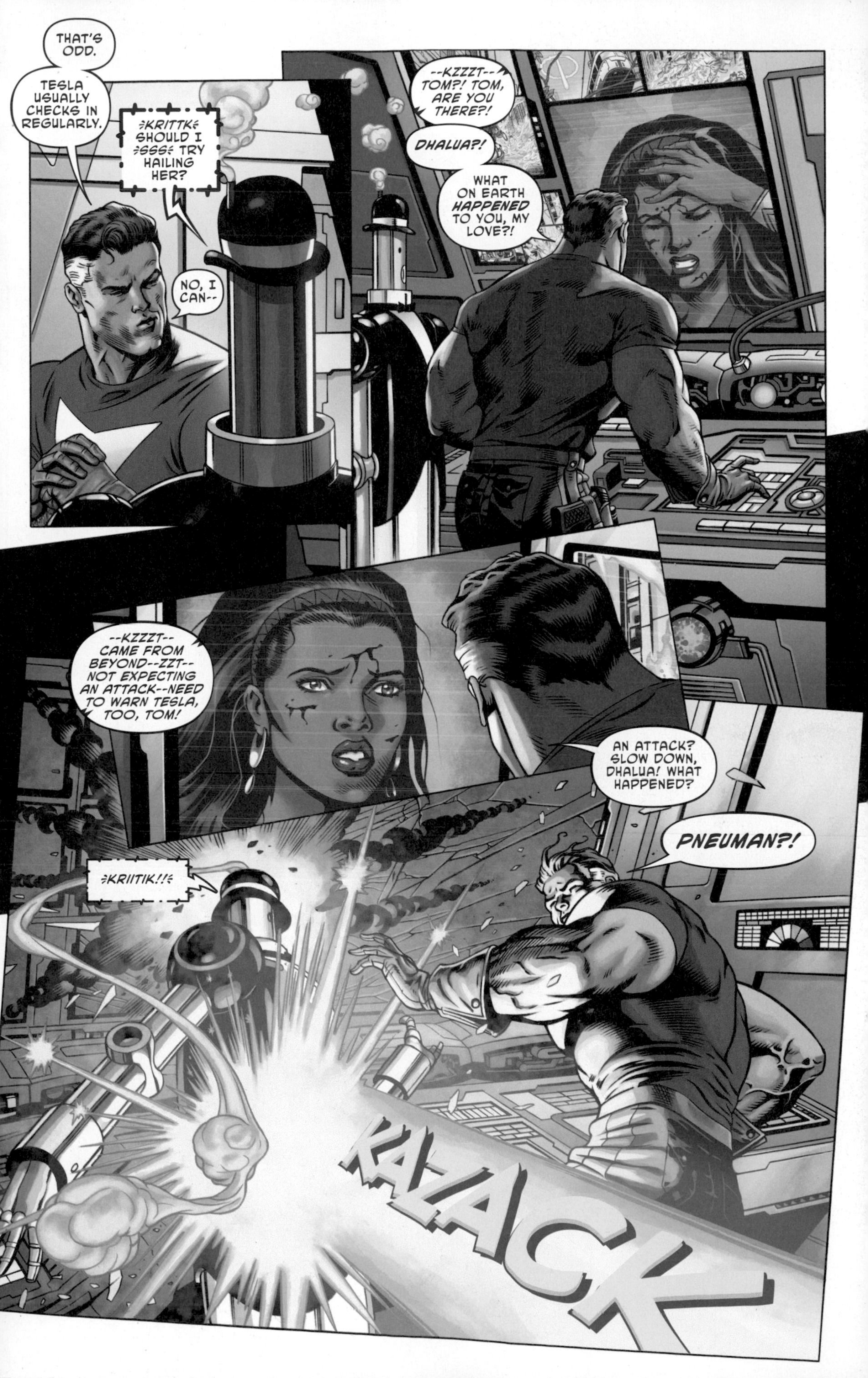
THAT'S ODD.
TESLA USUALLY CHECKS IN REGULARLY.
≠KRITTK≠ SHOULD I ≠SSS≠ TRY HAILING HER?
NO, I CAN--
--KZZZT-- TOM?! TOM, ARE YOU THERE?!
DHALUA?!
WHAT ON EARTH HAPPENED TO YOU, MY LOVE?!
--KZZZT-- CAME FROM BEYOND--ZZT-- NOT EXPECTING AN ATTACK--NEED TO WARN TESLA, TOO, TOM!
AN ATTACK? SLOW DOWN, DHALUA! WHAT HAPPENED?
PNEUMAN?!
≠KRIITIK!!≠
KAZACK

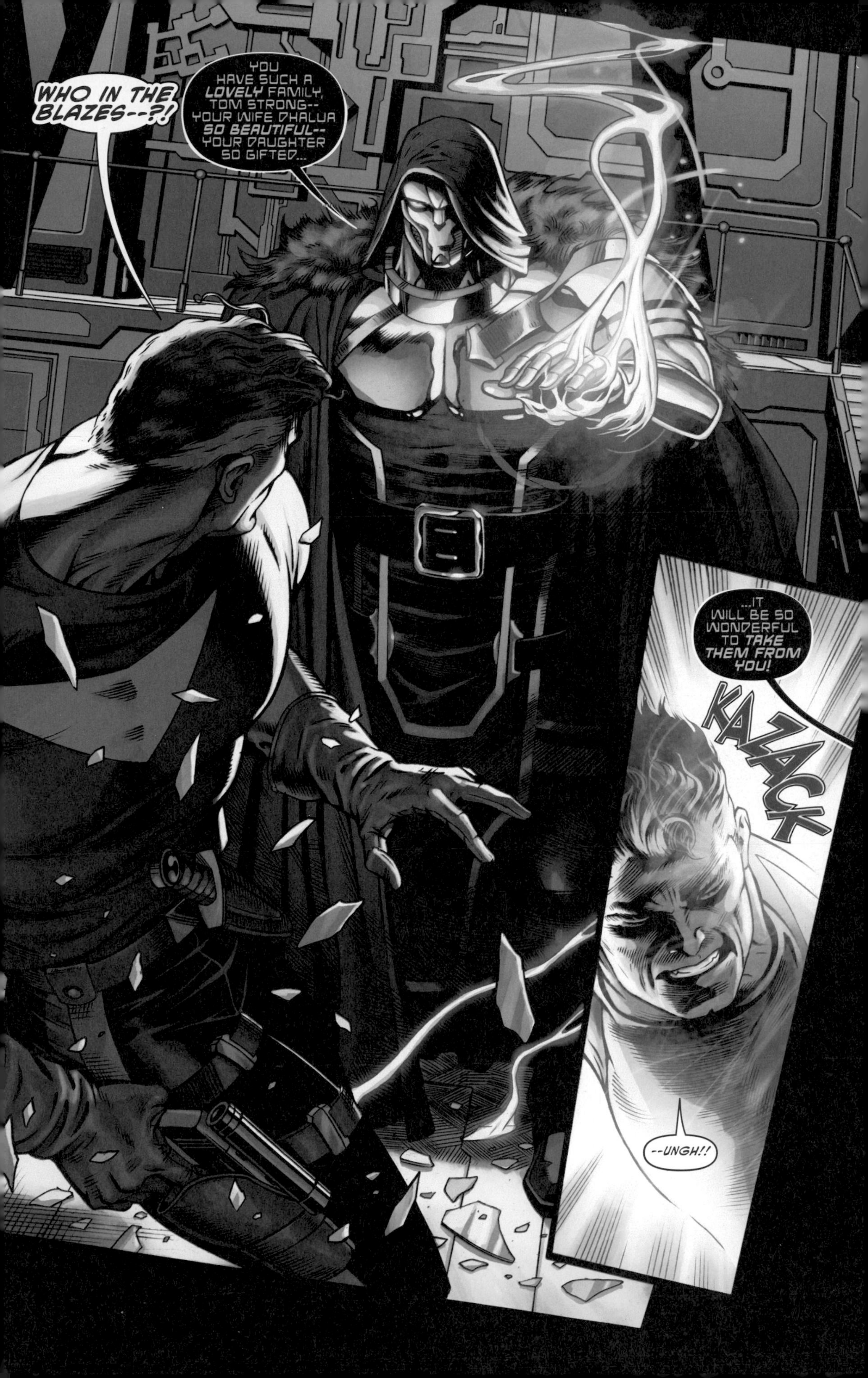
WHO IN THE BLAZES--?!
YOU HAVE SUCH A LOVELY FAMILY, TOM STRONG-- YOUR WIFE DHALUA SO BEAUTIFUL-- YOUR DAUGHTER SO GIFTED...
...IT WILL BE SO WONDERFUL TO TAKE THEM FROM YOU!
KAZACK
--UNGH!!

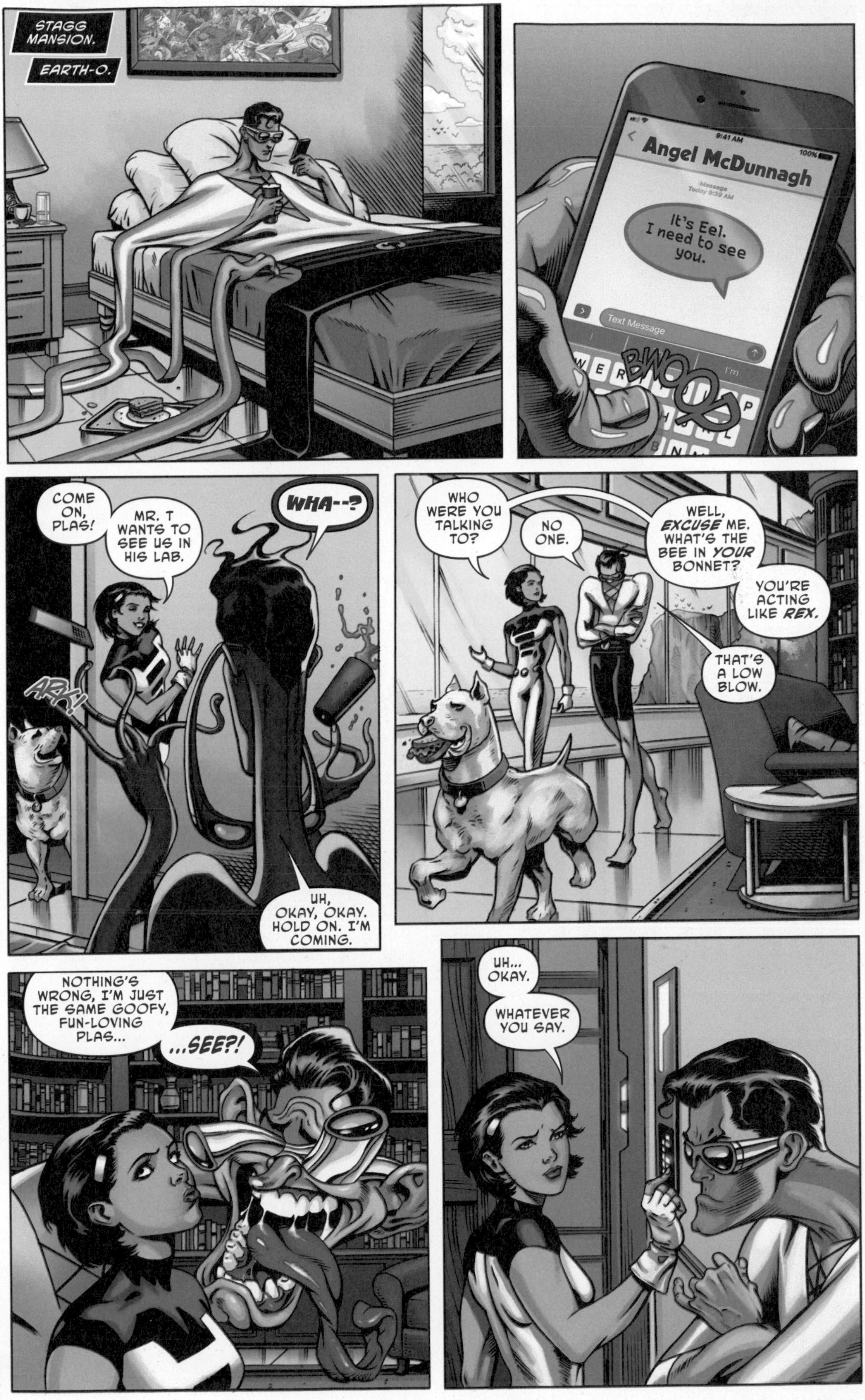
STAGG MANSION.
EARTH-0.
9:41 AM
Angel McDunnagh
100%
Message
Today 9:39 AM
It's Eel. I need to see you.
Text Message
BWOOP
COME ON, PLAS!
MR. T WANTS TO SEE US IN HIS LAB.
WHA--?
ARK!
UH, OKAY, OKAY. HOLD ON. I'M COMING.
WHO WERE YOU TALKING TO?
NO ONE.
WELL, EXCUSE ME. WHAT'S THE BEE IN YOUR BONNET?
YOU'RE ACTING LIKE REX.
THAT'S A LOW BLOW.
NOTHING'S WRONG, I'M JUST THE SAME GOOFY, FUN-LOVING PLAS...
...SEE?!
UH... OKAY.
WHATEVER YOU SAY.

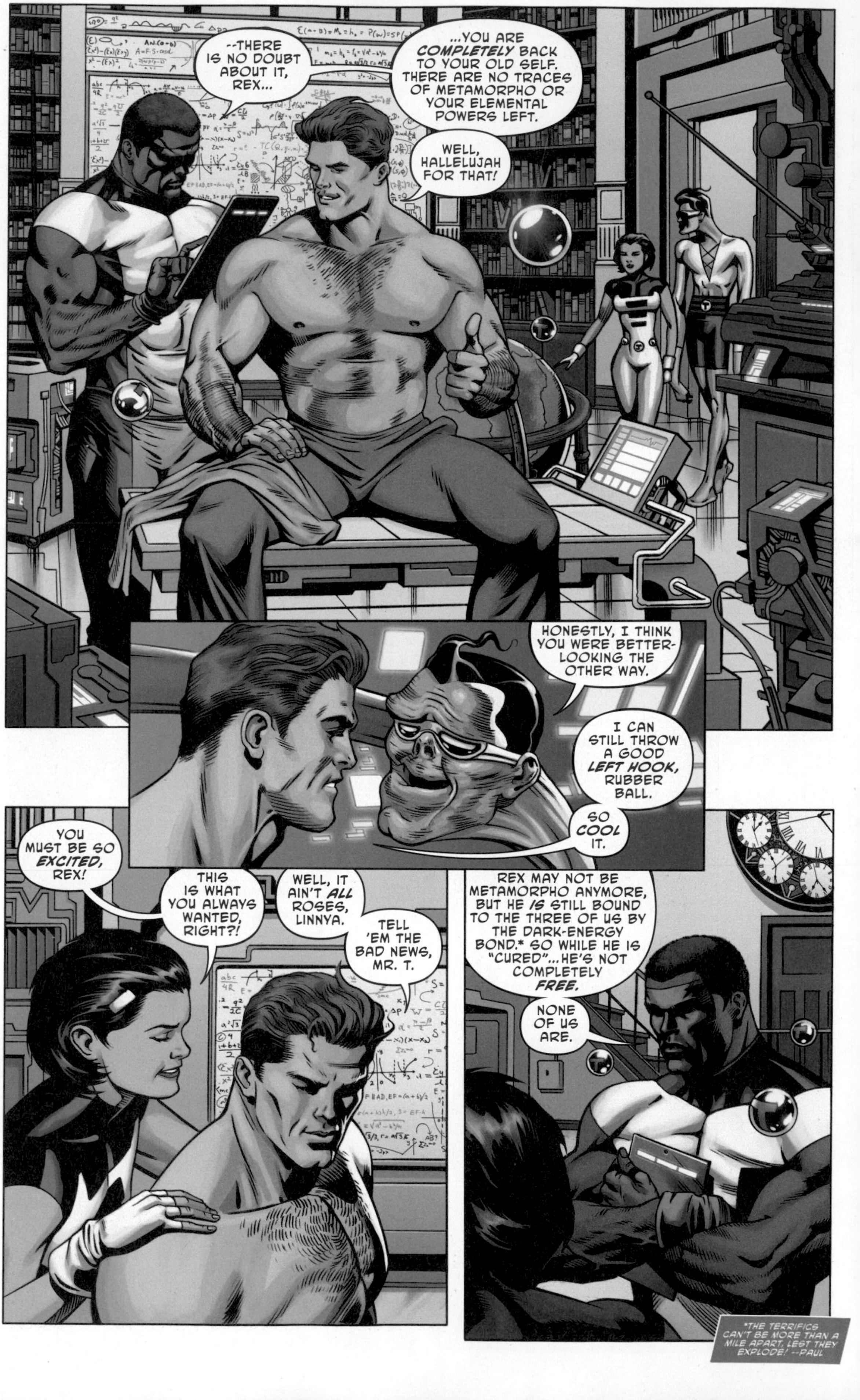
--THERE IS NO DOUBT ABOUT IT, REX...
...YOU ARE COMPLETELY BACK TO YOUR OLD SELF. THERE ARE NO TRACES OF METAMORPHO OR YOUR ELEMENTAL POWERS LEFT.
WELL, HALLELUJAH FOR THAT!
HONESTLY, I THINK YOU WERE BETTER-LOOKING THE OTHER WAY.
I CAN STILL THROW A GOOD LEFT HOOK, RUBBER BALL.
SO COOL IT.
YOU MUST BE SO EXCITED, REX!
THIS IS WHAT YOU ALWAYS WANTED, RIGHT?!
WELL, IT AIN'T ALL ROSES, LINNYA.
TELL 'EM THE BAD NEWS, MR. T.
REX MAY NOT BE METAMORPHO ANYMORE, BUT HE IS STILL BOUND TO THE THREE OF US BY THE DARK-ENERGY BOND.* SO WHILE HE IS "CURED"...HE'S NOT COMPLETELY FREE.
NONE OF US ARE.
*THE TERRIFICS CAN'T BE MORE THAN A MILE APART, LEST THEY EXPLODE! --PAUL

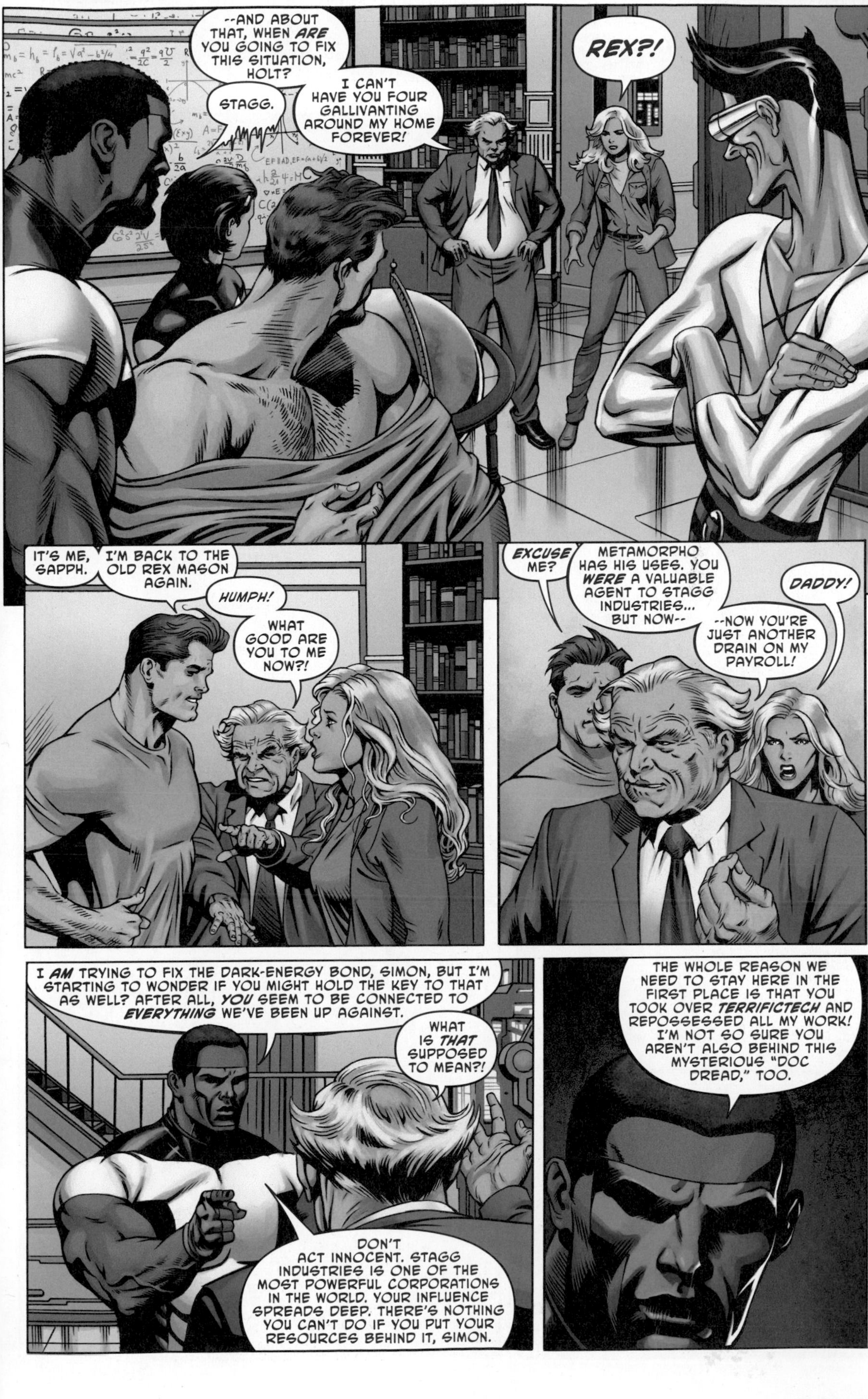
--AND ABOUT THAT, WHEN ARE YOU GOING TO FIX THIS SITUATION, HOLT?
STAGG.
I CAN'T HAVE YOU FOUR GALLIVANTING AROUND MY HOME FOREVER!
REX?!
IT'S ME, SAPPH.
I'M BACK TO THE OLD REX MASON AGAIN.
HUMPH!
WHAT GOOD ARE YOU TO ME NOW?!
EXCUSE ME?
METAMORPHO HAS HIS USES. YOU WERE A VALUABLE AGENT TO STAGG INDUSTRIES... BUT NOW--
--NOW YOU'RE JUST ANOTHER DRAIN ON MY PAYROLL!
DADDY!
I AM TRYING TO FIX THE DARK-ENERGY BOND, SIMON, BUT I'M STARTING TO WONDER IF YOU MIGHT HOLD THE KEY TO THAT AS WELL? AFTER ALL, YOU SEEM TO BE CONNECTED TO EVERYTHING WE'VE BEEN UP AGAINST.
WHAT IS THAT SUPPOSED TO MEAN?!
DON'T ACT INNOCENT. STAGG INDUSTRIES IS ONE OF THE MOST POWERFUL CORPORATIONS IN THE WORLD. YOUR INFLUENCE SPREADS DEEP. THERE'S NOTHING YOU CAN'T DO IF YOU PUT YOUR RESOURCES BEHIND IT, SIMON.
THE WHOLE REASON WE NEED TO STAY HERE IN THE FIRST PLACE IS THAT YOU TOOK OVER TERRIFICTECH AND REPOSSESSED ALL MY WORK! I'M NOT SO SURE YOU AREN'T ALSO BEHIND THIS MYSTERIOUS "DOC DREAD," TOO.

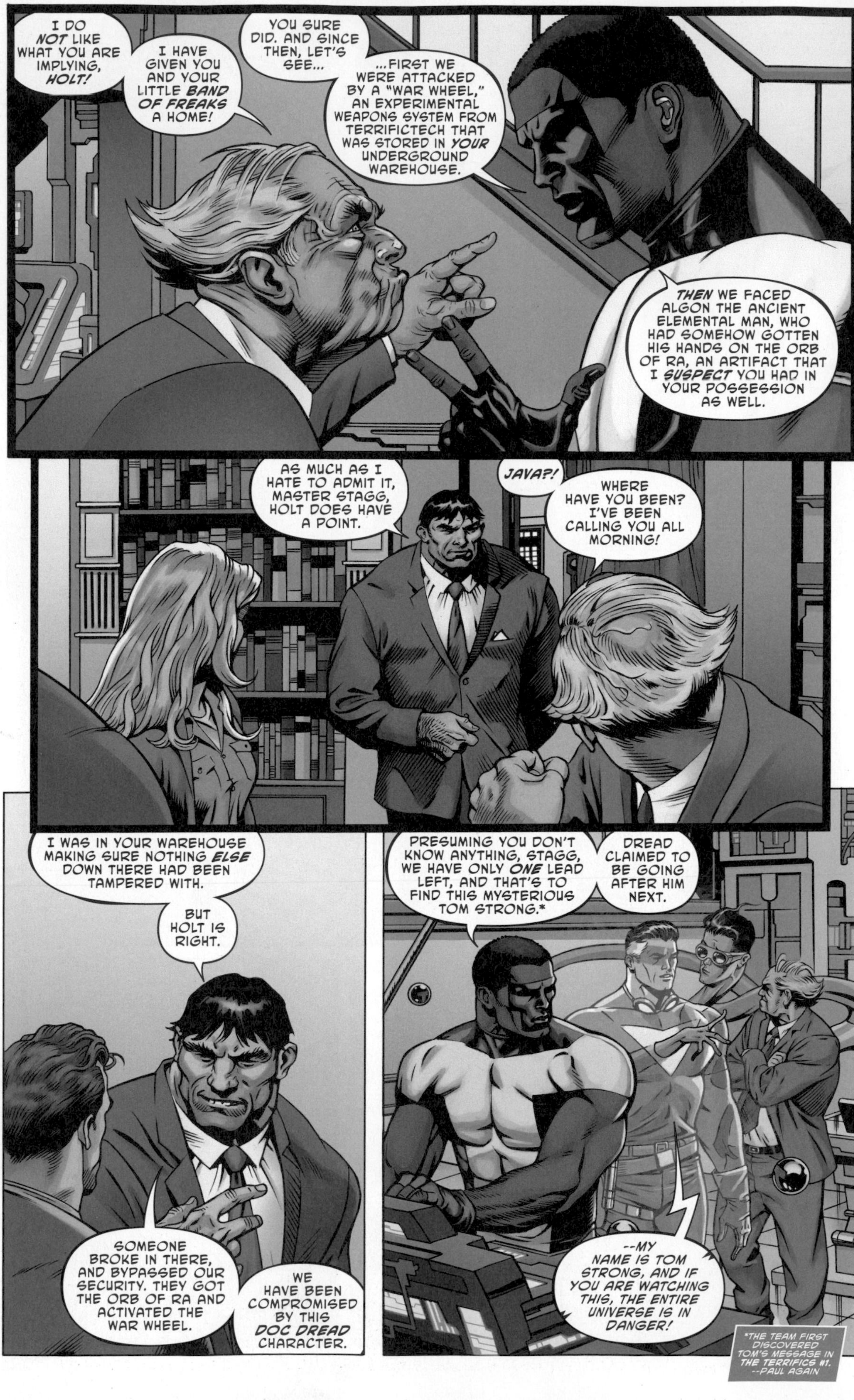
I DO NOT LIKE WHAT YOU ARE IMPLYING, HOLT!
I HAVE GIVEN YOU AND YOUR LITTLE BAND OF FREAKS A HOME!
YOU SURE DID. AND SINCE THEN, LET'S SEE...
...FIRST WE WERE ATTACKED BY A "WAR WHEEL," AN EXPERIMENTAL WEAPONS SYSTEM FROM TERRIFICTECH THAT WAS STORED IN YOUR UNDERGROUND WAREHOUSE.
THEN WE FACED ALGON THE ANCIENT ELEMENTAL MAN, WHO HAD SOMEHOW GOTTEN HIS HANDS ON THE ORB OF RA, AN ARTIFACT THAT I SUSPECT YOU HAD IN YOUR POSSESSION AS WELL.
AS MUCH AS I HATE TO ADMIT IT, MASTER STAGG, HOLT DOES HAVE A POINT.
JAVA?!
WHERE HAVE YOU BEEN? I'VE BEEN CALLING YOU ALL MORNING!
I WAS IN YOUR WAREHOUSE MAKING SURE NOTHING ELSE DOWN THERE HAD BEEN TAMPERED WITH.
BUT HOLT IS RIGHT.
SOMEONE BROKE IN THERE, AND BYPASSED OUR SECURITY. THEY GOT THE ORB OF RA AND ACTIVATED THE WAR WHEEL.
WE HAVE BEEN COMPROMISED BY THIS DOC DREAD CHARACTER.
PRESUMING YOU DON'T KNOW ANYTHING, STAGG, WE HAVE ONLY ONE LEAD LEFT, AND THAT'S TO FIND THIS MYSTERIOUS TOM STRONG.*
DREAD CLAIMED TO BE GOING AFTER HIM NEXT.
--MY NAME IS TOM STRONG, AND IF YOU ARE WATCHING THIS, THE ENTIRE UNIVERSE IS IN DANGER!
*THE TEAM FIRST DISCOVERED TOM'S MESSAGE IN THE TERRIFICS #1. --PAUL AGAIN

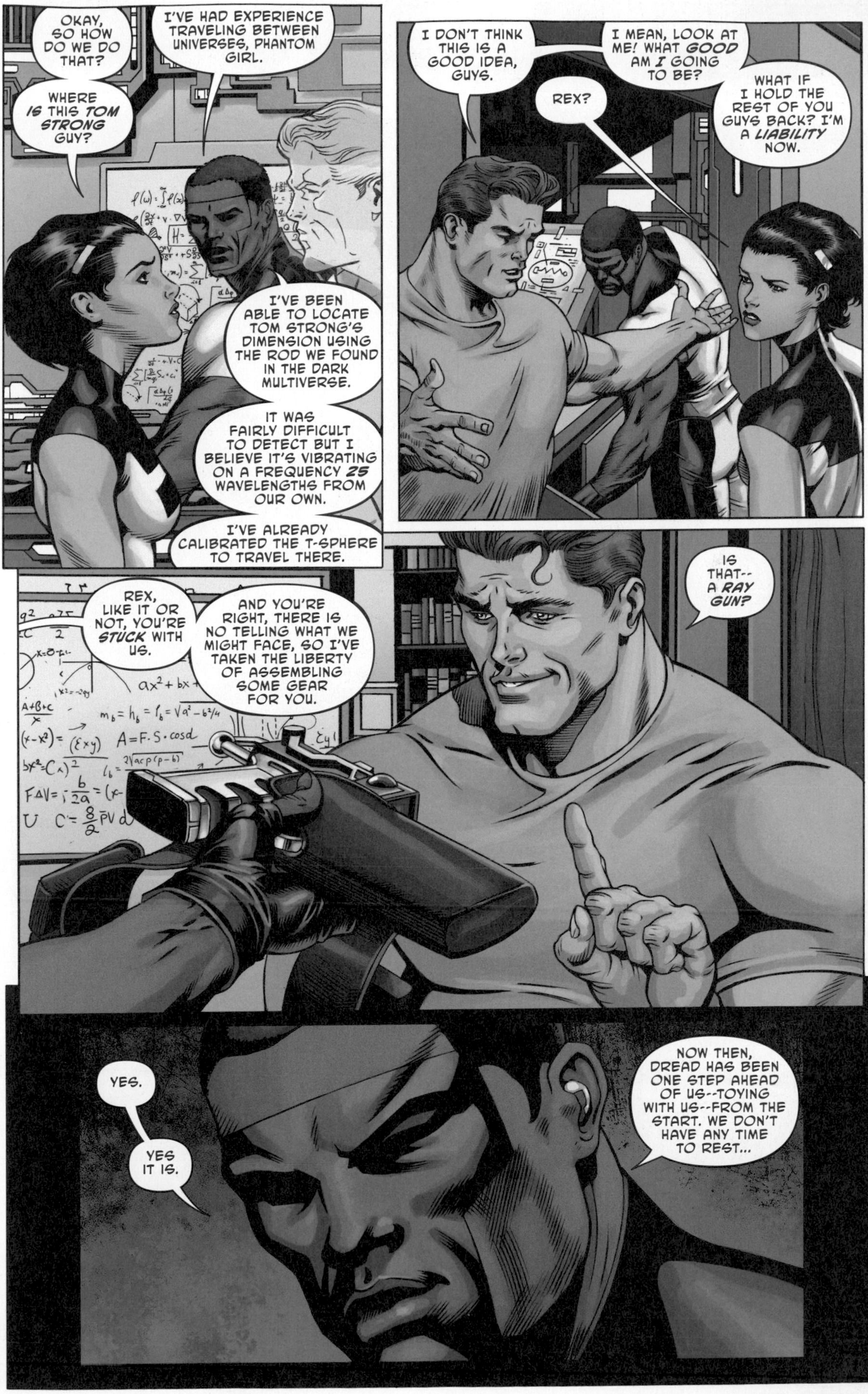
OKAY, SO HOW DO WE DO THAT?
I'VE HAD EXPERIENCE TRAVELING BETWEEN UNIVERSES, PHANTOM GIRL.
WHERE *IS* THIS *TOM STRONG* GUY?
I'VE BEEN ABLE TO LOCATE TOM STRONG'S DIMENSION USING THE ROD WE FOUND IN THE DARK MULTIVERSE.
IT WAS FAIRLY DIFFICULT TO DETECT BUT I BELIEVE IT'S VIBRATING ON A FREQUENCY *25* WAVELENGTHS FROM OUR OWN.
I'VE ALREADY CALIBRATED THE T-SPHERE TO TRAVEL THERE.
I DON'T THINK THIS IS A GOOD IDEA, GUYS.
I MEAN, LOOK AT ME! WHAT *GOOD* AM *I* GOING TO BE?
REX?
WHAT IF I HOLD THE REST OF YOU GUYS BACK? I'M A *LIABILITY* NOW.
REX, LIKE IT OR NOT, YOU'RE *STUCK* WITH US.
AND YOU'RE RIGHT, THERE IS NO TELLING WHAT WE MIGHT FACE, SO I'VE TAKEN THE LIBERTY OF ASSEMBLING SOME GEAR FOR YOU.
IS THAT-- A *RAY GUN?*
YES.
YES IT IS.
NOW THEN, DREAD HAS BEEN ONE STEP AHEAD OF US--TOYING WITH US--FROM THE START. WE DON'T HAVE ANY TIME TO REST...

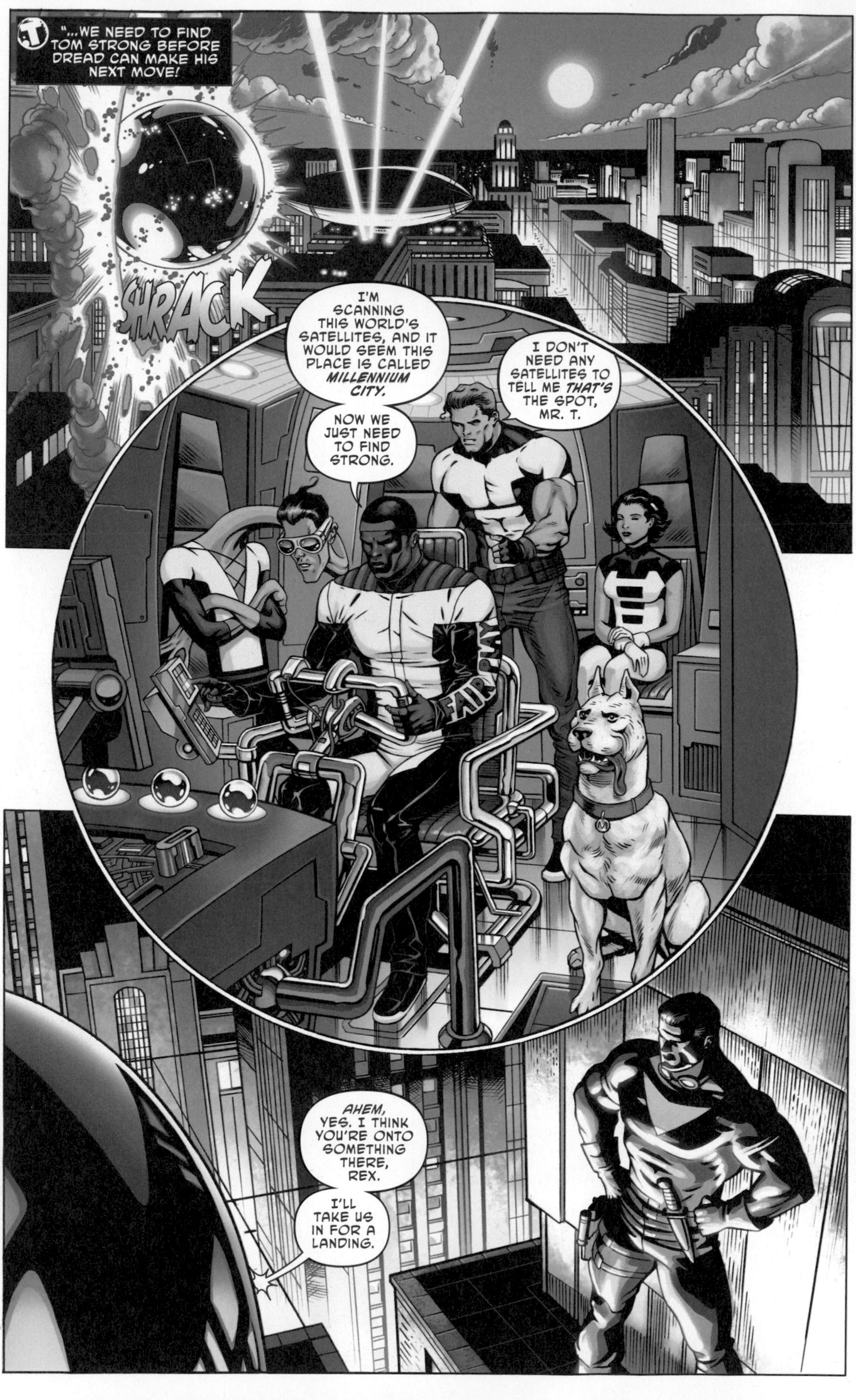
"...WE NEED TO FIND TOM STRONG BEFORE DREAD CAN MAKE HIS NEXT MOVE!
SHRACK
I'M SCANNING THIS WORLD'S SATELLITES, AND IT WOULD SEEM THIS PLACE IS CALLED MILLENNIUM CITY.
NOW WE JUST NEED TO FIND STRONG.
I DON'T NEED ANY SATELLITES TO TELL ME THAT'S THE SPOT, MR. T.
AHEM, YES. I THINK YOU'RE ONTO SOMETHING THERE, REX.
I'LL TAKE US IN FOR A LANDING.

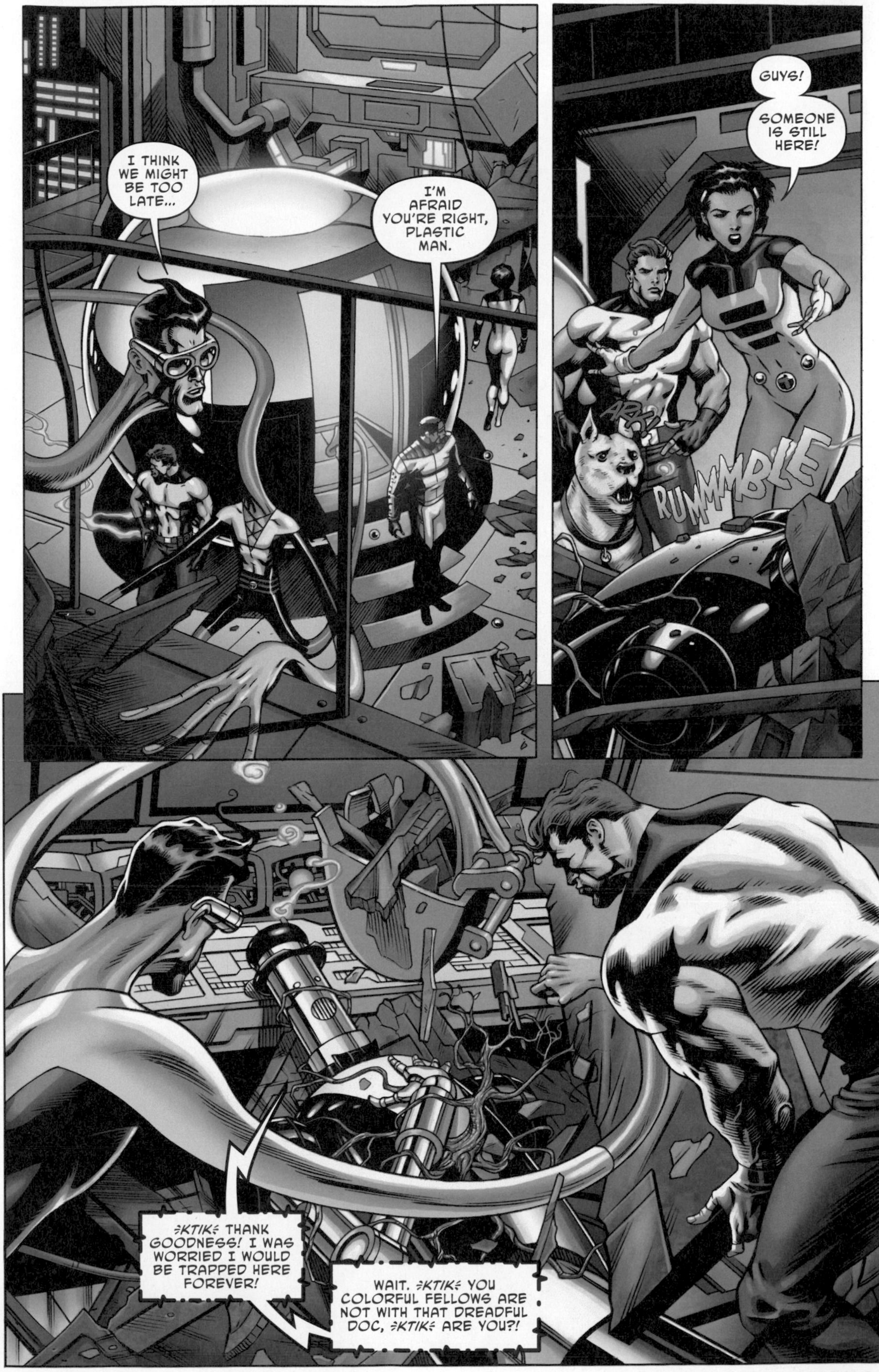
I THINK WE MIGHT BE TOO LATE...
I'M AFRAID YOU'RE RIGHT, PLASTIC MAN.
GUYS!
SOMEONE IS STILL HERE!
ARK!
RUMMMBLE
=KTIK= THANK GOODNESS! I WAS WORRIED I WOULD BE TRAPPED HERE FOREVER!
WAIT. =KTIK= YOU COLORFUL FELLOWS ARE NOT WITH THAT DREADFUL DOC, =KTIK= ARE YOU?!

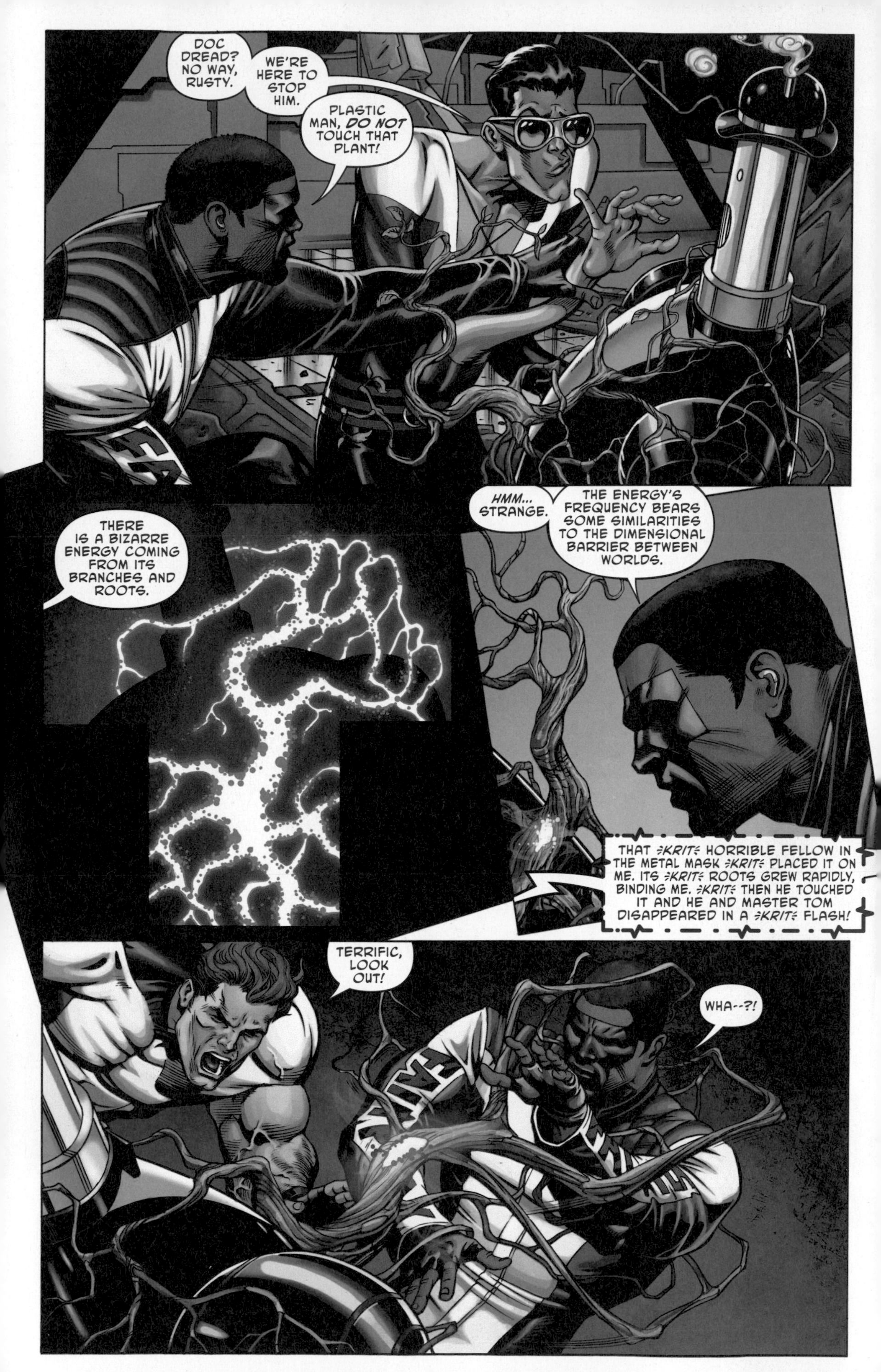
DOC DREAD? NO WAY, RUSTY.
WE'RE HERE TO STOP HIM.
PLASTIC MAN, *DO NOT* TOUCH THAT PLANT!
THERE IS A BIZARRE ENERGY COMING FROM ITS BRANCHES AND ROOTS.
HMM... STRANGE.
THE ENERGY'S FREQUENCY BEARS SOME SIMILARITIES TO THE DIMENSIONAL BARRIER BETWEEN WORLDS.
THAT *KRIT* HORRIBLE FELLOW IN THE METAL MASK *KRIT* PLACED IT ON ME. ITS *KRIT* ROOTS GREW RAPIDLY, BINDING ME. *KRIT* THEN HE TOUCHED IT AND HE AND MASTER TOM DISAPPEARED IN A *KRIT* FLASH!
TERRIFIC, LOOK OUT!
WHA--?!

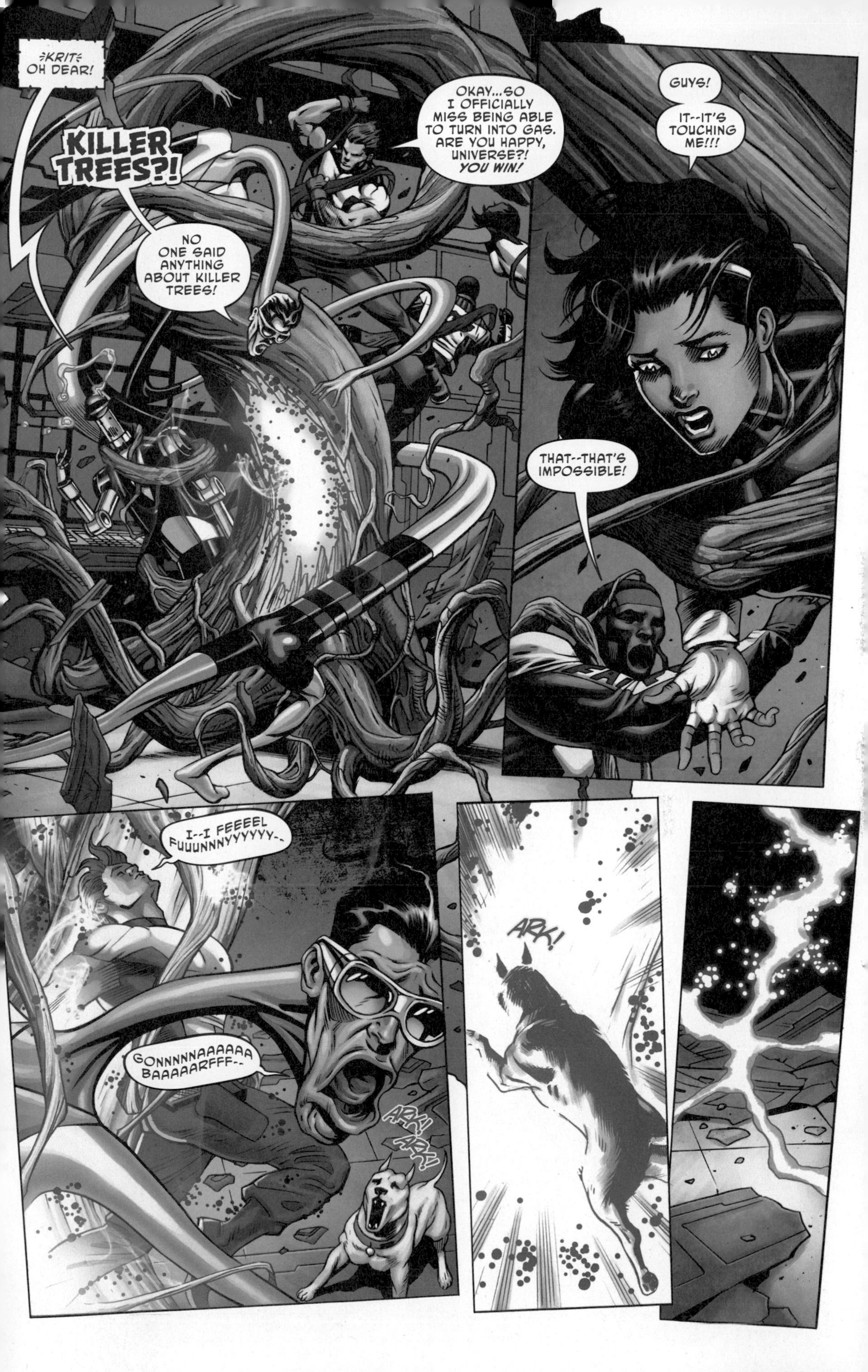

=KRIT= OH DEAR!
KILLER TREES?!
NO ONE SAID ANYTHING ABOUT KILLER TREES!
OKAY...SO I OFFICIALLY MISS BEING ABLE TO TURN INTO GAS. ARE YOU HAPPY, UNIVERSE?! YOU WIN!
GUYS!
IT--IT'S TOUCHING ME!!!
THAT--THAT'S IMPOSSIBLE!
I--I FEEEEL FUUUNNNYYYYYY--
GONNNNNAAAAAA BAAAAARFFF--
ARK! ARK!
ARK!

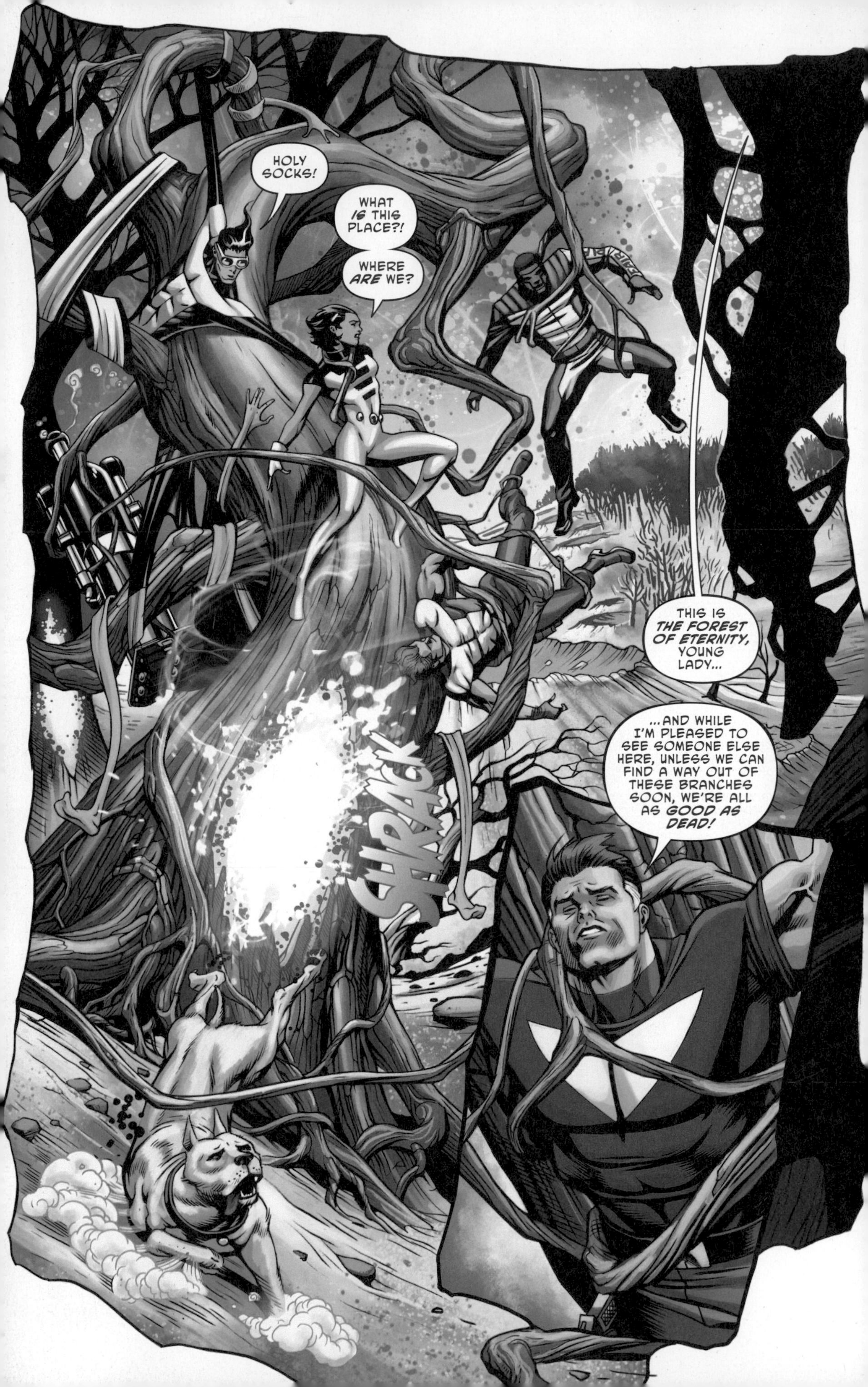
HOLY SOCKS!
WHAT *IS* THIS PLACE?!
WHERE *ARE* WE?
SHRAACK
THIS IS *THE FOREST OF ETERNITY,* YOUNG LADY...
...AND WHILE I'M PLEASED TO SEE SOMEONE ELSE HERE, UNLESS WE CAN FIND A WAY OUT OF THESE BRANCHES SOON, WE'RE ALL AS *GOOD AS DEAD!*

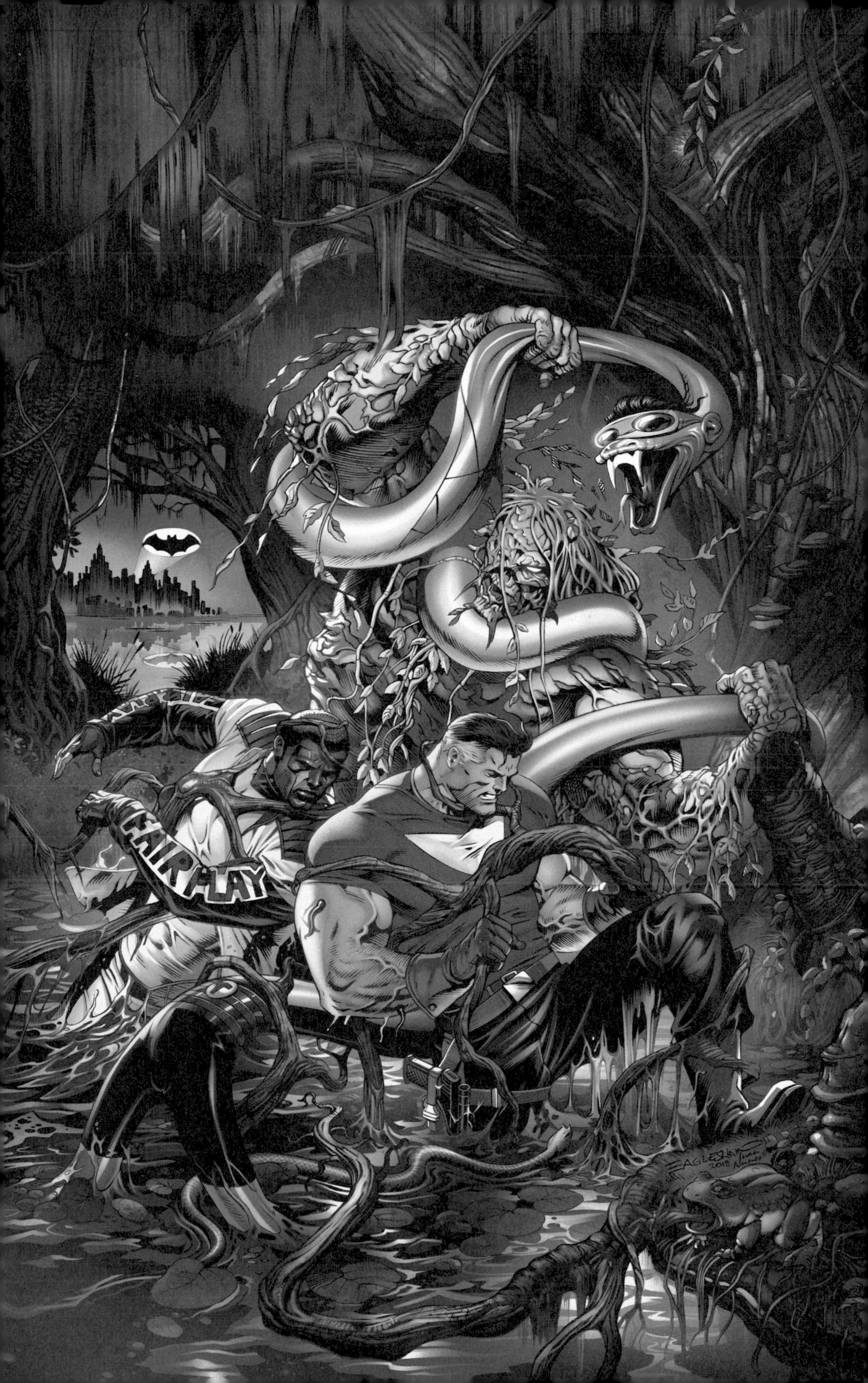
FAIR PLAY

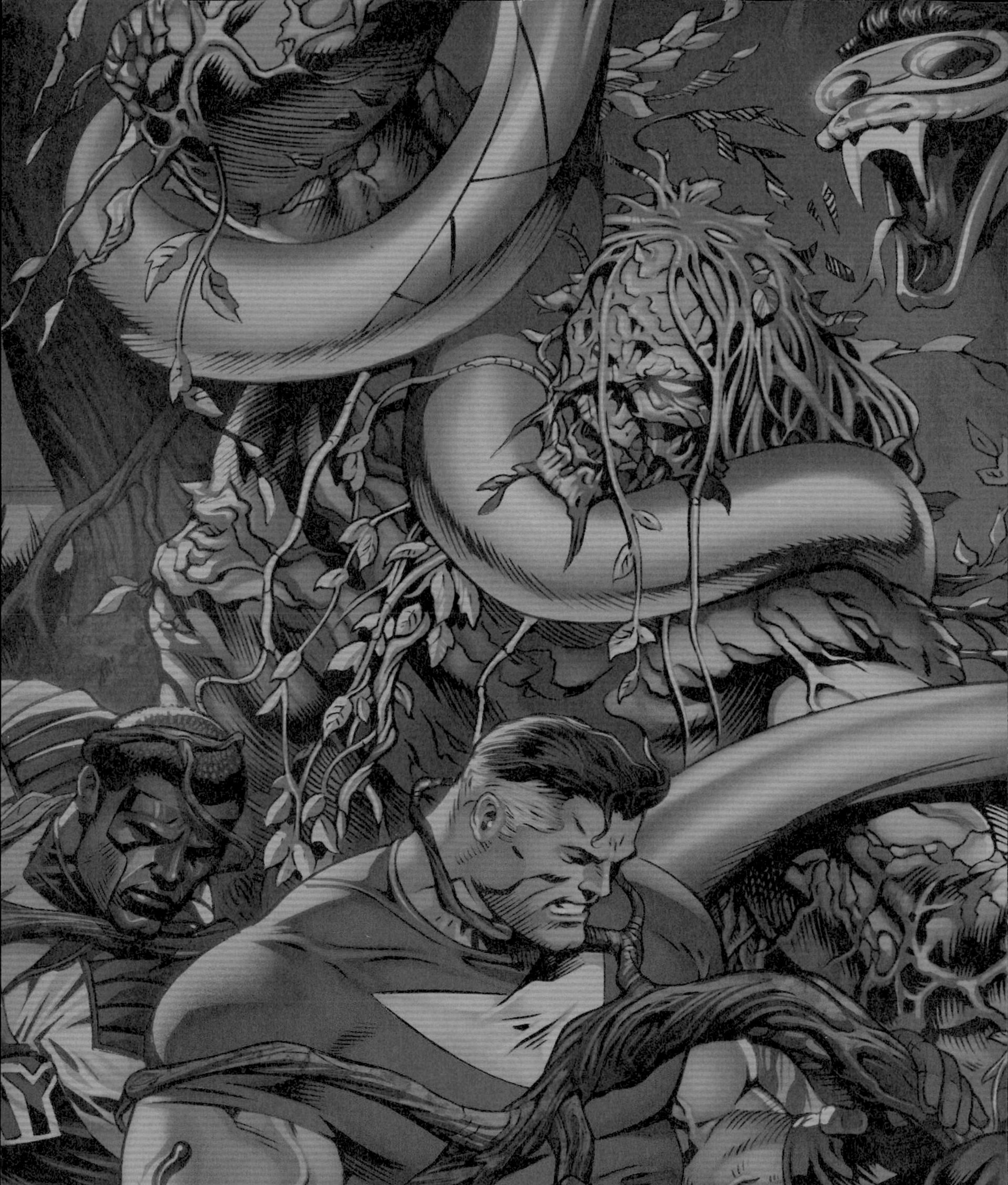

THE TERRIFICS
#8

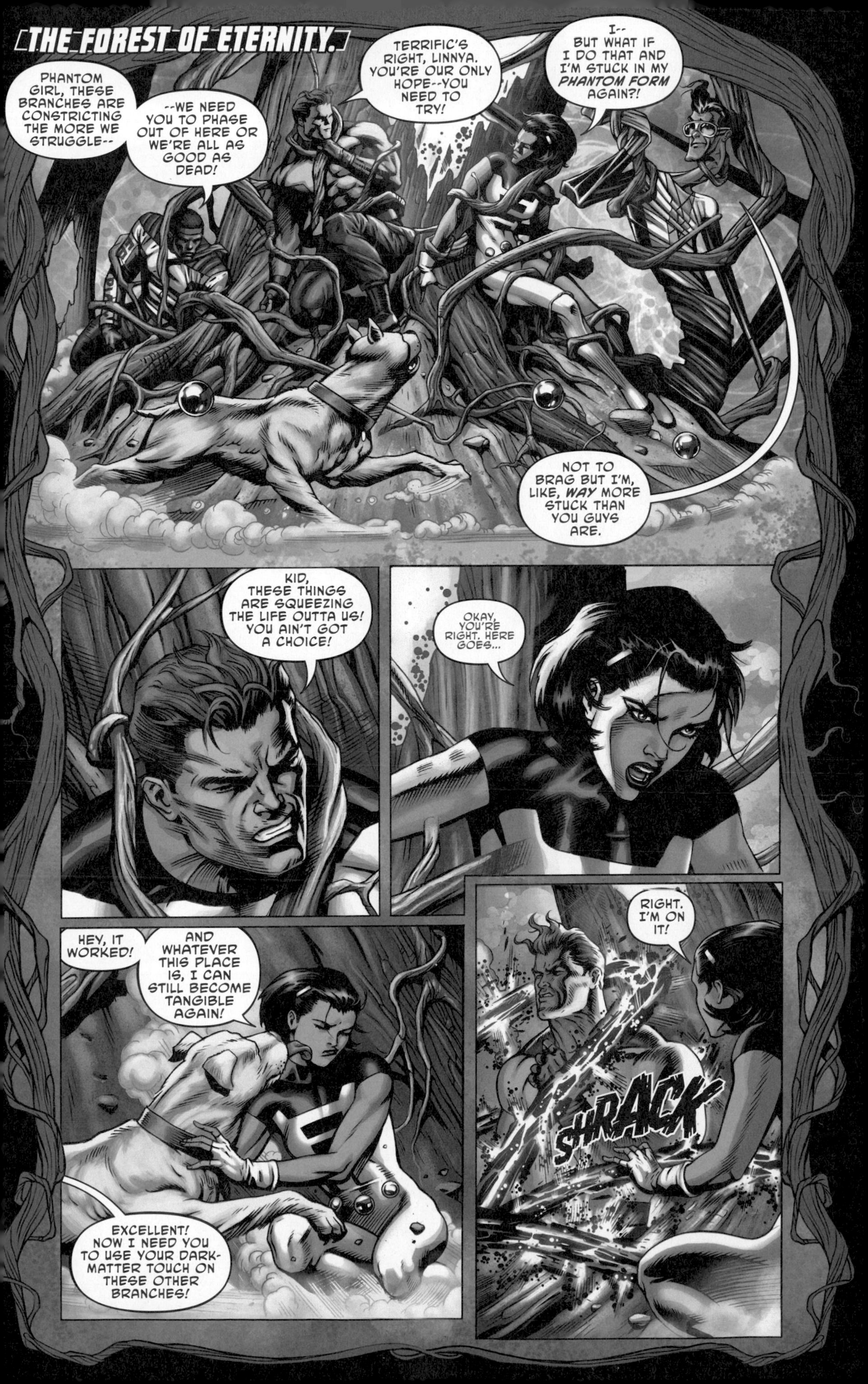
THE FOREST OF ETERNITY.
PHANTOM GIRL, THESE BRANCHES ARE CONSTRICTING THE MORE WE STRUGGLE--
--WE NEED YOU TO PHASE OUT OF HERE OR WE'RE ALL AS GOOD AS DEAD!
TERRIFIC'S RIGHT, LINNYA. YOU'RE OUR ONLY HOPE--YOU NEED TO TRY!
I-- BUT WHAT IF I DO THAT AND I'M STUCK IN MY PHANTOM FORM AGAIN?!
NOT TO BRAG BUT I'M, LIKE, WAY MORE STUCK THAN YOU GUYS ARE.
KID, THESE THINGS ARE SQUEEZING THE LIFE OUTTA US! YOU AIN'T GOT A CHOICE!
OKAY, YOU'RE RIGHT. HERE GOES...
HEY, IT WORKED!
AND WHATEVER THIS PLACE IS, I CAN STILL BECOME TANGIBLE AGAIN!
EXCELLENT! NOW I NEED YOU TO USE YOUR DARK-MATTER TOUCH ON THESE OTHER BRANCHES!
RIGHT. I'M ON IT!
SHRACK

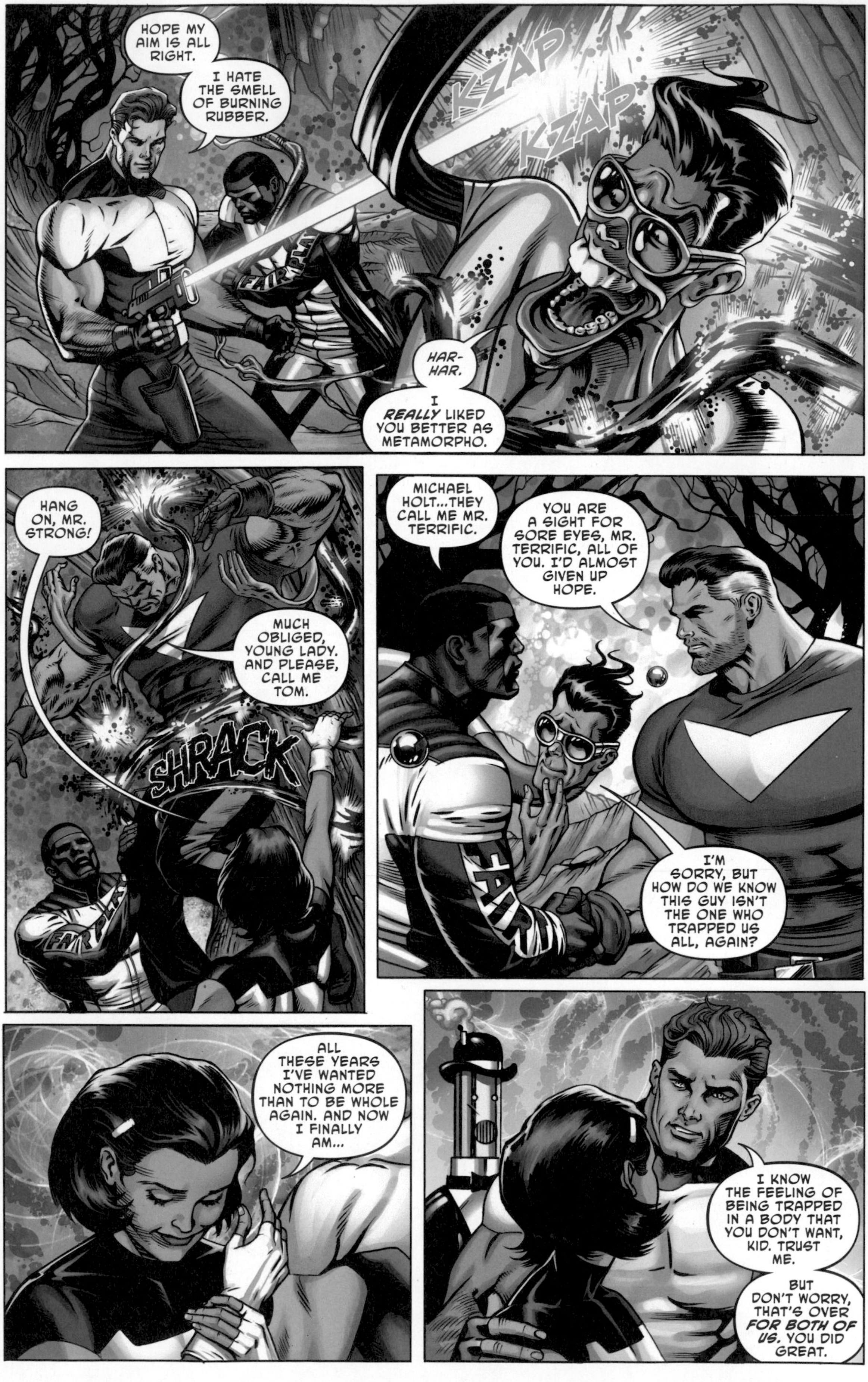
HOPE MY AIM IS ALL RIGHT.
I HATE THE SMELL OF BURNING RUBBER.
KZAP
KZAP
HAR-HAR.
I *REALLY* LIKED YOU BETTER AS METAMORPHO.
HANG ON, MR. STRONG!
MUCH OBLIGED, YOUNG LADY. AND PLEASE, CALL ME TOM.
SHRACK
MICHAEL HOLT...THEY CALL ME MR. TERRIFIC.
YOU ARE A SIGHT FOR SORE EYES, MR. TERRIFIC, ALL OF YOU. I'D ALMOST GIVEN UP HOPE.
I'M SORRY, BUT HOW DO WE KNOW THIS GUY ISN'T THE ONE WHO TRAPPED US ALL, AGAIN?
ALL THESE YEARS I'VE WANTED NOTHING MORE THAN TO BE WHOLE AGAIN. AND NOW I FINALLY AM...
I KNOW THE FEELING OF BEING TRAPPED IN A BODY THAT YOU DON'T WANT, KID. TRUST ME.
BUT DON'T WORRY, THAT'S OVER *FOR BOTH OF US.* YOU DID GREAT.

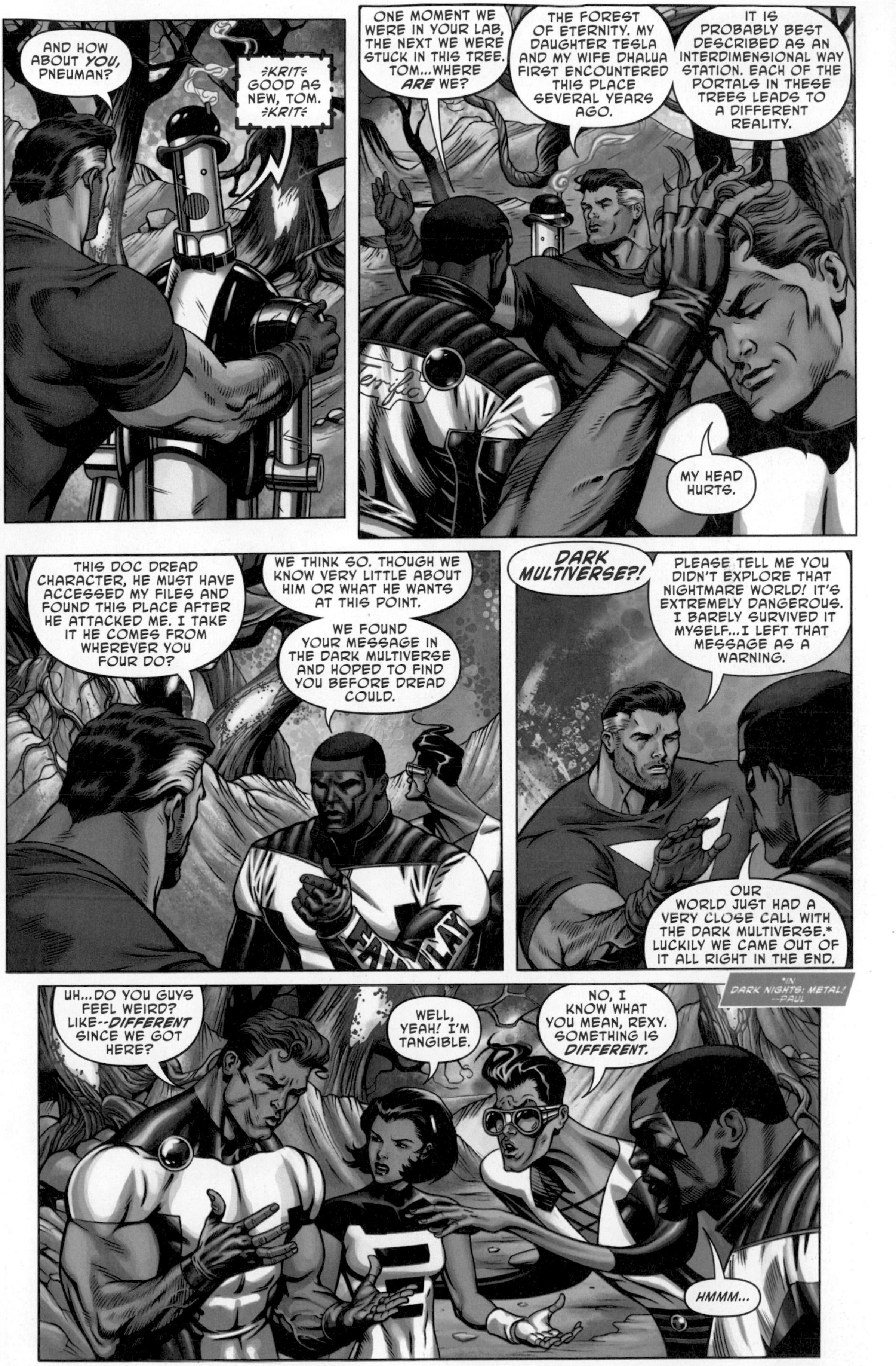
AND HOW ABOUT *YOU,* PNEUMAN?
≠KRIT≠ GOOD AS NEW, TOM. ≠KRIT≠
ONE MOMENT WE WERE IN YOUR LAB, THE NEXT WE WERE STUCK IN THIS TREE. TOM...WHERE *ARE* WE?
THE FOREST OF ETERNITY. MY DAUGHTER TESLA AND MY WIFE DHALUA FIRST ENCOUNTERED THIS PLACE SEVERAL YEARS AGO.
IT IS PROBABLY BEST DESCRIBED AS AN INTERDIMENSIONAL WAY STATION. EACH OF THE PORTALS IN THESE TREES LEADS TO A DIFFERENT REALITY.
MY HEAD HURTS.
THIS DOC DREAD CHARACTER, HE MUST HAVE ACCESSED MY FILES AND FOUND THIS PLACE AFTER HE ATTACKED ME. I TAKE IT HE COMES FROM WHEREVER YOU FOUR DO?
WE THINK SO. THOUGH WE KNOW VERY LITTLE ABOUT HIM OR WHAT HE WANTS AT THIS POINT.
WE FOUND YOUR MESSAGE IN THE DARK MULTIVERSE AND HOPED TO FIND YOU BEFORE DREAD COULD.
DARK MULTIVERSE?!
PLEASE TELL ME YOU DIDN'T EXPLORE THAT NIGHTMARE WORLD! IT'S EXTREMELY DANGEROUS. I BARELY SURVIVED IT MYSELF...I LEFT THAT MESSAGE AS A WARNING.
OUR WORLD JUST HAD A VERY CLOSE CALL WITH THE DARK MULTIVERSE.* LUCKILY WE CAME OUT OF IT ALL RIGHT IN THE END.
*IN *DARK NIGHTS: METAL!* --PAUL
UH...DO YOU GUYS FEEL WEIRD? LIKE--*DIFFERENT* SINCE WE GOT HERE?
WELL, *YEAH!* I'M TANGIBLE.
NO, I KNOW WHAT YOU MEAN, REXY. SOMETHING IS *DIFFERENT.*
HMMM...

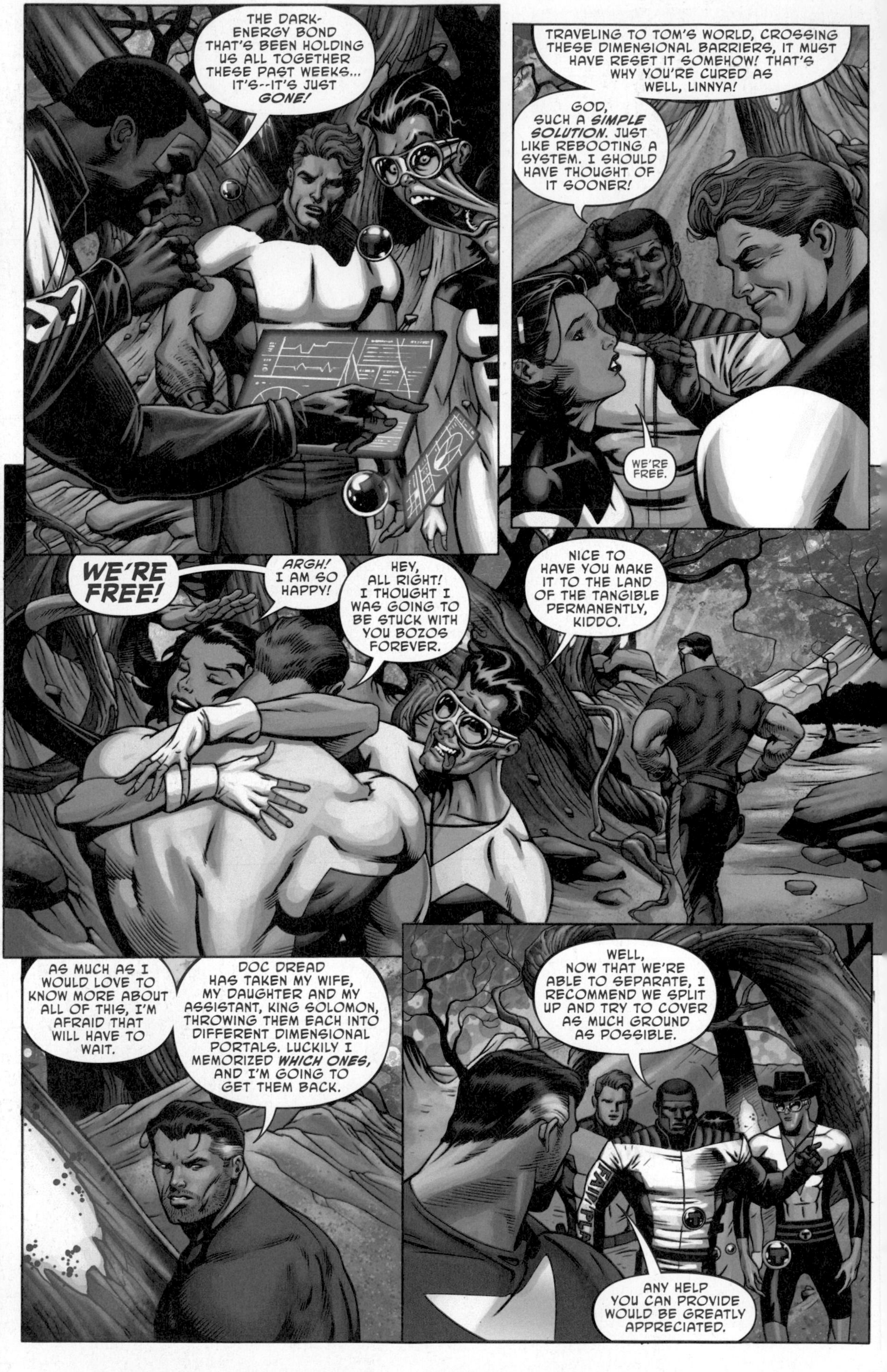
THE DARK-ENERGY BOND THAT'S BEEN HOLDING US ALL TOGETHER THESE PAST WEEKS... IT'S--IT'S JUST GONE!
TRAVELING TO TOM'S WORLD, CROSSING THESE DIMENSIONAL BARRIERS, IT MUST HAVE RESET IT SOMEHOW! THAT'S WHY YOU'RE CURED AS WELL, LINNYA!
GOD, SUCH A SIMPLE SOLUTION. JUST LIKE REBOOTING A SYSTEM. I SHOULD HAVE THOUGHT OF IT SOONER!
WE'RE FREE.
WE'RE FREE!
ARGH! I AM SO HAPPY!
HEY, ALL RIGHT! I THOUGHT I WAS GOING TO BE STUCK WITH YOU BOZOS FOREVER.
NICE TO HAVE YOU MAKE IT TO THE LAND OF THE TANGIBLE PERMANENTLY, KIDDO.
AS MUCH AS I WOULD LOVE TO KNOW MORE ABOUT ALL OF THIS, I'M AFRAID THAT WILL HAVE TO WAIT.
DOC DREAD HAS TAKEN MY WIFE, MY DAUGHTER AND MY ASSISTANT, KING SOLOMON, THROWING THEM EACH INTO DIFFERENT DIMENSIONAL PORTALS. LUCKILY I MEMORIZED WHICH ONES, AND I'M GOING TO GET THEM BACK.
WELL, NOW THAT WE'RE ABLE TO SEPARATE, I RECOMMEND WE SPLIT UP AND TRY TO COVER AS MUCH GROUND AS POSSIBLE.
ANY HELP YOU CAN PROVIDE WOULD BE GREATLY APPRECIATED.

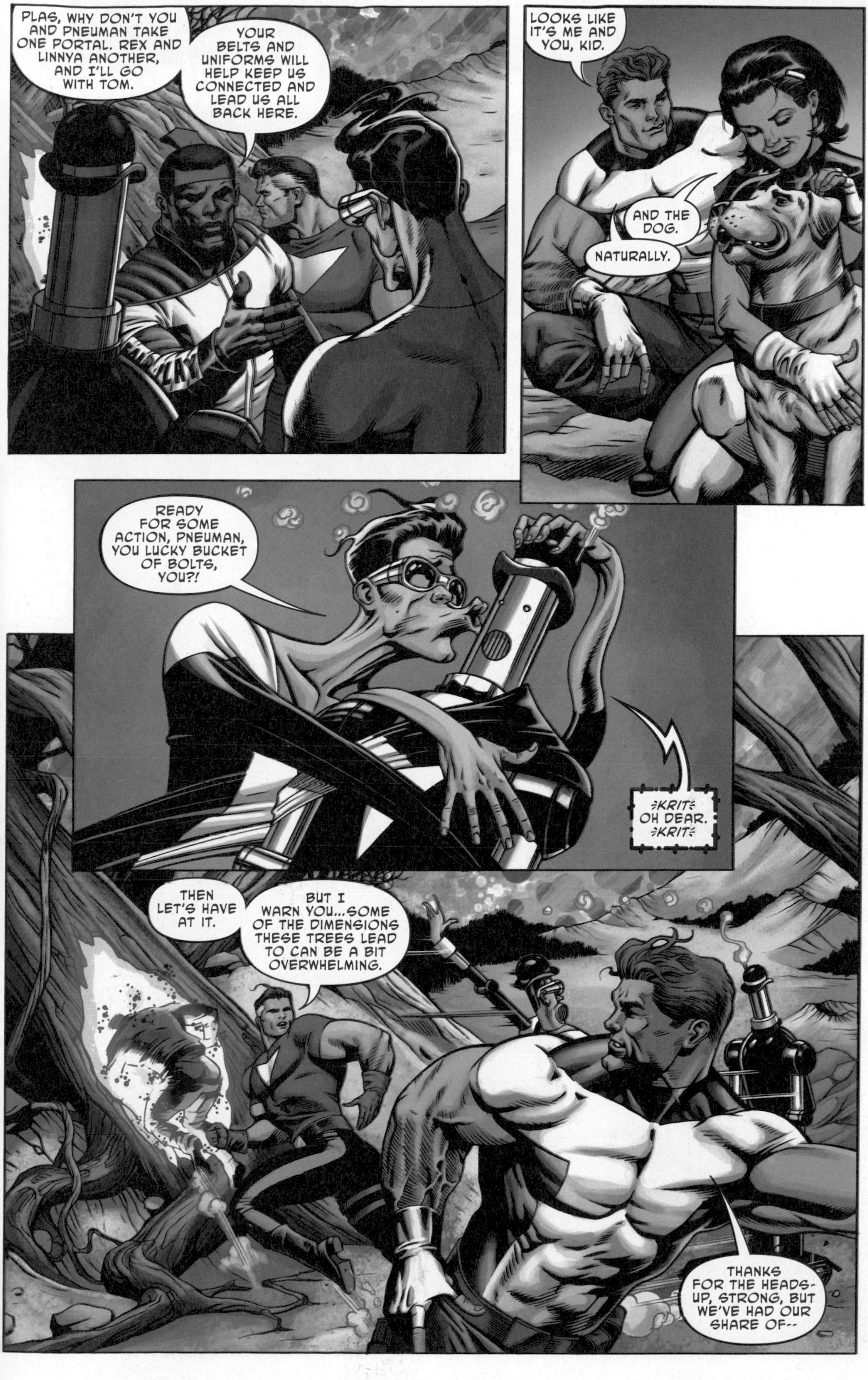
PLAS, WHY DON'T YOU AND PNEUMAN TAKE ONE PORTAL. REX AND LINNYA ANOTHER, AND I'LL GO WITH TOM.
YOUR BELTS AND UNIFORMS WILL HELP KEEP US CONNECTED AND LEAD US ALL BACK HERE.
LOOKS LIKE IT'S ME AND YOU, KID.
AND THE DOG.
NATURALLY.
READY FOR SOME ACTION, PNEUMAN, YOU LUCKY BUCKET OF BOLTS, YOU?!
KRIT OH DEAR. KRIT
THEN LET'S HAVE AT IT.
BUT I WARN YOU...SOME OF THE DIMENSIONS THESE TREES LEAD TO CAN BE A BIT OVERWHELMING.
THANKS FOR THE HEADS-UP, STRONG, BUT WE'VE HAD OUR SHARE OF--

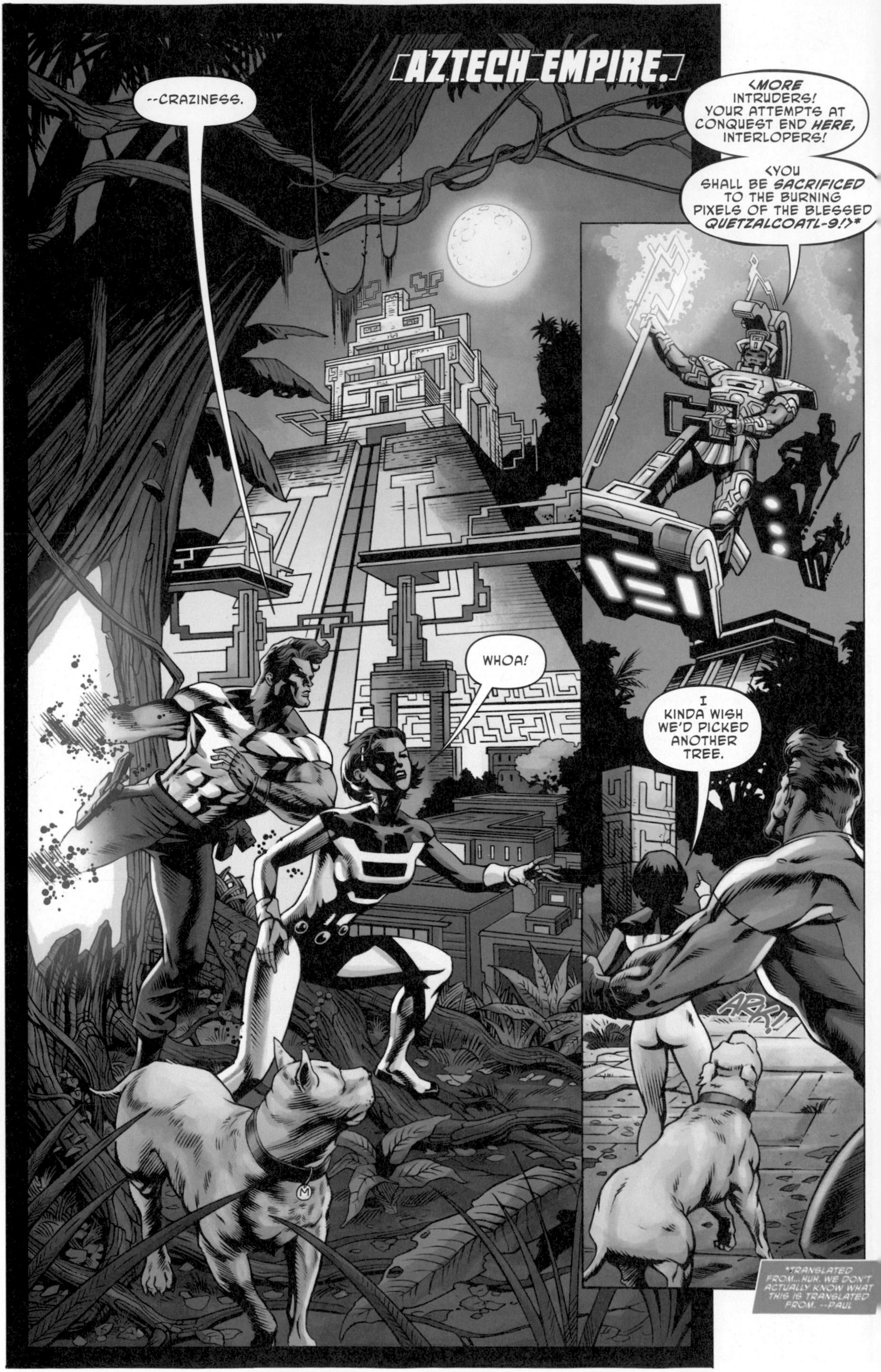
AZTECH EMPIRE.
--CRAZINESS.
<MORE INTRUDERS! YOUR ATTEMPTS AT CONQUEST END HERE, INTERLOPERS!
<YOU SHALL BE SACRIFICED TO THE BURNING PIXELS OF THE BLESSED QUETZALCOATL-9!>*
WHOA!
I KINDA WISH WE'D PICKED ANOTHER TREE.
ARK!!
*TRANSLATED FROM...HUH. WE DON'T ACTUALLY KNOW WHAT THIS IS TRANSLATED FROM. --PAUL

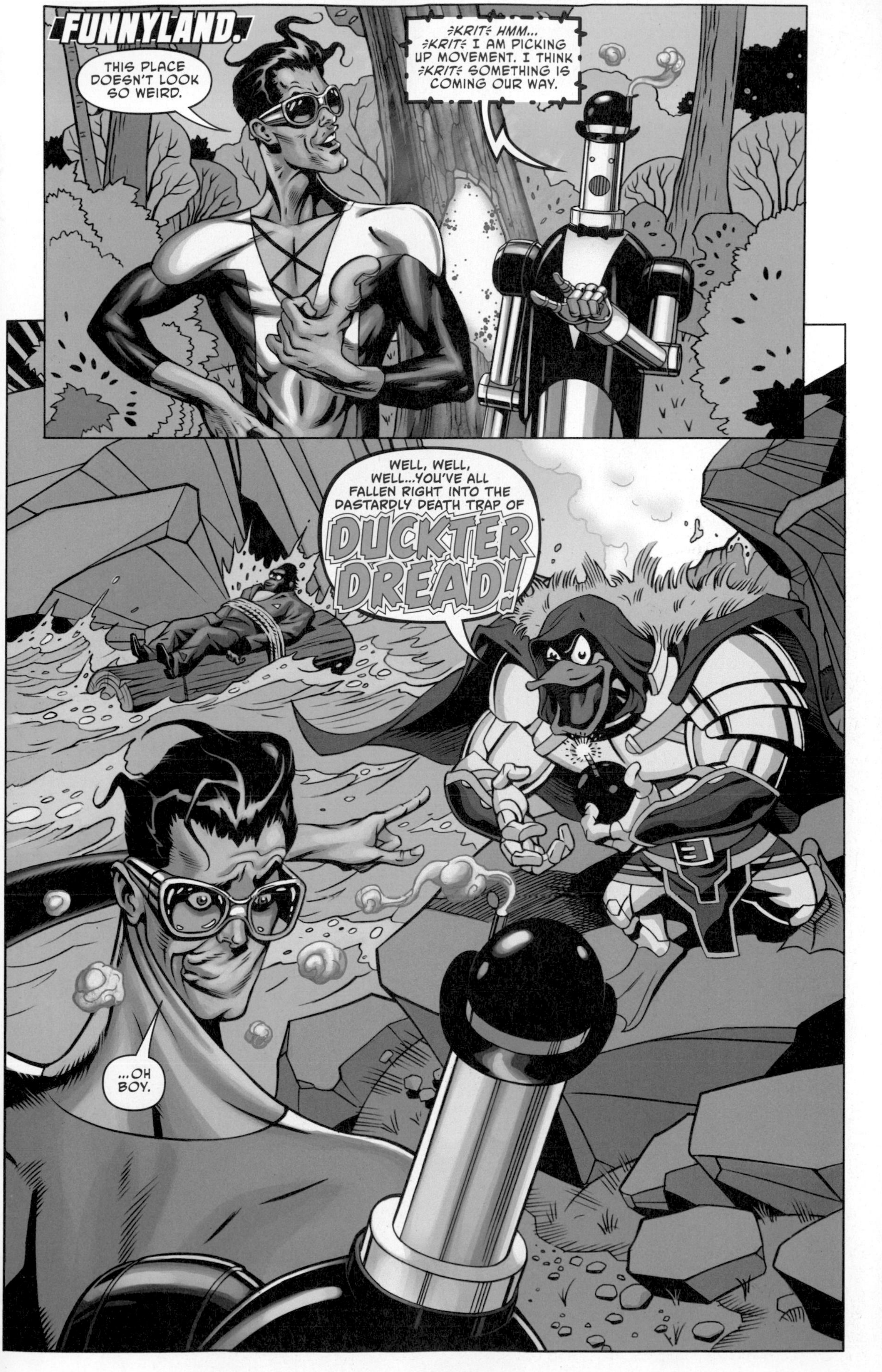
FUNNYLAND.
THIS PLACE DOESN'T LOOK SO WEIRD.
≠KRIT≠ HMM... ≠KRIT≠ I AM PICKING UP MOVEMENT. I THINK ≠KRIT≠ SOMETHING IS COMING OUR WAY.
WELL, WELL, WELL...YOU'VE ALL FALLEN RIGHT INTO THE DASTARDLY DEATH TRAP OF DUCKTER DREAD!
...OH BOY.

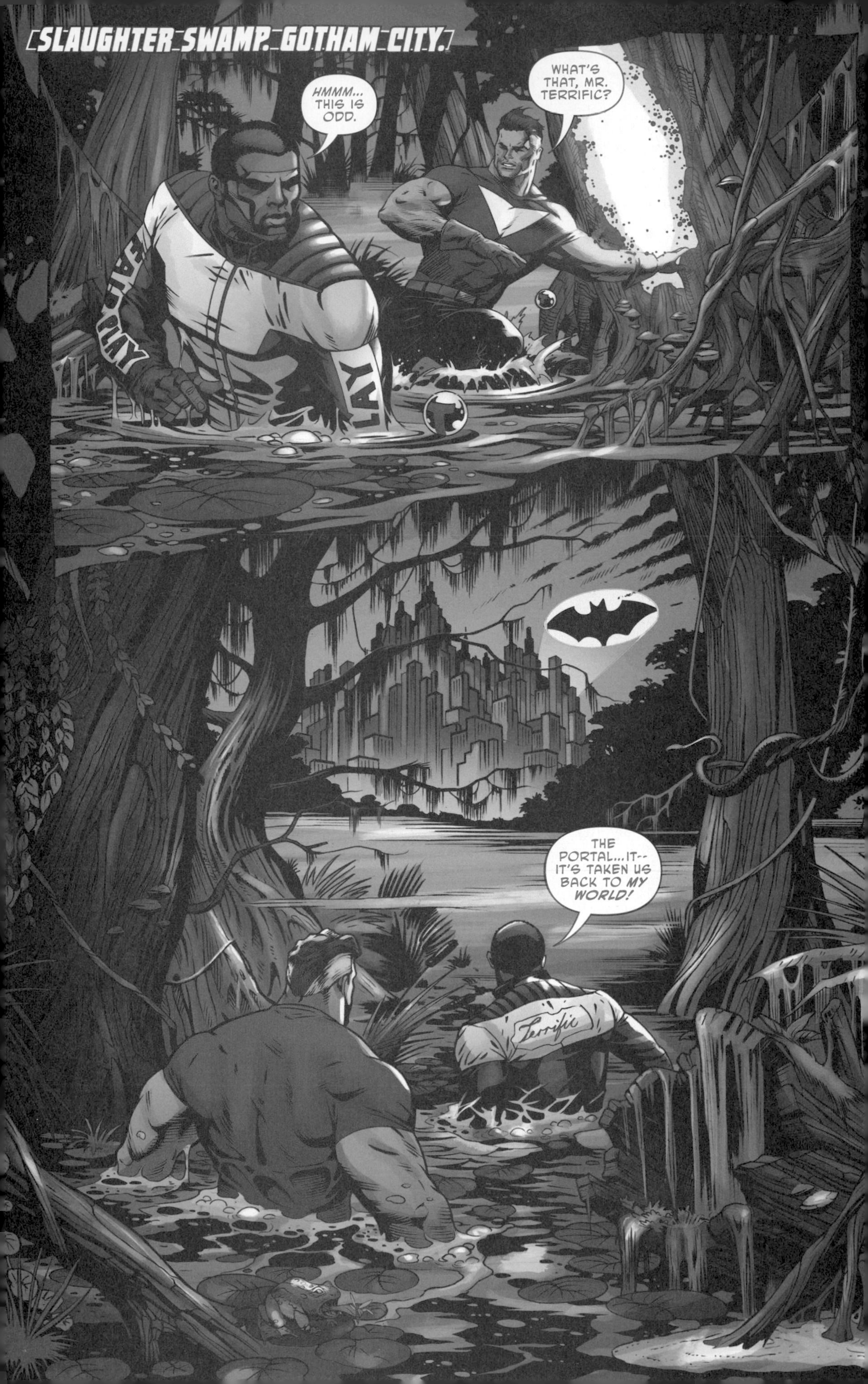
SLAUGHTER SWAMP, GOTHAM CITY.
HMMM... THIS IS ODD.
WHAT'S THAT, MR. TERRIFIC?
THE PORTAL...IT-- IT'S TAKEN US BACK TO *MY WORLD!*

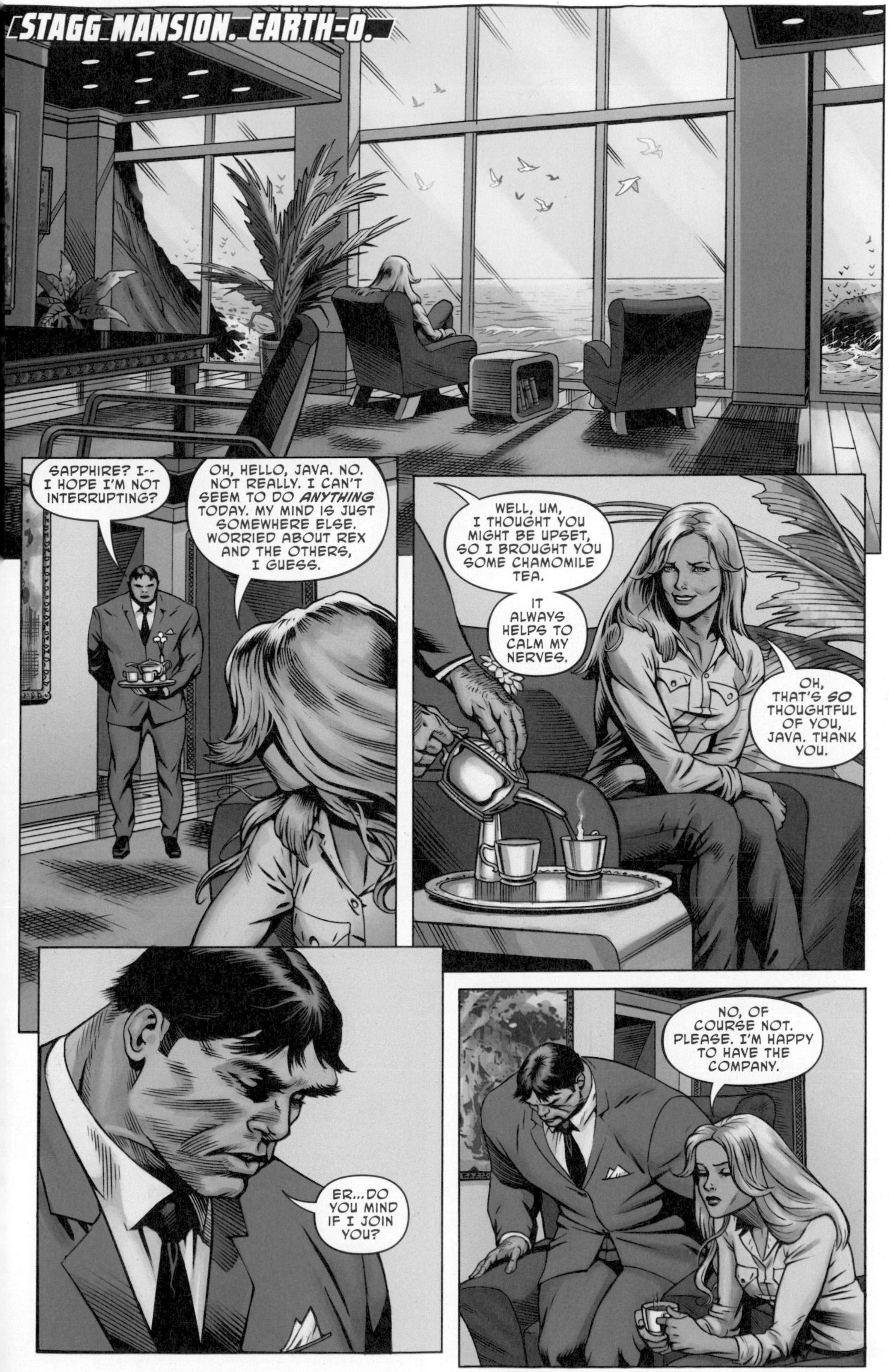
STAGG MANSION. EARTH-0.
SAPPHIRE? I-- I HOPE I'M NOT INTERRUPTING?
OH, HELLO, JAVA. NO. NOT REALLY. I CAN'T SEEM TO DO *ANYTHING* TODAY. MY MIND IS JUST SOMEWHERE ELSE. WORRIED ABOUT REX AND THE OTHERS, I GUESS.
WELL, UM, I THOUGHT YOU MIGHT BE UPSET, SO I BROUGHT YOU SOME CHAMOMILE TEA.
IT ALWAYS HELPS TO CALM MY NERVES.
OH, THAT'S *SO* THOUGHTFUL OF YOU, JAVA. THANK YOU.
ER...DO YOU MIND IF I JOIN YOU?
NO, OF COURSE NOT. PLEASE. I'M HAPPY TO HAVE THE COMPANY.

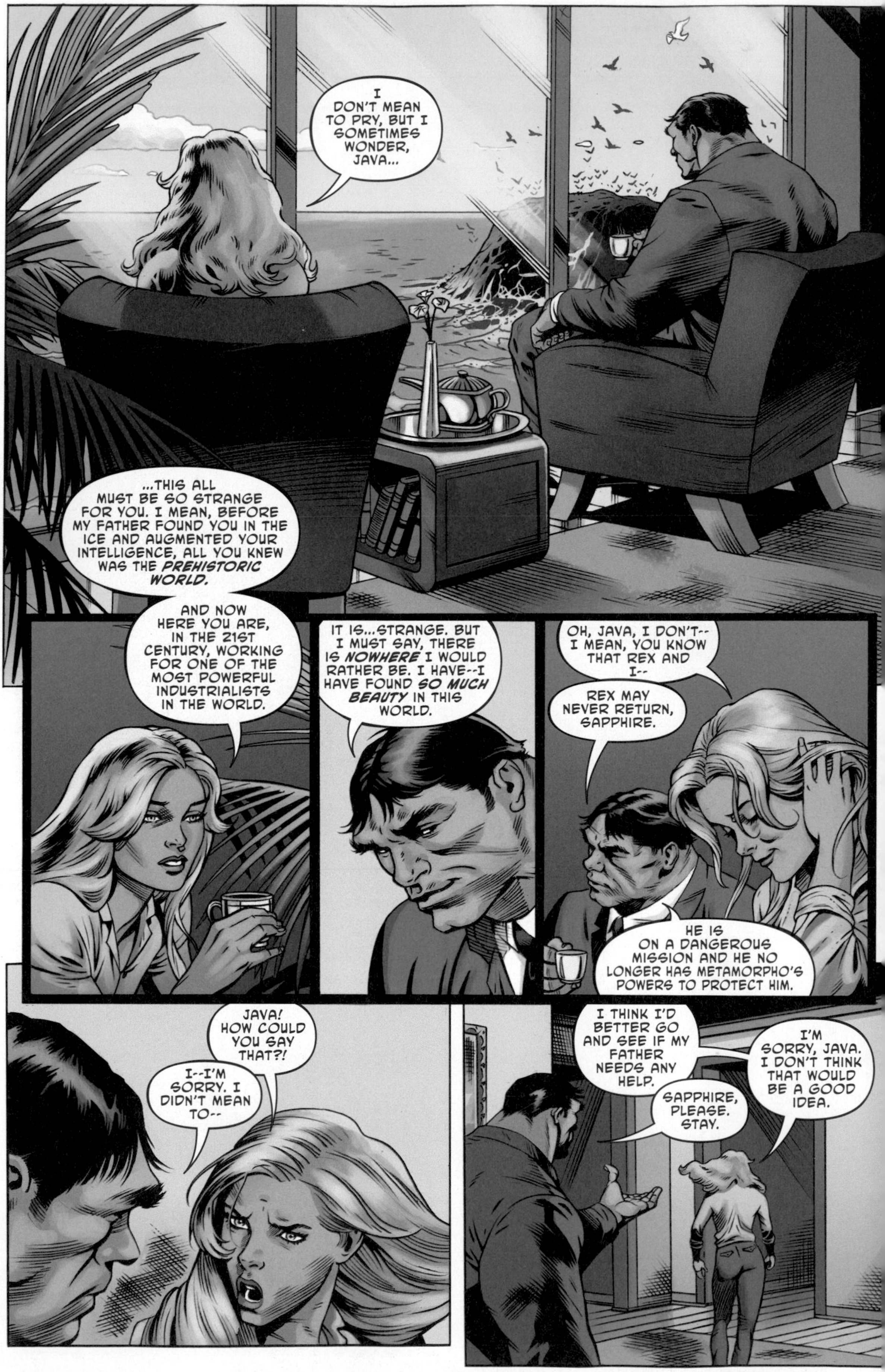
I DON'T MEAN TO PRY, BUT I SOMETIMES WONDER, JAVA...
...THIS ALL MUST BE SO STRANGE FOR YOU. I MEAN, BEFORE MY FATHER FOUND YOU IN THE ICE AND AUGMENTED YOUR INTELLIGENCE, ALL YOU KNEW WAS THE PREHISTORIC WORLD.
AND NOW HERE YOU ARE, IN THE 21ST CENTURY, WORKING FOR ONE OF THE MOST POWERFUL INDUSTRIALISTS IN THE WORLD.
IT IS...STRANGE. BUT I MUST SAY, THERE IS NOWHERE I WOULD RATHER BE. I HAVE--I HAVE FOUND SO MUCH BEAUTY IN THIS WORLD.
OH, JAVA, I DON'T-- I MEAN, YOU KNOW THAT REX AND I--
REX MAY NEVER RETURN, SAPPHIRE.
HE IS ON A DANGEROUS MISSION AND HE NO LONGER HAS METAMORPHO'S POWERS TO PROTECT HIM.
JAVA! HOW COULD YOU SAY THAT?!
I--I'M SORRY. I DIDN'T MEAN TO--
I THINK I'D BETTER GO AND SEE IF MY FATHER NEEDS ANY HELP.
SAPPHIRE, PLEASE. STAY.
I'M SORRY, JAVA. I DON'T THINK THAT WOULD BE A GOOD IDEA.

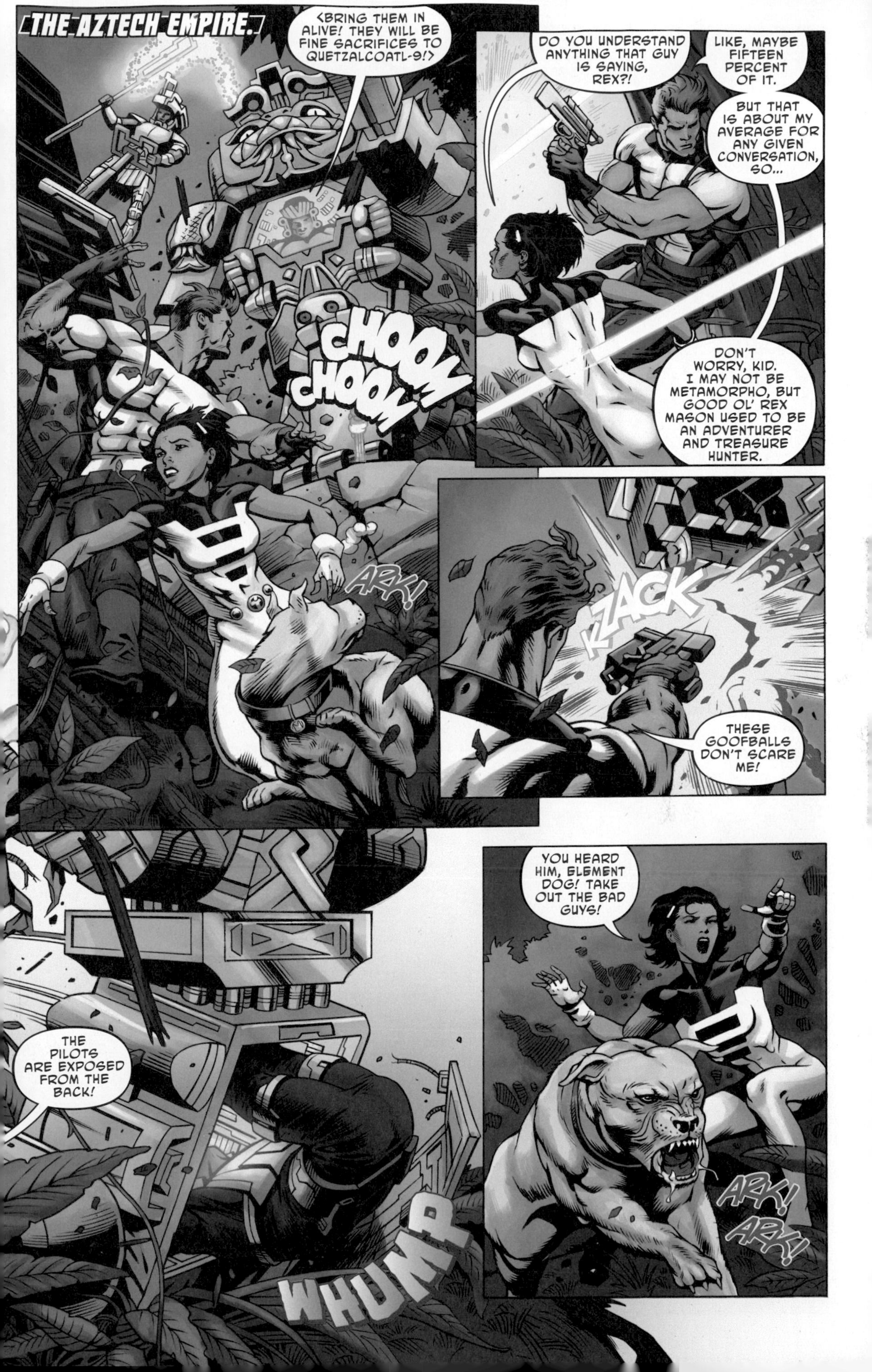
THE AZTECH EMPIRE.
<BRING THEM IN ALIVE! THEY WILL BE FINE SACRIFICES TO QUETZALCOATL-9!>
CHOOM CHOOM
ARK!
DO YOU UNDERSTAND ANYTHING THAT GUY IS SAYING, REX?!
LIKE, MAYBE FIFTEEN PERCENT OF IT.
BUT THAT IS ABOUT MY AVERAGE FOR ANY GIVEN CONVERSATION, SO...
DON'T WORRY, KID. I MAY NOT BE METAMORPHO, BUT GOOD OL' REX MASON USED TO BE AN ADVENTURER AND TREASURE HUNTER.
KZACK
THESE GOOFBALLS DON'T SCARE ME!
THE PILOTS ARE EXPOSED FROM THE BACK!
WHUMP
YOU HEARD HIM, ELEMENT DOG! TAKE OUT THE BAD GUYS!
ARK! ARK!

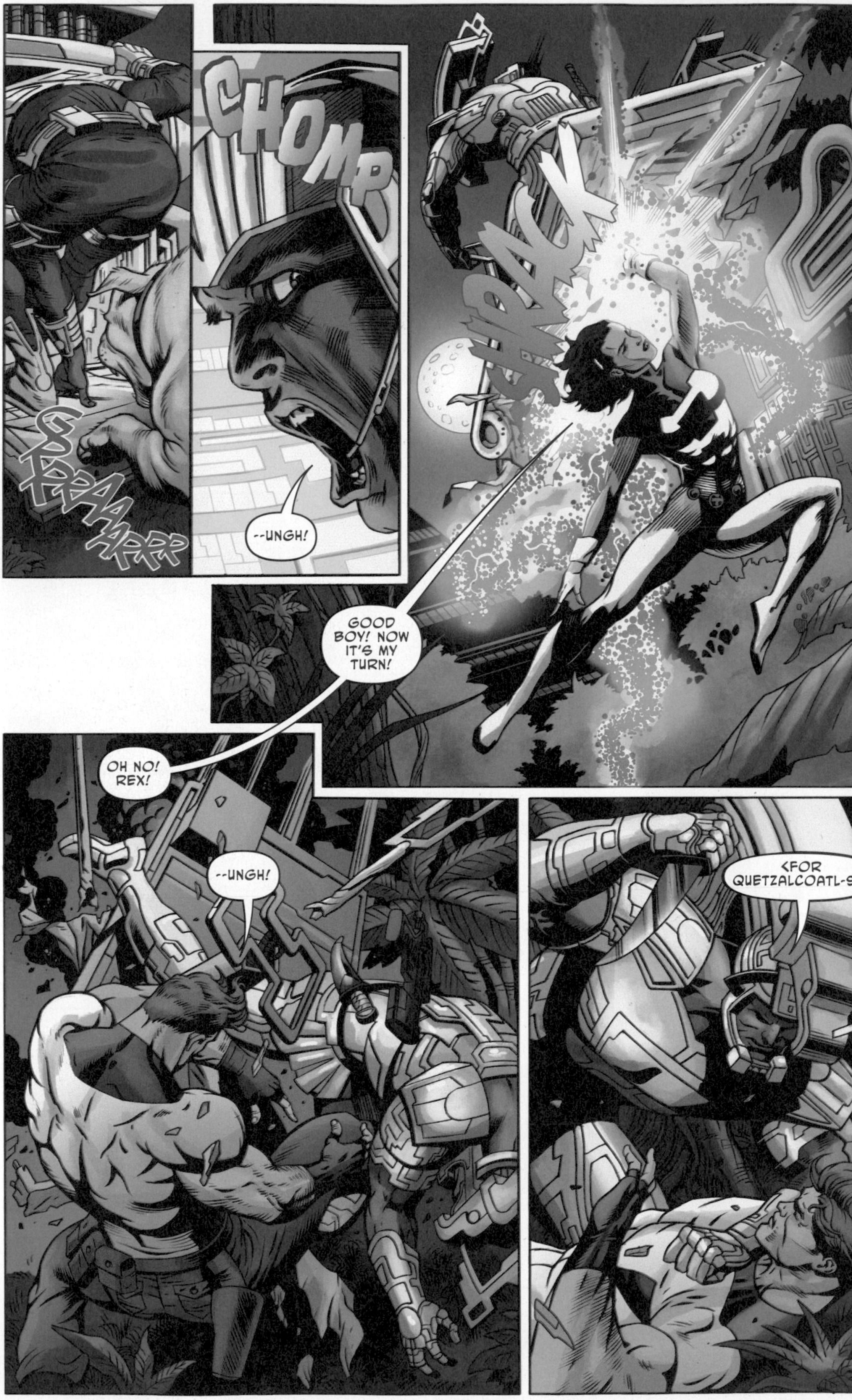
SKRAAARRR
CHOMP
--UNGH!
KRACK
GOOD BOY! NOW IT'S MY TURN!
OH NO! REX!
--UNGH!
<FOR QUETZALCOATL-9!>

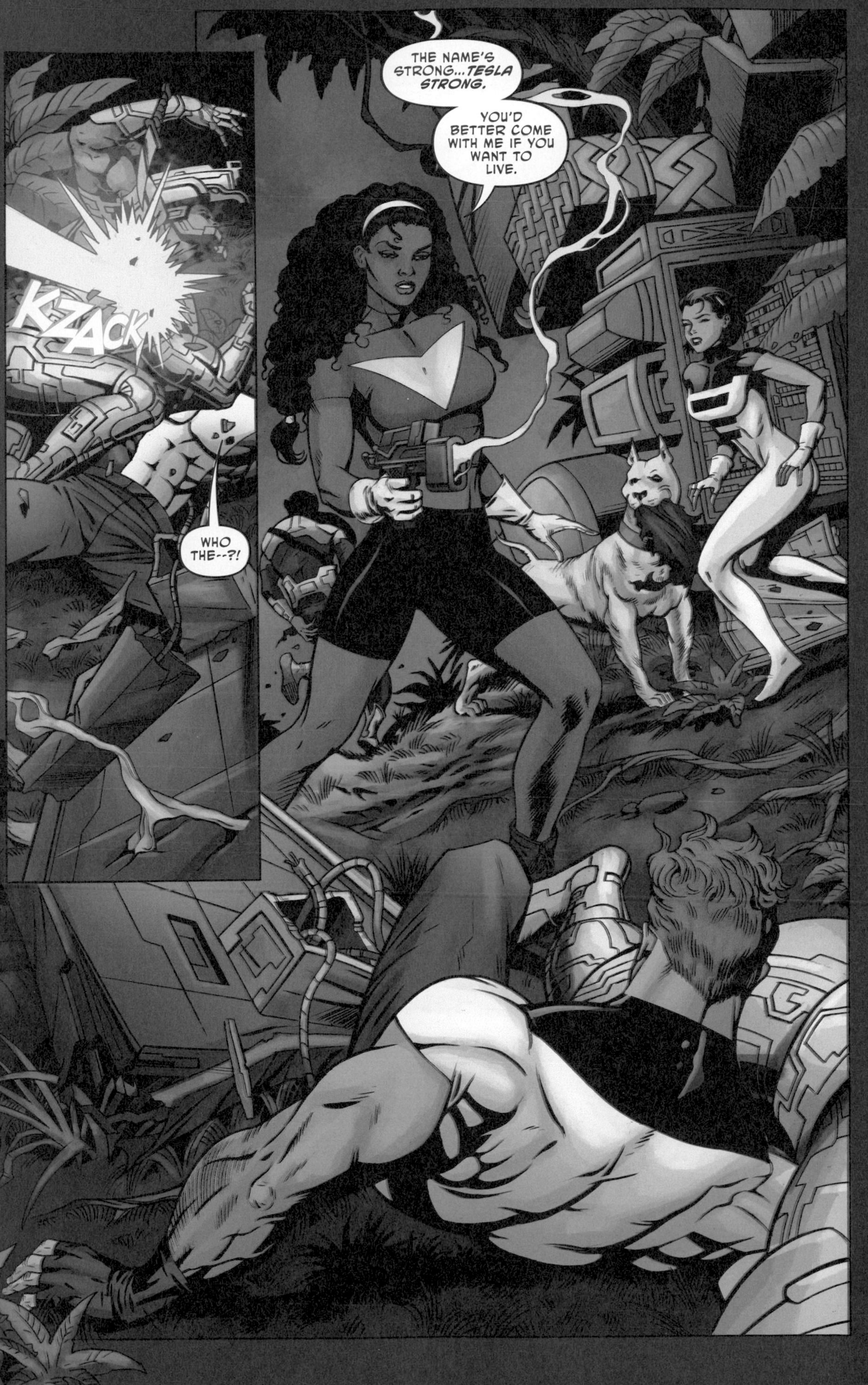

K-ZACK
WHO THE--?!
THE NAME'S STRONG...TESLA STRONG.
YOU'D BETTER COME WITH ME IF YOU WANT TO LIVE.

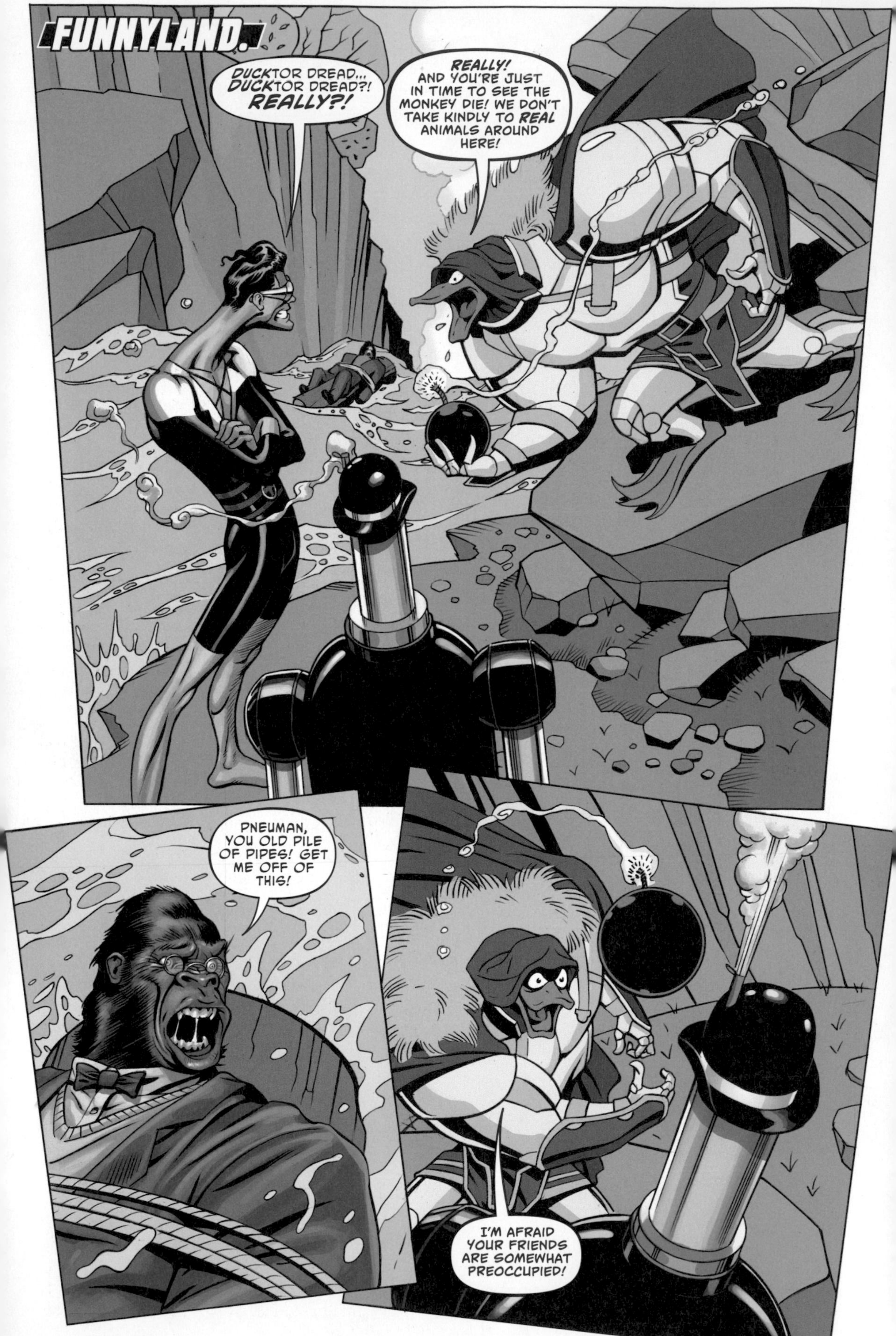
FUNNYLAND.
DUCKTOR DREAD... DUCKTOR DREAD?! REALLY?!
REALLY! AND YOU'RE JUST IN TIME TO SEE THE MONKEY DIE! WE DON'T TAKE KINDLY TO REAL ANIMALS AROUND HERE!
PNEUMAN, YOU OLD PILE OF PIPES! GET ME OFF OF THIS!
I'M AFRAID YOUR FRIENDS ARE SOMEWHAT PREOCCUPIED!

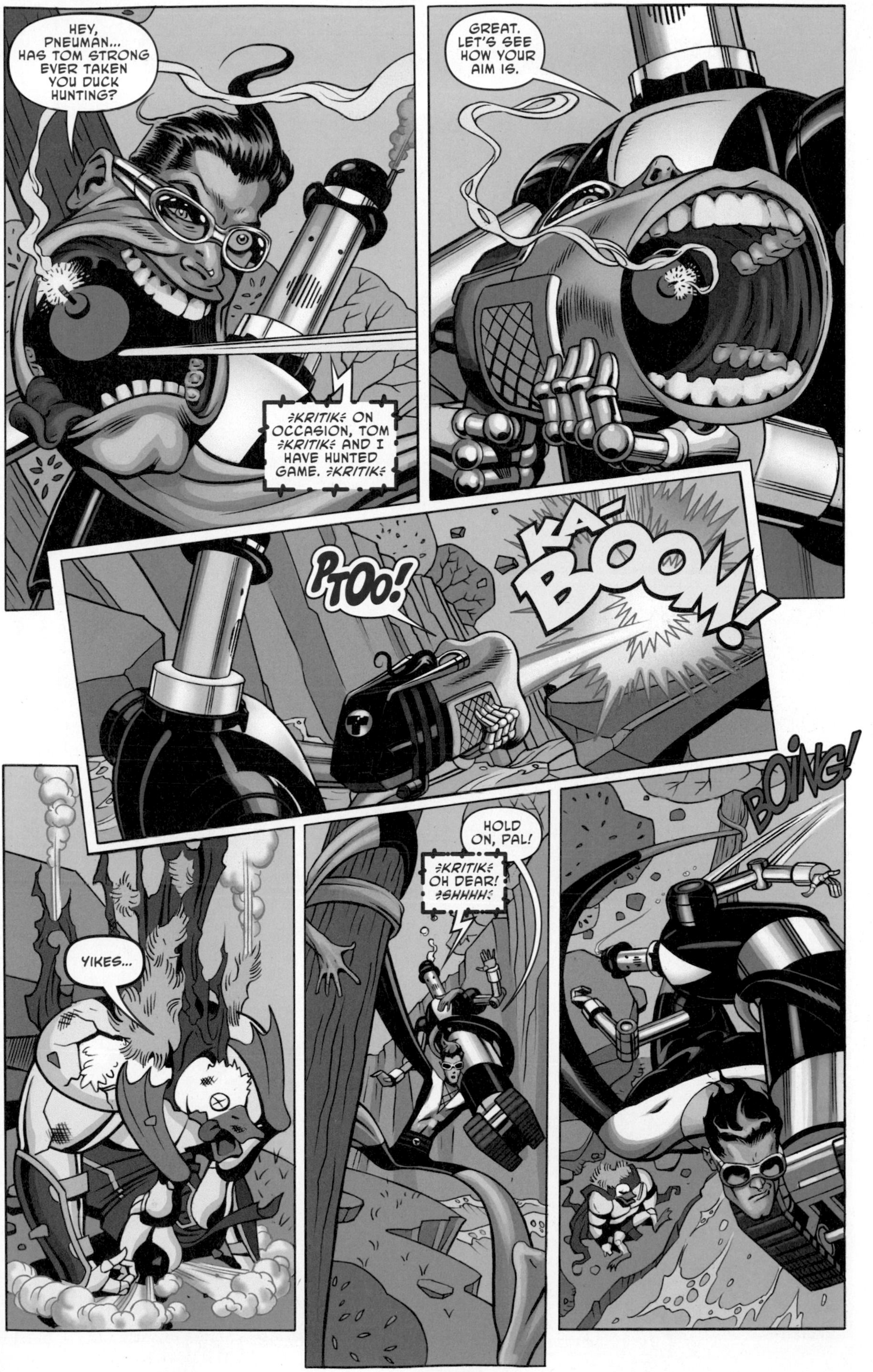
HEY, PNEUMAN... HAS TOM STRONG EVER TAKEN YOU DUCK HUNTING?
⌁KRITIK⌁ ON OCCASION, TOM ⌁KRITIK⌁ AND I HAVE HUNTED GAME. ⌁KRITIK⌁
GREAT. LET'S SEE HOW YOUR AIM IS.
PTOO!
KA-BOOM!
YIKES...
HOLD ON, PAL!
⌁KRITIK⌁ OH DEAR! ⌁SHHHH⌁
BOING!

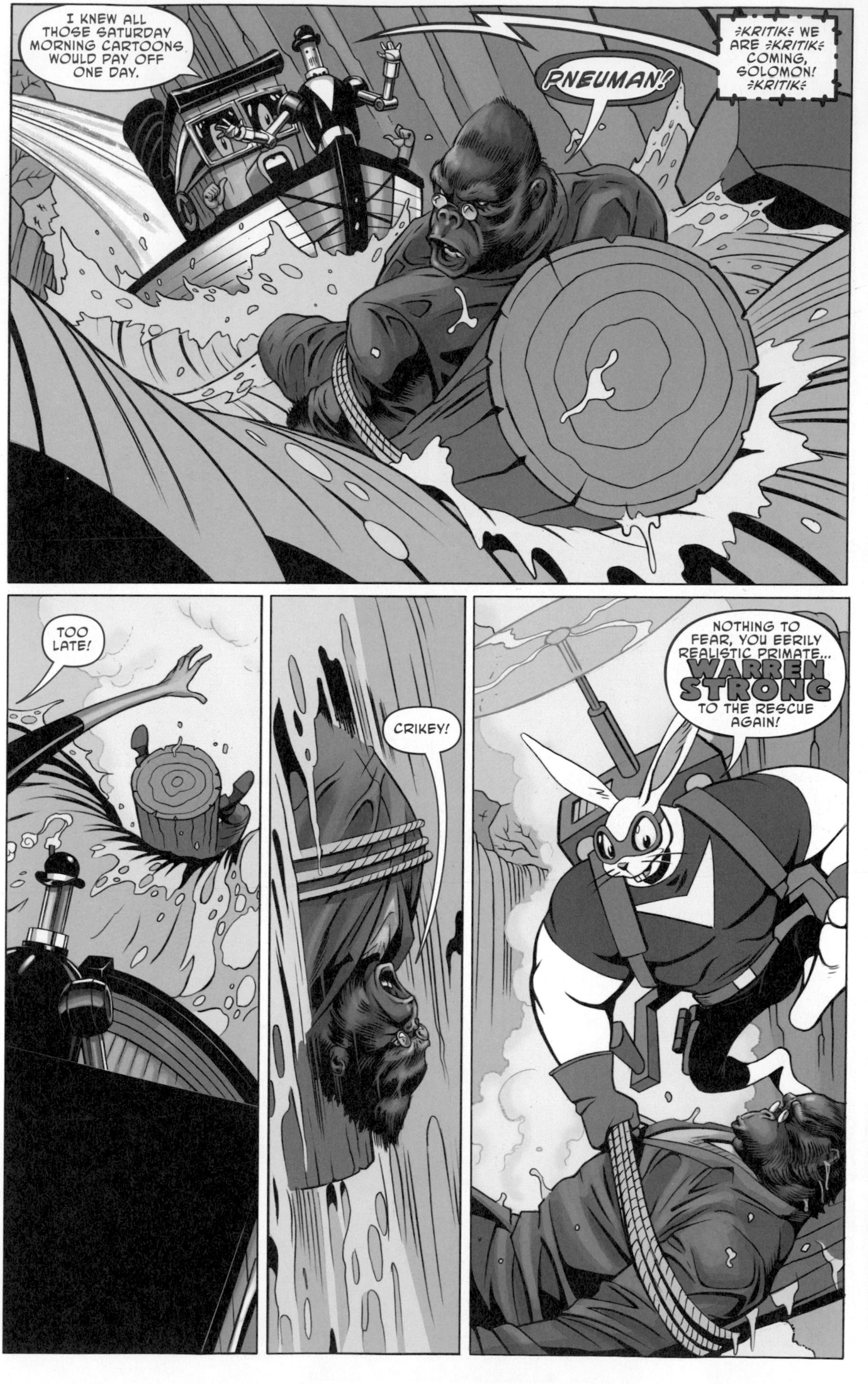
I KNEW ALL THOSE SATURDAY MORNING CARTOONS WOULD PAY OFF ONE DAY.
PNEUMAN!
⇒KRITIK⇐ WE ARE ⇒KRITIK⇐ COMING, SOLOMON! ⇒KRITIK⇐
TOO LATE!
CRIKEY!
NOTHING TO FEAR, YOU EERILY REALISTIC PRIMATE... WARREN STRONG TO THE RESCUE AGAIN!

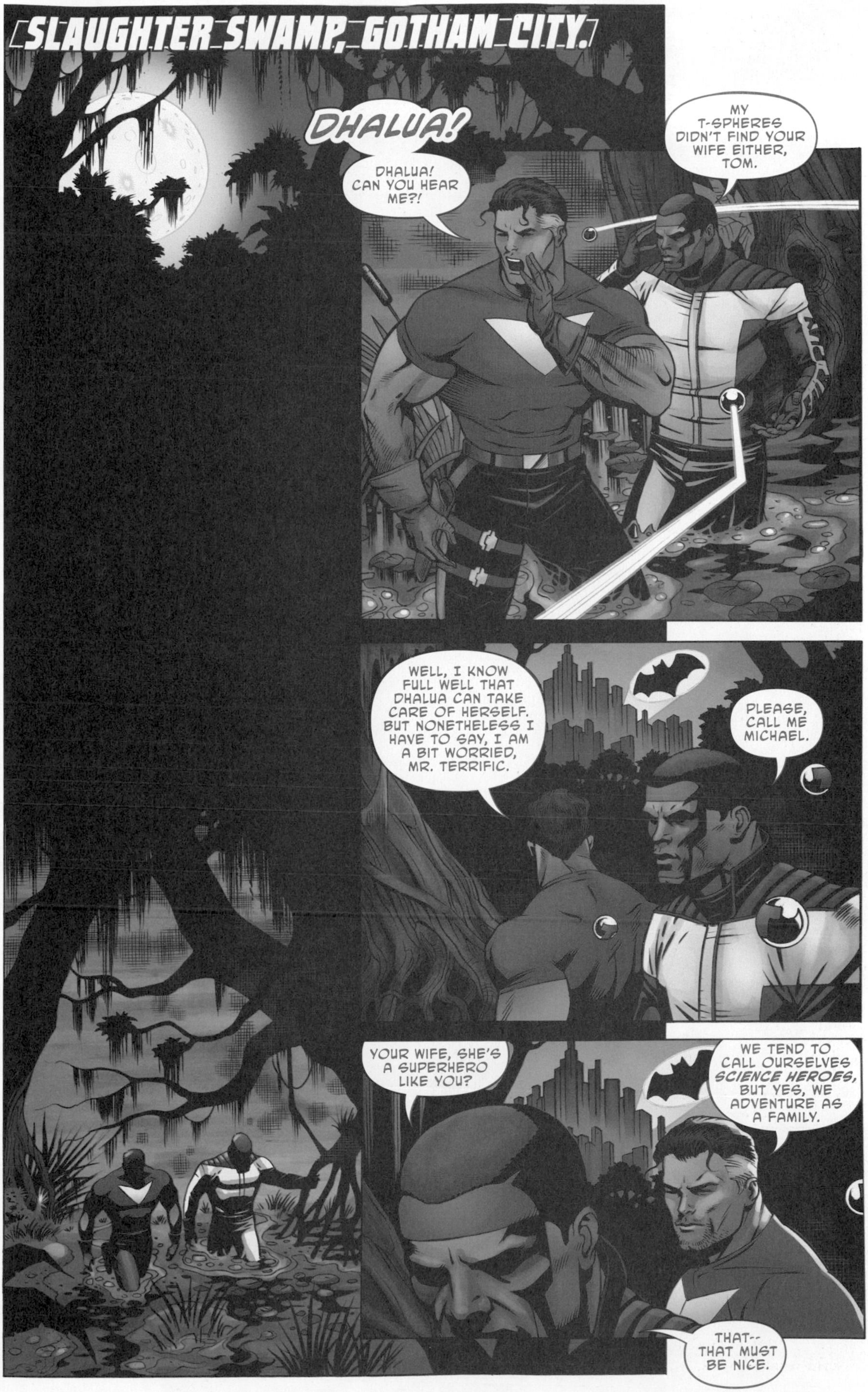
SLAUGHTER SWAMP, GOTHAM CITY.
DHALUA!
DHALUA! CAN YOU HEAR ME?!
MY T-SPHERES DIDN'T FIND YOUR WIFE EITHER, TOM.
WELL, I KNOW FULL WELL THAT DHALUA CAN TAKE CARE OF HERSELF. BUT NONETHELESS I HAVE TO SAY, I AM A BIT WORRIED, MR. TERRIFIC.
PLEASE, CALL ME MICHAEL.
YOUR WIFE, SHE'S A SUPERHERO LIKE YOU?
WE TEND TO CALL OURSELVES *SCIENCE HEROES*, BUT YES, WE ADVENTURE AS A FAMILY.
THAT-- THAT MUST BE NICE.

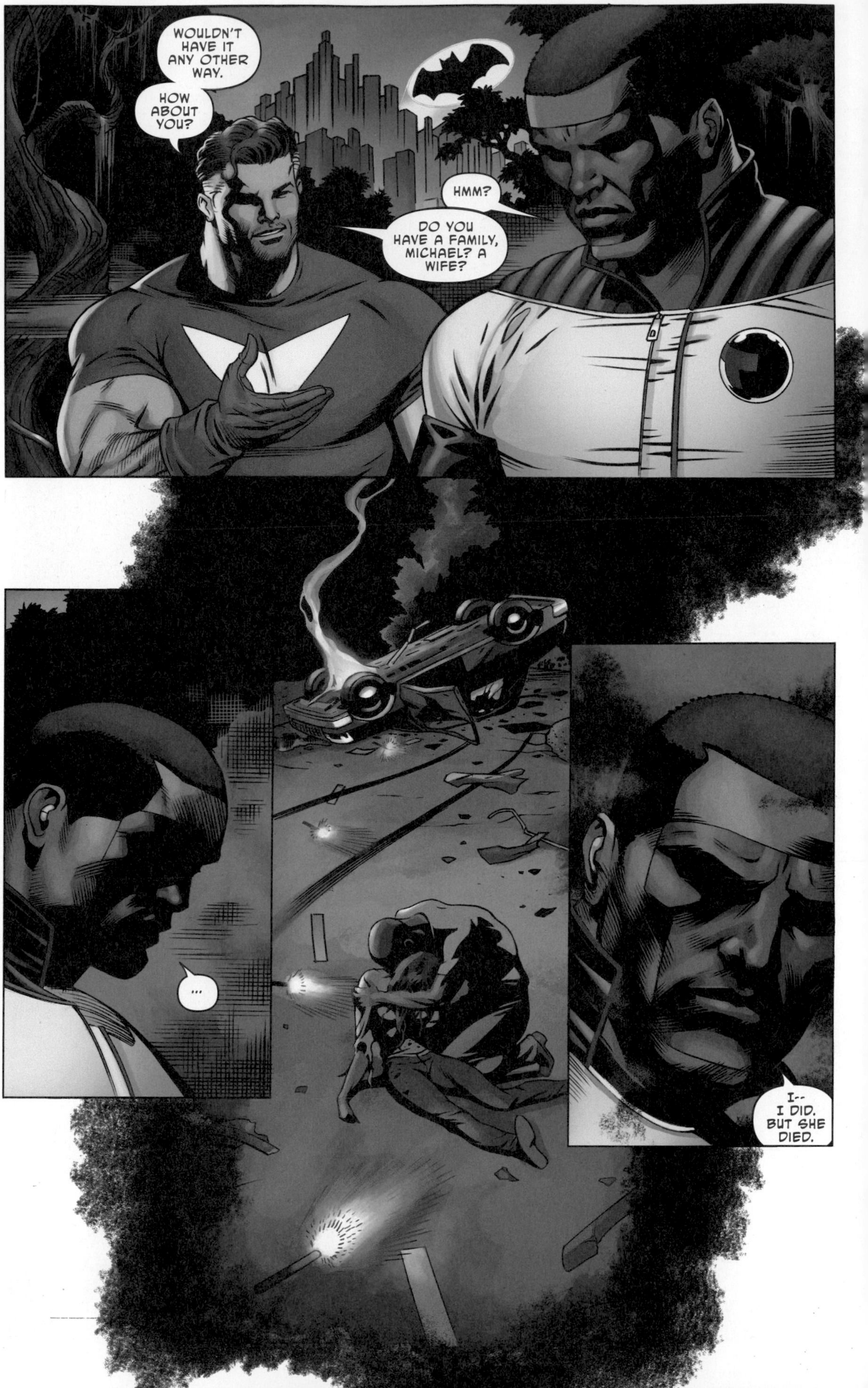
WOULDN'T HAVE IT ANY OTHER WAY.
HOW ABOUT YOU?
HMM?
DO YOU HAVE A FAMILY, MICHAEL? A WIFE?
...
I-- I DID. BUT SHE DIED.

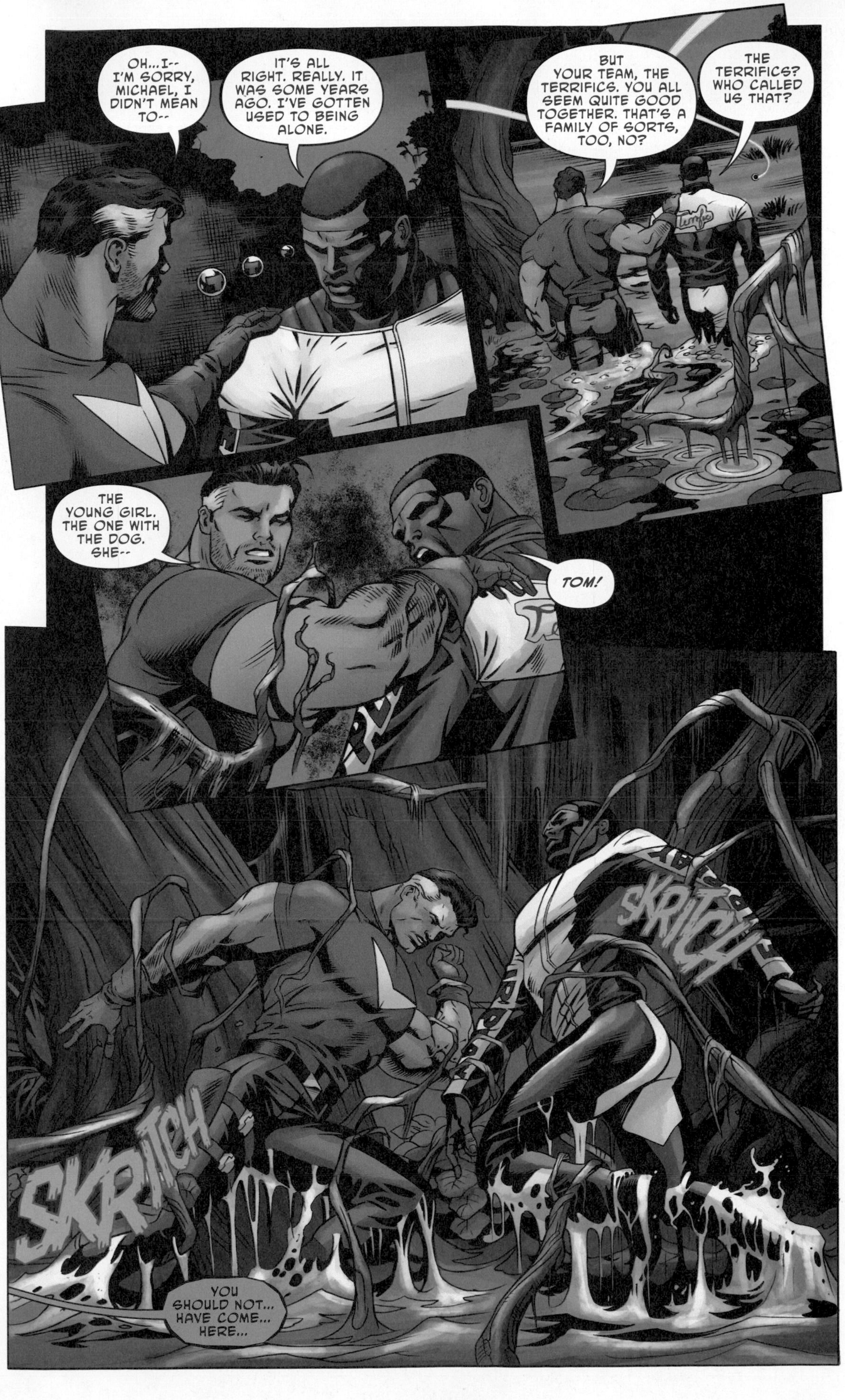
OH...I--
I'M SORRY, MICHAEL, I DIDN'T MEAN TO--
IT'S ALL RIGHT. REALLY. IT WAS SOME YEARS AGO. I'VE GOTTEN USED TO BEING ALONE.
BUT YOUR TEAM, THE TERRIFICS. YOU ALL SEEM QUITE GOOD TOGETHER. THAT'S A FAMILY OF SORTS, TOO, NO?
THE TERRIFICS? WHO CALLED US THAT?
THE YOUNG GIRL. THE ONE WITH THE DOG. SHE--
TOM!
SKRITCH
SKRITCH
YOU SHOULD NOT... HAVE COME... HERE...

THIS PLACE...IS SACRED...
I WILL NOT HAVE IT...DEFILED BY THE LIKES OF YOU!
TOM STRONG & THE TERRIFICS
PART TWO
DALE EAGLESHAM & JEFF LEMIRE STORYTELLERS
MICHAEL ATIYEH COLORS TOM NAPOLITANO LETTERS
DALE EAGLESHAM & IVAN NUNES COVER
ANDREW MARINO ASSISTANT EDITOR
PAUL KAMINSKI EDITOR MARIE JAVINS GROUP EDITOR

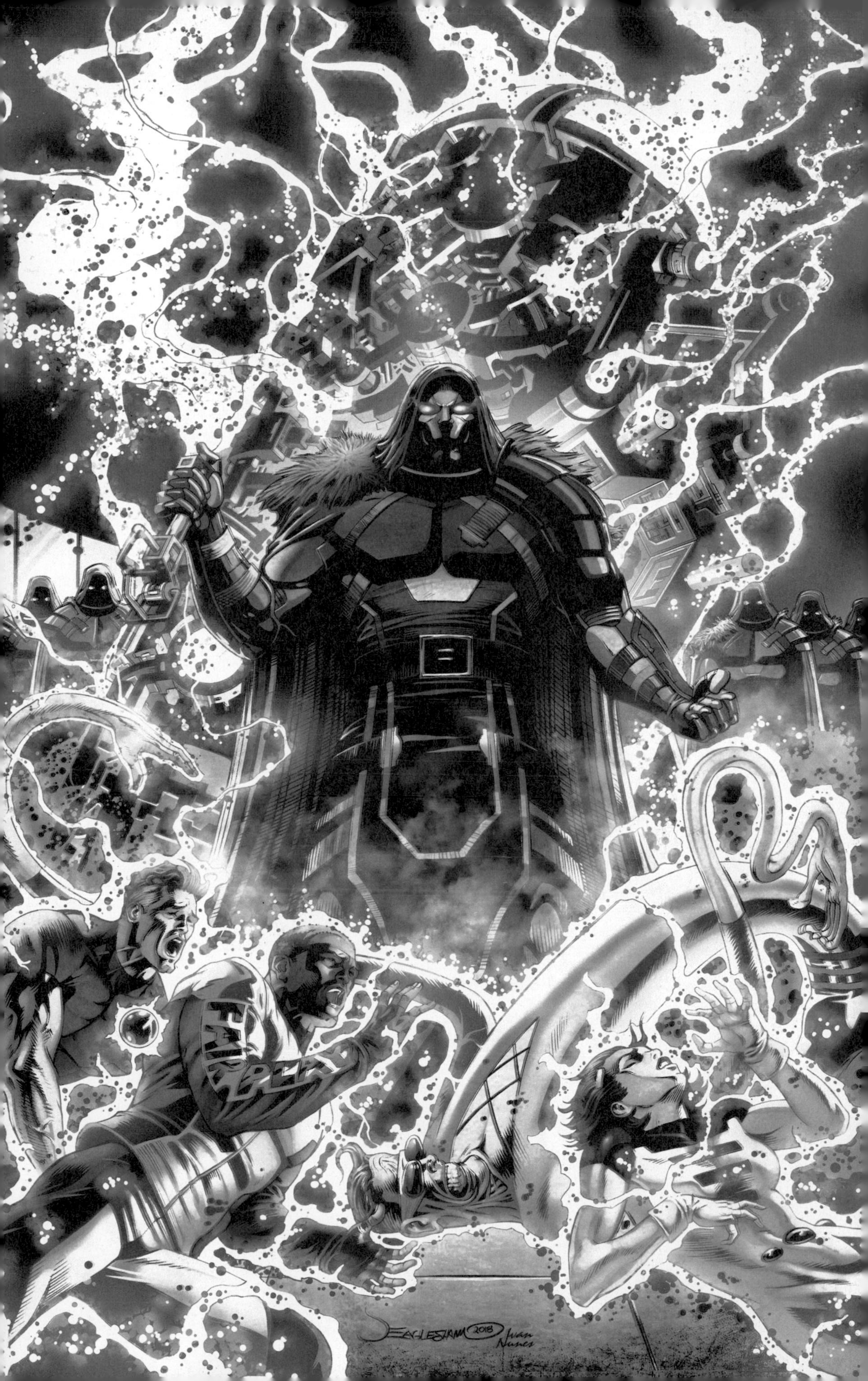

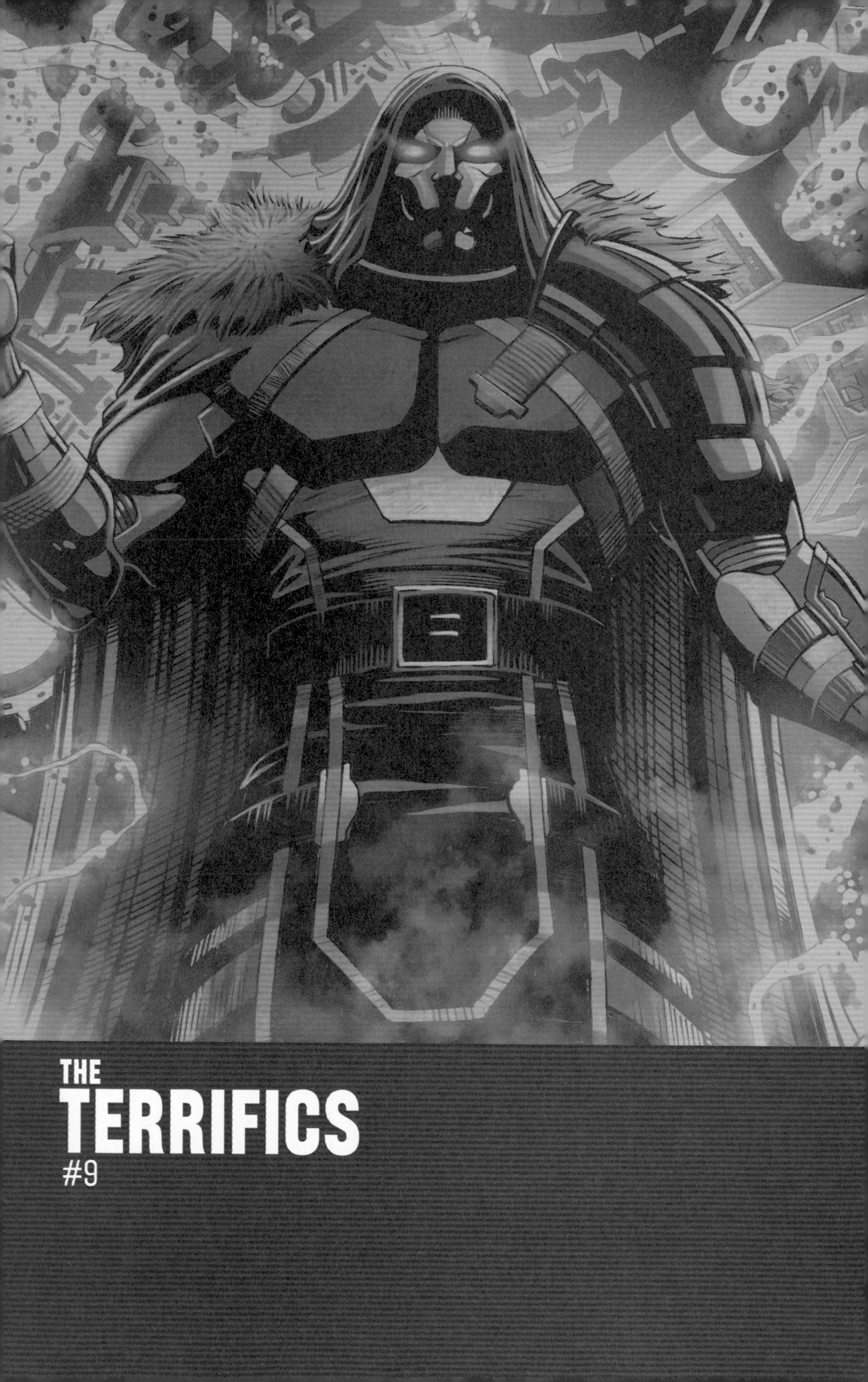

THE TERRIFICS
#9

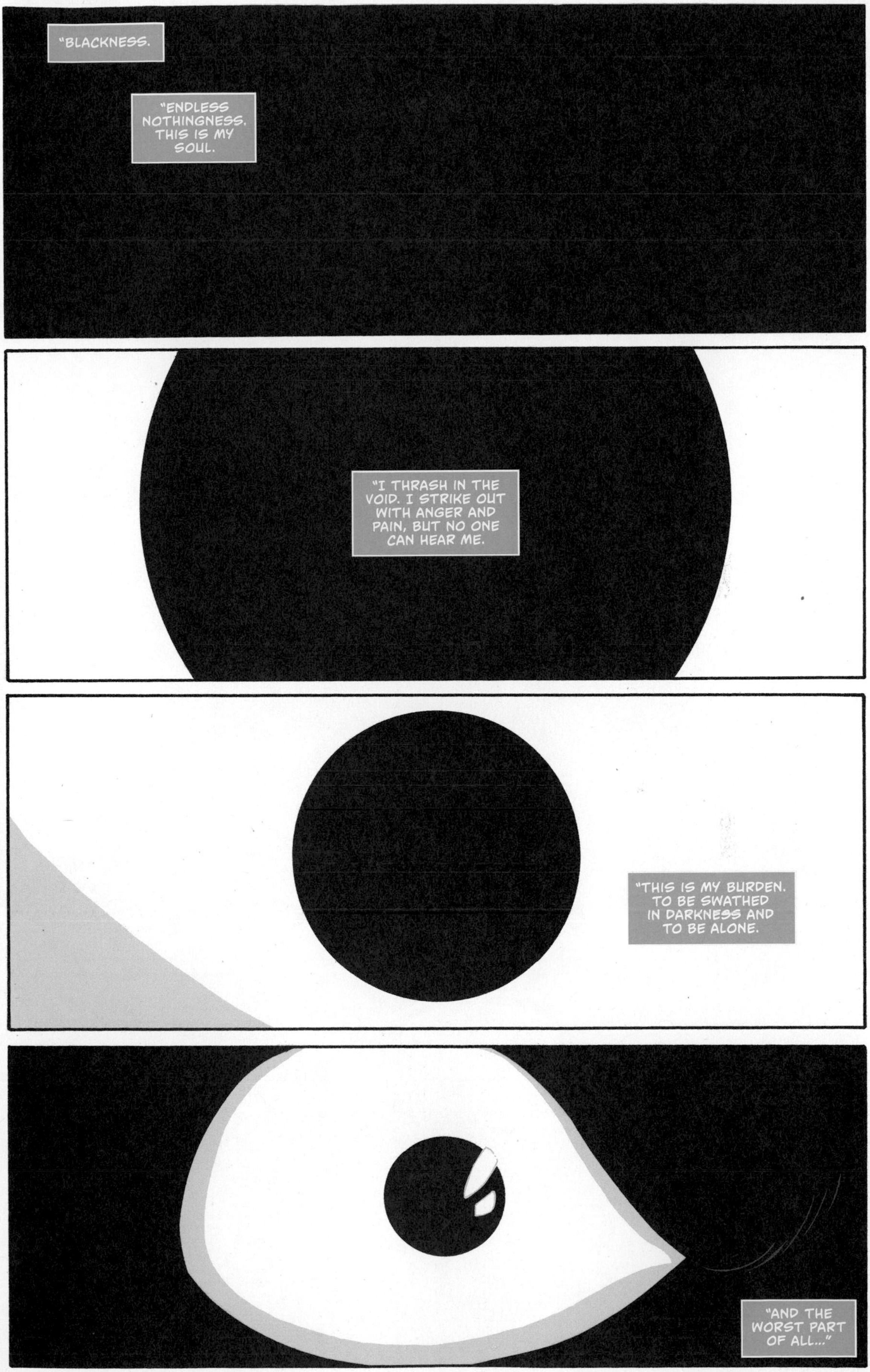
"BLACKNESS.
"ENDLESS NOTHINGNESS. THIS IS MY SOUL.
"I THRASH IN THE VOID. I STRIKE OUT WITH ANGER AND PAIN, BUT NO ONE CAN HEAR ME.
"THIS IS MY BURDEN. TO BE SWATHED IN DARKNESS AND TO BE ALONE.
"AND THE WORST PART OF ALL..."

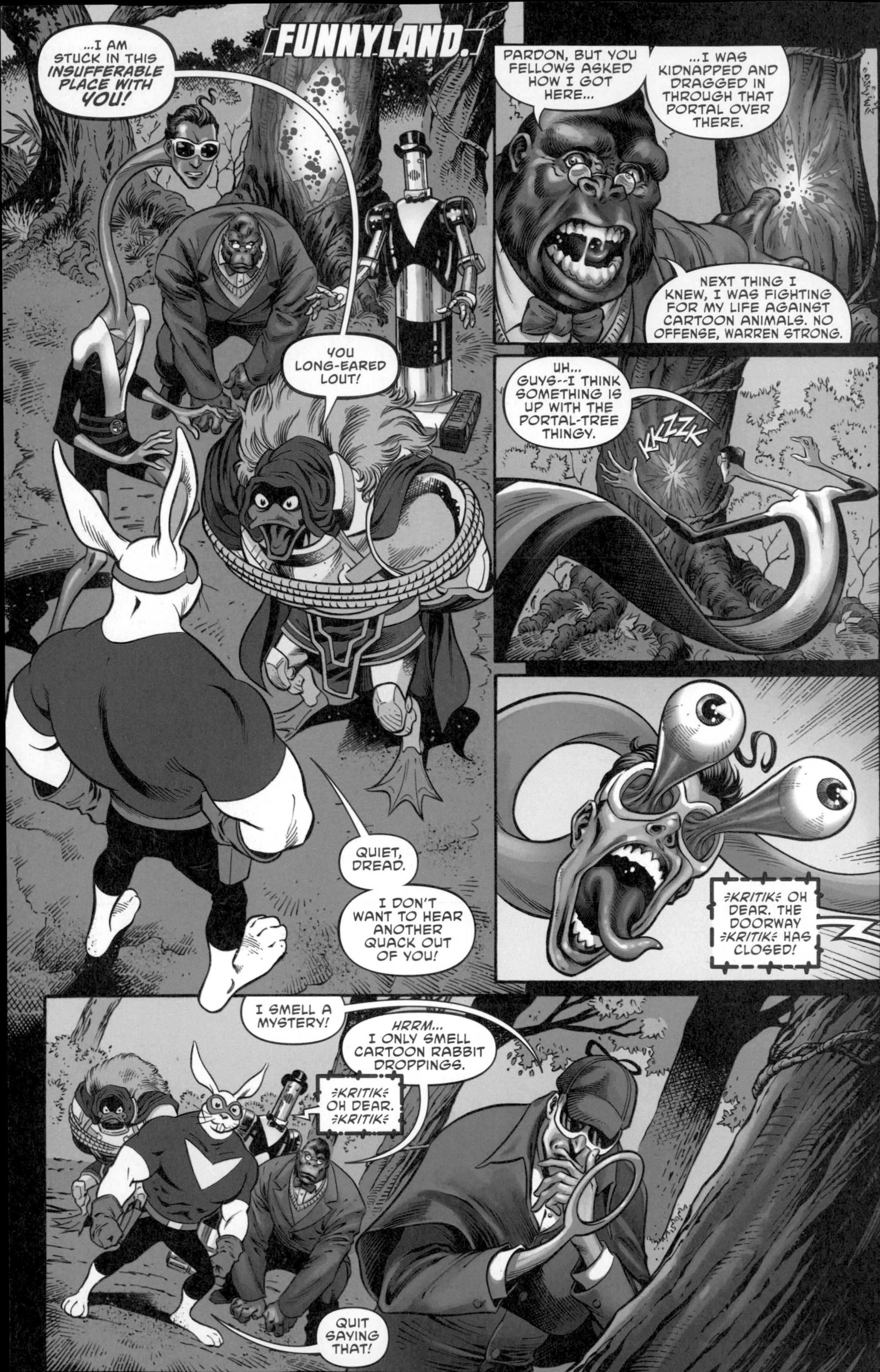
FUNNYLAND.
...I AM STUCK IN THIS INSUFFERABLE PLACE WITH YOU!
YOU LONG-EARED LOUT!
QUIET, DREAD.
I DON'T WANT TO HEAR ANOTHER QUACK OUT OF YOU!
PARDON, BUT YOU FELLOWS ASKED HOW I GOT HERE...
...I WAS KIDNAPPED AND DRAGGED IN THROUGH THAT PORTAL OVER THERE.
NEXT THING I KNEW, I WAS FIGHTING FOR MY LIFE AGAINST CARTOON ANIMALS. NO OFFENSE, WARREN STRONG.
UH... GUYS--I THINK SOMETHING IS UP WITH THE PORTAL-TREE THINGY.
KKZZZK
≠KRITIK≠ OH DEAR. THE DOORWAY ≠KRITIK≠ HAS CLOSED!
I SMELL A MYSTERY!
HRRM... I ONLY SMELL CARTOON RABBIT DROPPINGS.
≠KRITIK≠ OH DEAR. ≠KRITIK≠
QUIT SAYING THAT!

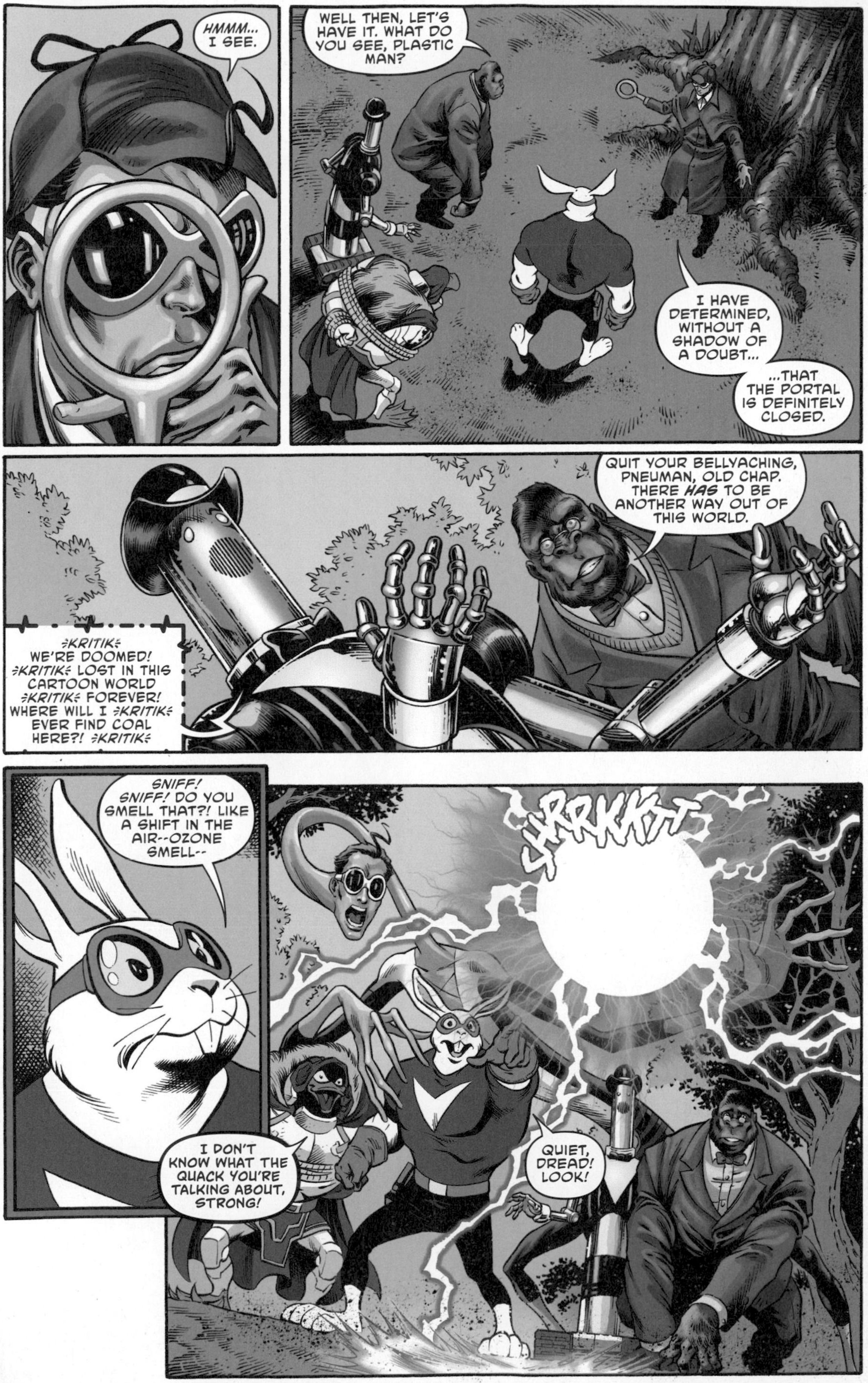
HMMM... I SEE.
WELL THEN, LET'S HAVE IT. WHAT DO YOU SEE, PLASTIC MAN?
I HAVE DETERMINED, WITHOUT A SHADOW OF A DOUBT...
...THAT THE PORTAL IS DEFINITELY CLOSED.
=KRITIK= WE'RE DOOMED! =KRITIK= LOST IN THIS CARTOON WORLD =KRITIK= FOREVER! WHERE WILL I =KRITIK= EVER FIND COAL HERE?! =KRITIK=
QUIT YOUR BELLYACHING, PNEUMAN, OLD CHAP. THERE HAS TO BE ANOTHER WAY OUT OF THIS WORLD.
SNIFF! SNIFF! DO YOU SMELL THAT?! LIKE A SHIFT IN THE AIR--OZONE SMELL--
SKRRKKT
I DON'T KNOW WHAT THE QUACK YOU'RE TALKING ABOUT, STRONG!
QUIET, DREAD! LOOK!

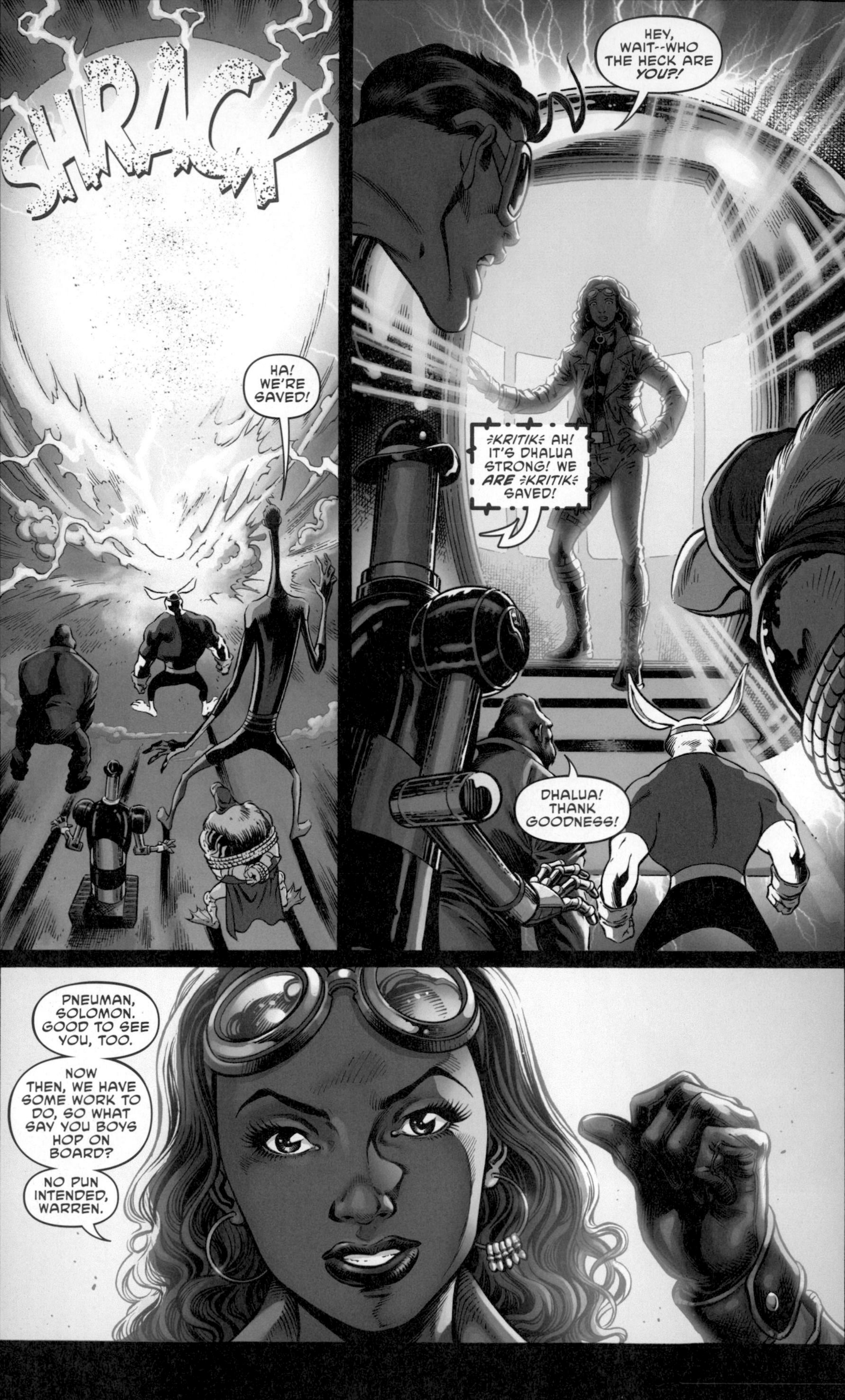
SHRACK
HA! WE'RE SAVED!
HEY, WAIT--WHO THE HECK ARE *YOU?!*
⇌KRITIK⇌ AH! IT'S DHALUA STRONG! WE *ARE* ⇌KRITIK⇌ SAVED!
DHALUA! THANK GOODNESS!
PNEUMAN, SOLOMON. GOOD TO SEE YOU, TOO.
NOW THEN, WE HAVE SOME WORK TO DO, SO WHAT SAY YOU BOYS HOP ON BOARD?
NO PUN INTENDED, WARREN.

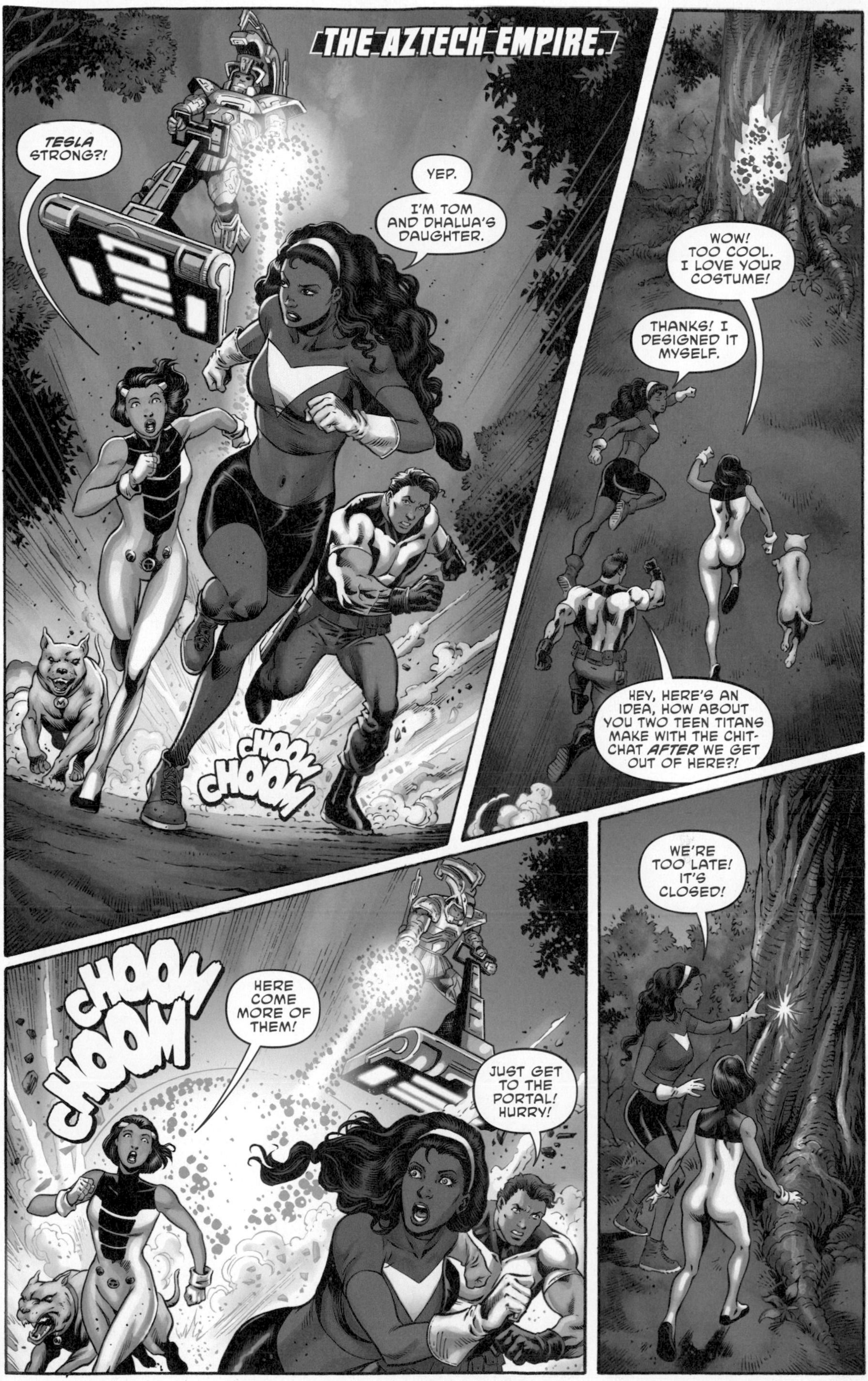
THE AZTECH EMPIRE.
TESLA STRONG?!
YEP.
I'M TOM AND DHALUA'S DAUGHTER.
CHOOM CHOOM
WOW! TOO COOL. I LOVE YOUR COSTUME!
THANKS! I DESIGNED IT MYSELF.
HEY, HERE'S AN IDEA, HOW ABOUT YOU TWO TEEN TITANS MAKE WITH THE CHIT-CHAT AFTER WE GET OUT OF HERE?!
CHOOM CHOOM
HERE COME MORE OF THEM!
JUST GET TO THE PORTAL! HURRY!
WE'RE TOO LATE! IT'S CLOSED!

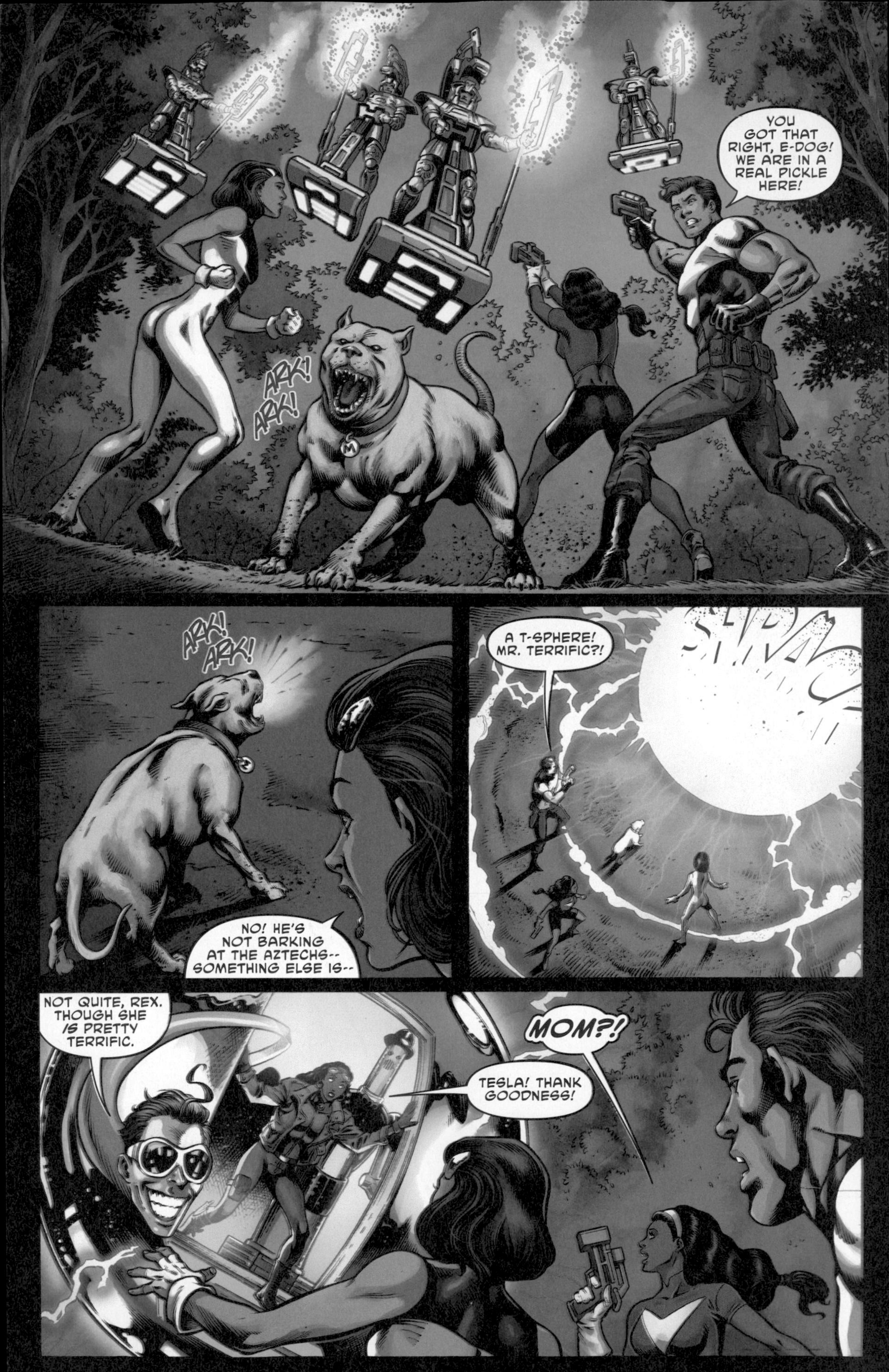
YOU GOT THAT RIGHT, E-DOG! WE ARE IN A REAL PICKLE HERE!
ARK! ARK!
ARK! ARK!
NO! HE'S NOT BARKING AT THE AZTECHS-- SOMETHING ELSE IS--
A T-SPHERE! MR. TERRIFIC?!
NOT QUITE, REX. THOUGH SHE *IS* PRETTY TERRIFIC.
MOM?!
TESLA! THANK GOODNESS!

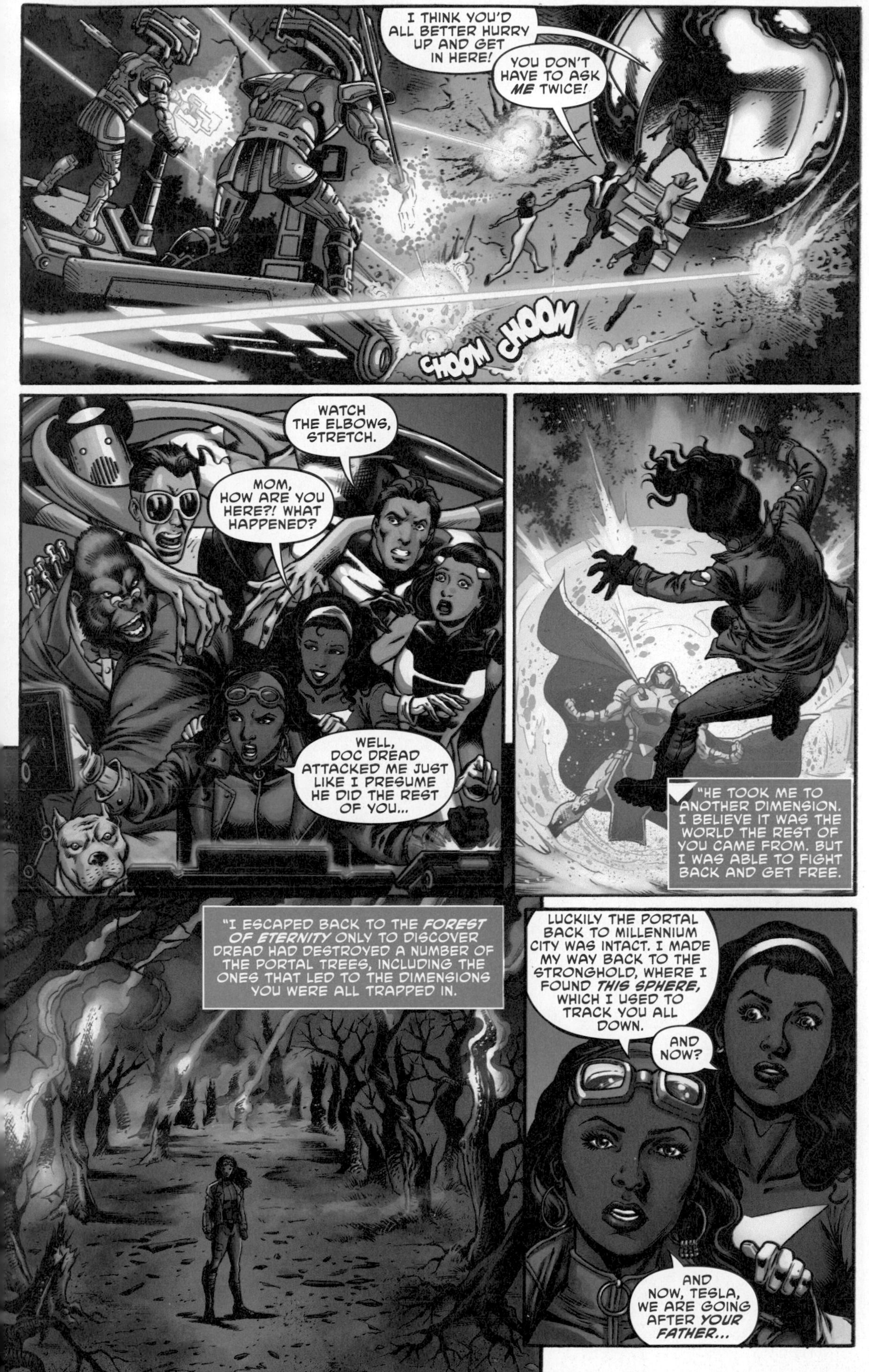

I THINK YOU'D ALL BETTER HURRY UP AND GET IN HERE!
YOU DON'T HAVE TO ASK *ME* TWICE!
CHOOM CHOOM
WATCH THE ELBOWS, STRETCH.
MOM, HOW ARE YOU HERE?! WHAT HAPPENED?
WELL, DOC DREAD ATTACKED ME JUST LIKE I PRESUME HE DID THE REST OF YOU...
"HE TOOK ME TO ANOTHER DIMENSION. I BELIEVE IT WAS THE WORLD THE REST OF YOU CAME FROM. BUT I WAS ABLE TO FIGHT BACK AND GET FREE.
"I ESCAPED BACK TO THE *FOREST OF ETERNITY* ONLY TO DISCOVER DREAD HAD DESTROYED A NUMBER OF THE PORTAL TREES, INCLUDING THE ONES THAT LED TO THE DIMENSIONS YOU WERE ALL TRAPPED IN.
LUCKILY THE PORTAL BACK TO MILLENNIUM CITY WAS INTACT. I MADE MY WAY BACK TO THE STRONGHOLD, WHERE I FOUND *THIS SPHERE,* WHICH I USED TO TRACK YOU ALL DOWN.
AND NOW?
AND NOW, TESLA, WE ARE GOING AFTER *YOUR FATHER*...

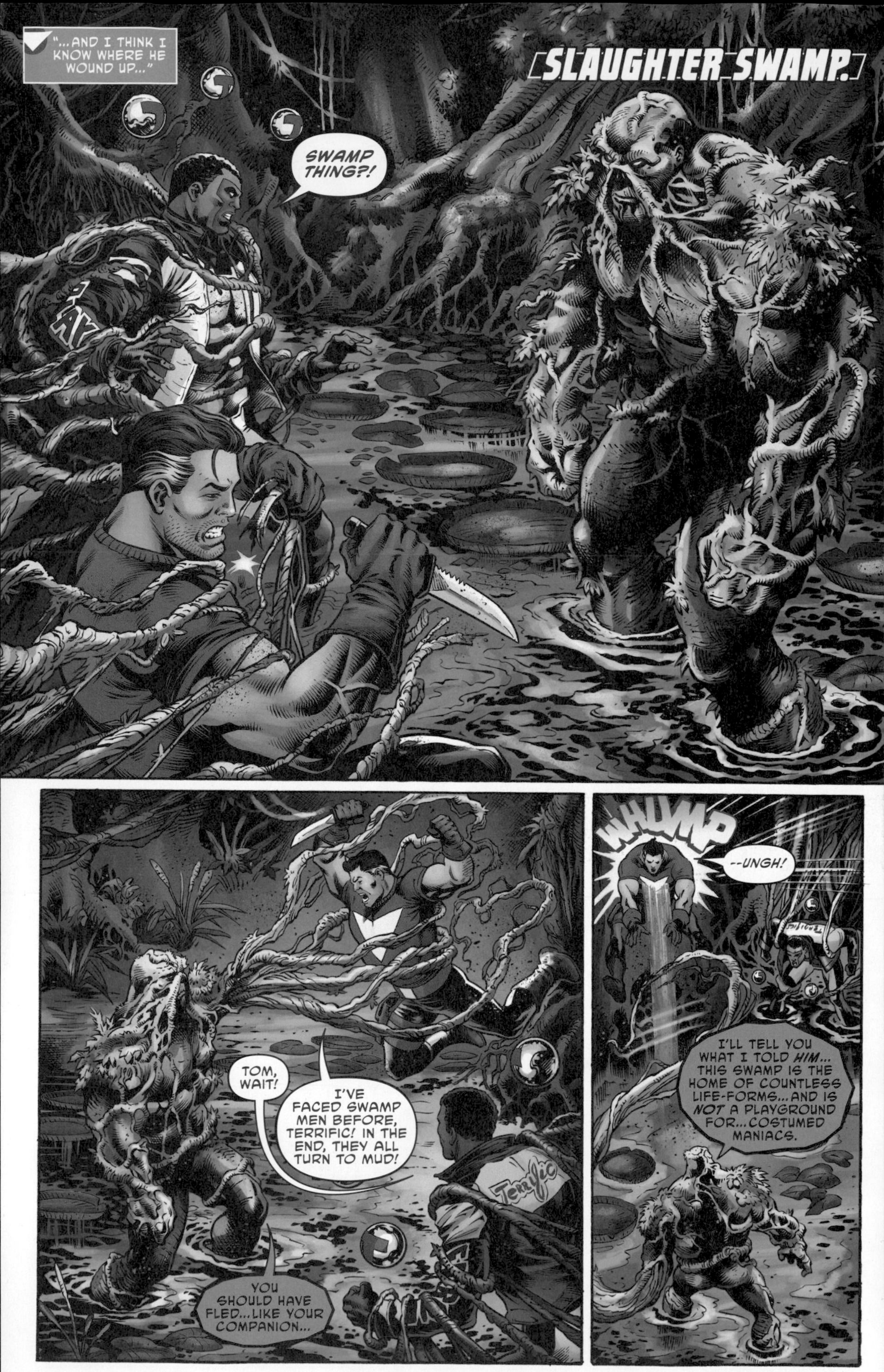
"...AND I THINK I KNOW WHERE HE WOUND UP..."
SLAUGHTER SWAMP.
SWAMP THING?!
TOM, WAIT!
I'VE FACED SWAMP MEN BEFORE, TERRIFIC! IN THE END, THEY ALL TURN TO MUD!
YOU SHOULD HAVE FLED...LIKE YOUR COMPANION...
WHUMP
--UNGH!
I'LL TELL YOU WHAT I TOLD HIM... THIS SWAMP IS THE HOME OF COUNTLESS LIFE-FORMS...AND IS NOT A PLAYGROUND FOR...COSTUMED MANIACS.

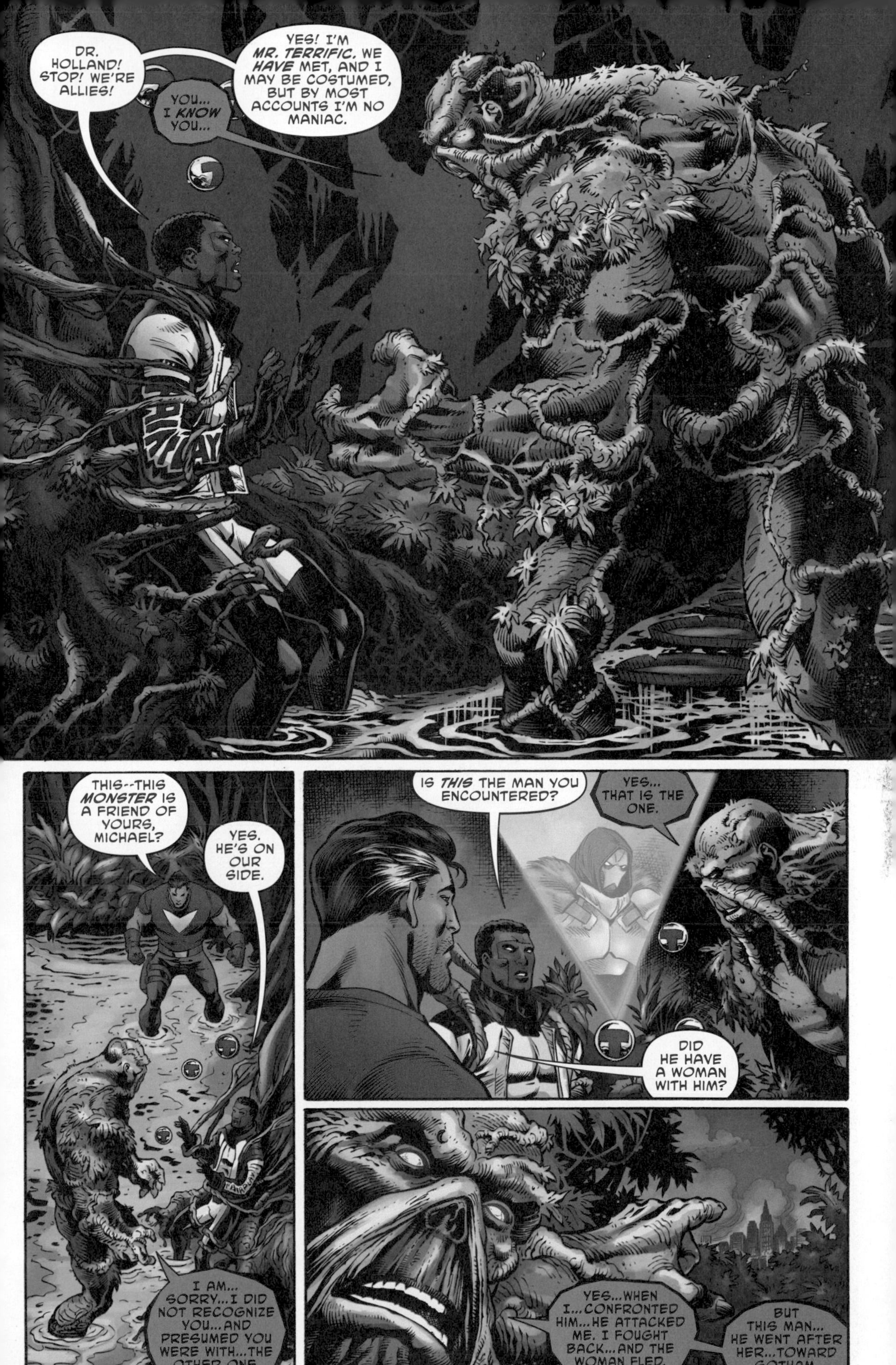

DR. HOLLAND! STOP! WE'RE ALLIES!
YOU... I KNOW YOU...
YES! I'M MR. TERRIFIC. WE HAVE MET, AND I MAY BE COSTUMED, BUT BY MOST ACCOUNTS I'M NO MANIAC.
THIS--THIS MONSTER IS A FRIEND OF YOURS, MICHAEL?
YES. HE'S ON OUR SIDE.
I AM... SORRY... I DID NOT RECOGNIZE YOU... AND PRESUMED YOU WERE WITH... THE OTHER ONE.
IS THIS THE MAN YOU ENCOUNTERED?
YES... THAT IS THE ONE.
DID HE HAVE A WOMAN WITH HIM?
YES... WHEN I... CONFRONTED HIM... HE ATTACKED ME. I FOUGHT BACK... AND THE WOMAN FLED.
BUT THIS MAN... HE WENT AFTER HER... TOWARD GOTHAM.

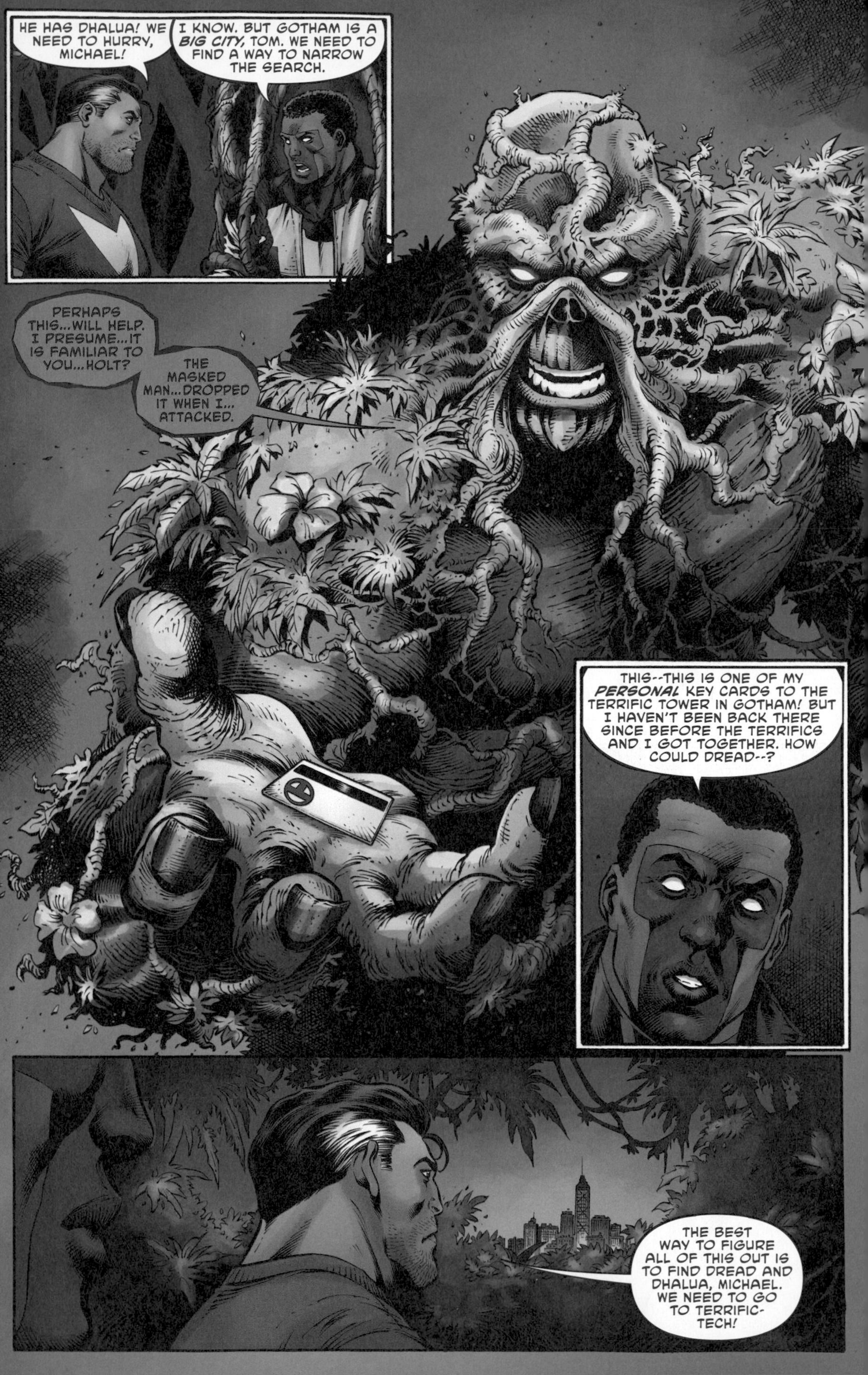
HE HAS DHALUA! WE NEED TO HURRY, MICHAEL!
I KNOW. BUT GOTHAM IS A *BIG CITY,* TOM. WE NEED TO FIND A WAY TO NARROW THE SEARCH.
PERHAPS THIS...WILL HELP. I PRESUME...IT IS FAMILIAR TO YOU...HOLT?
THE MASKED MAN...DROPPED IT WHEN I... ATTACKED.
THIS--THIS IS ONE OF MY *PERSONAL* KEY CARDS TO THE TERRIFIC TOWER IN GOTHAM! BUT I HAVEN'T BEEN BACK THERE SINCE BEFORE THE TERRIFICS AND I GOT TOGETHER. HOW COULD DREAD--?
THE BEST WAY TO FIGURE ALL OF THIS OUT IS TO FIND DREAD AND DHALUA, MICHAEL. WE NEED TO GO TO TERRIFIC-TECH!

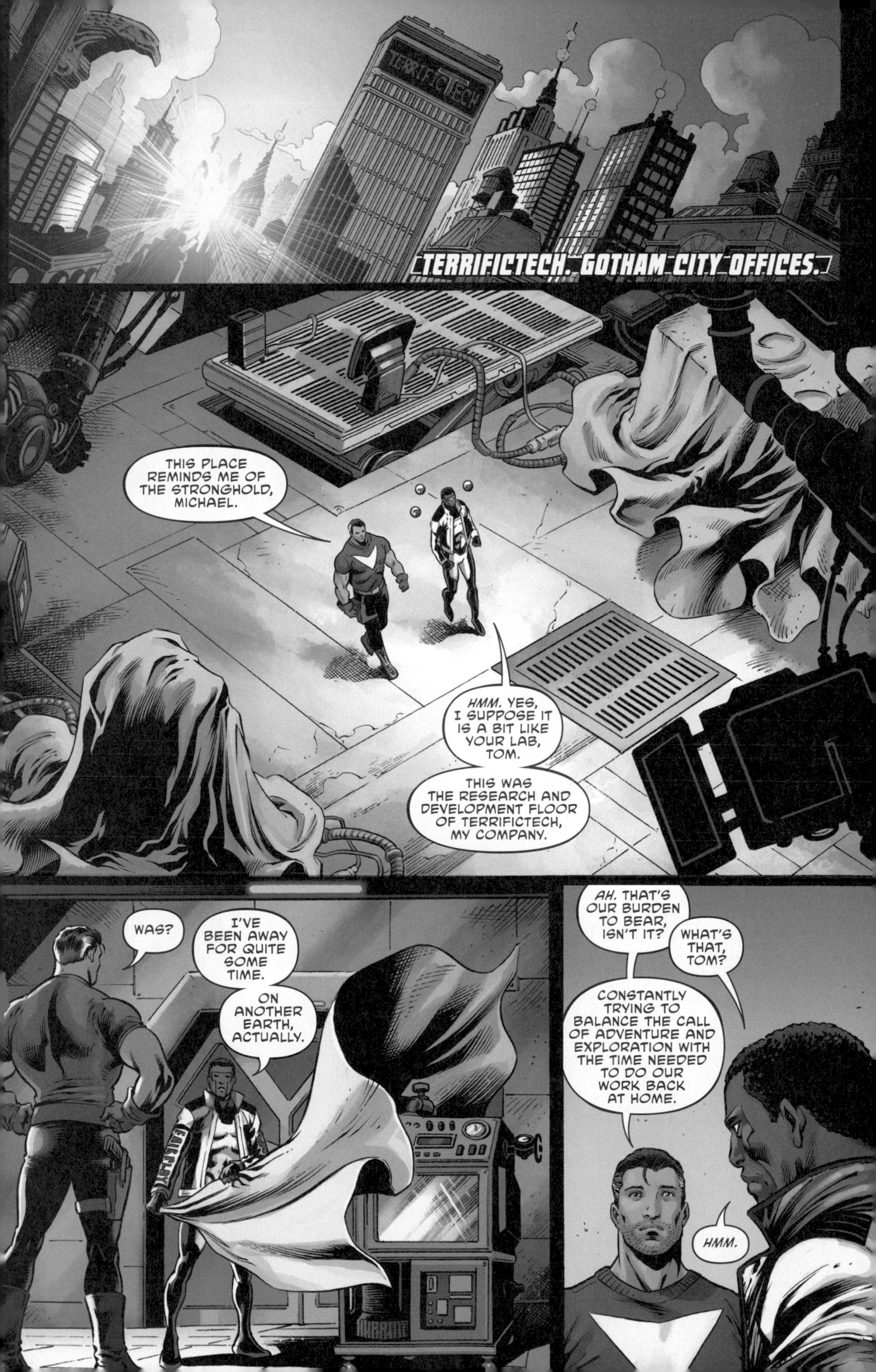
TERRIFICTECH
TERRIFICTECH. GOTHAM CITY OFFICES.
THIS PLACE REMINDS ME OF THE STRONGHOLD, MICHAEL.
HMM. YES, I SUPPOSE IT IS A BIT LIKE YOUR LAB, TOM.
THIS WAS THE RESEARCH AND DEVELOPMENT FLOOR OF TERRIFICTECH, MY COMPANY.
WAS?
I'VE BEEN AWAY FOR QUITE SOME TIME.
ON ANOTHER EARTH, ACTUALLY.
AH. THAT'S OUR BURDEN TO BEAR, ISN'T IT?
WHAT'S THAT, TOM?
CONSTANTLY TRYING TO BALANCE THE CALL OF ADVENTURE AND EXPLORATION WITH THE TIME NEEDED TO DO OUR WORK BACK AT HOME.
HMM.

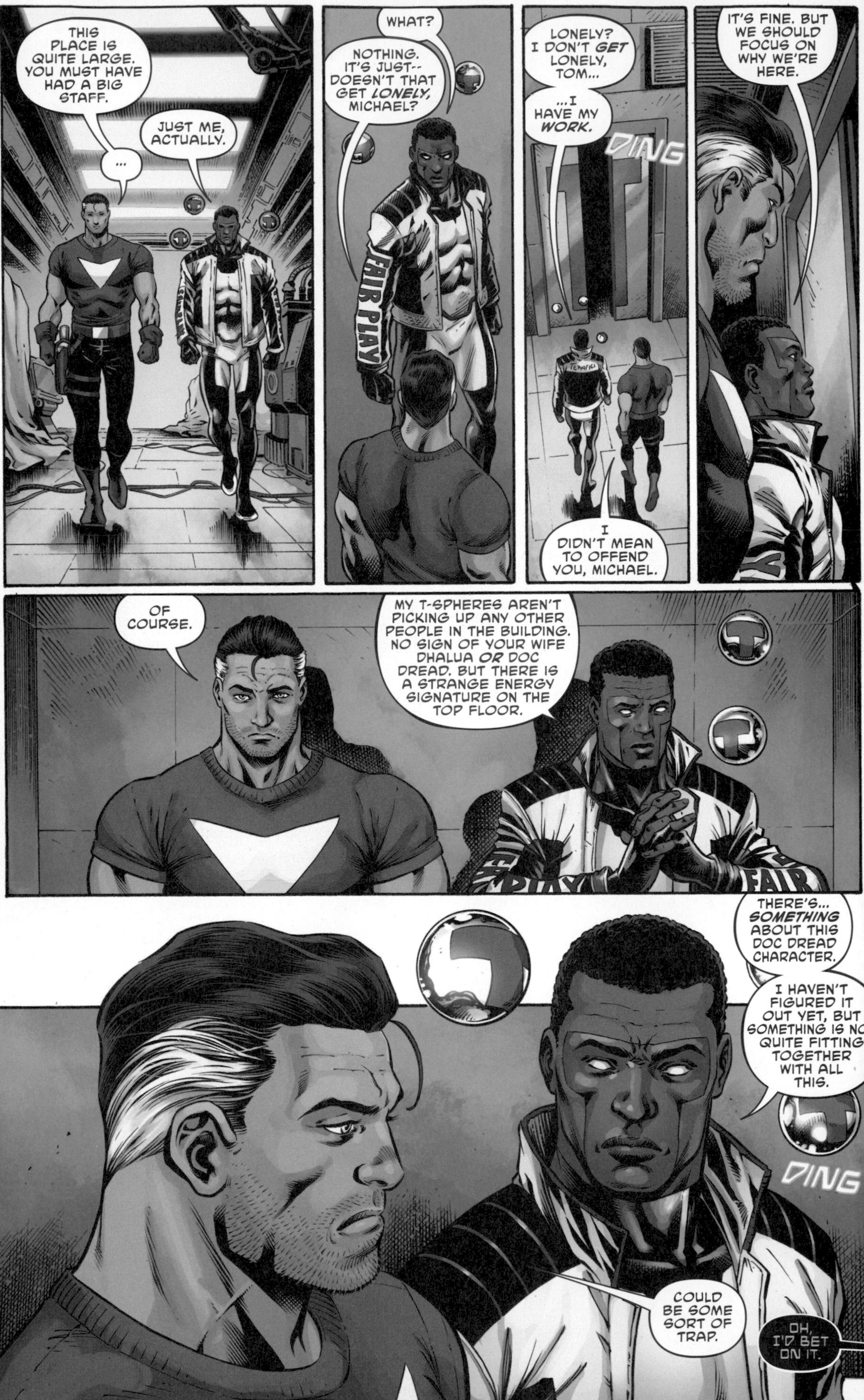
THIS PLACE IS QUITE LARGE. YOU MUST HAVE HAD A BIG STAFF.
JUST ME, ACTUALLY.
...
WHAT?
NOTHING. IT'S JUST-- DOESN'T THAT GET *LONELY,* MICHAEL?
LONELY? I DON'T *GET* LONELY, TOM...
...I HAVE MY *WORK.*
DING
I DIDN'T MEAN TO OFFEND YOU, MICHAEL.
IT'S FINE. BUT WE SHOULD FOCUS ON WHY WE'RE HERE.
OF COURSE.
MY T-SPHERES AREN'T PICKING UP ANY OTHER PEOPLE IN THE BUILDING. NO SIGN OF YOUR WIFE DHALUA *OR* DOC DREAD. BUT THERE IS A STRANGE ENERGY SIGNATURE ON THE TOP FLOOR.
THERE'S... *SOMETHING* ABOUT THIS DOC DREAD CHARACTER.
I HAVEN'T FIGURED IT OUT YET, BUT SOMETHING IS NO QUITE FITTING TOGETHER WITH ALL THIS.
DING
COULD BE SOME SORT OF TRAP.
OH, I'D BET ON IT.

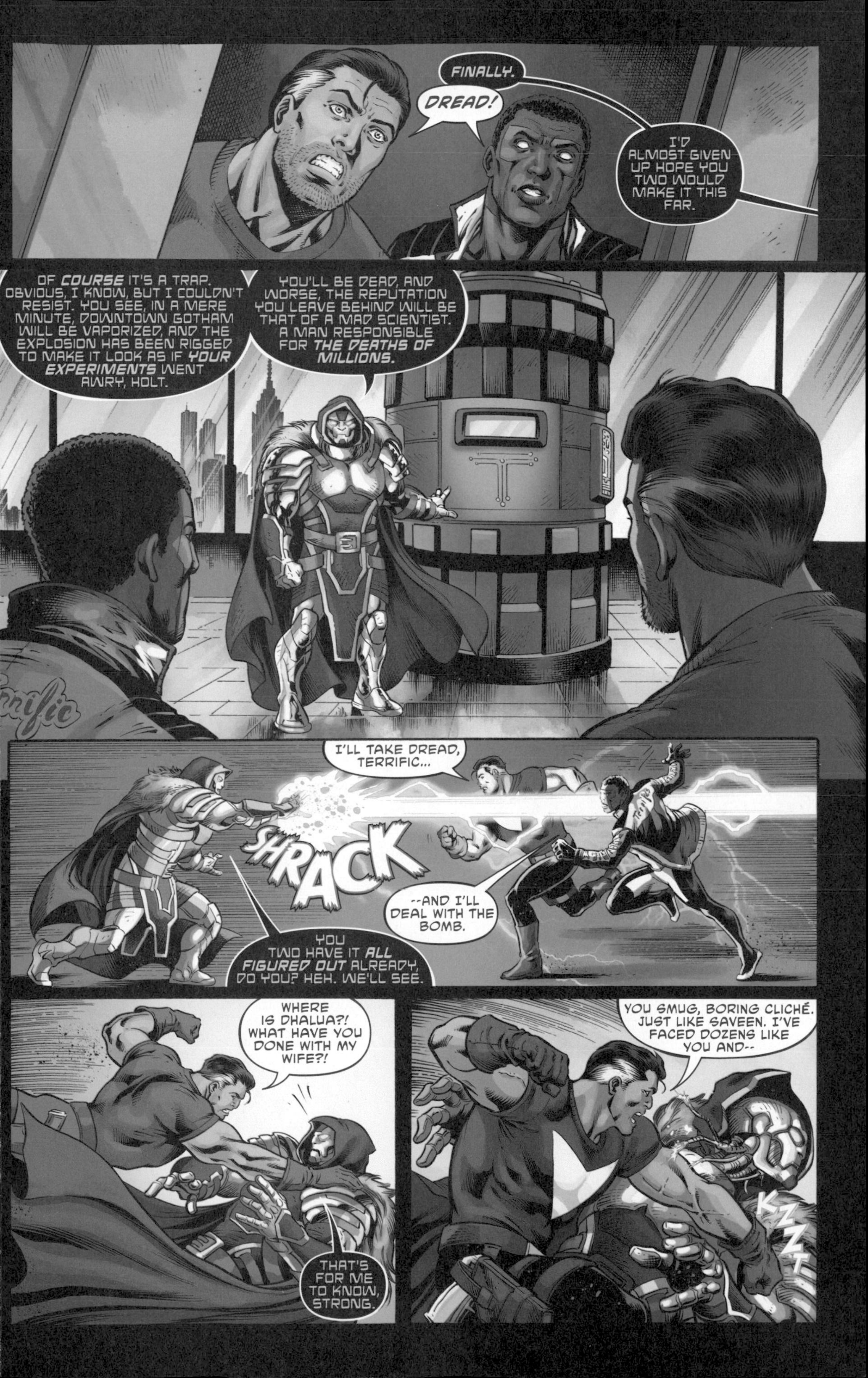
FINALLY.
DREAD!
I'D ALMOST GIVEN UP HOPE YOU TWO WOULD MAKE IT THIS FAR.
OF COURSE IT'S A TRAP. OBVIOUS, I KNOW, BUT I COULDN'T RESIST. YOU SEE, IN A MERE MINUTE, DOWNTOWN GOTHAM WILL BE VAPORIZED, AND THE EXPLOSION HAS BEEN RIGGED TO MAKE IT LOOK AS IF YOUR EXPERIMENTS WENT AWRY, HOLT.
YOU'LL BE DEAD, AND WORSE, THE REPUTATION YOU LEAVE BEHIND WILL BE THAT OF A MAD SCIENTIST. A MAN RESPONSIBLE FOR THE DEATHS OF MILLIONS.
I'LL TAKE DREAD, TERRIFIC...
SHRACK
--AND I'LL DEAL WITH THE BOMB.
YOU TWO HAVE IT ALL FIGURED OUT ALREADY, DO YOU? HEH. WE'LL SEE.
WHERE IS DHALUA?! WHAT HAVE YOU DONE WITH MY WIFE?!
THAT'S FOR ME TO KNOW, STRONG.
YOU SMUG, BORING CLICHÉ. JUST LIKE SAVEEN. I'VE FACED DOZENS LIKE YOU AND--
KZZT

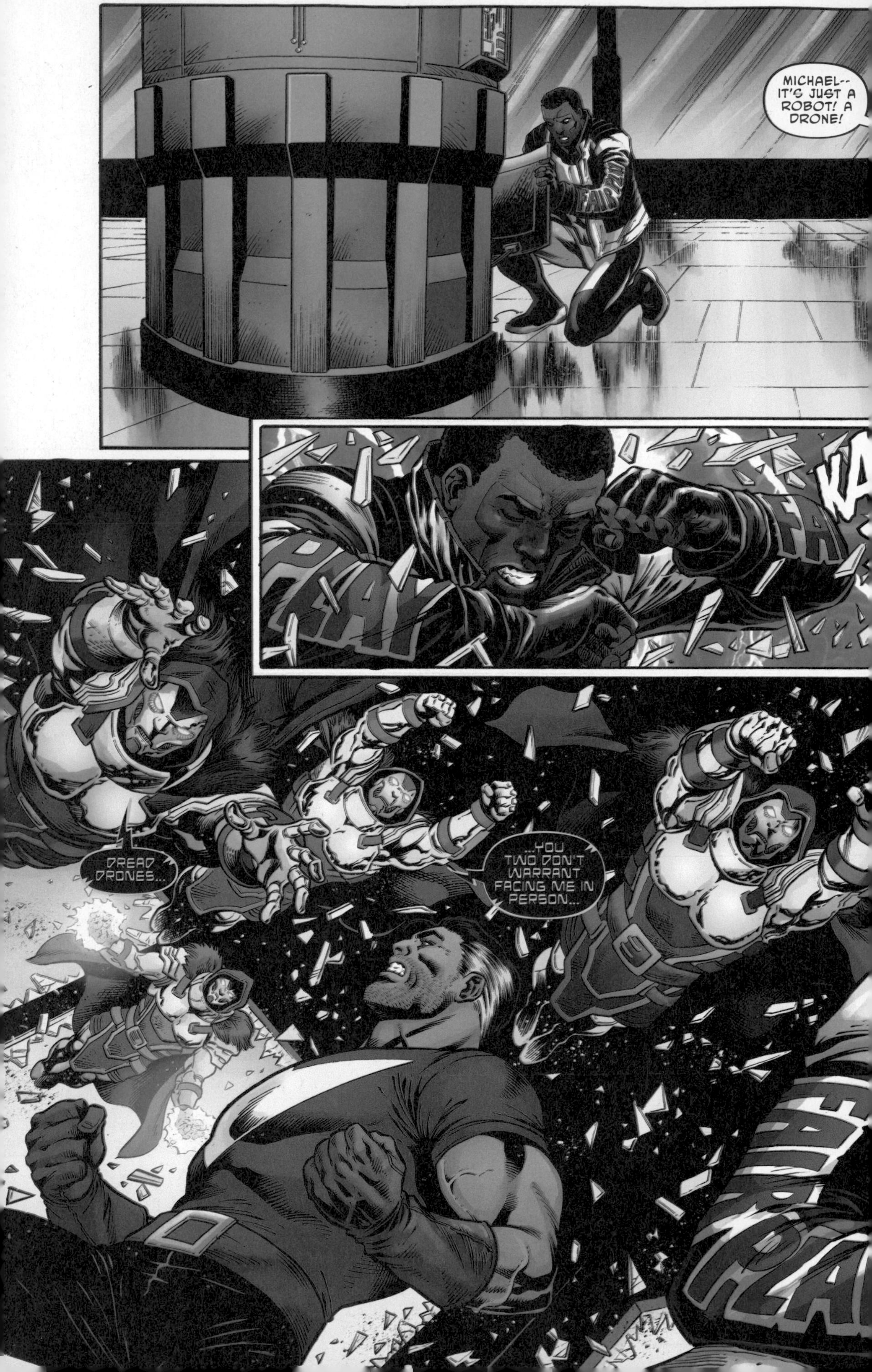
MICHAEL--
IT'S JUST A ROBOT! A DRONE!
KA
DREAD DRONES...
...YOU TWO DON'T WARRANT FACING ME IN PERSON...

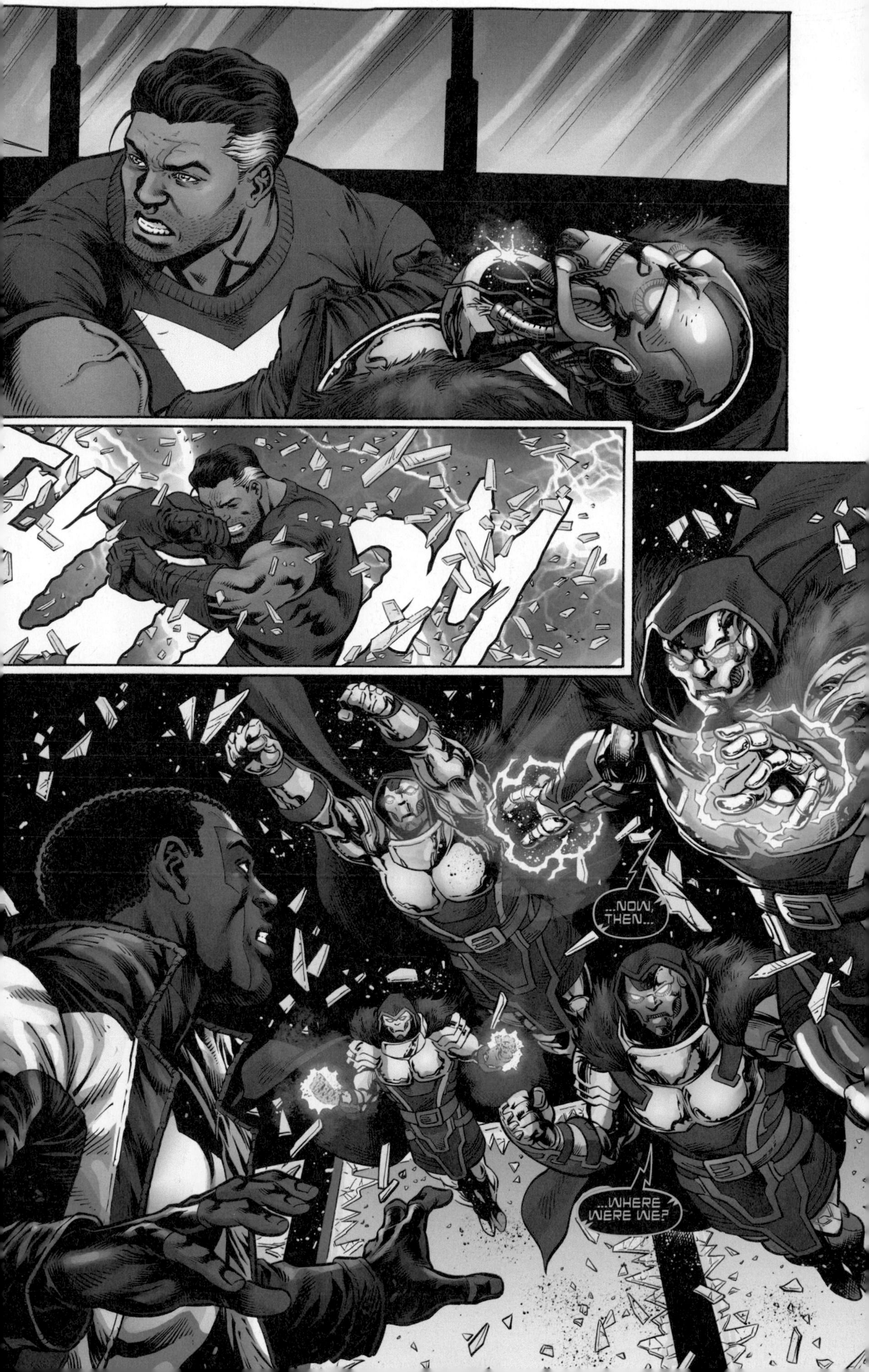
...NOW, THEN...
...WHERE WERE WE?

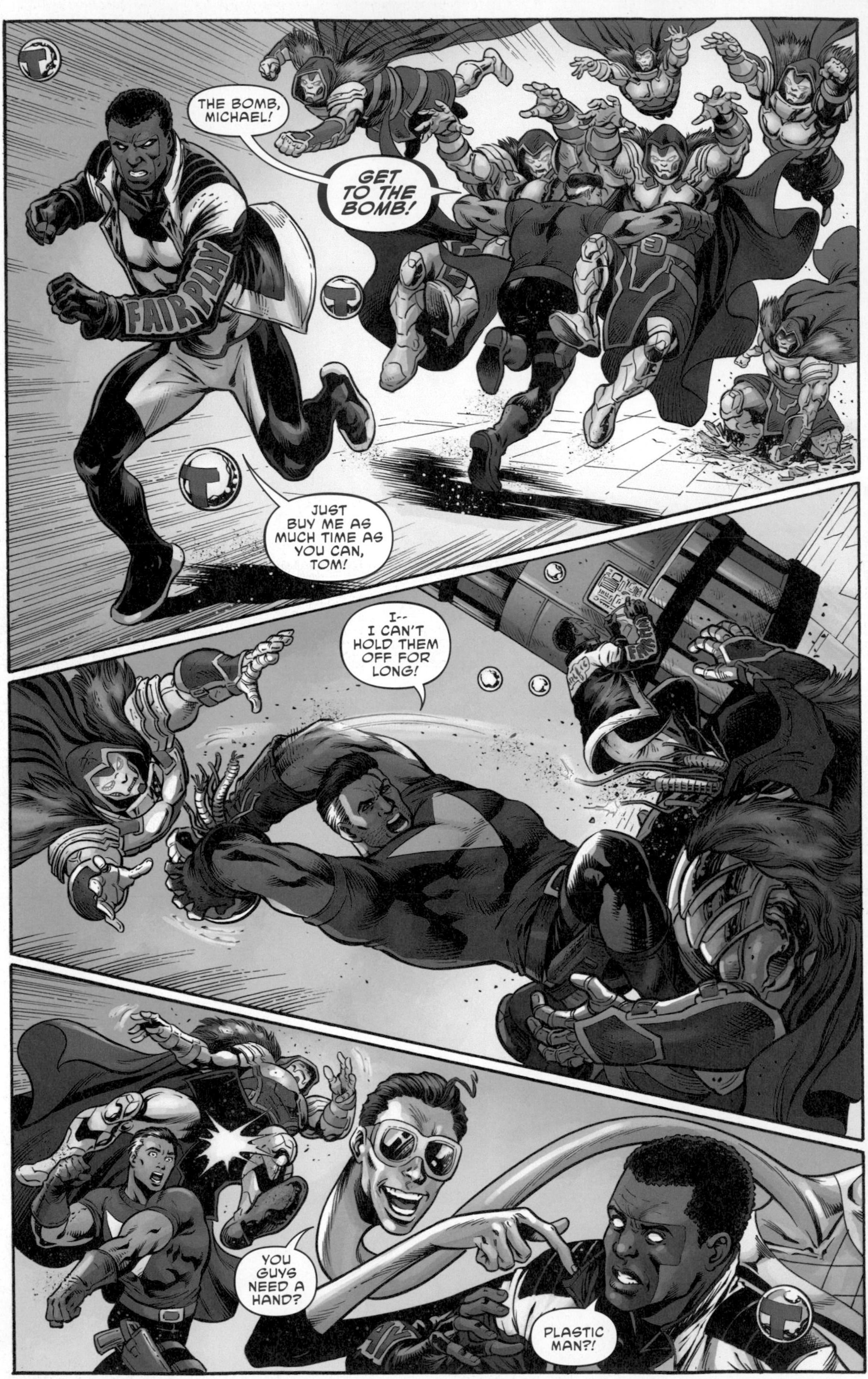
THE BOMB, MICHAEL!
GET TO THE BOMB!
JUST BUY ME AS MUCH TIME AS YOU CAN, TOM!
FAIR PLAY
I-- I CAN'T HOLD THEM OFF FOR LONG!
YOU GUYS NEED A HAND?
PLASTIC MAN?!

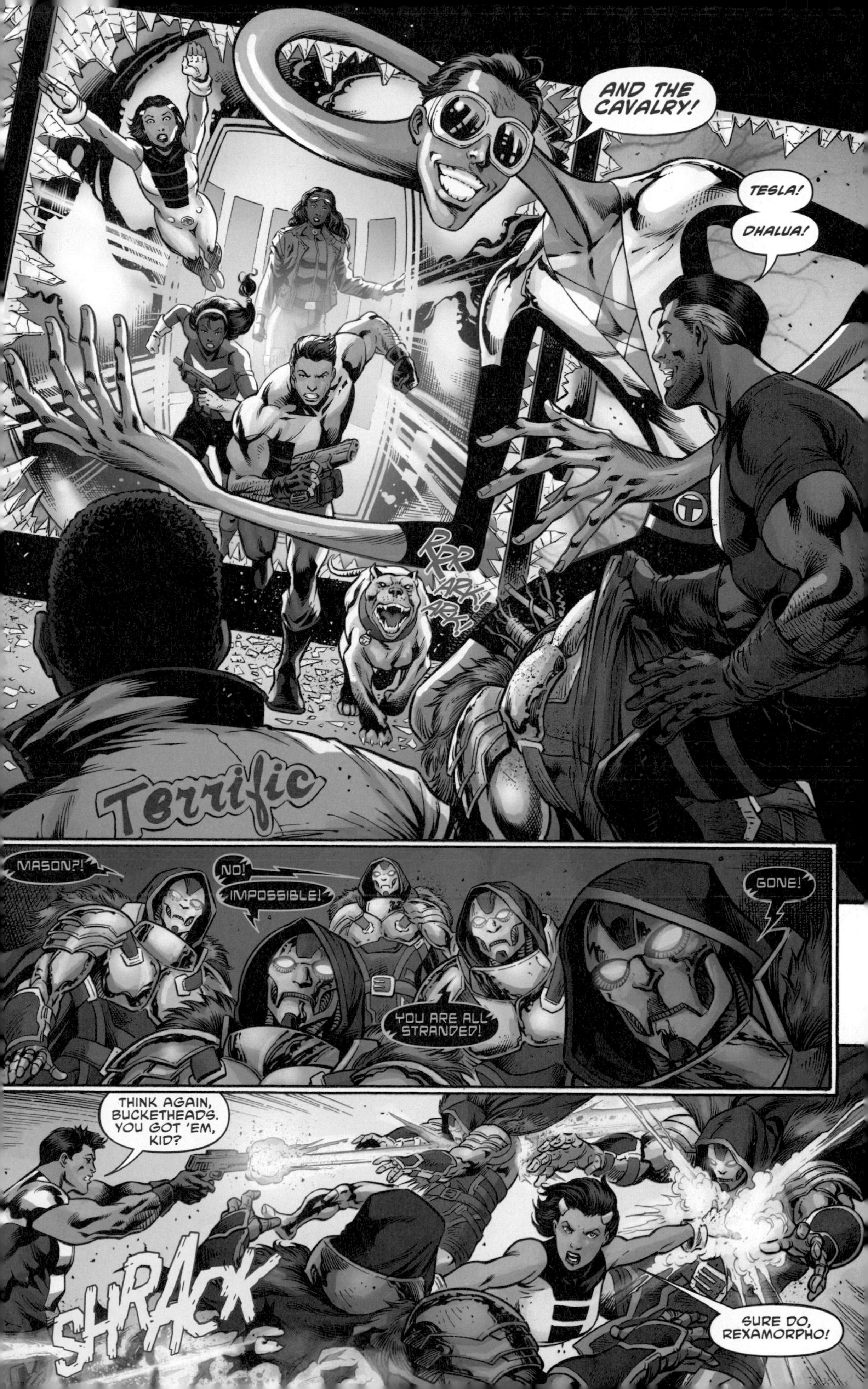
AND THE CAVALRY!
TESLA!
DHALUA!
RRR RARK! ARK!
Terrific
MASON?!
NO!
IMPOSSIBLE!
GONE!
YOU ARE ALL STRANDED!
THINK AGAIN, BUCKETHEADS. YOU GOT 'EM, KID?
SHRACK
SURE DO, REXAMORPHO!

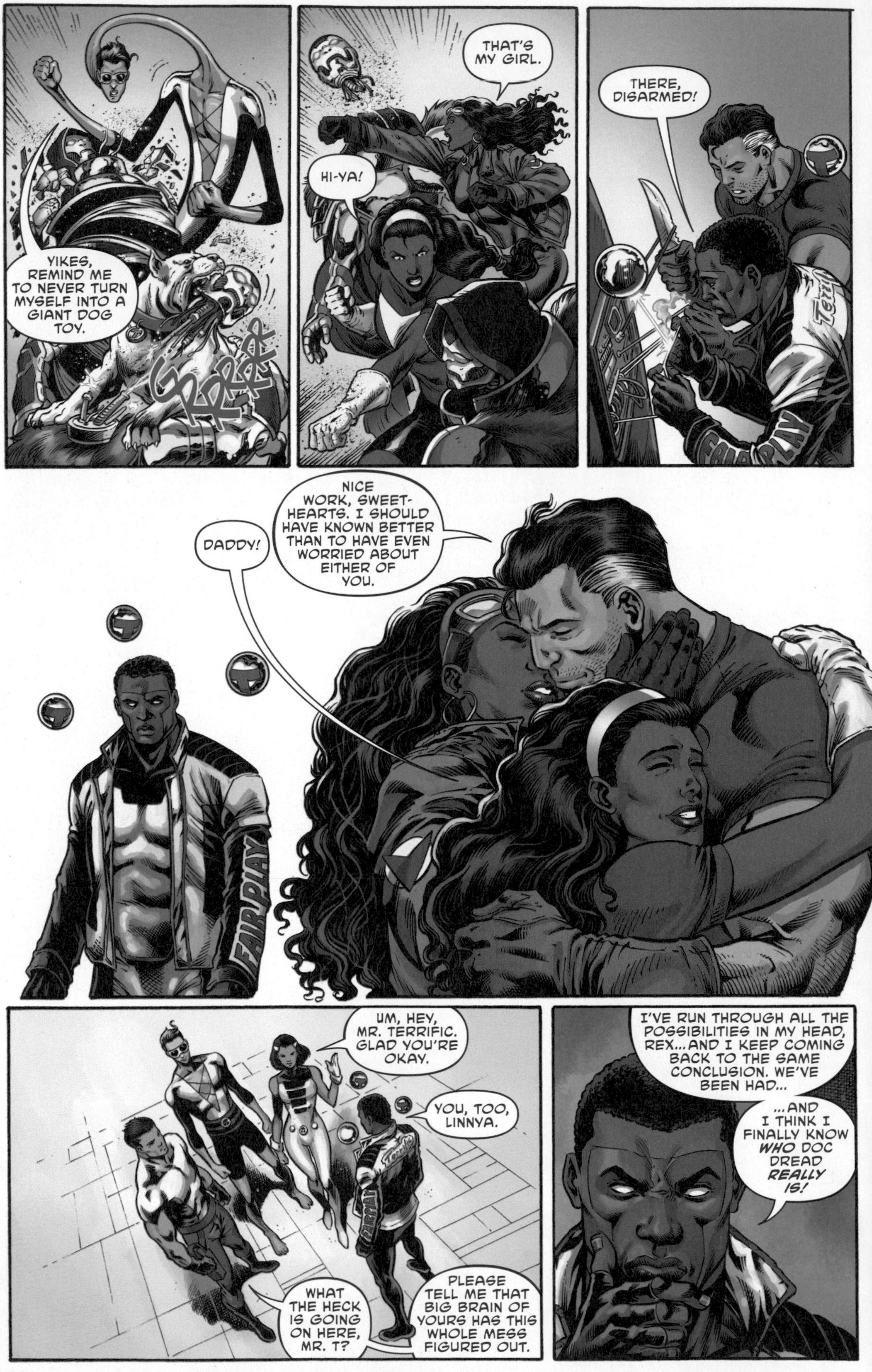
YIKES, REMIND ME TO NEVER TURN MYSELF INTO A GIANT DOG TOY.
GRRRRR
THAT'S MY GIRL.
HI-YA!
THERE, DISARMED!
FAIR PLAY
NICE WORK, SWEET-HEARTS. I SHOULD HAVE KNOWN BETTER THAN TO HAVE EVEN WORRIED ABOUT EITHER OF YOU.
DADDY!
FAIR PLAY
UM, HEY, MR. TERRIFIC. GLAD YOU'RE OKAY.
YOU, TOO, LINNYA.
WHAT THE HECK IS GOING ON HERE, MR. T?
PLEASE TELL ME THAT BIG BRAIN OF YOURS HAS THIS WHOLE MESS FIGURED OUT.
I'VE RUN THROUGH ALL THE POSSIBILITIES IN MY HEAD, REX...AND I KEEP COMING BACK TO THE SAME CONCLUSION. WE'VE BEEN HAD...
...AND I THINK I FINALLY KNOW *WHO* DOC DREAD *REALLY* IS!

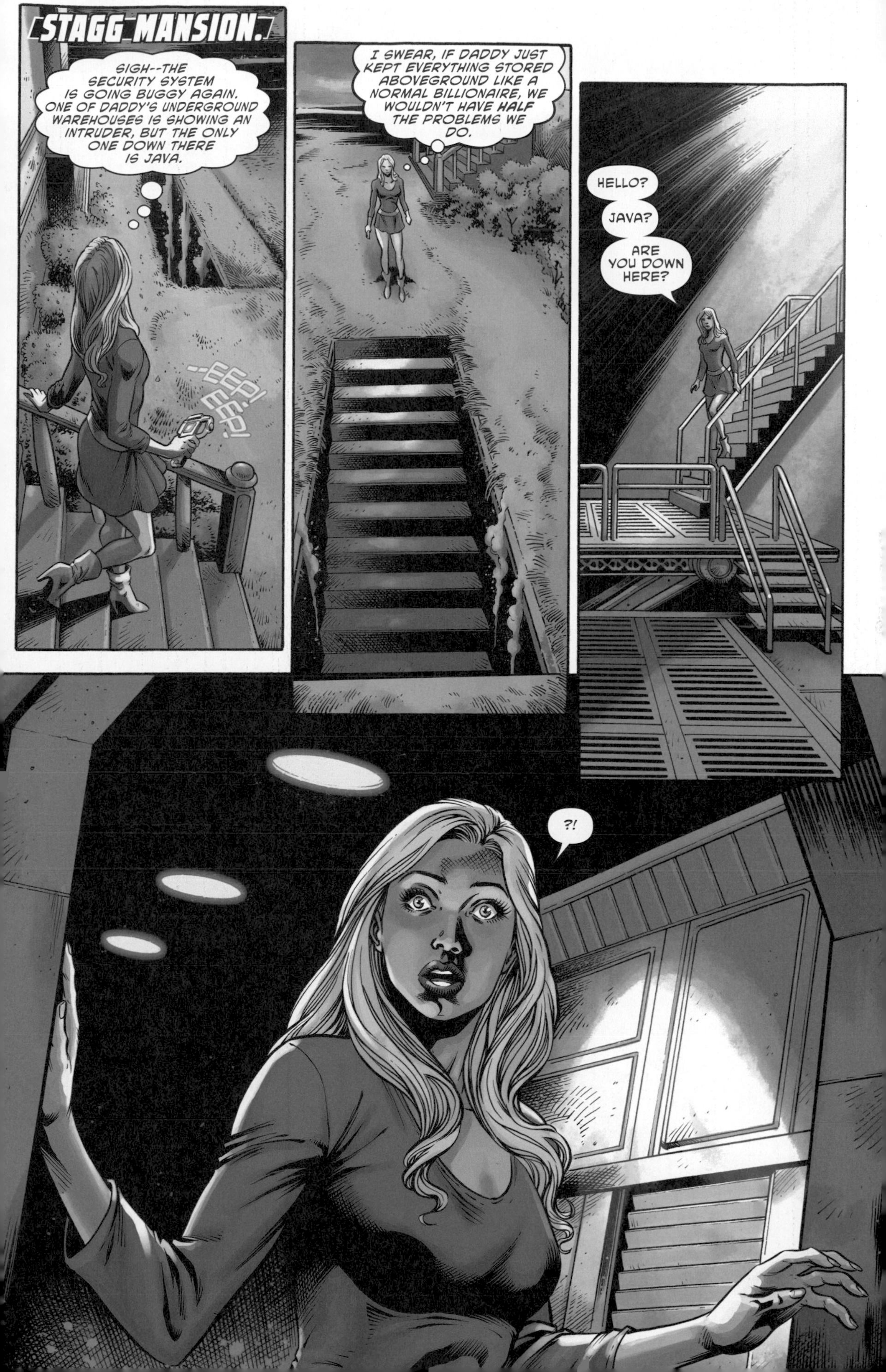
STAGG MANSION.
SIGH--THE SECURITY SYSTEM IS GOING BUGGY AGAIN. ONE OF DADDY'S UNDERGROUND WAREHOUSES IS SHOWING AN INTRUDER, BUT THE ONLY ONE DOWN THERE IS JAVA.
--EEP! EEP!
I SWEAR, IF DADDY JUST KEPT EVERYTHING STORED ABOVEGROUND LIKE A NORMAL BILLIONAIRE, WE WOULDN'T HAVE HALF THE PROBLEMS WE DO.
HELLO?
JAVA?
ARE YOU DOWN HERE?
?!

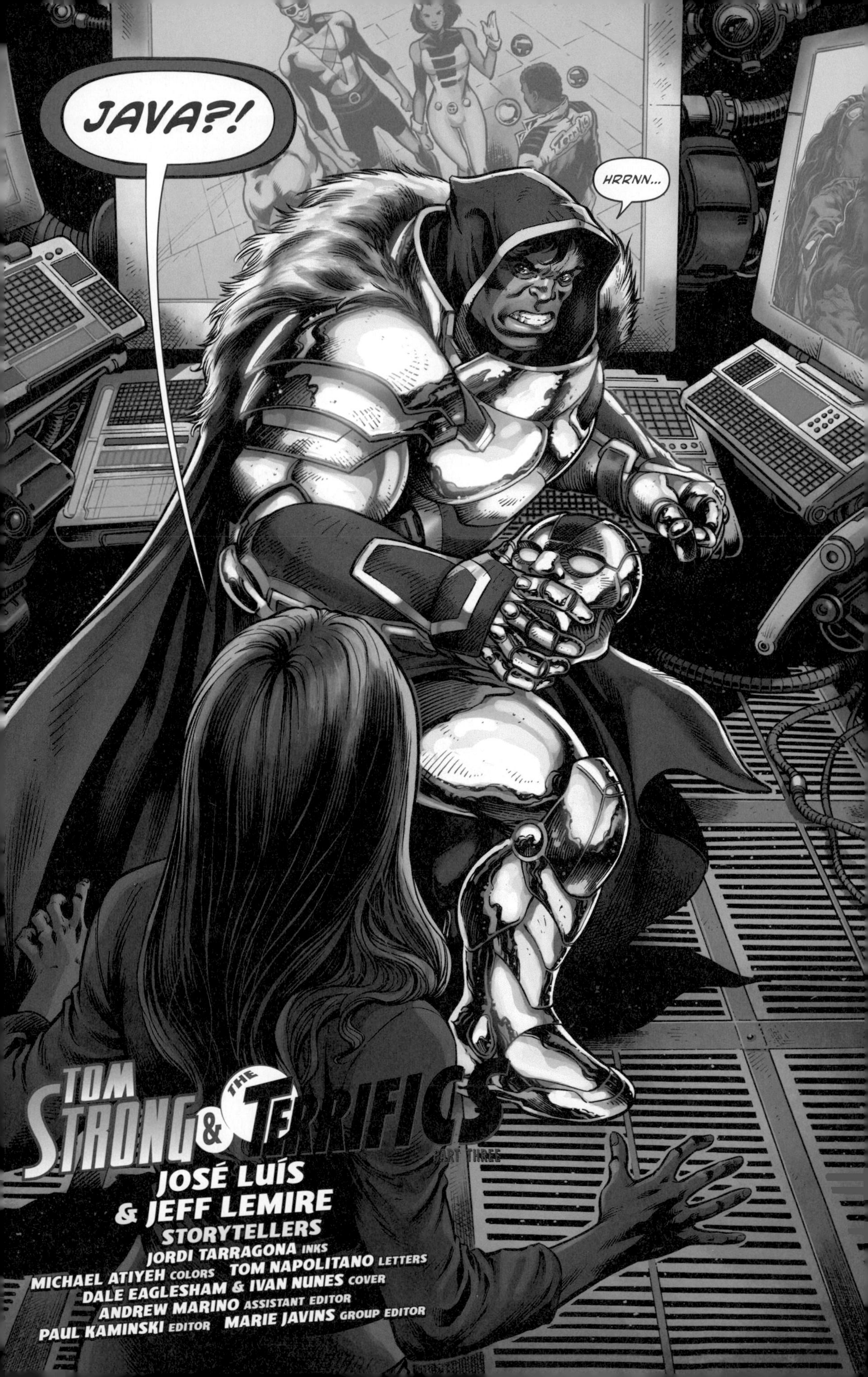
JAVA?!
HRRNN...
TOM STRONG & THE TERRIFICS
PART THREE
JOSÉ LUÍS & JEFF LEMIRE STORYTELLERS
JORDI TARRAGONA INKS
MICHAEL ATIYEH COLORS TOM NAPOLITANO LETTERS
DALE EAGLESHAM & IVAN NUNES COVER
ANDREW MARINO ASSISTANT EDITOR
PAUL KAMINSKI EDITOR MARIE JAVINS GROUP EDITOR

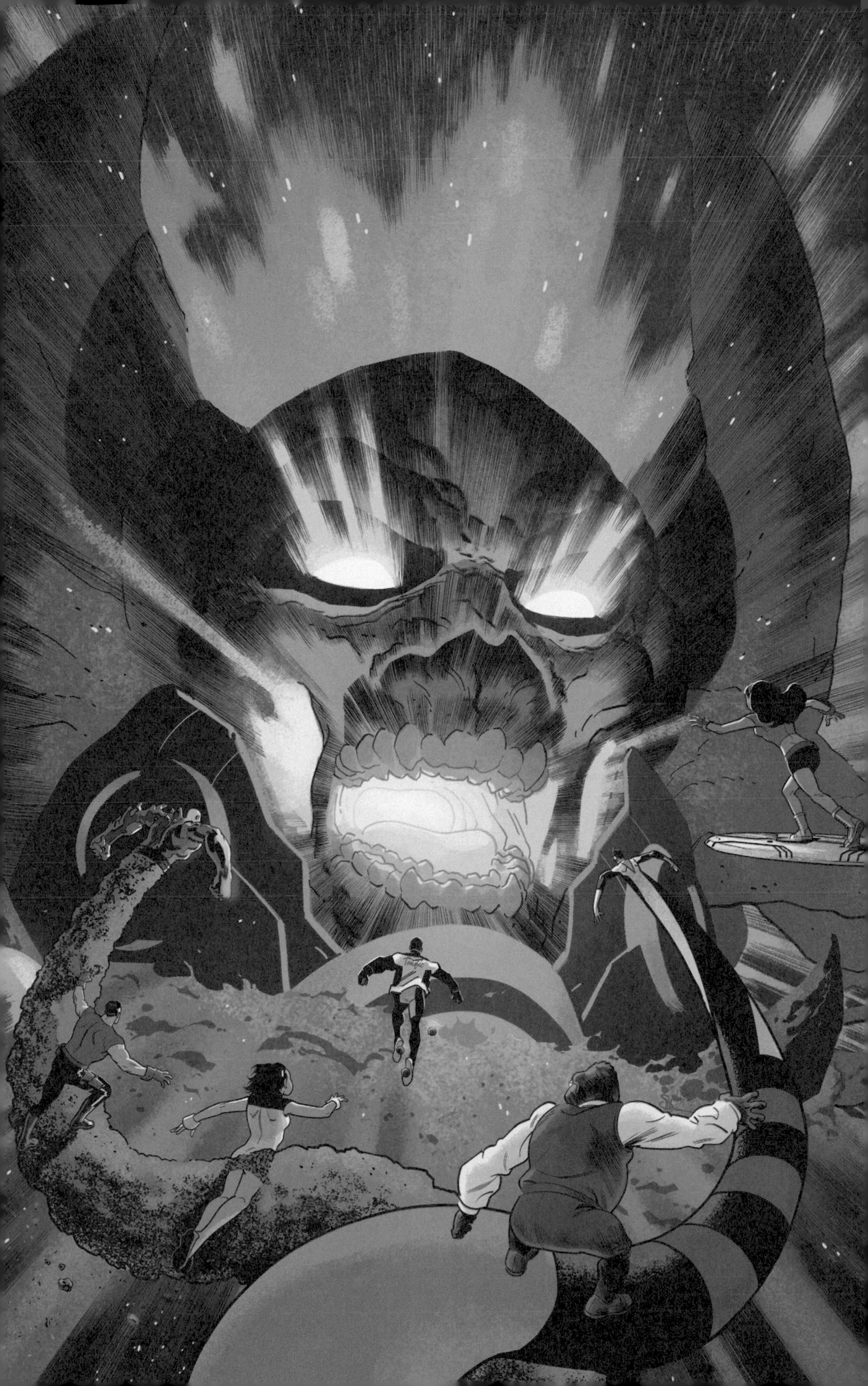

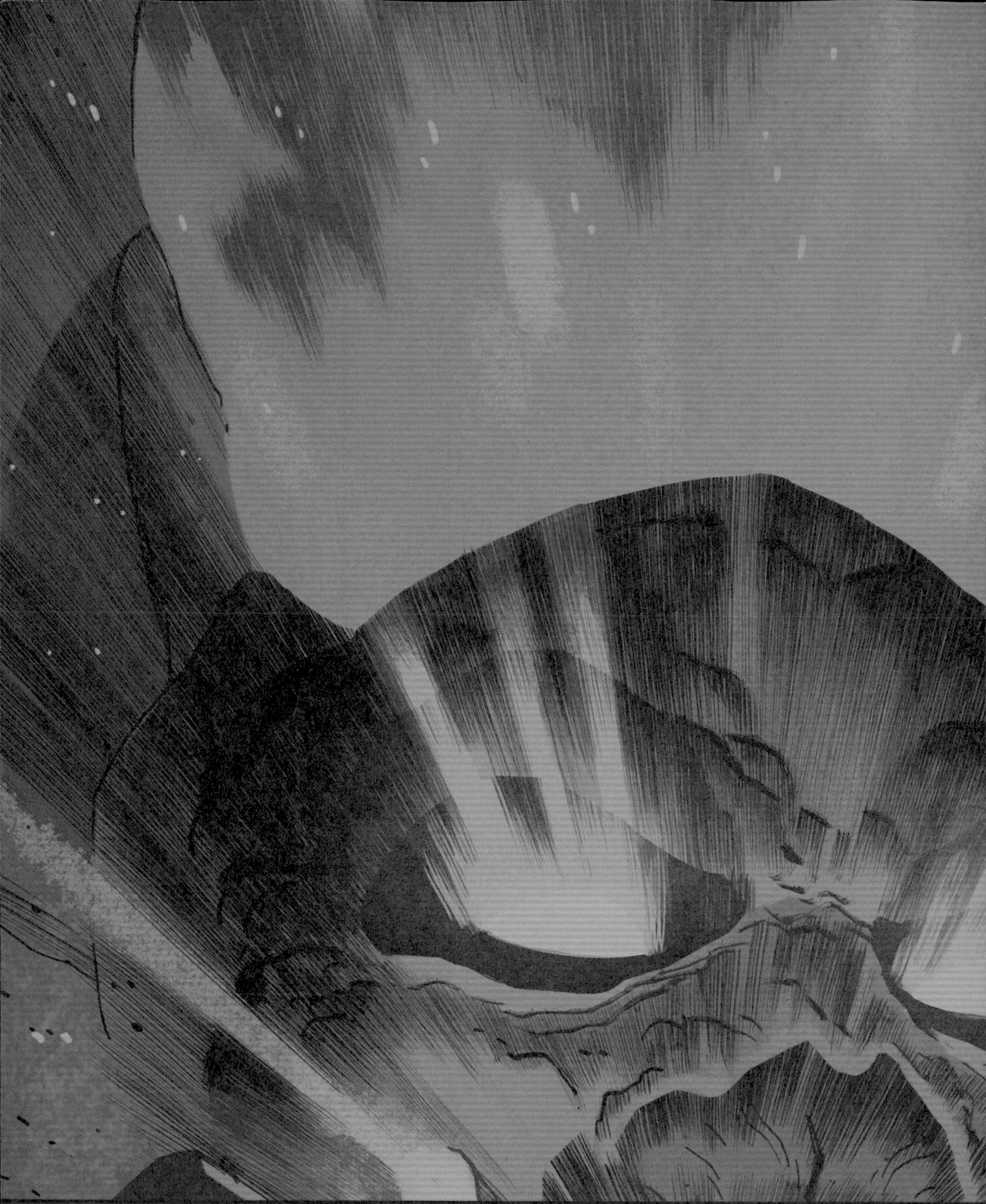

THE TERRIFICS

#10

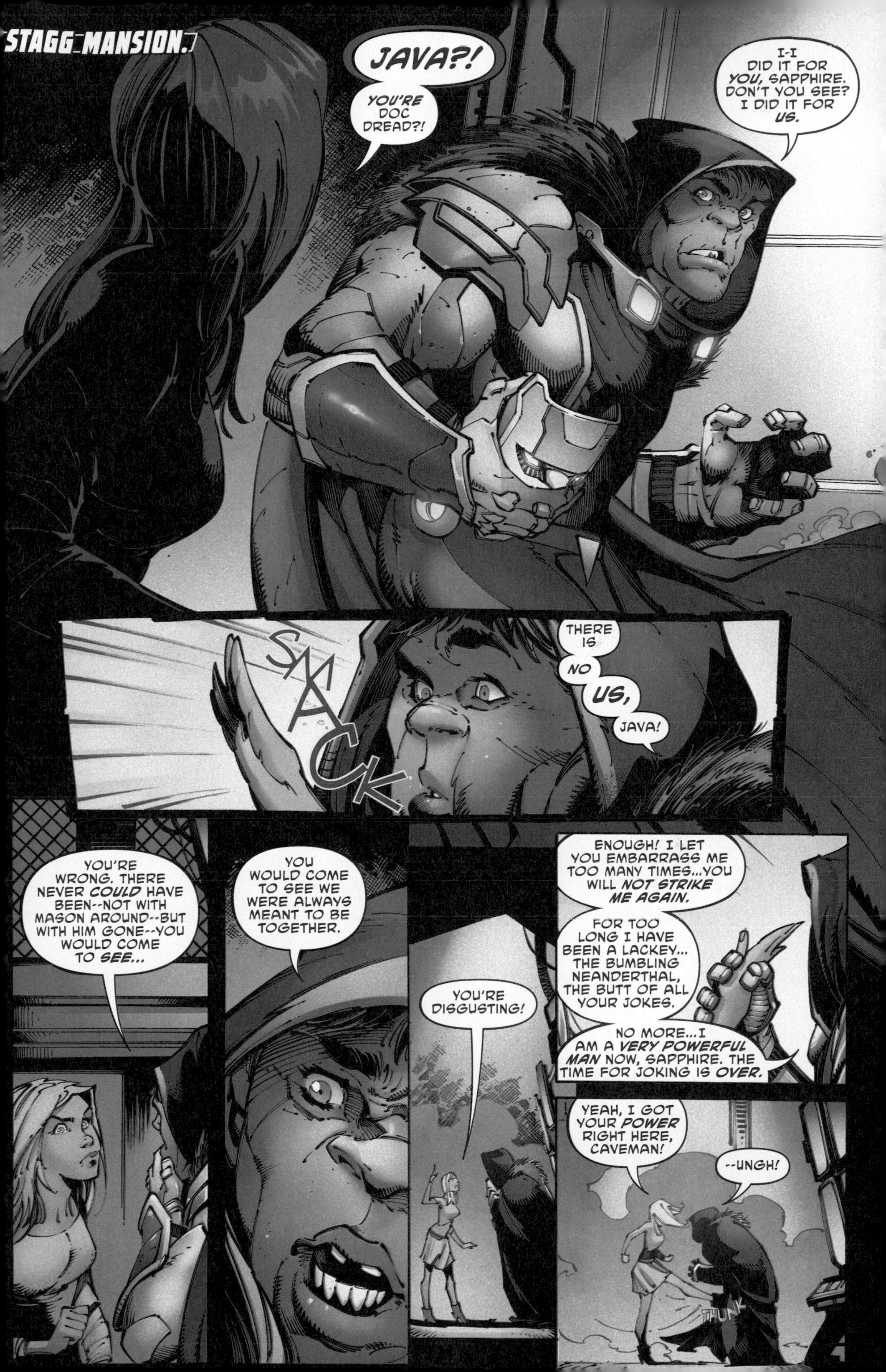
STAGG MANSION.
JAVA?!
YOU'RE DOC DREAD?!
I-I DID IT FOR YOU, SAPPHIRE. DON'T YOU SEE? I DID IT FOR US.
SMACK
THERE IS NO US, JAVA!
YOU'RE WRONG. THERE NEVER COULD HAVE BEEN--NOT WITH MASON AROUND--BUT WITH HIM GONE--YOU WOULD COME TO SEE...
YOU WOULD COME TO SEE WE WERE ALWAYS MEANT TO BE TOGETHER.
YOU'RE DISGUSTING!
ENOUGH! I LET YOU EMBARRASS ME TOO MANY TIMES...YOU WILL NOT STRIKE ME AGAIN.
FOR TOO LONG I HAVE BEEN A LACKEY... THE BUMBLING NEANDERTHAL, THE BUTT OF ALL YOUR JOKES.
NO MORE...I AM A VERY POWERFUL MAN NOW, SAPPHIRE. THE TIME FOR JOKING IS OVER.
YEAH, I GOT YOUR POWER RIGHT HERE, CAVEMAN!
--UNGH!
THUNK

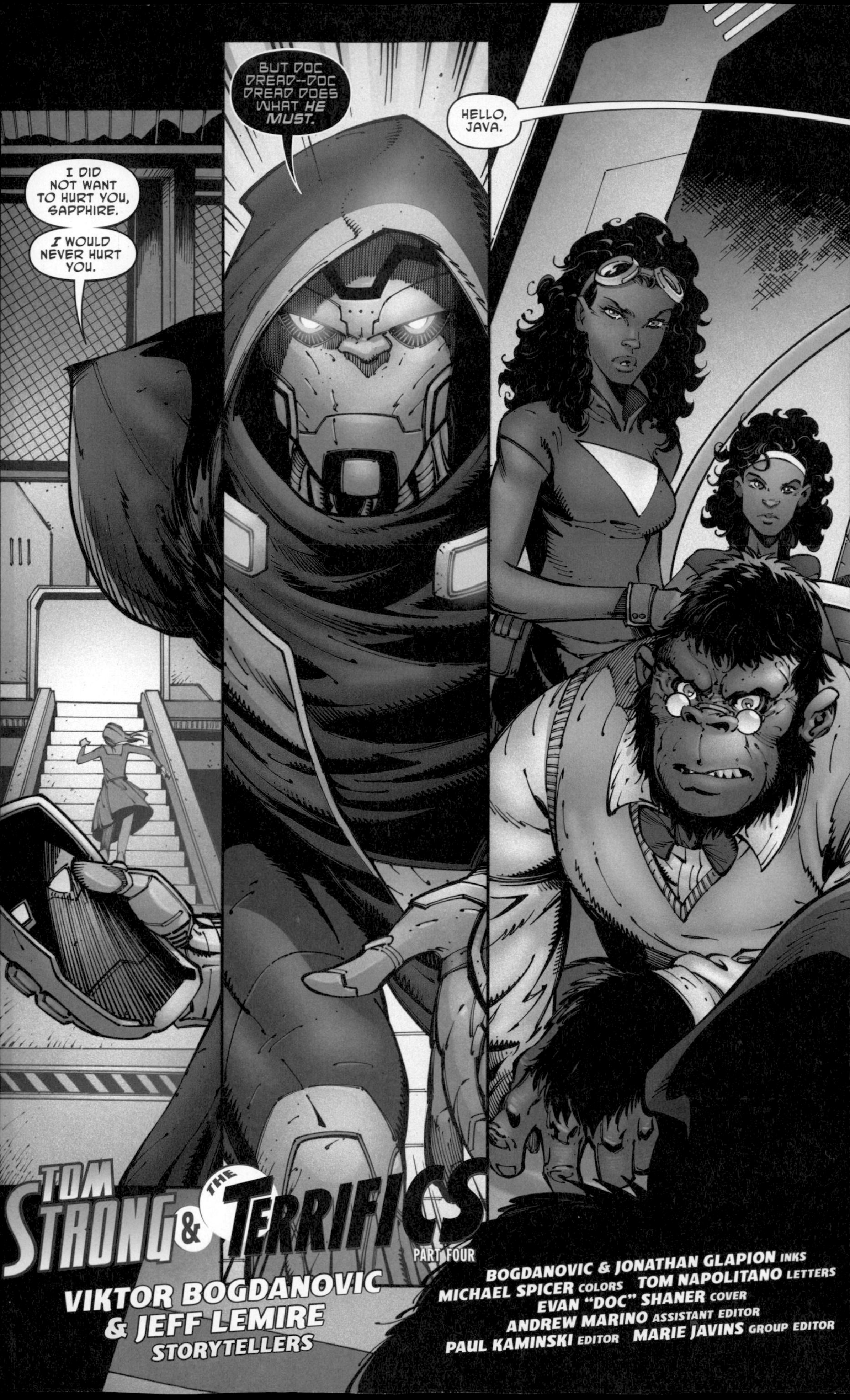
I DID NOT WANT TO HURT YOU, SAPPHIRE.
I WOULD NEVER HURT YOU.
BUT DOC DREAD--DOC DREAD DOES WHAT HE MUST.
HELLO, JAVA.
TOM STRONG & THE TERRIFICS
PART FOUR
VIKTOR BOGDANOVIC & JEFF LEMIRE STORYTELLERS
BOGDANOVIC & JONATHAN GLAPION INKS
MICHAEL SPICER COLORS TOM NAPOLITANO LETTERS
EVAN "DOC" SHANER COVER
ANDREW MARINO ASSISTANT EDITOR
PAUL KAMINSKI EDITOR MARIE JAVINS GROUP EDITOR

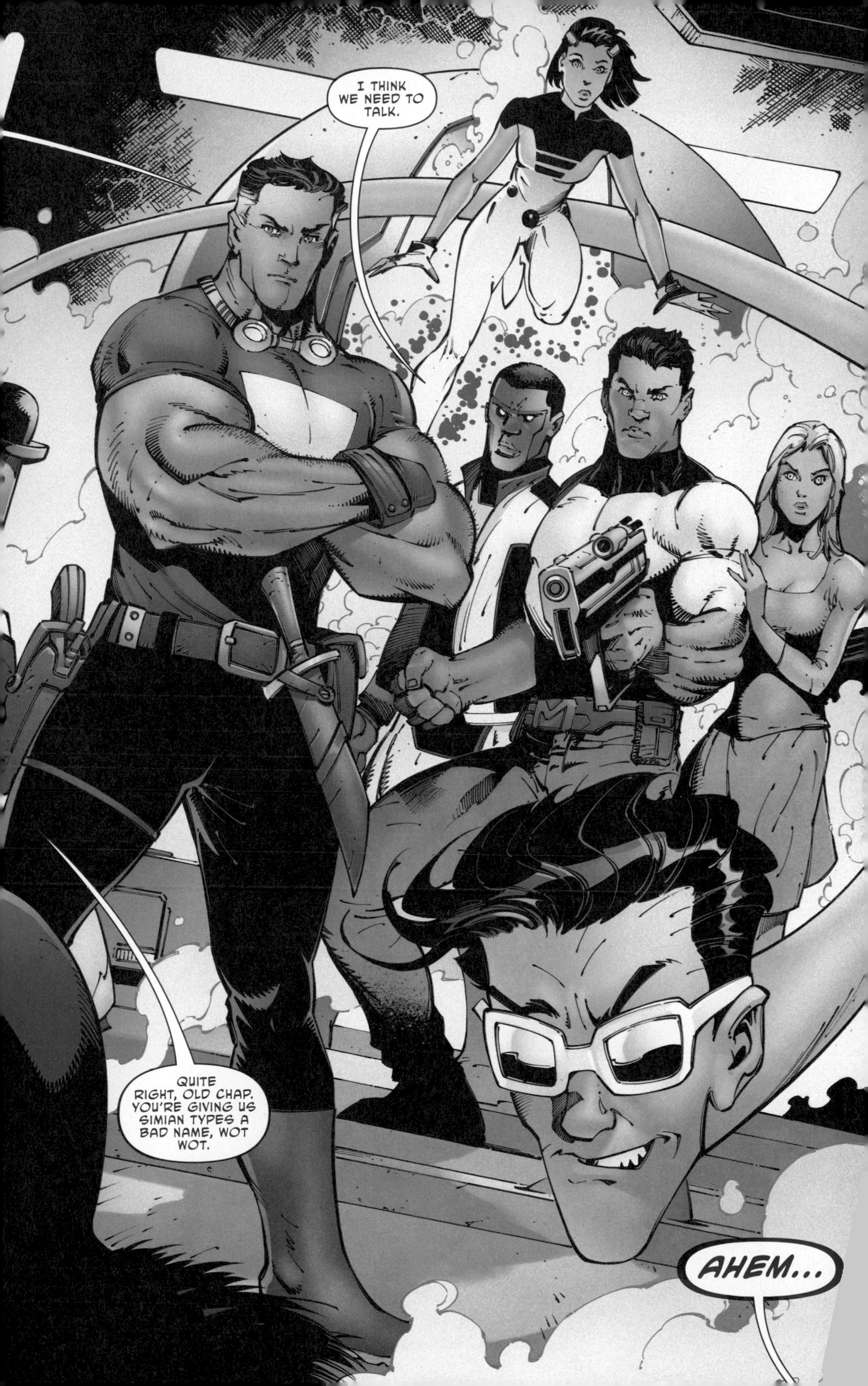
I THINK WE NEED TO TALK.
QUITE RIGHT, OLD CHAP. YOU'RE GIVING US SIMIAN TYPES A BAD NAME, WOT WOT.
AHEM...

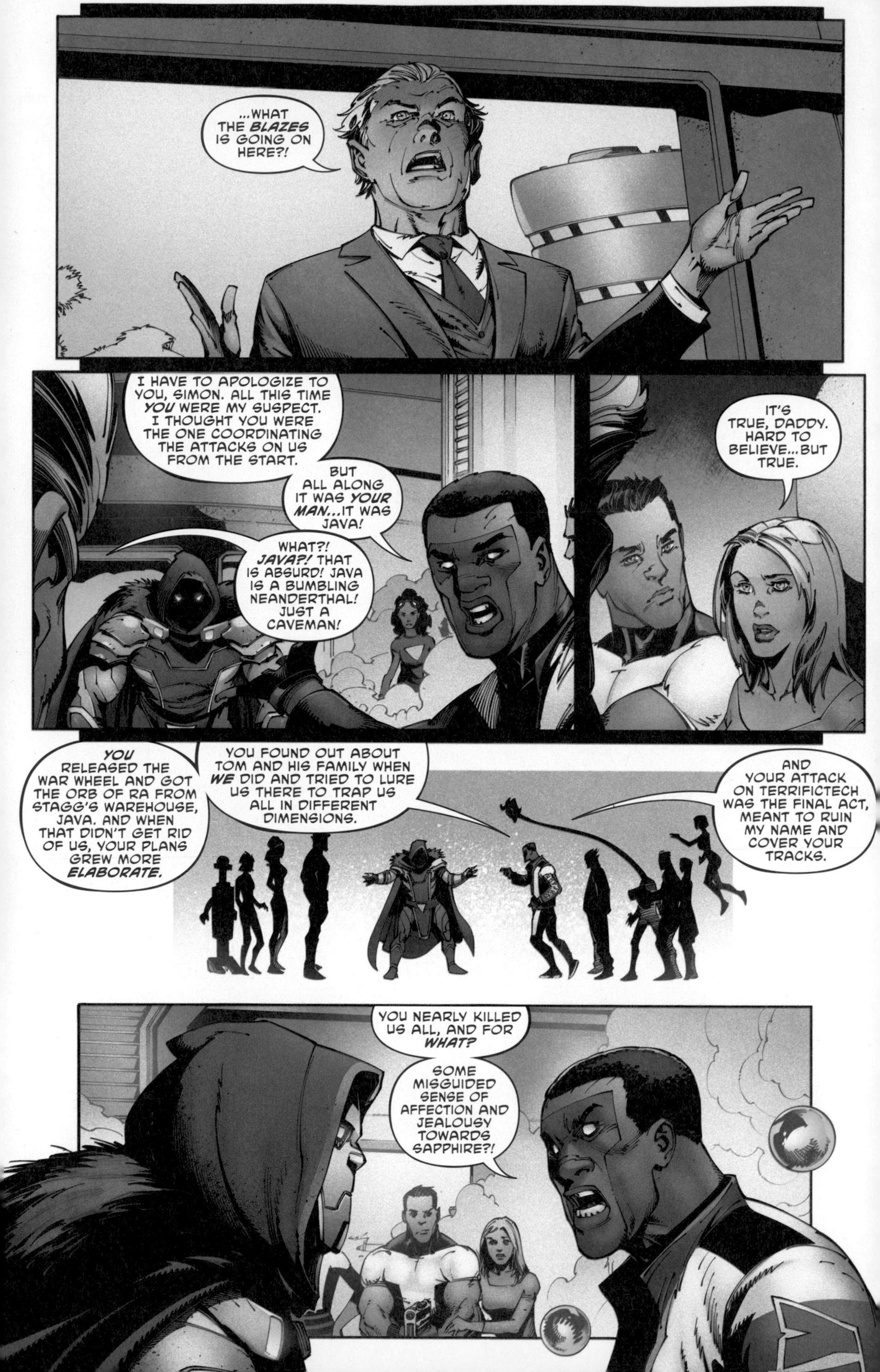
...WHAT THE BLAZES IS GOING ON HERE?!
I HAVE TO APOLOGIZE TO YOU, SIMON. ALL THIS TIME YOU WERE MY SUSPECT. I THOUGHT YOU WERE THE ONE COORDINATING THE ATTACKS ON US FROM THE START.
BUT ALL ALONG IT WAS YOUR MAN...IT WAS JAVA!
WHAT?! JAVA?! THAT IS ABSURD! JAVA IS A BUMBLING NEANDERTHAL! JUST A CAVEMAN!
IT'S TRUE, DADDY. HARD TO BELIEVE...BUT TRUE.
YOU RELEASED THE WAR WHEEL AND GOT THE ORB OF RA FROM STAGG'S WAREHOUSE, JAVA. AND WHEN THAT DIDN'T GET RID OF US, YOUR PLANS GREW MORE ELABORATE.
YOU FOUND OUT ABOUT TOM AND HIS FAMILY WHEN WE DID AND TRIED TO LURE US THERE TO TRAP US ALL IN DIFFERENT DIMENSIONS.
AND YOUR ATTACK ON TERRIFICTECH WAS THE FINAL ACT, MEANT TO RUIN MY NAME AND COVER YOUR TRACKS.
YOU NEARLY KILLED US ALL, AND FOR WHAT?
SOME MISGUIDED SENSE OF AFFECTION AND JEALOUSY TOWARDS SAPPHIRE?!

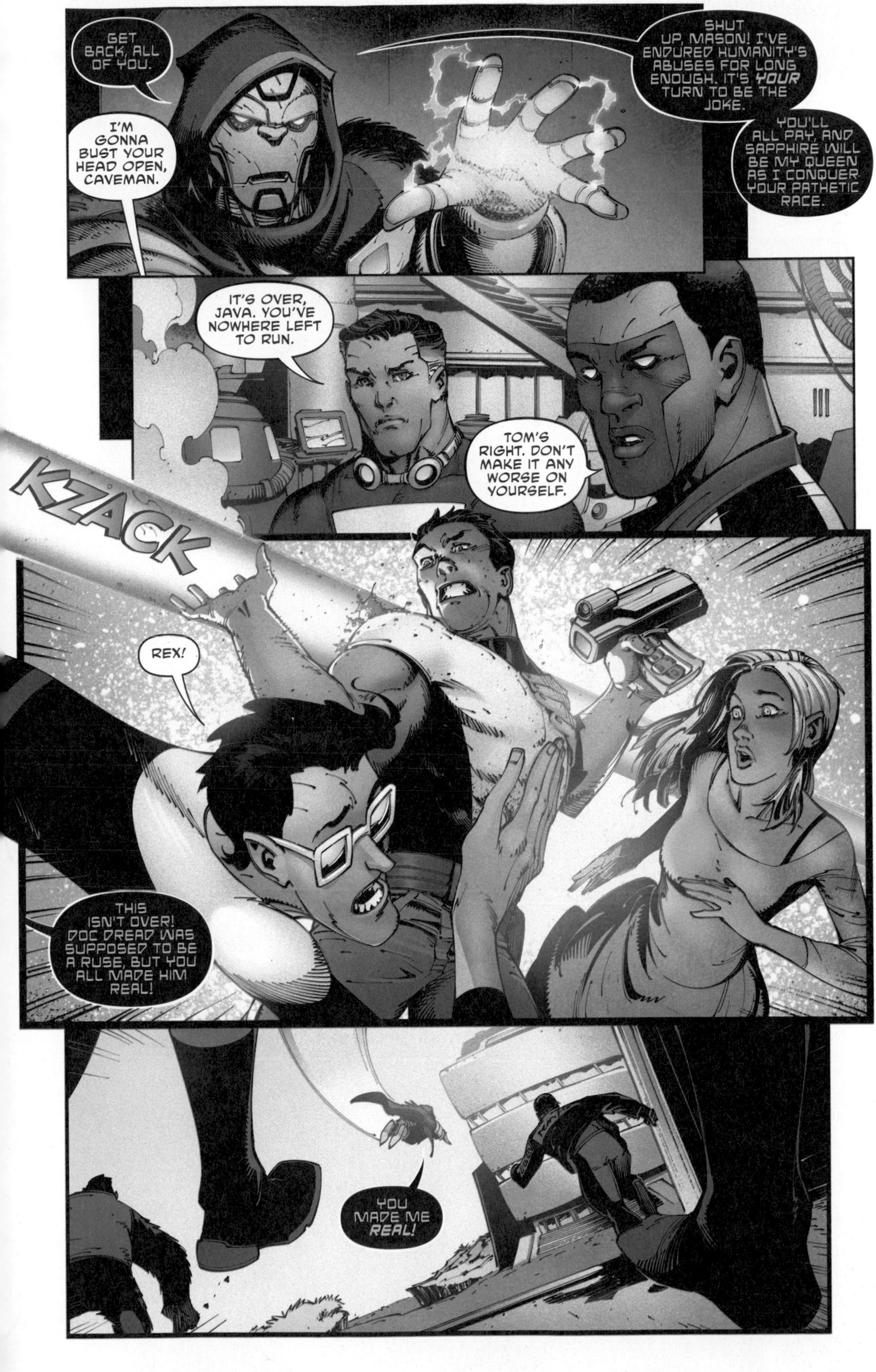
GET BACK, ALL OF YOU.
SHUT UP, MASON! I'VE ENDURED HUMANITY'S ABUSES FOR LONG ENOUGH. IT'S *YOUR* TURN TO BE THE JOKE.
I'M GONNA BUST YOUR HEAD OPEN, CAVEMAN.
YOU'LL ALL PAY, AND SAPPHIRE WILL BE MY QUEEN AS I CONQUER YOUR PATHETIC RACE.
IT'S OVER, JAVA. YOU'VE NOWHERE LEFT TO RUN.
TOM'S RIGHT. DON'T MAKE IT ANY WORSE ON YOURSELF.
KZACK
REX!
THIS ISN'T OVER! DOC DREAD WAS SUPPOSED TO BE A RUSE, BUT YOU ALL MADE HIM REAL!
YOU MADE ME *REAL!*

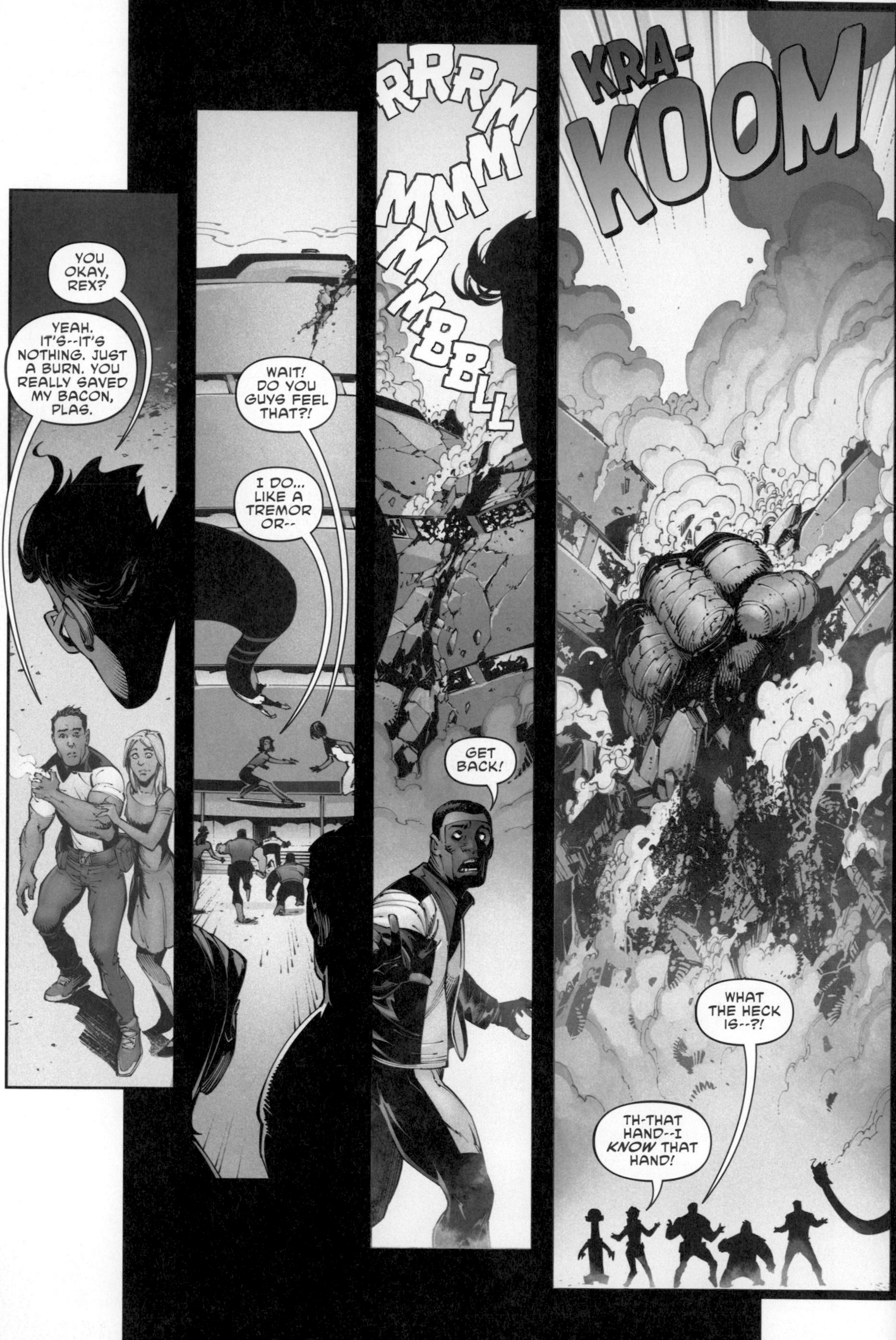
YOU OKAY, REX?
YEAH. IT'S--IT'S NOTHING. JUST A BURN. YOU REALLY SAVED MY BACON, PLAS.
WAIT! DO YOU GUYS FEEL THAT?!
I DO... LIKE A TREMOR OR--
RRRRMMMMMMMBBLL
GET BACK!
KRA-KOOM
WHAT THE HECK IS--?!
TH-THAT HAND--I *KNOW* THAT HAND!

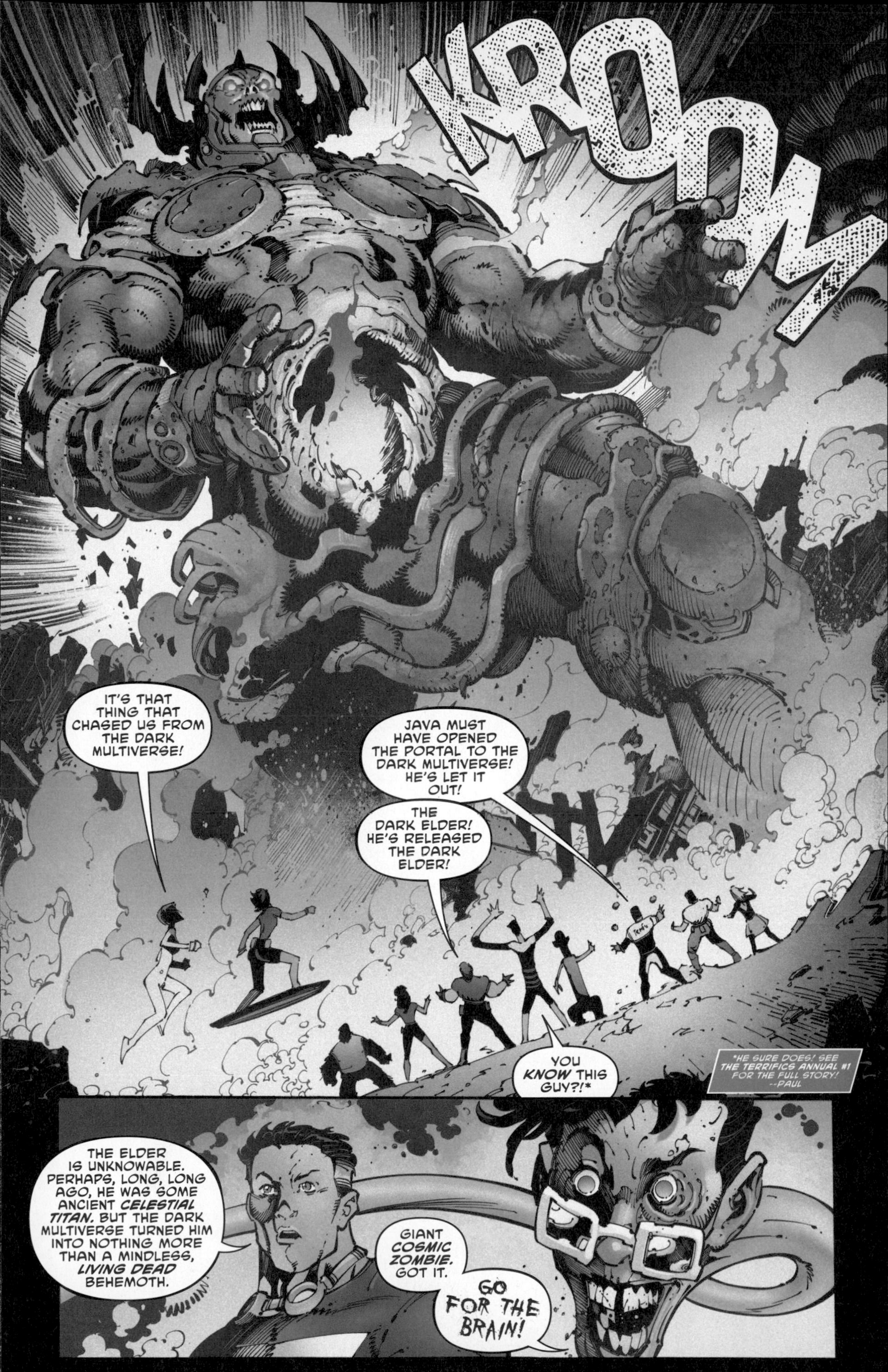
KROOM
IT'S THAT THING THAT CHASED US FROM THE DARK MULTIVERSE!
JAVA MUST HAVE OPENED THE PORTAL TO THE DARK MULTIVERSE! HE'S LET IT OUT!
THE DARK ELDER! HE'S RELEASED THE DARK ELDER!
YOU KNOW THIS GUY?!*
*HE SURE DOES! SEE THE TERRIFICS ANNUAL #1 FOR THE FULL STORY! --PAUL
THE ELDER IS UNKNOWABLE. PERHAPS, LONG, LONG AGO, HE WAS SOME ANCIENT CELESTIAL TITAN. BUT THE DARK MULTIVERSE TURNED HIM INTO NOTHING MORE THAN A MINDLESS, LIVING DEAD BEHEMOTH.
GIANT COSMIC ZOMBIE. GOT IT.
GO FOR THE BRAIN!

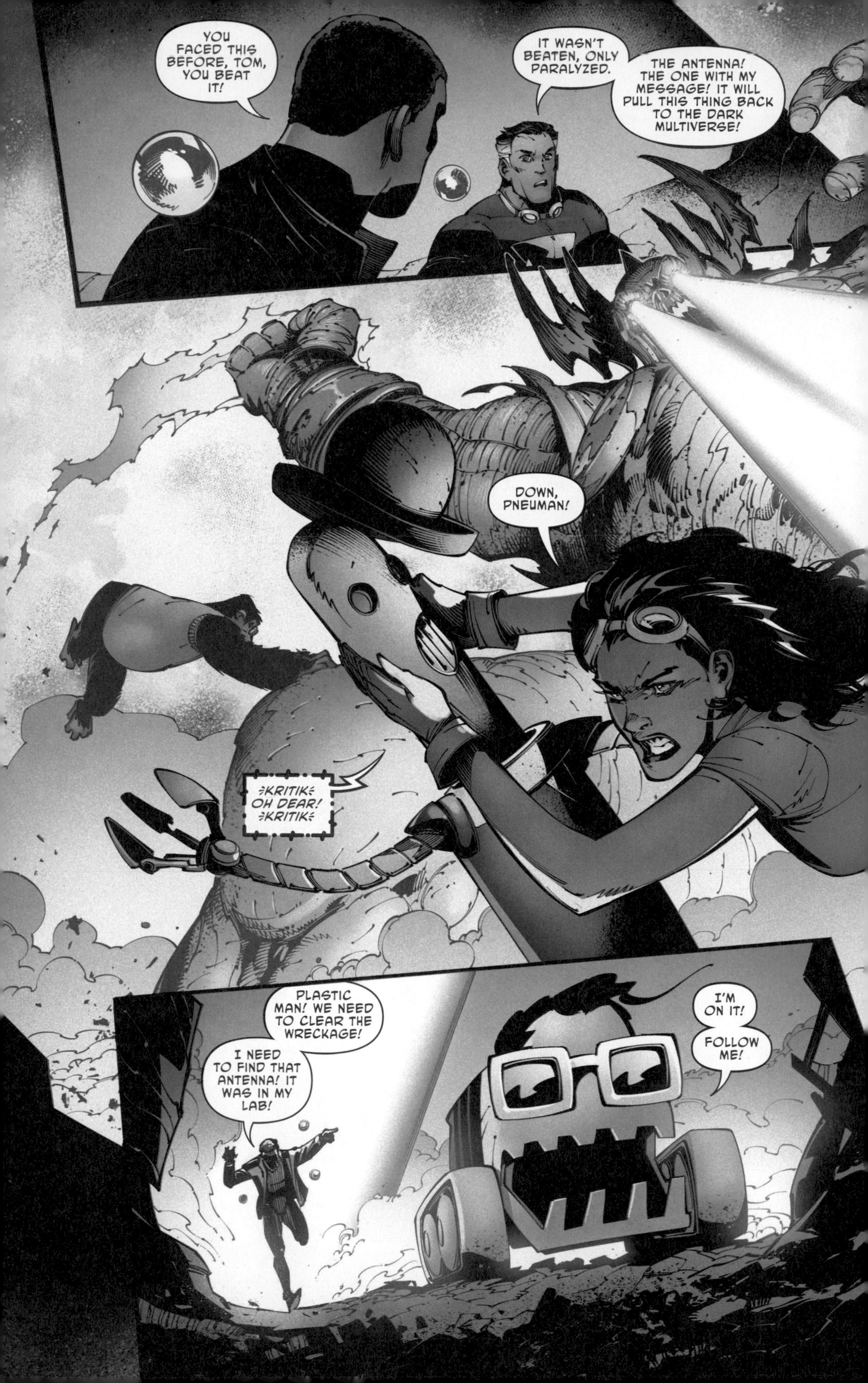
YOU FACED THIS BEFORE, TOM, YOU BEAT IT!
IT WASN'T BEATEN, ONLY PARALYZED.
THE ANTENNA! THE ONE WITH MY MESSAGE! IT WILL PULL THIS THING BACK TO THE DARK MULTIVERSE!
DOWN, PNEUMAN!
KRITIK OH DEAR! KRITIK
PLASTIC MAN! WE NEED TO CLEAR THE WRECKAGE!
I NEED TO FIND THAT ANTENNA! IT WAS IN MY LAB!
I'M ON IT!
FOLLOW ME!

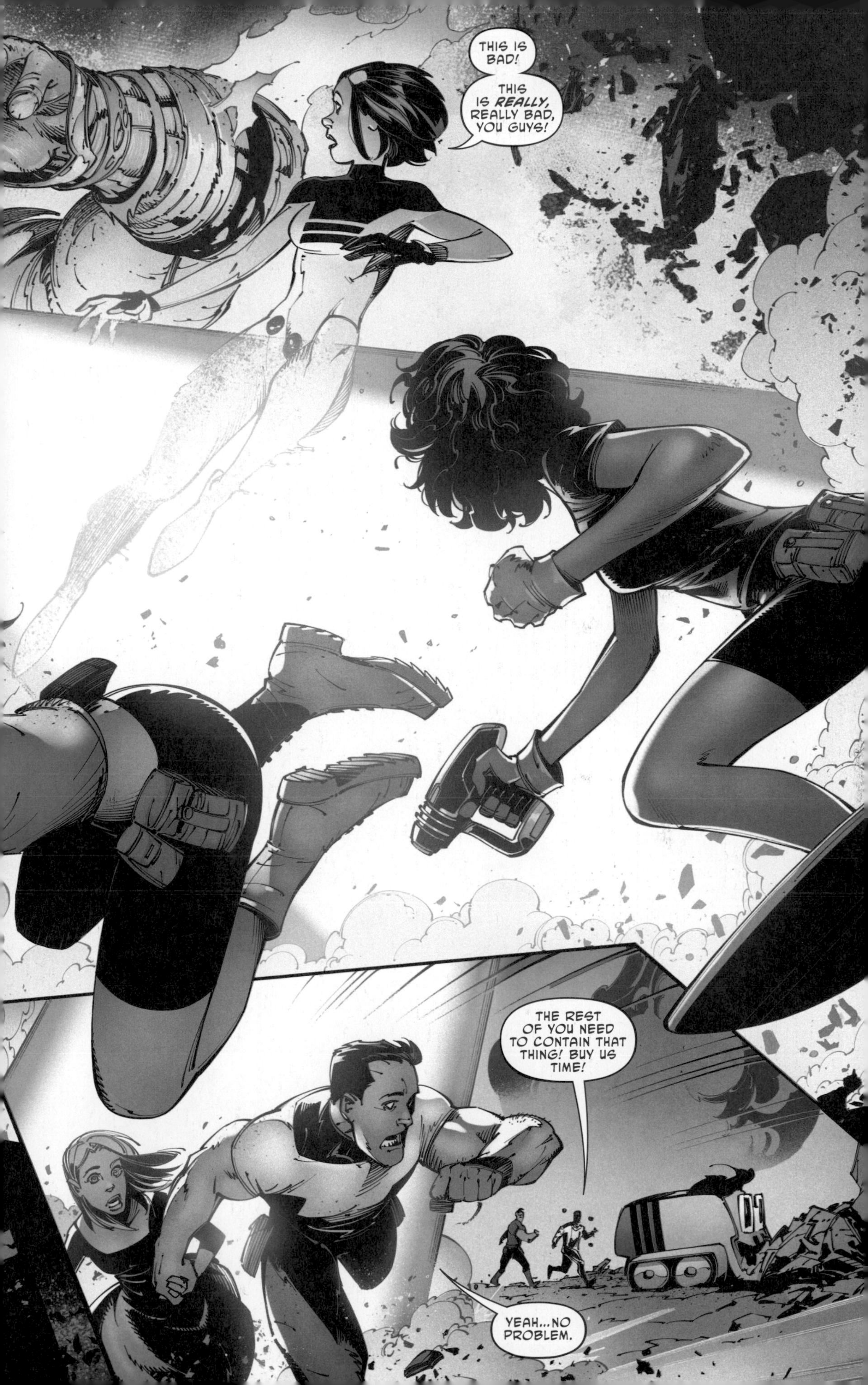
THIS IS BAD!
THIS IS *REALLY,* REALLY BAD, YOU GUYS!
THE REST OF YOU NEED TO CONTAIN THAT THING! BUY US TIME!
YEAH...NO PROBLEM.

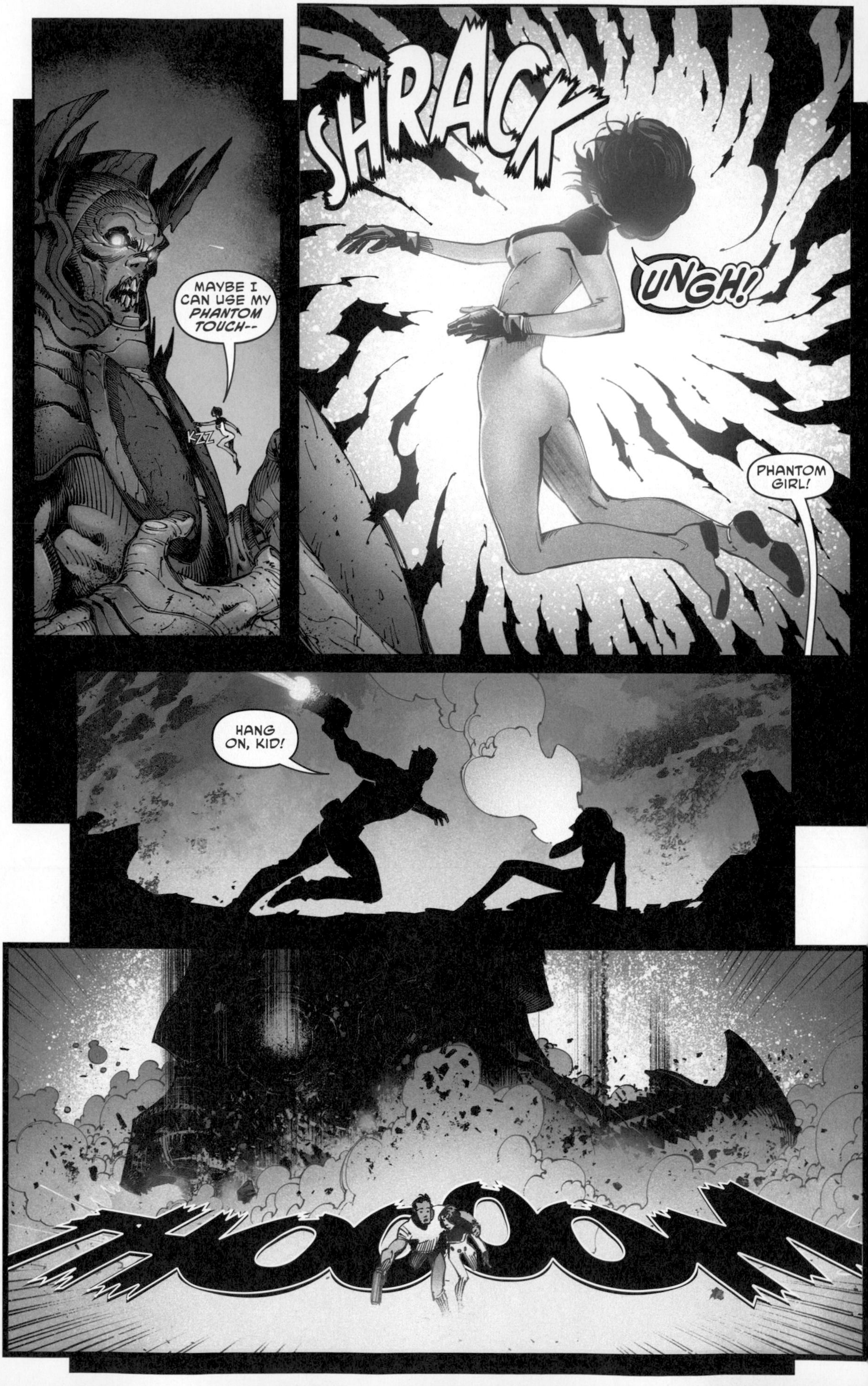
MAYBE I CAN USE MY PHANTOM TOUCH--
KZZ
SHRACK
UNGH!
PHANTOM GIRL!
HANG ON, KID!

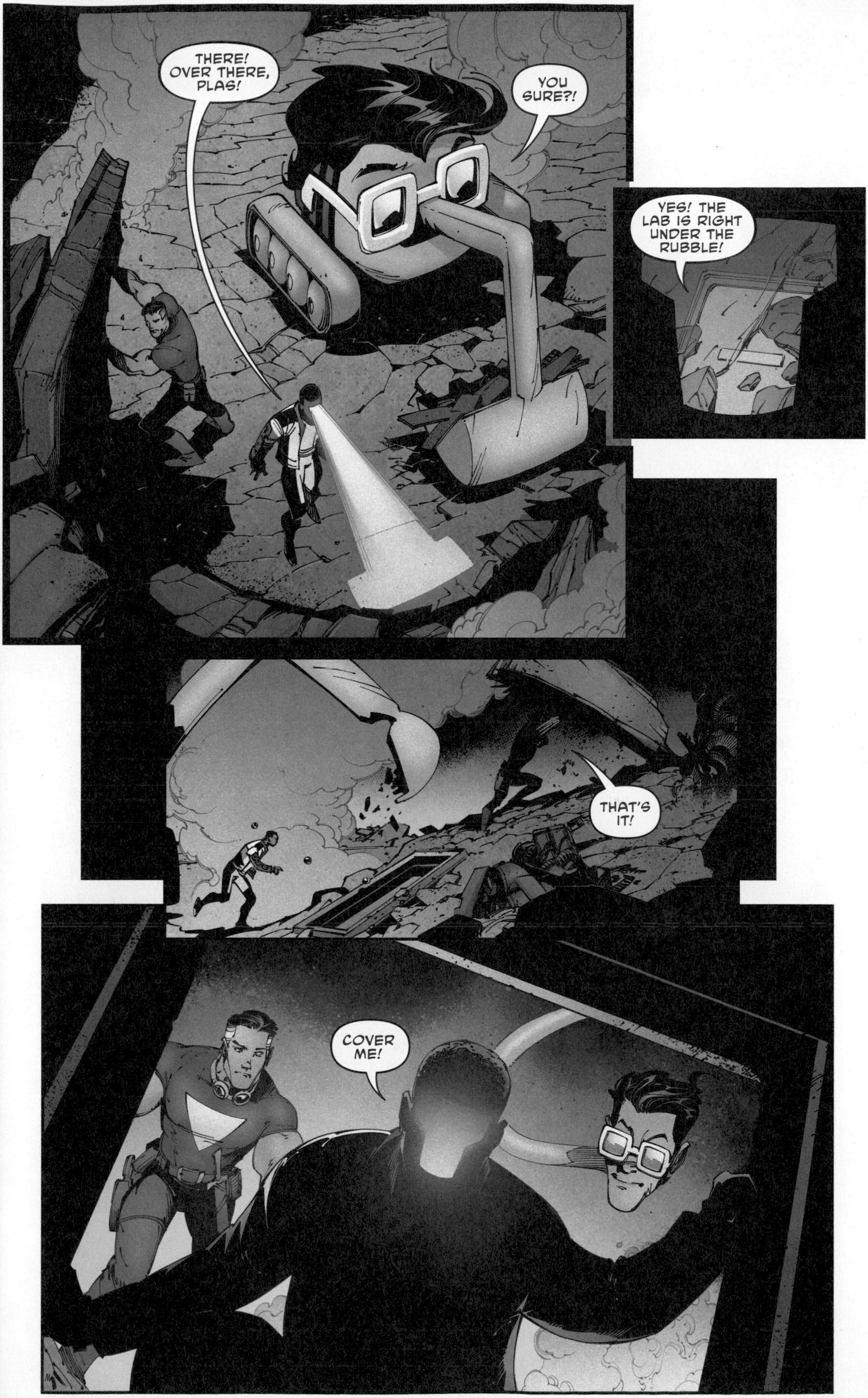
THERE! OVER THERE, PLAS!
YOU SURE?!
YES! THE LAB IS RIGHT UNDER THE RUBBLE!
THAT'S IT!
COVER ME!

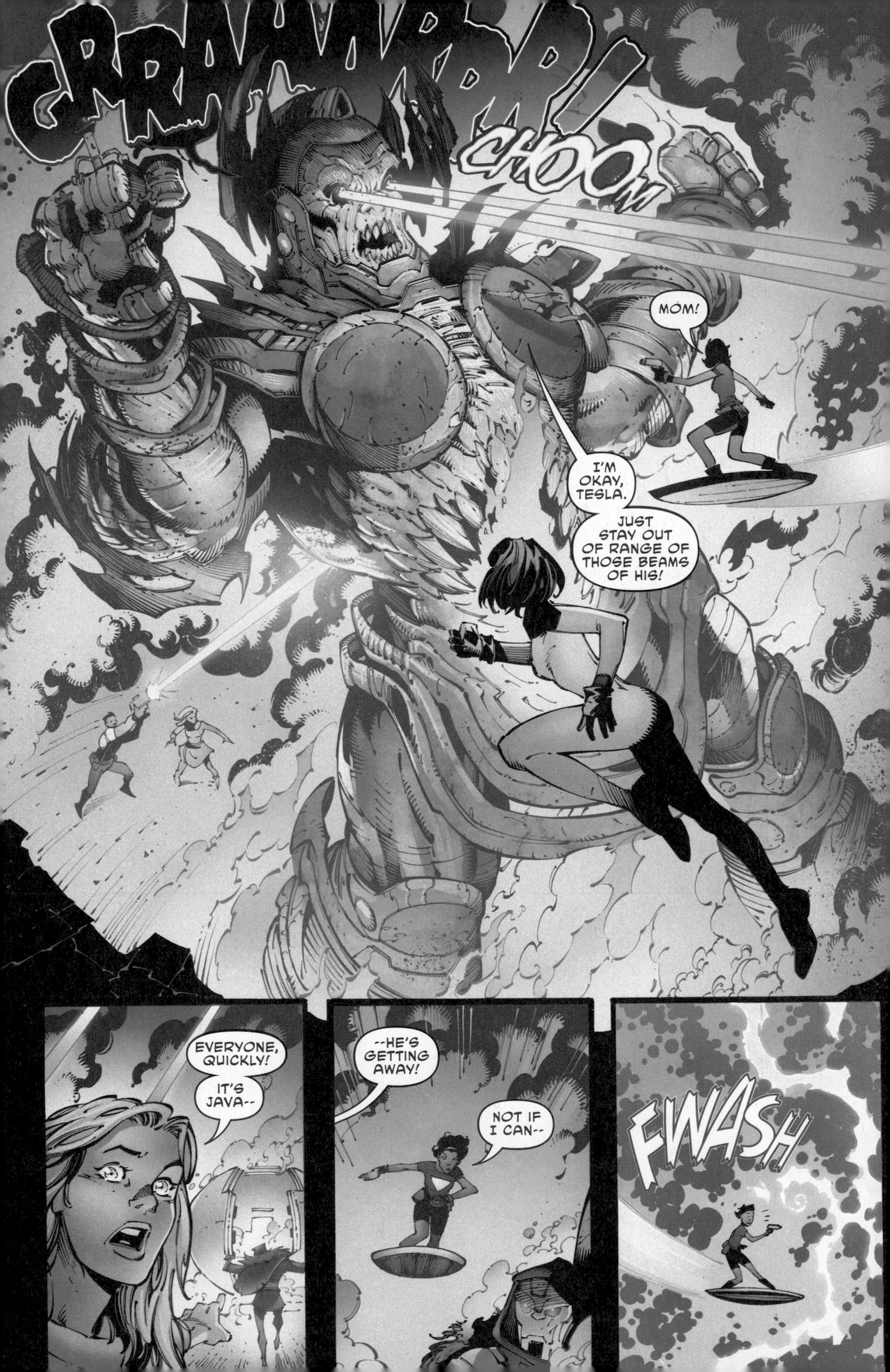
CRAAAARRP!
CHOOM
MOM!
I'M OKAY, TESLA.
JUST STAY OUT OF RANGE OF THOSE BEAMS OF HIS!
EVERYONE, QUICKLY!
IT'S JAVA--
--HE'S GETTING AWAY!
NOT IF I CAN--
FWASH

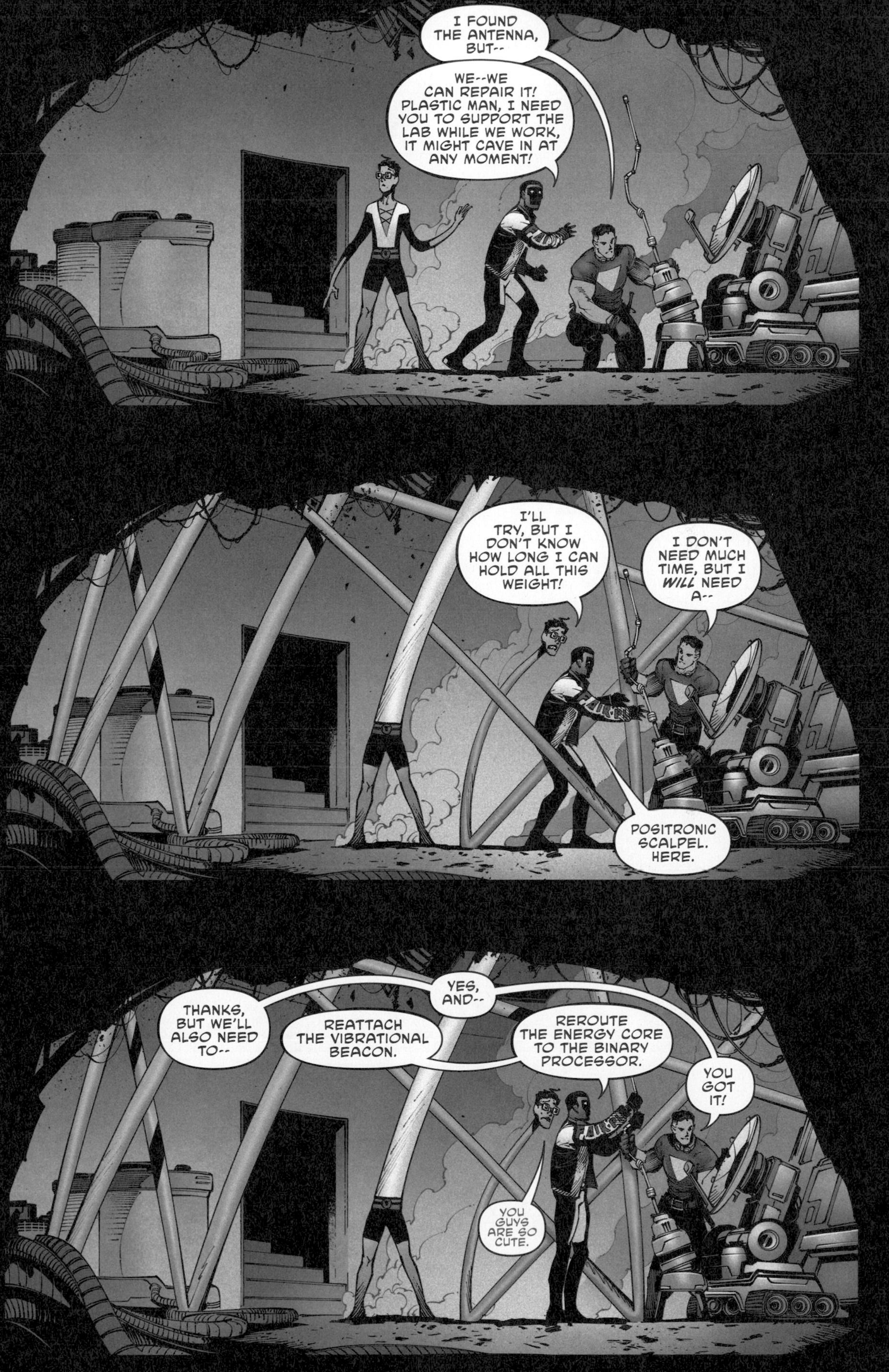
I FOUND THE ANTENNA, BUT--
WE--WE CAN REPAIR IT! PLASTIC MAN, I NEED YOU TO SUPPORT THE LAB WHILE WE WORK, IT MIGHT CAVE IN AT ANY MOMENT!
I'LL TRY, BUT I DON'T KNOW HOW LONG I CAN HOLD ALL THIS WEIGHT!
I DON'T NEED MUCH TIME, BUT I *WILL* NEED A--
POSITRONIC SCALPEL. HERE.
THANKS, BUT WE'LL ALSO NEED TO--
YES, AND--
REATTACH THE VIBRATIONAL BEACON.
REROUTE THE ENERGY CORE TO THE BINARY PROCESSOR.
YOU GOT IT!
YOU GUYS ARE SO CUTE.

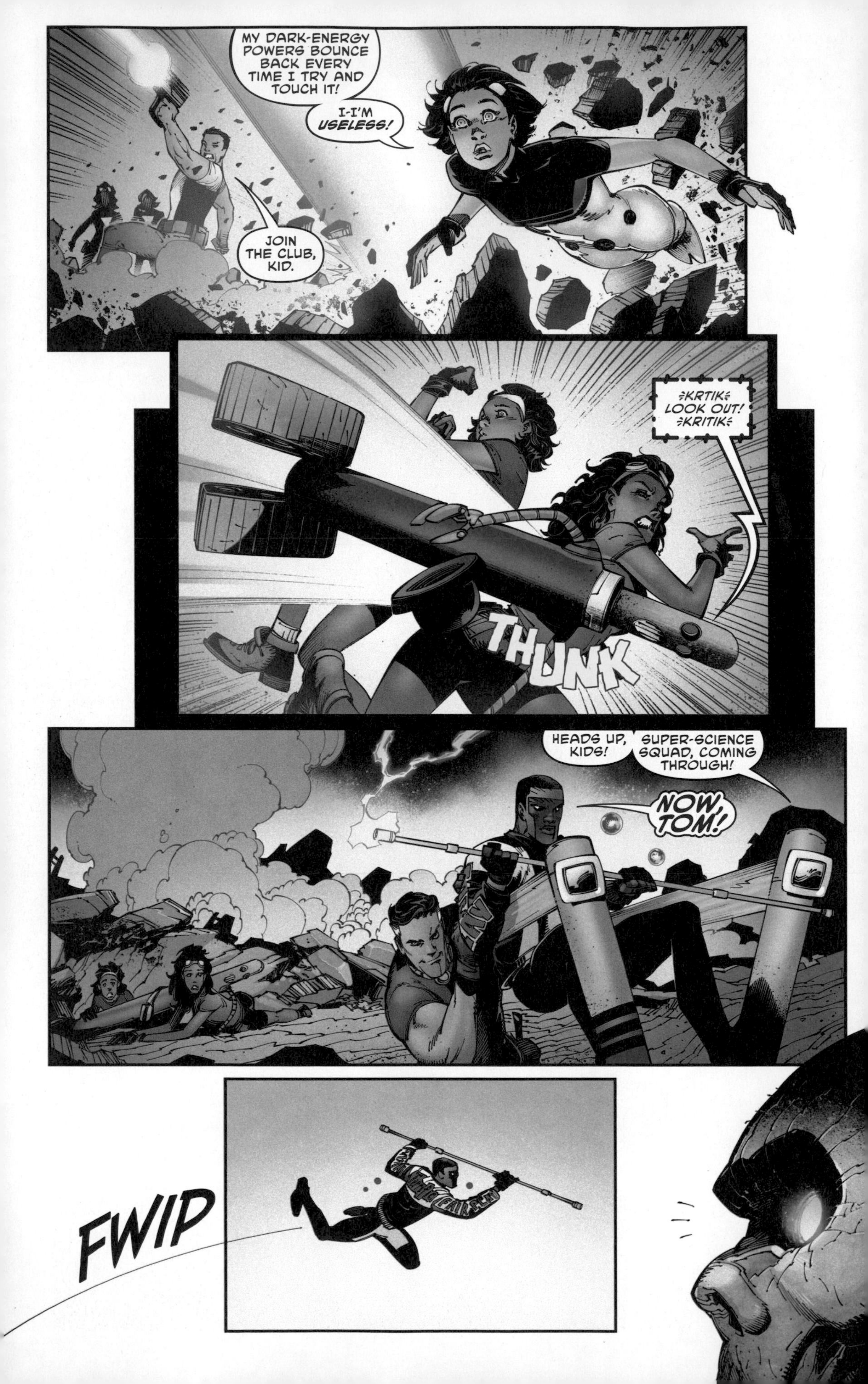
MY DARK-ENERGY POWERS BOUNCE BACK EVERY TIME I TRY AND TOUCH IT!
I-I'M USELESS!
JOIN THE CLUB, KID.
KRTIK LOOK OUT! KRITIK
THUNK
HEADS UP, KIDS!
SUPER-SCIENCE SQUAD, COMING THROUGH!
NOW, TOM!
FWIP

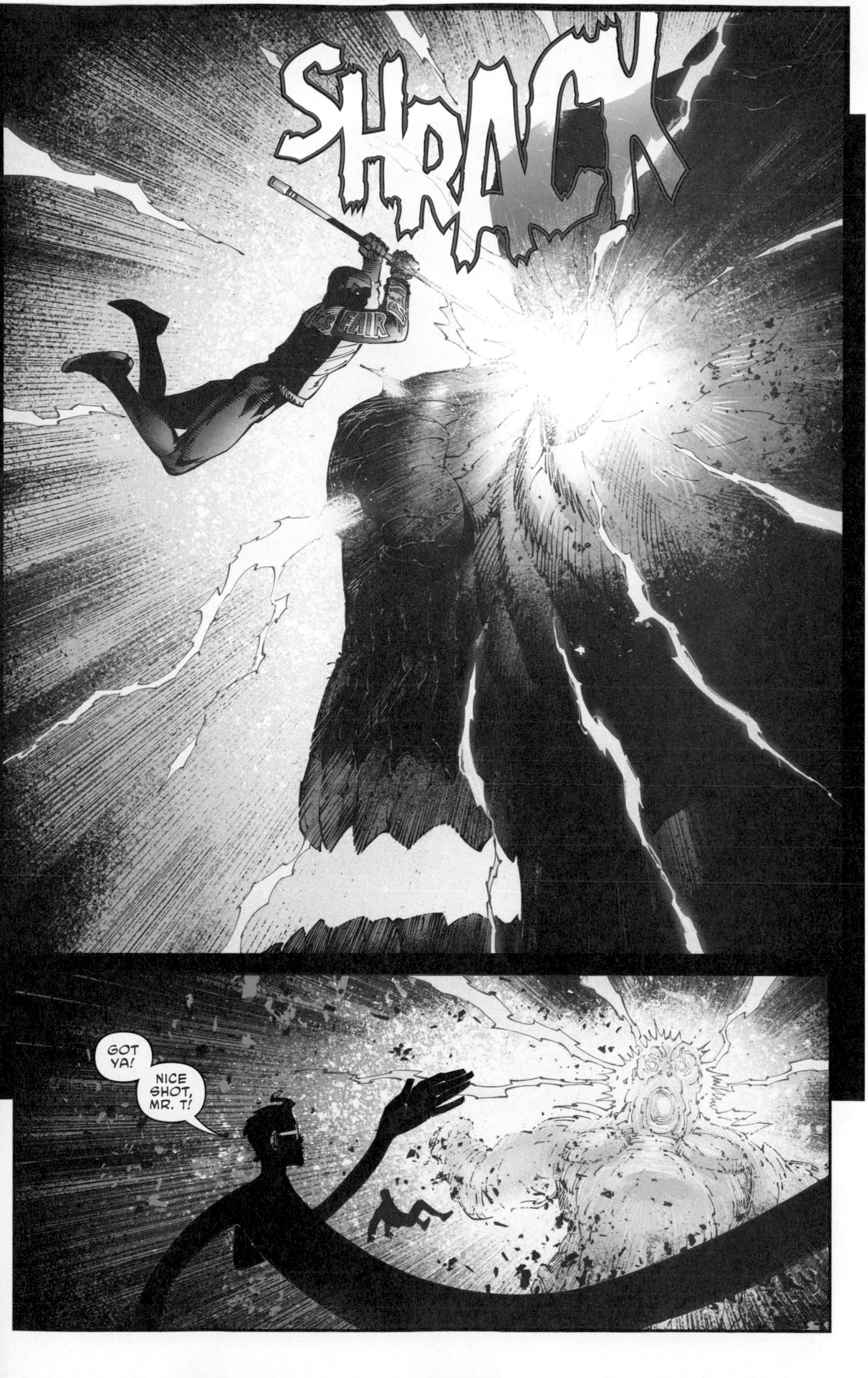
SHRACK
GOT YA!
NICE SHOT, MR. T!

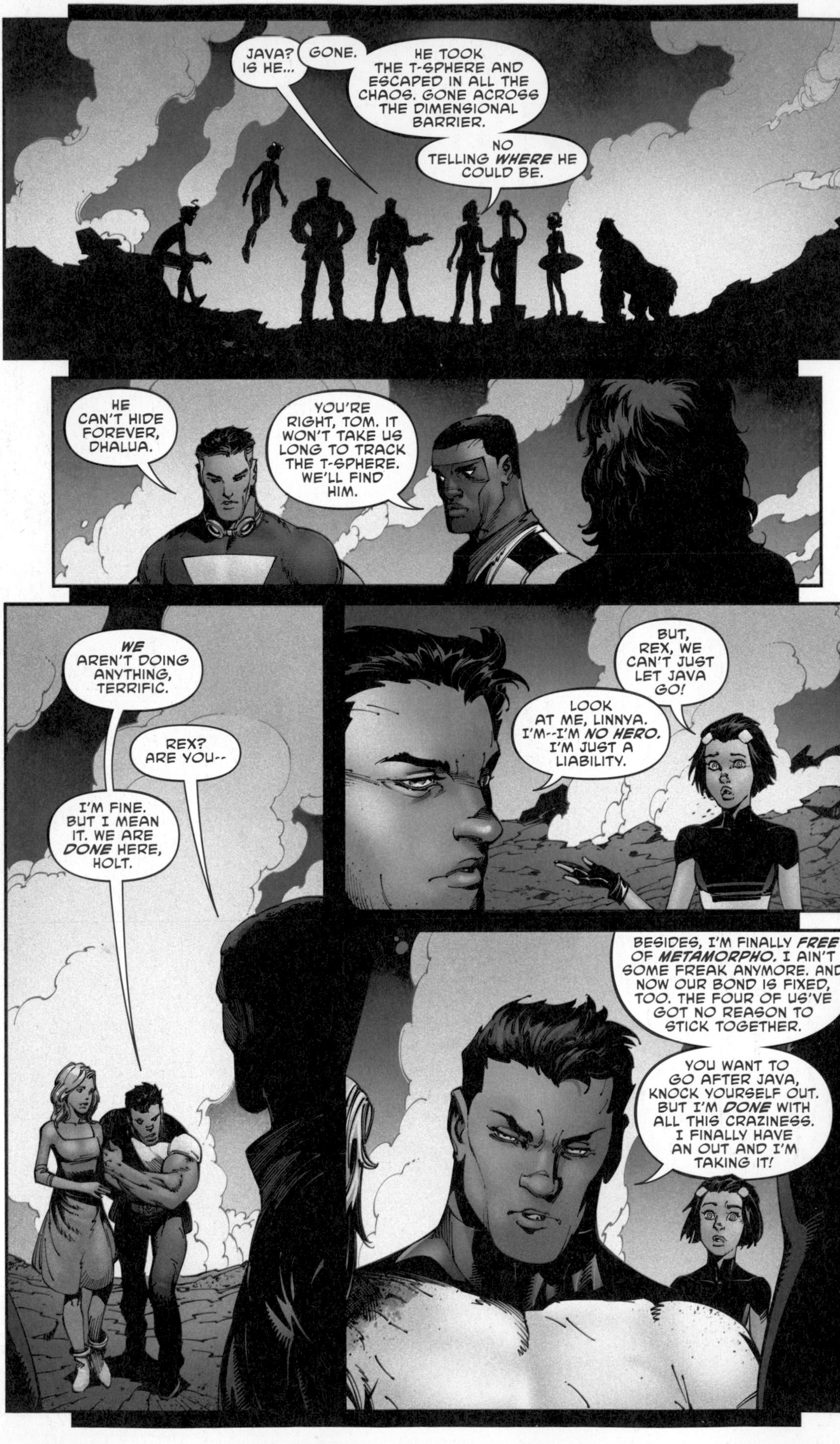
JAVA? IS HE...
GONE.
HE TOOK THE T-SPHERE AND ESCAPED IN ALL THE CHAOS. GONE ACROSS THE DIMENSIONAL BARRIER.
NO TELLING WHERE HE COULD BE.
HE CAN'T HIDE FOREVER, DHALUA.
YOU'RE RIGHT, TOM. IT WON'T TAKE US LONG TO TRACK THE T-SPHERE. WE'LL FIND HIM.
WE AREN'T DOING ANYTHING, TERRIFIC.
REX? ARE YOU--
I'M FINE. BUT I MEAN IT. WE ARE DONE HERE, HOLT.
BUT, REX, WE CAN'T JUST LET JAVA GO!
LOOK AT ME, LINNYA. I'M--I'M NO HERO. I'M JUST A LIABILITY.
BESIDES, I'M FINALLY FREE OF METAMORPHO. I AIN'T SOME FREAK ANYMORE. AND NOW OUR BOND IS FIXED, TOO. THE FOUR OF US'VE GOT NO REASON TO STICK TOGETHER.
YOU WANT TO GO AFTER JAVA, KNOCK YOURSELF OUT. BUT I'M DONE WITH ALL THIS CRAZINESS. I FINALLY HAVE AN OUT AND I'M TAKING IT!

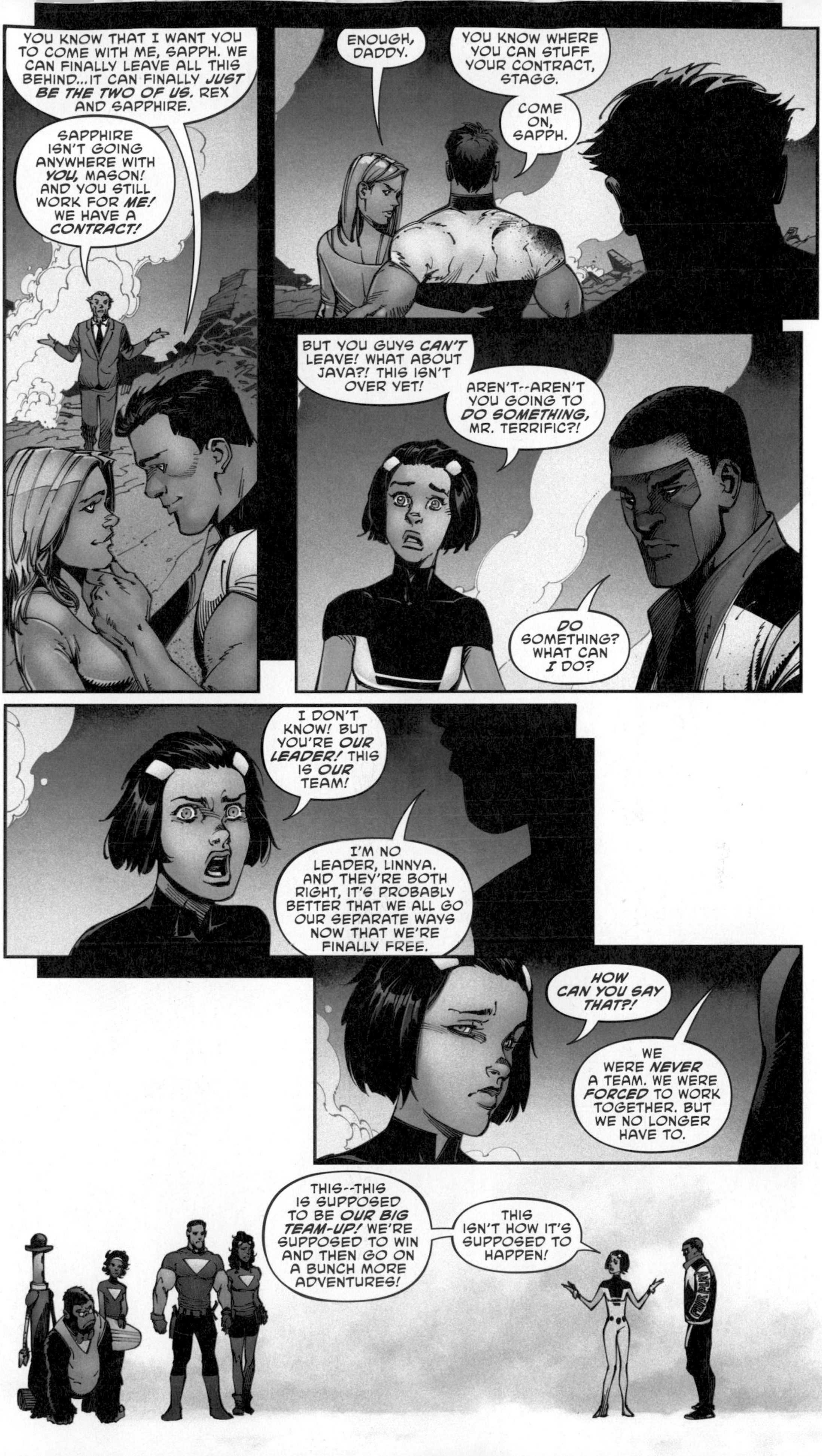
YOU KNOW THAT I WANT YOU TO COME WITH ME, SAPPH. WE CAN FINALLY LEAVE ALL THIS BEHIND...IT CAN FINALLY JUST BE THE TWO OF US. REX AND SAPPHIRE.
SAPPHIRE ISN'T GOING ANYWHERE WITH YOU, MASON! AND YOU STILL WORK FOR ME! WE HAVE A CONTRACT!
ENOUGH, DADDY.
YOU KNOW WHERE YOU CAN STUFF YOUR CONTRACT, STAGG.
COME ON, SAPPH.
BUT YOU GUYS CAN'T LEAVE! WHAT ABOUT JAVA?! THIS ISN'T OVER YET!
AREN'T--AREN'T YOU GOING TO DO SOMETHING, MR. TERRIFIC?!
DO SOMETHING? WHAT CAN I DO?
I DON'T KNOW! BUT YOU'RE OUR LEADER! THIS IS OUR TEAM!
I'M NO LEADER, LINNYA. AND THEY'RE BOTH RIGHT, IT'S PROBABLY BETTER THAT WE ALL GO OUR SEPARATE WAYS NOW THAT WE'RE FINALLY FREE.
HOW CAN YOU SAY THAT?!
WE WERE NEVER A TEAM. WE WERE FORCED TO WORK TOGETHER. BUT WE NO LONGER HAVE TO.
THIS--THIS IS SUPPOSED TO BE OUR BIG TEAM-UP! WE'RE SUPPOSED TO WIN AND THEN GO ON A BUNCH MORE ADVENTURES!
THIS ISN'T HOW IT'S SUPPOSED TO HAPPEN!

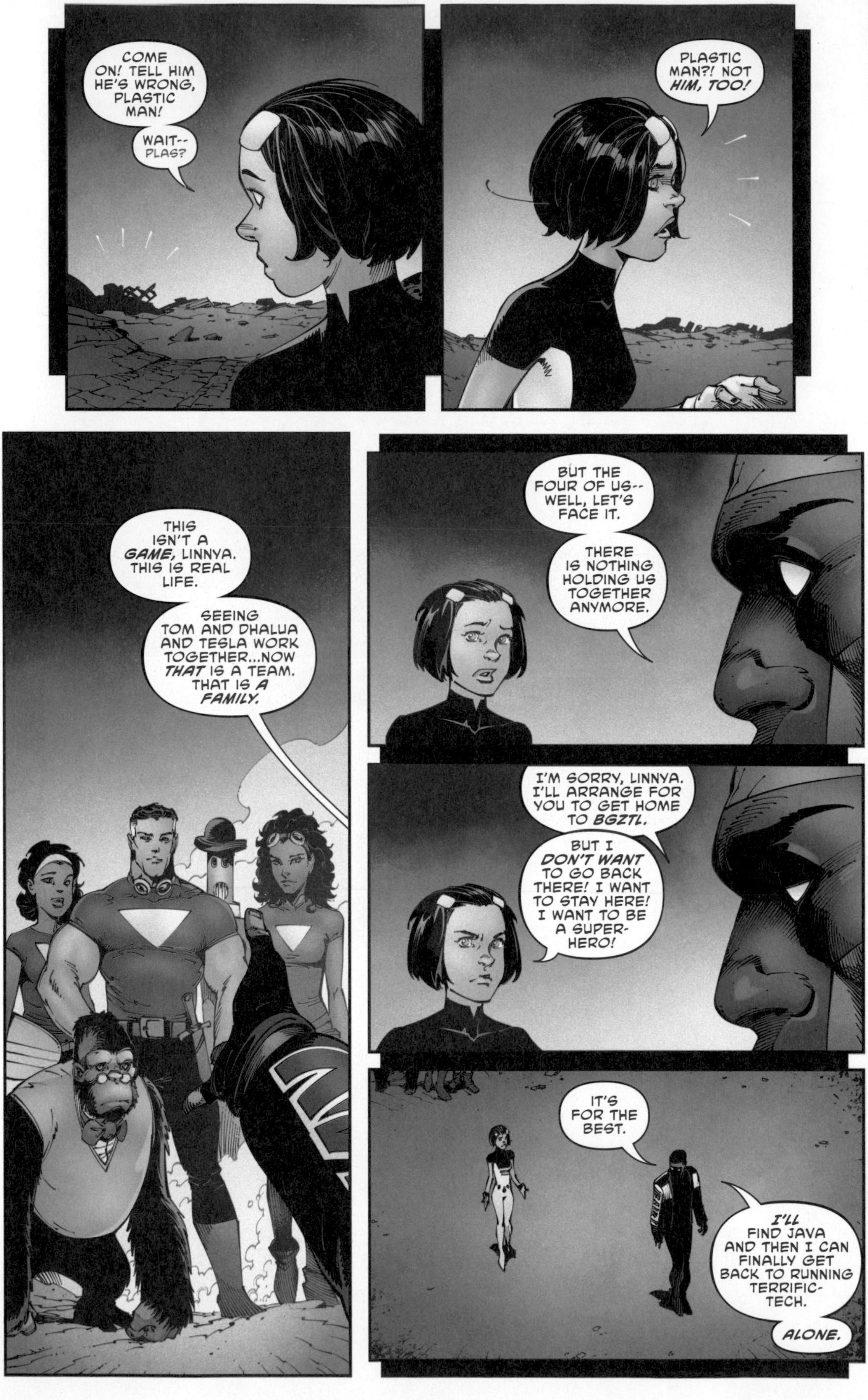

COME ON! TELL HIM HE'S WRONG, PLASTIC MAN!
WAIT-- PLAS?
PLASTIC MAN?! NOT *HIM, TOO!*
THIS ISN'T A *GAME,* LINNYA. THIS IS REAL LIFE.
SEEING TOM AND DHALUA AND TESLA WORK TOGETHER...NOW *THAT* IS A TEAM. THAT IS *A FAMILY.*
BUT THE FOUR OF US-- WELL, LET'S FACE IT.
THERE IS NOTHING HOLDING US TOGETHER ANYMORE.
I'M SORRY, LINNYA. I'LL ARRANGE FOR YOU TO GET HOME TO *BGZTL.*
BUT I *DON'T WANT* TO GO BACK THERE! I WANT TO STAY HERE! I WANT TO BE A SUPER-HERO!
IT'S FOR THE BEST.
I'LL FIND JAVA AND THEN I CAN FINALLY GET BACK TO RUNNING TERRIFIC-TECH.
ALONE.

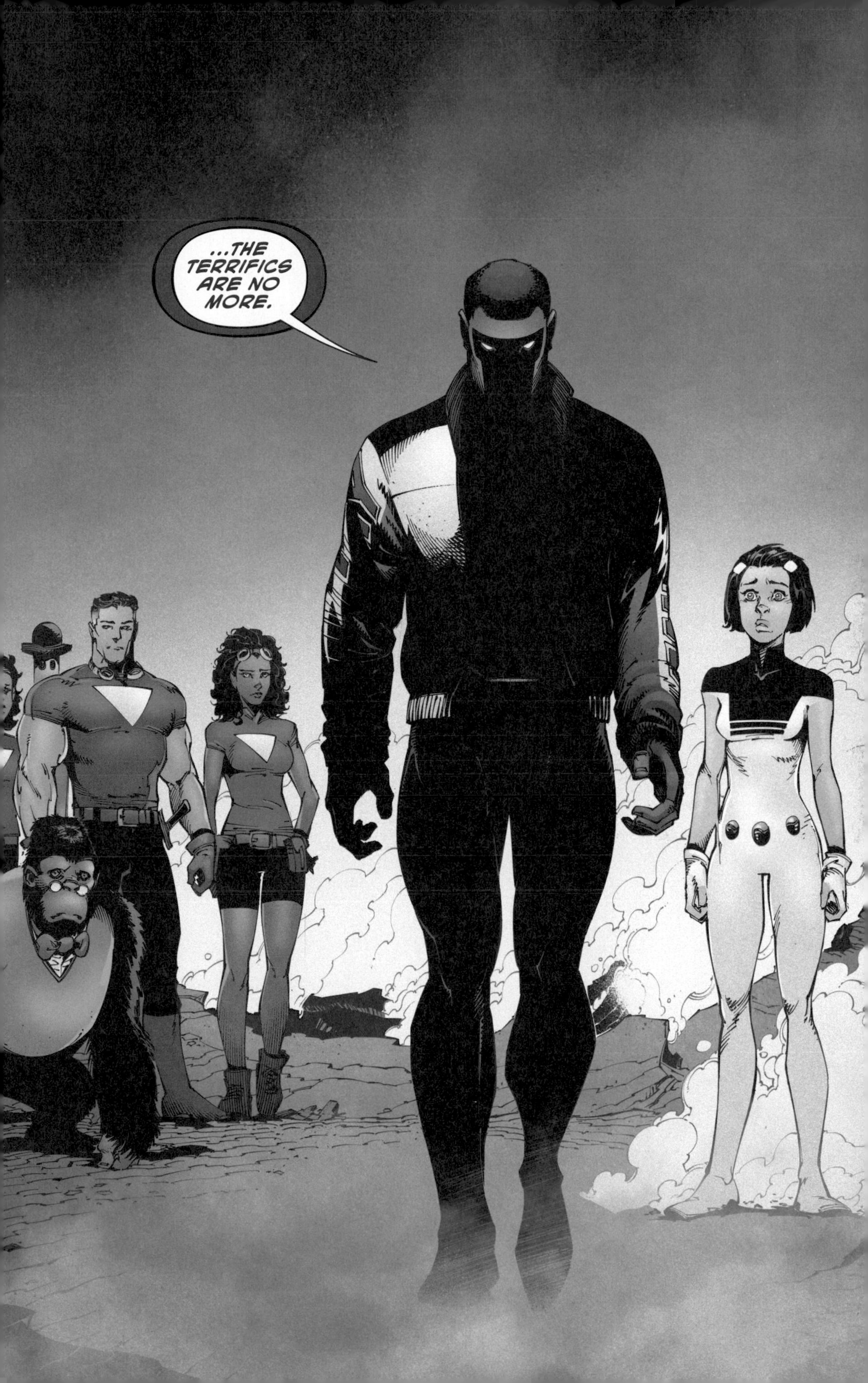
...THE TERRIFICS ARE NO MORE.

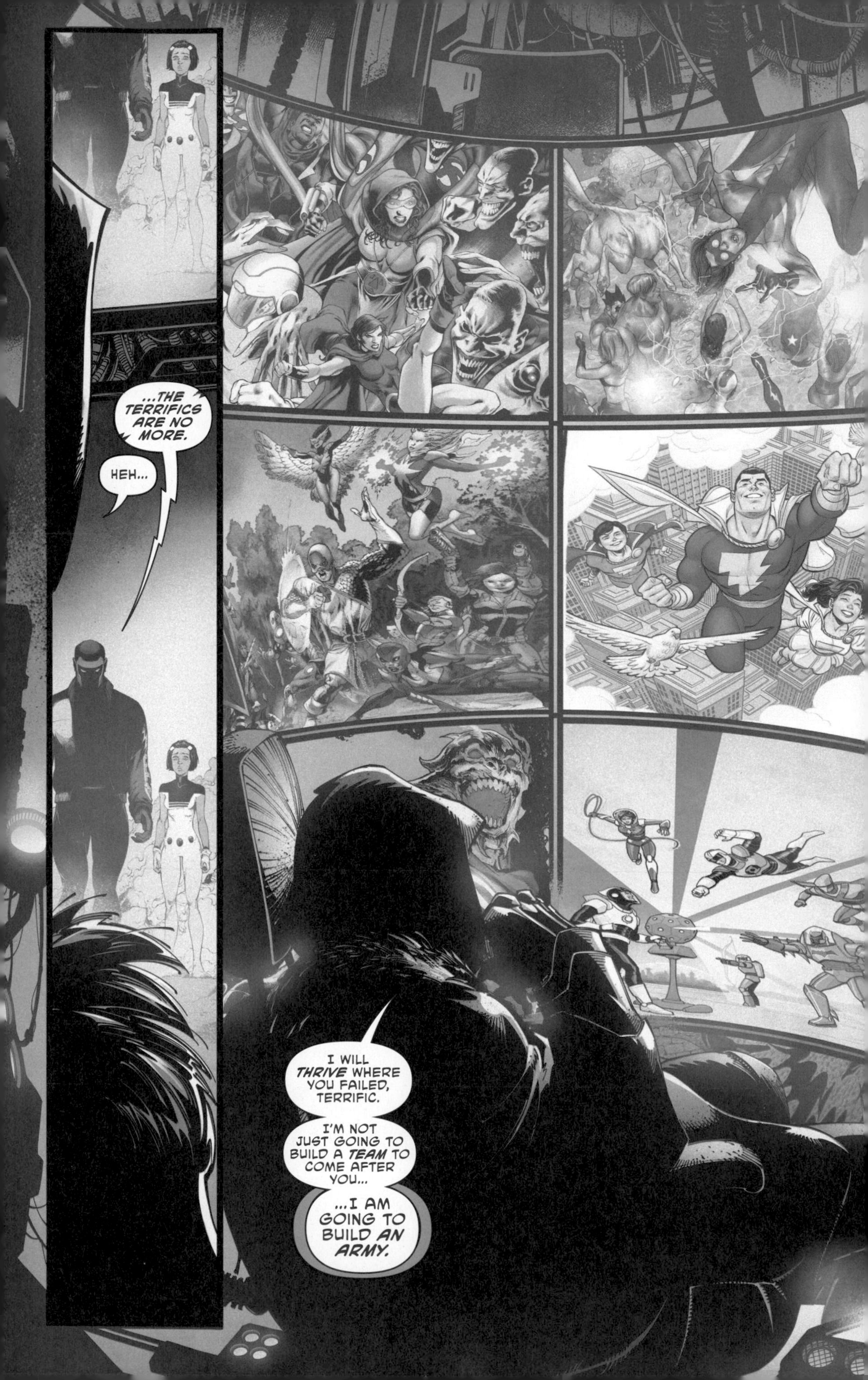
...THE TERRIFICS ARE NO MORE.
HEH...
I WILL THRIVE WHERE YOU FAILED, TERRIFIC.
I'M NOT JUST GOING TO BUILD A TEAM TO COME AFTER YOU...
...I AM GOING TO BUILD AN ARMY.

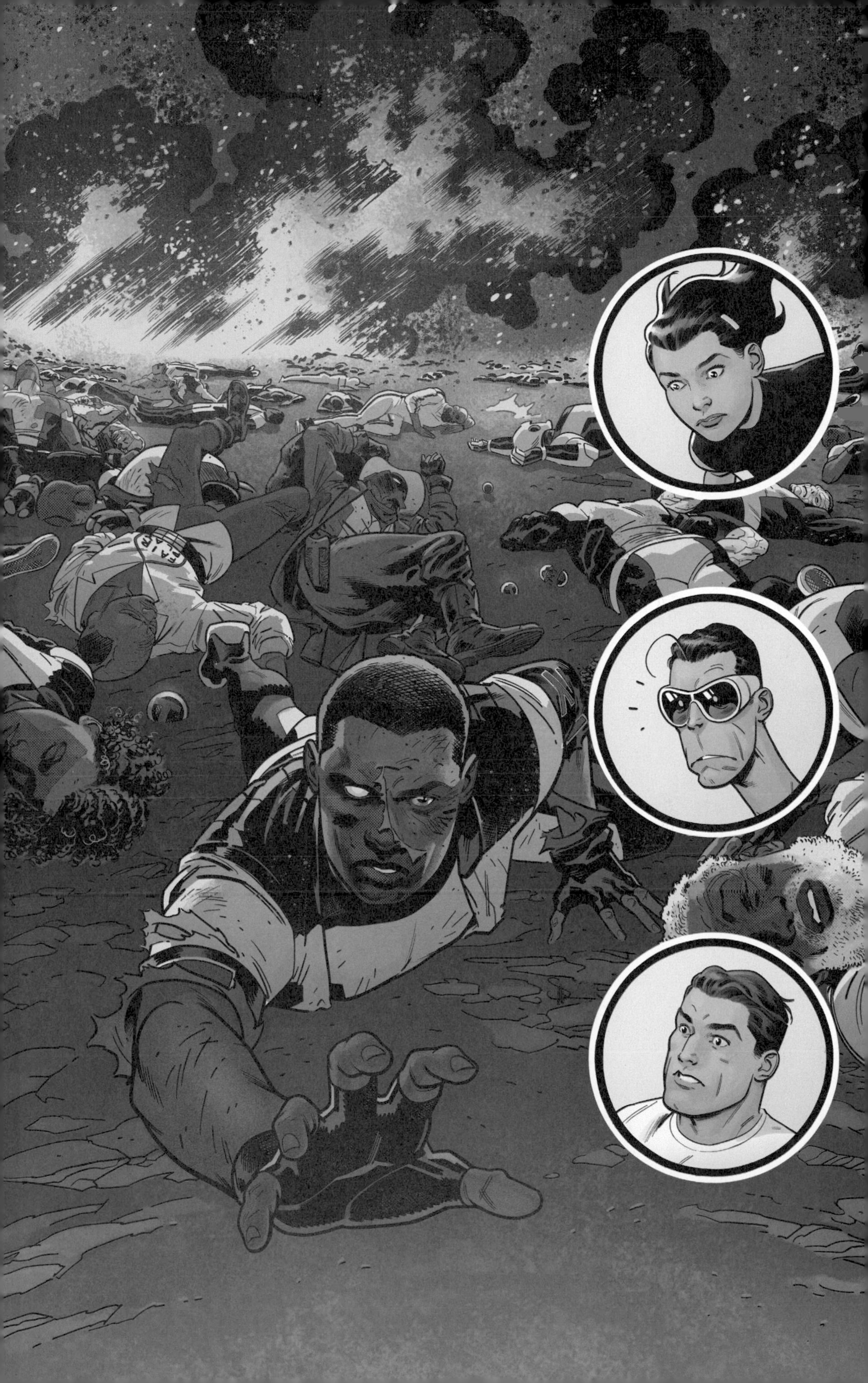

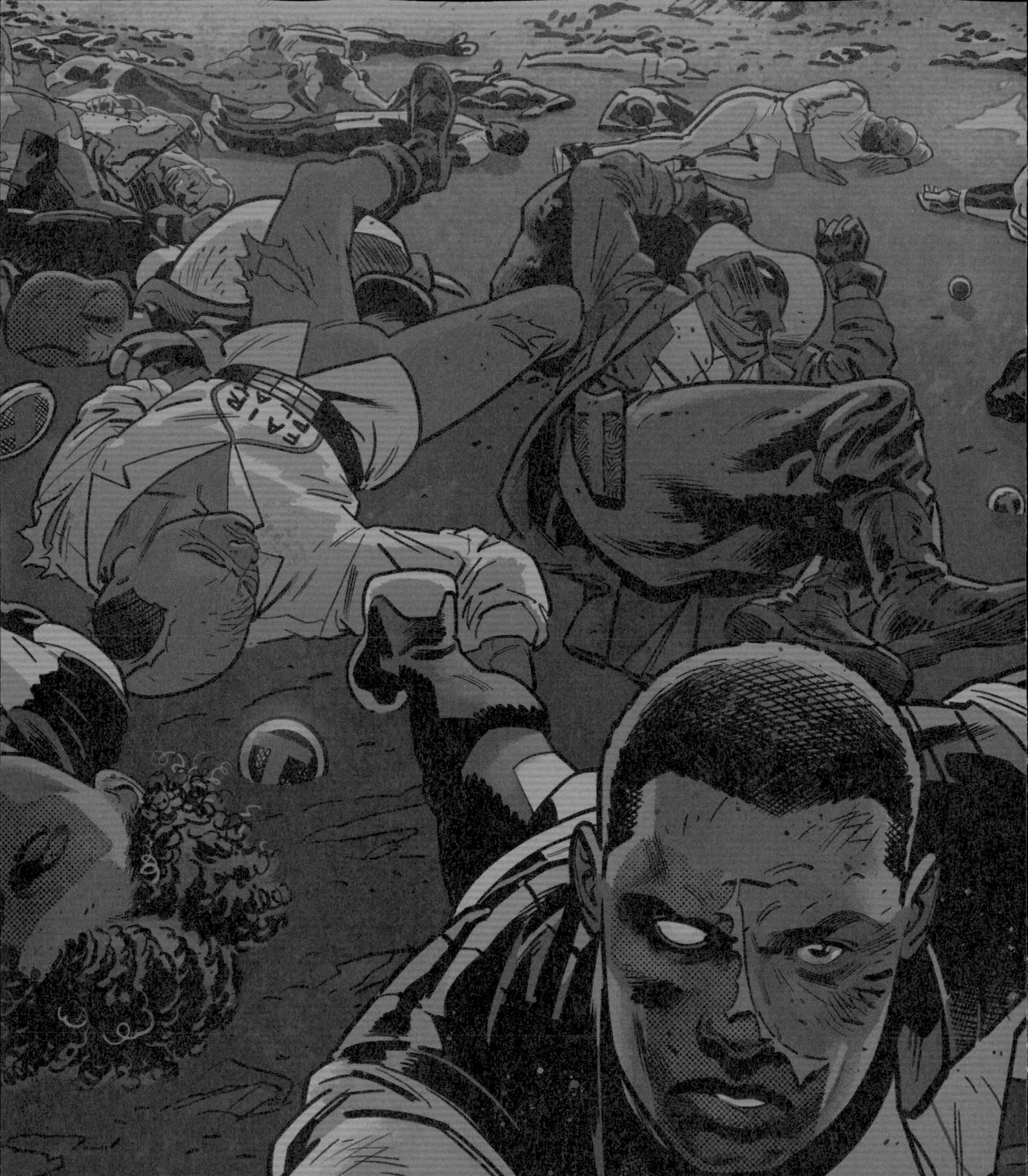

THE TERRIFICS
#11

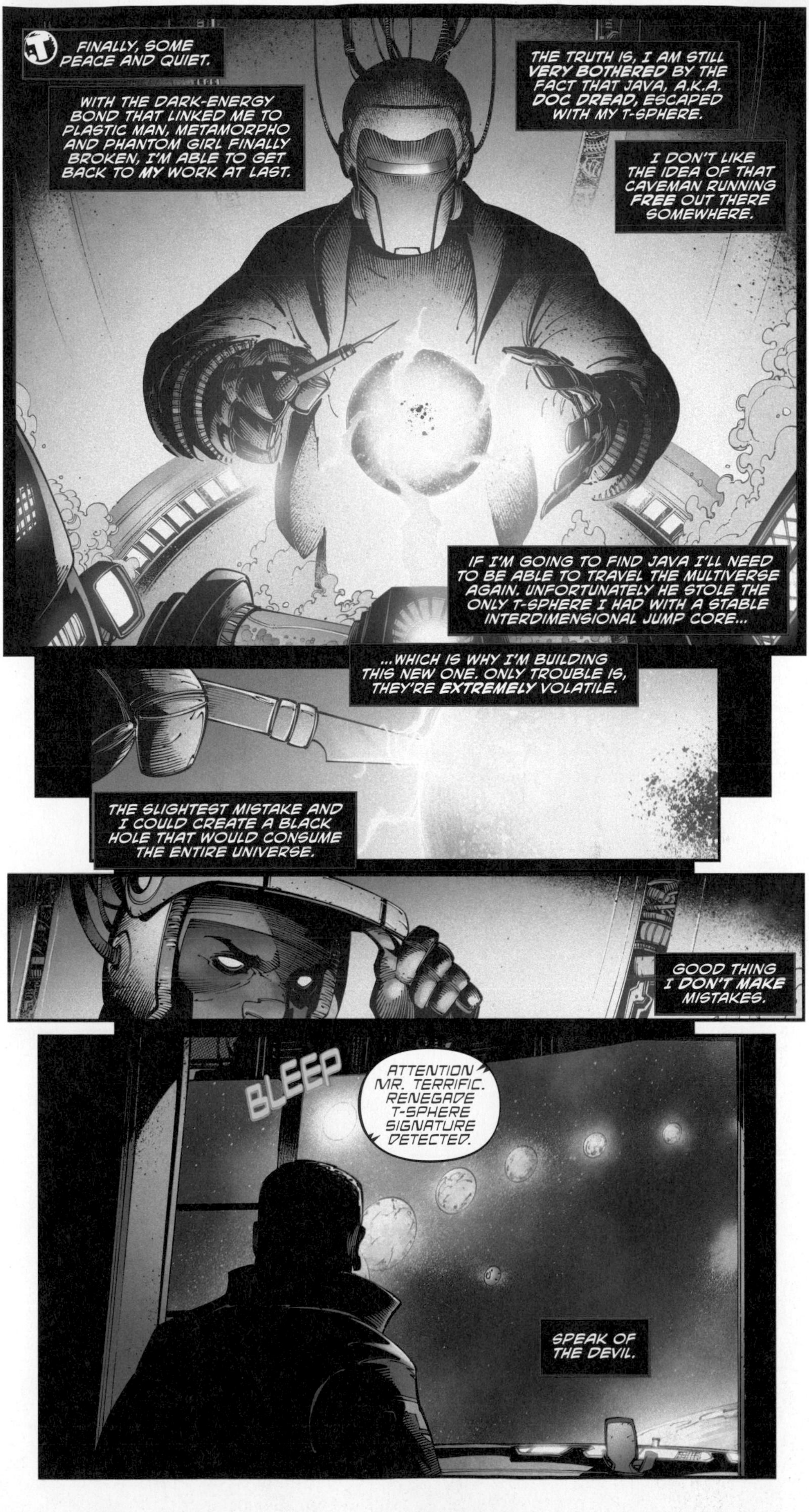
FINALLY, SOME PEACE AND QUIET.
WITH THE DARK-ENERGY BOND THAT LINKED ME TO PLASTIC MAN, METAMORPHO AND PHANTOM GIRL FINALLY BROKEN, I'M ABLE TO GET BACK TO MY WORK AT LAST.
THE TRUTH IS, I AM STILL VERY BOTHERED BY THE FACT THAT JAVA, A.K.A. DOC DREAD, ESCAPED WITH MY T-SPHERE.
I DON'T LIKE THE IDEA OF THAT CAVEMAN RUNNING FREE OUT THERE SOMEWHERE.
IF I'M GOING TO FIND JAVA I'LL NEED TO BE ABLE TO TRAVEL THE MULTIVERSE AGAIN. UNFORTUNATELY HE STOLE THE ONLY T-SPHERE I HAD WITH A STABLE INTERDIMENSIONAL JUMP CORE...
...WHICH IS WHY I'M BUILDING THIS NEW ONE. ONLY TROUBLE IS, THEY'RE EXTREMELY VOLATILE.
THE SLIGHTEST MISTAKE AND I COULD CREATE A BLACK HOLE THAT WOULD CONSUME THE ENTIRE UNIVERSE.
GOOD THING I DON'T MAKE MISTAKES.
BLEEP
ATTENTION MR. TERRIFIC. RENEGADE T-SPHERE SIGNATURE DETECTED.
SPEAK OF THE DEVIL.

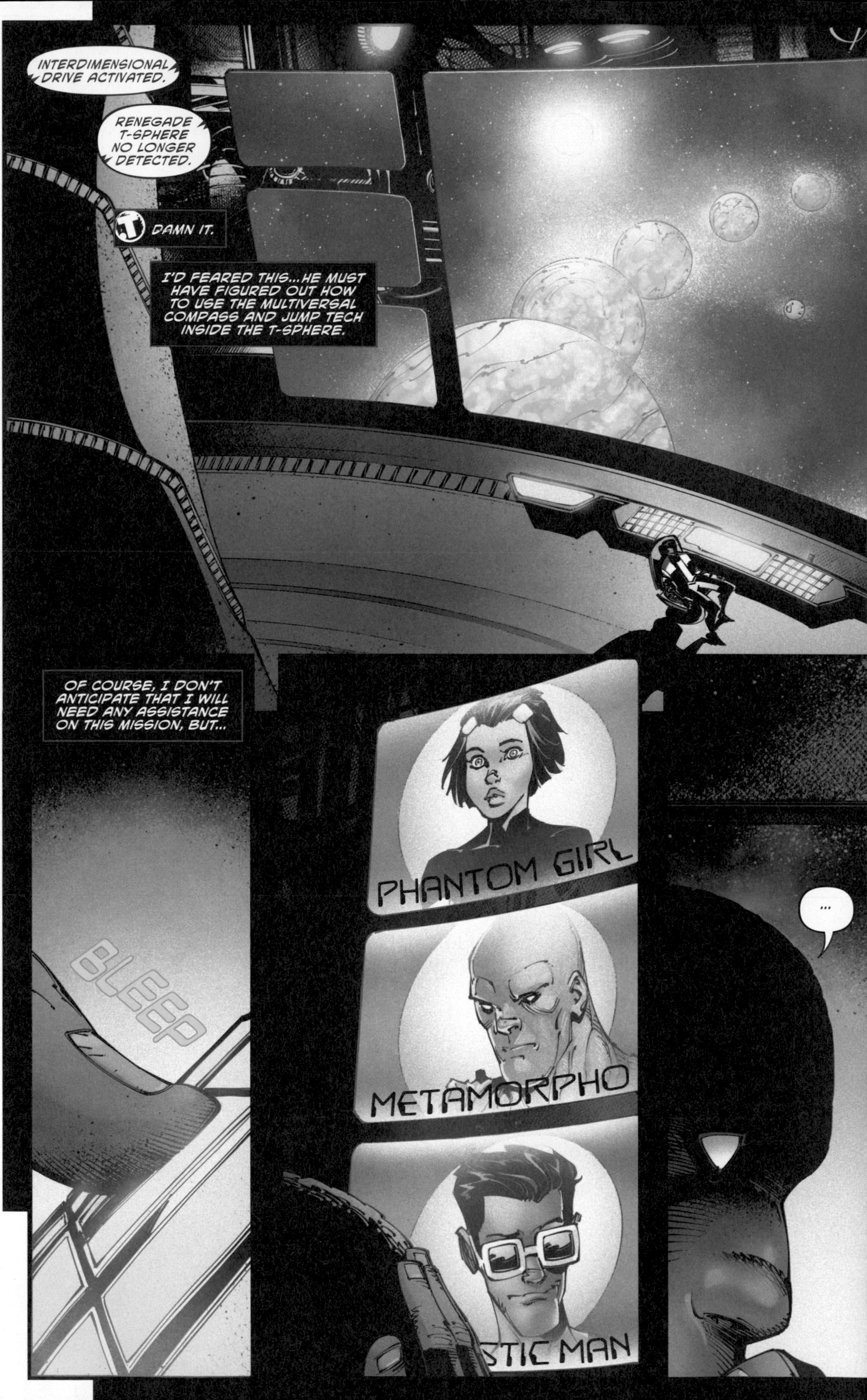
INTERDIMENSIONAL DRIVE ACTIVATED.
RENEGADE T-SPHERE NO LONGER DETECTED.
DAMN IT.
I'D FEARED THIS...HE MUST HAVE FIGURED OUT HOW TO USE THE MULTIVERSAL COMPASS AND JUMP TECH INSIDE THE T-SPHERE.
OF COURSE, I DON'T ANTICIPATE THAT I WILL NEED ANY ASSISTANCE ON THIS MISSION, BUT...
BLEEP
PHANTOM GIRL
METAMORPHO
STIC MAN
...

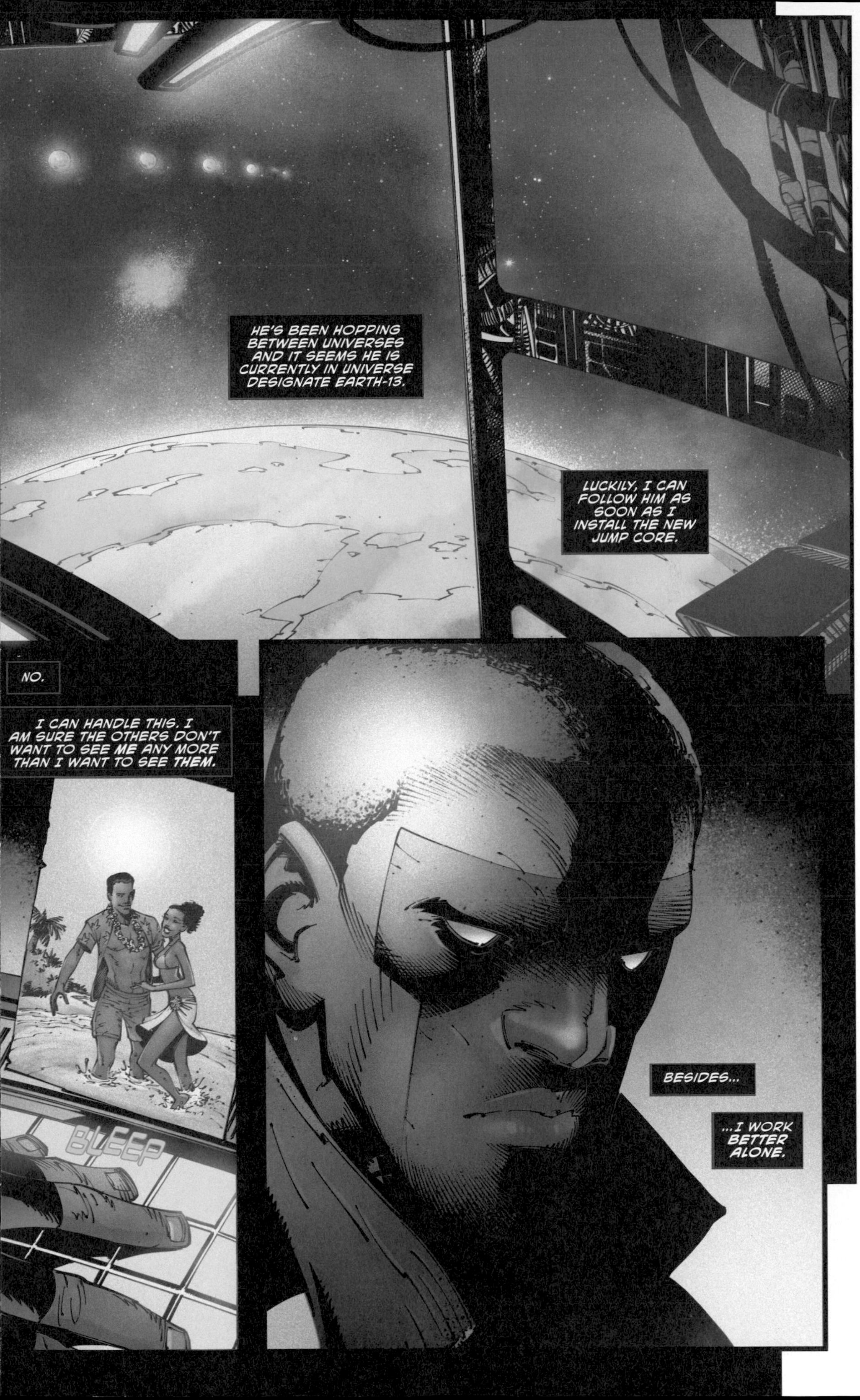
HE'S BEEN HOPPING BETWEEN UNIVERSES AND IT SEEMS HE IS CURRENTLY IN UNIVERSE DESIGNATE EARTH-13.
LUCKILY, I CAN FOLLOW HIM AS SOON AS I INSTALL THE NEW JUMP CORE.
NO.
I CAN HANDLE THIS. I AM SURE THE OTHERS DON'T WANT TO SEE ME ANY MORE THAN I WANT TO SEE THEM.
BLEEP
BESIDES...
...I WORK BETTER ALONE.

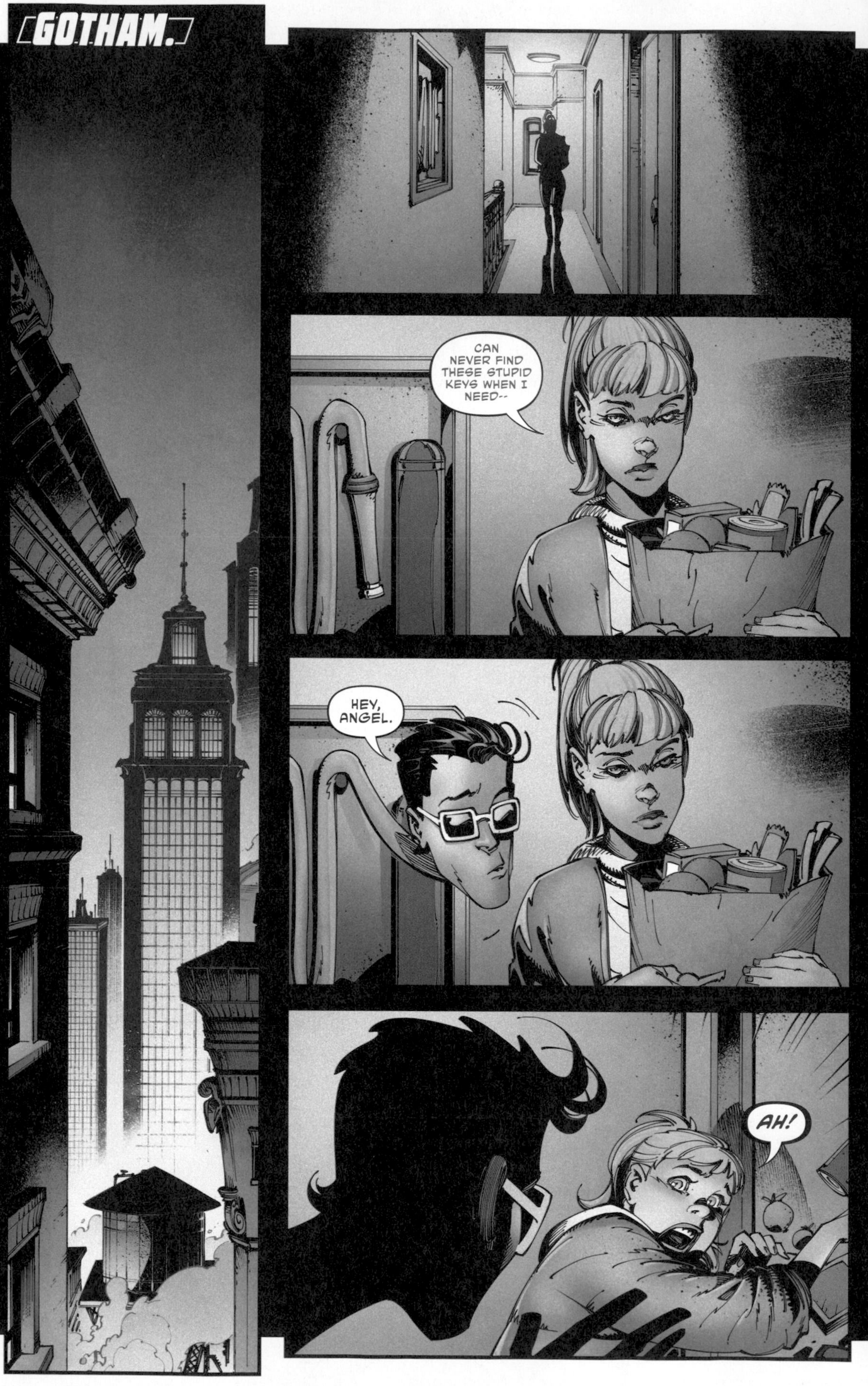
GOTHAM.
CAN NEVER FIND THESE STUPID KEYS WHEN I NEED--
HEY, ANGEL.
AH!

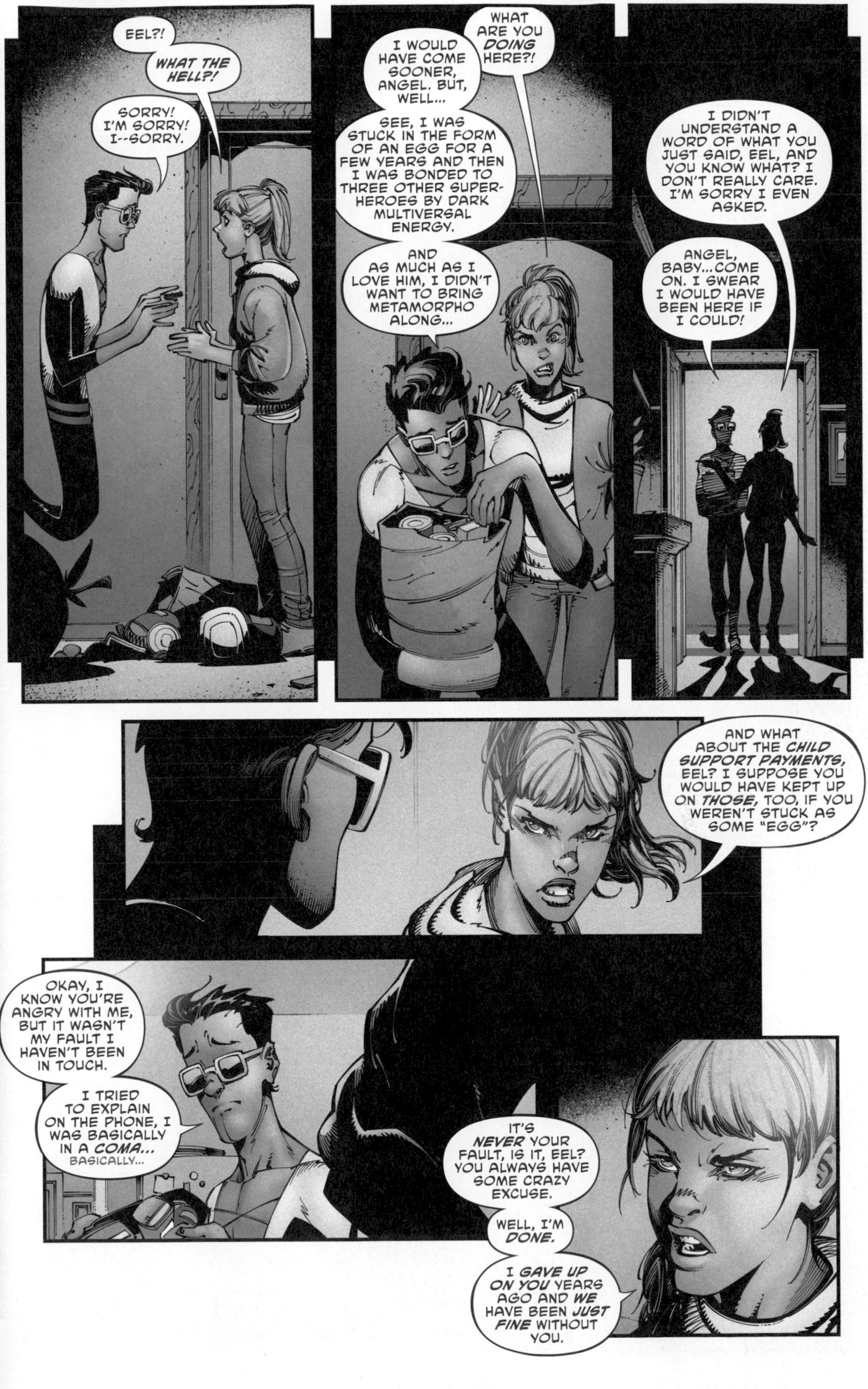
EEL?!
WHAT THE HELL?!
SORRY! I'M SORRY! I--SORRY.
WHAT ARE YOU DOING HERE?!
I WOULD HAVE COME SOONER, ANGEL. BUT, WELL...
SEE, I WAS STUCK IN THE FORM OF AN EGG FOR A FEW YEARS AND THEN I WAS BONDED TO THREE OTHER SUPER-HEROES BY DARK MULTIVERSAL ENERGY.
AND AS MUCH AS I LOVE HIM, I DIDN'T WANT TO BRING METAMORPHO ALONG...
I DIDN'T UNDERSTAND A WORD OF WHAT YOU JUST SAID, EEL, AND YOU KNOW WHAT? I DON'T REALLY CARE. I'M SORRY I EVEN ASKED.
ANGEL, BABY...COME ON. I SWEAR I WOULD HAVE BEEN HERE IF I COULD!
AND WHAT ABOUT THE CHILD SUPPORT PAYMENTS, EEL? I SUPPOSE YOU WOULD HAVE KEPT UP ON THOSE, TOO, IF YOU WEREN'T STUCK AS SOME "EGG"?
OKAY, I KNOW YOU'RE ANGRY WITH ME, BUT IT WASN'T MY FAULT I HAVEN'T BEEN IN TOUCH.
I TRIED TO EXPLAIN ON THE PHONE, I WAS BASICALLY IN A COMA... BASICALLY...
IT'S NEVER YOUR FAULT, IS IT, EEL? YOU ALWAYS HAVE SOME CRAZY EXCUSE.
WELL, I'M DONE.
I GAVE UP ON YOU YEARS AGO AND WE HAVE BEEN JUST FINE WITHOUT YOU.

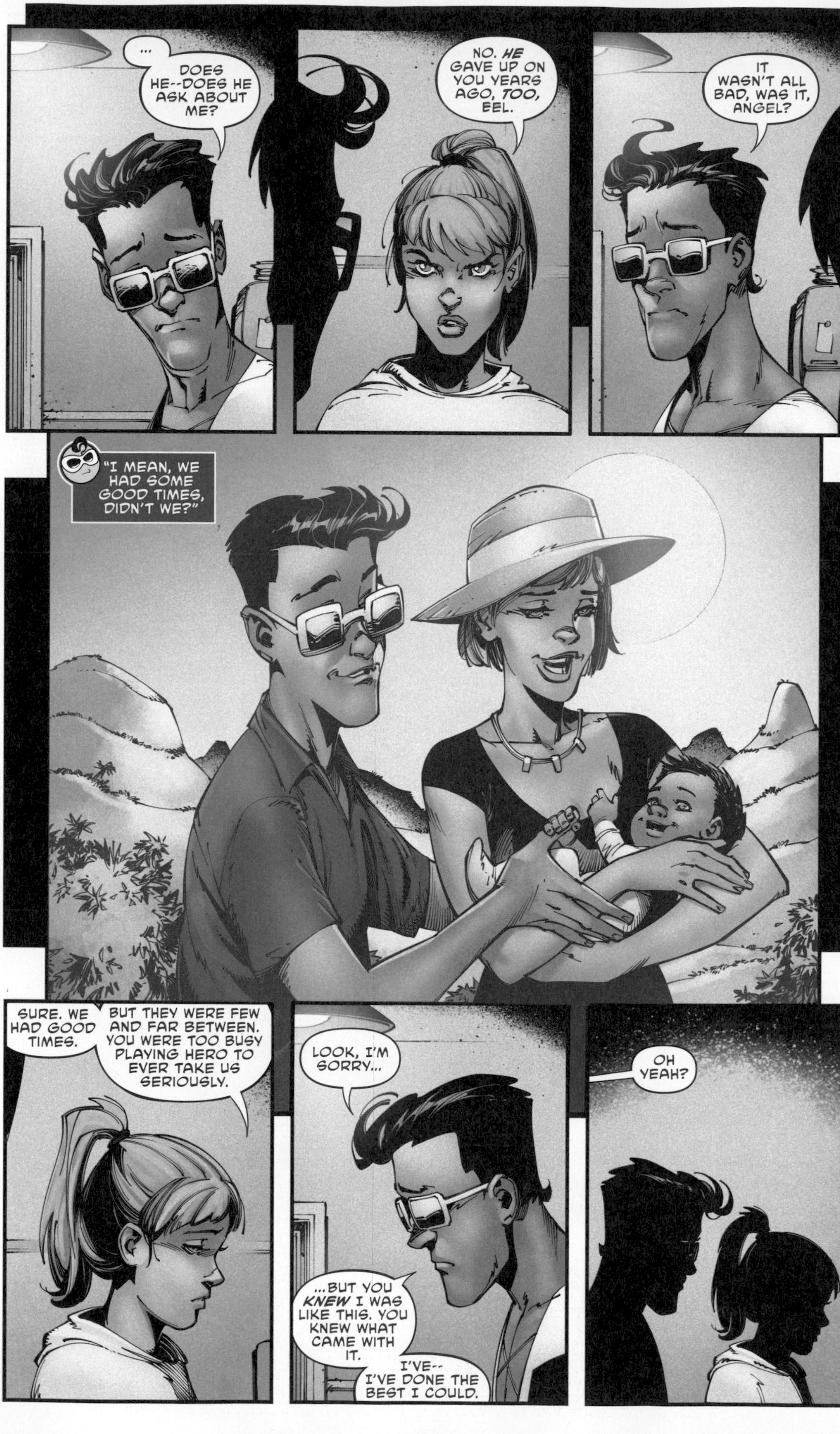
...
DOES HE--DOES HE ASK ABOUT ME?
NO. HE GAVE UP ON YOU YEARS AGO, TOO, EEL.
IT WASN'T ALL BAD, WAS IT, ANGEL?
"I MEAN, WE HAD SOME GOOD TIMES, DIDN'T WE?"
SURE. WE HAD GOOD TIMES.
BUT THEY WERE FEW AND FAR BETWEEN. YOU WERE TOO BUSY PLAYING HERO TO EVER TAKE US SERIOUSLY.
LOOK, I'M SORRY...
...BUT YOU KNEW I WAS LIKE THIS. YOU KNEW WHAT CAME WITH IT.
I'VE-- I'VE DONE THE BEST I COULD.
OH YEAH?

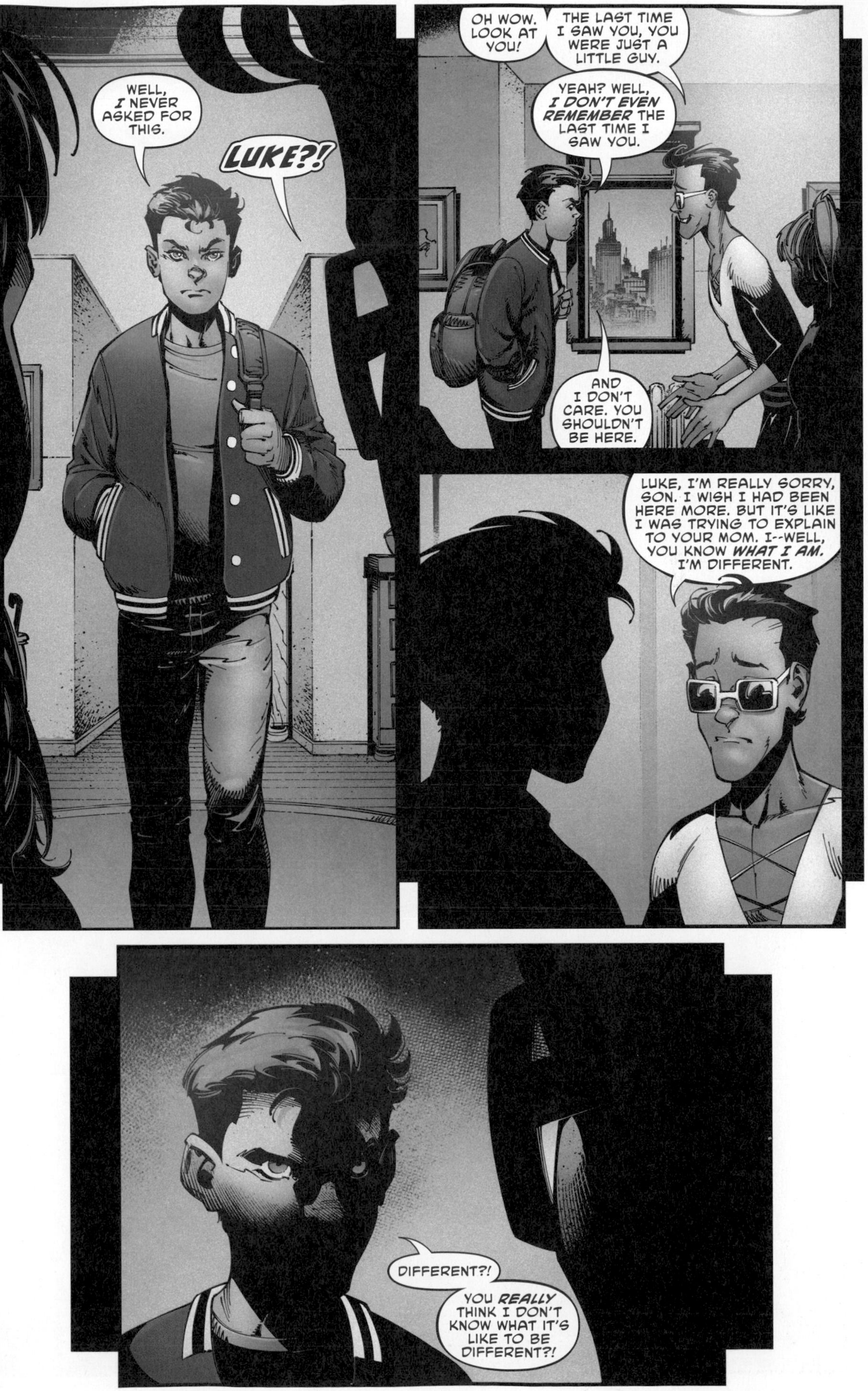
WELL, I NEVER ASKED FOR THIS.
LUKE?!
OH WOW. LOOK AT YOU!
THE LAST TIME I SAW YOU, YOU WERE JUST A LITTLE GUY.
YEAH? WELL, I DON'T EVEN REMEMBER THE LAST TIME I SAW YOU.
AND I DON'T CARE. YOU SHOULDN'T BE HERE.
LUKE, I'M REALLY SORRY, SON. I WISH I HAD BEEN HERE MORE. BUT IT'S LIKE I WAS TRYING TO EXPLAIN TO YOUR MOM. I--WELL, YOU KNOW WHAT I AM. I'M DIFFERENT.
DIFFERENT?!
YOU REALLY THINK I DON'T KNOW WHAT IT'S LIKE TO BE DIFFERENT?!

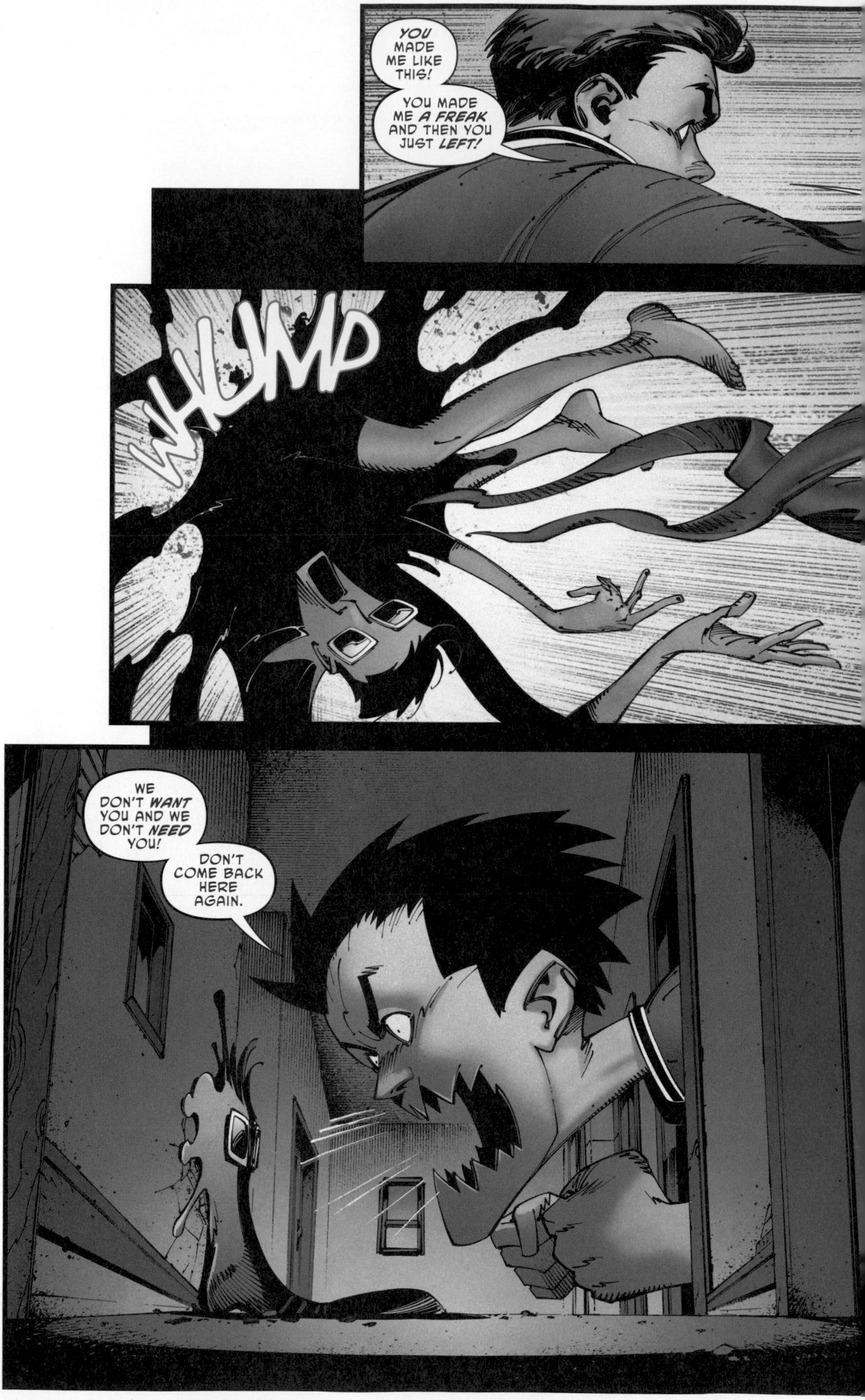
YOU MADE ME LIKE THIS!
YOU MADE ME A FREAK AND THEN YOU JUST LEFT!
WHUMP
WE DON'T WANT YOU AND WE DON'T NEED YOU!
DON'T COME BACK HERE AGAIN.

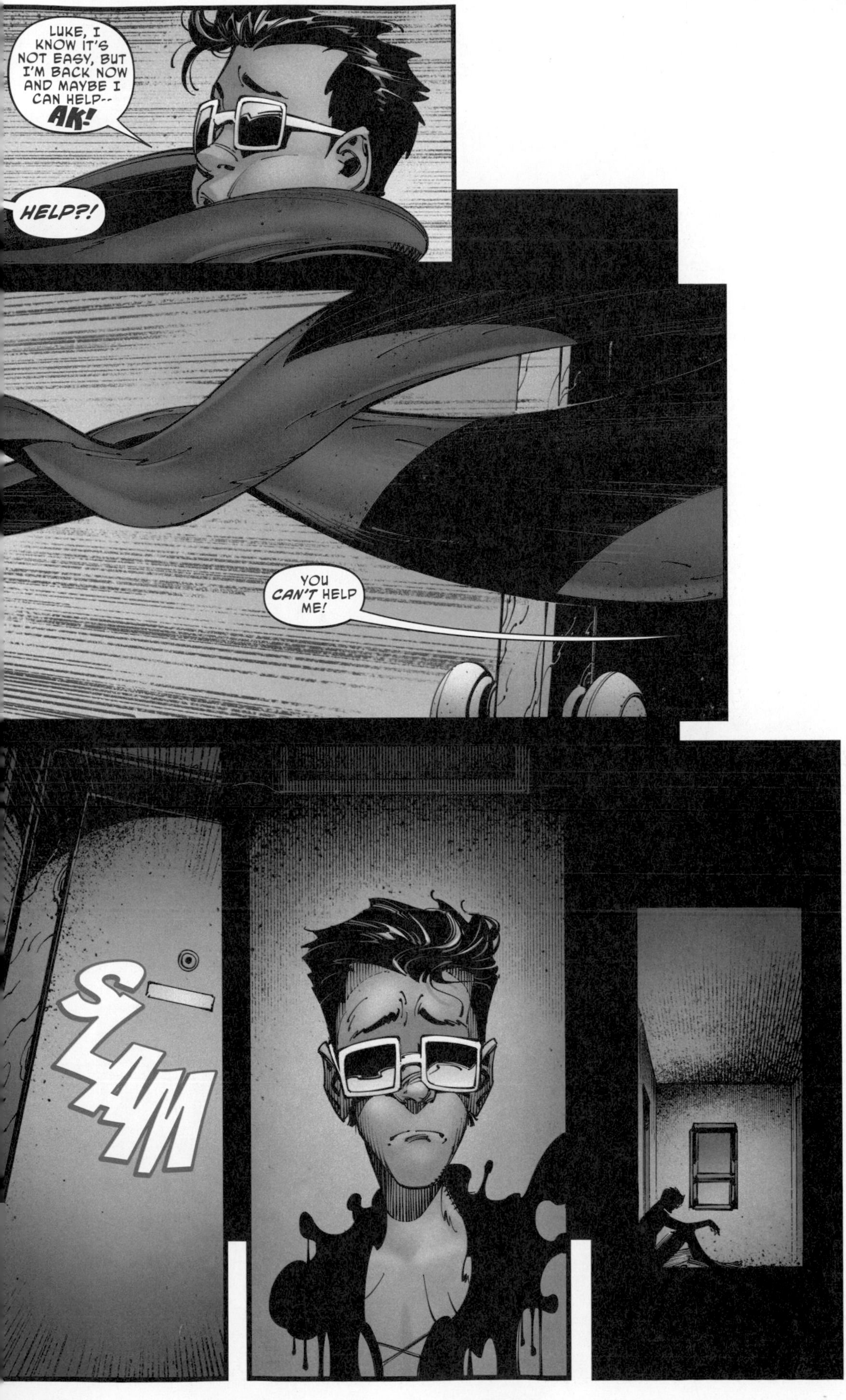
LUKE, I KNOW IT'S NOT EASY, BUT I'M BACK NOW AND MAYBE I CAN HELP-- AK!
HELP?!
YOU CAN'T HELP ME!
SLAM

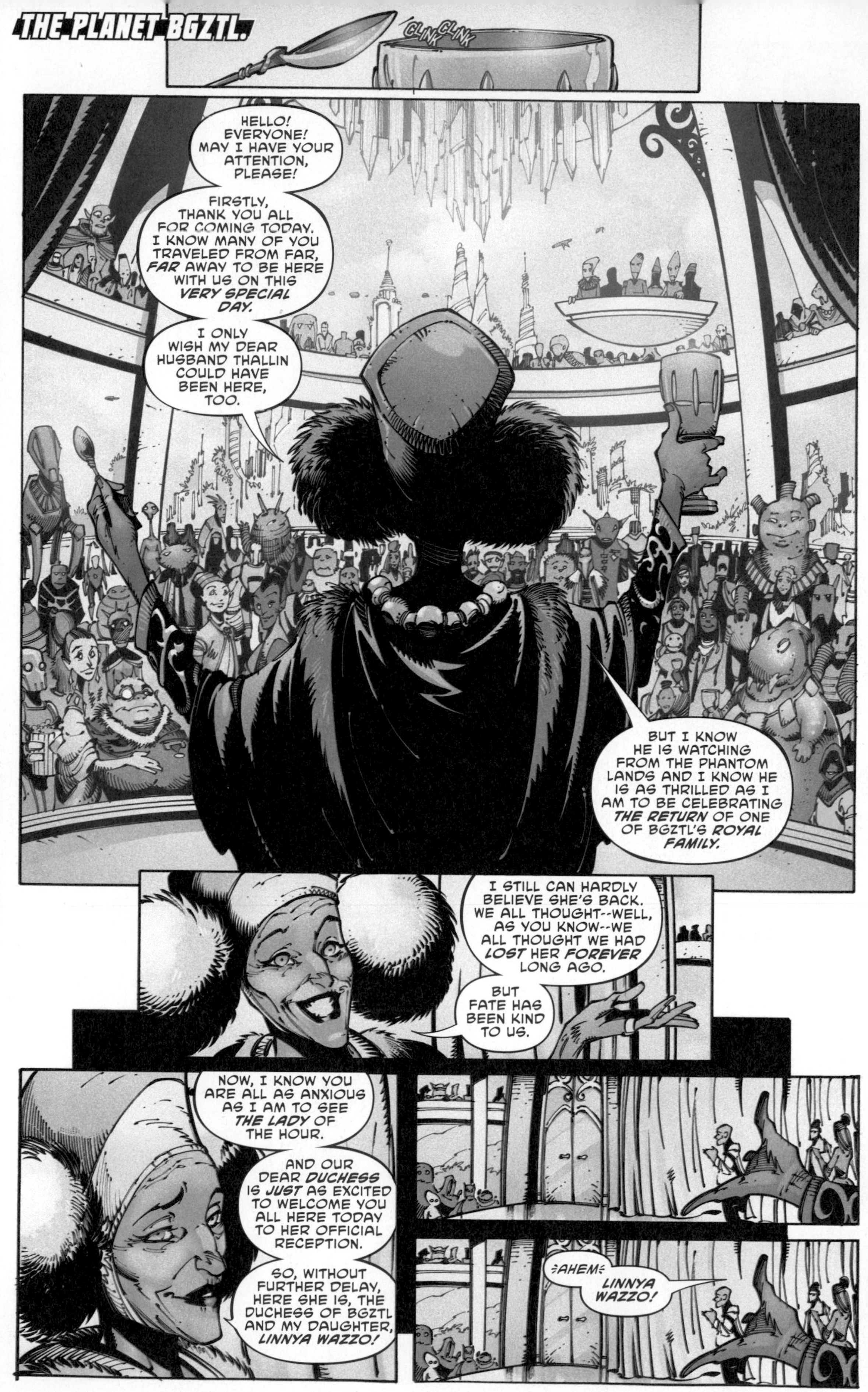
THE PLANET BGZTL.
CLINK CLINK CLINK
HELLO! EVERYONE! MAY I HAVE YOUR ATTENTION, PLEASE!
FIRSTLY, THANK YOU ALL FOR COMING TODAY. I KNOW MANY OF YOU TRAVELED FROM FAR, FAR AWAY TO BE HERE WITH US ON THIS VERY SPECIAL DAY.
I ONLY WISH MY DEAR HUSBAND THALLIN COULD HAVE BEEN HERE, TOO.
BUT I KNOW HE IS WATCHING FROM THE PHANTOM LANDS AND I KNOW HE IS AS THRILLED AS I AM TO BE CELEBRATING THE RETURN OF ONE OF BGZTL'S ROYAL FAMILY.
I STILL CAN HARDLY BELIEVE SHE'S BACK. WE ALL THOUGHT--WELL, AS YOU KNOW--WE ALL THOUGHT WE HAD LOST HER FOREVER LONG AGO.
BUT FATE HAS BEEN KIND TO US.
NOW, I KNOW YOU ARE ALL AS ANXIOUS AS I AM TO SEE THE LADY OF THE HOUR.
AND OUR DEAR DUCHESS IS JUST AS EXCITED TO WELCOME YOU ALL HERE TODAY TO HER OFFICIAL RECEPTION.
SO, WITHOUT FURTHER DELAY, HERE SHE IS, THE DUCHESS OF BGZTL AND MY DAUGHTER, LINNYA WAZZO!
AHEM
LINNYA WAZZO!

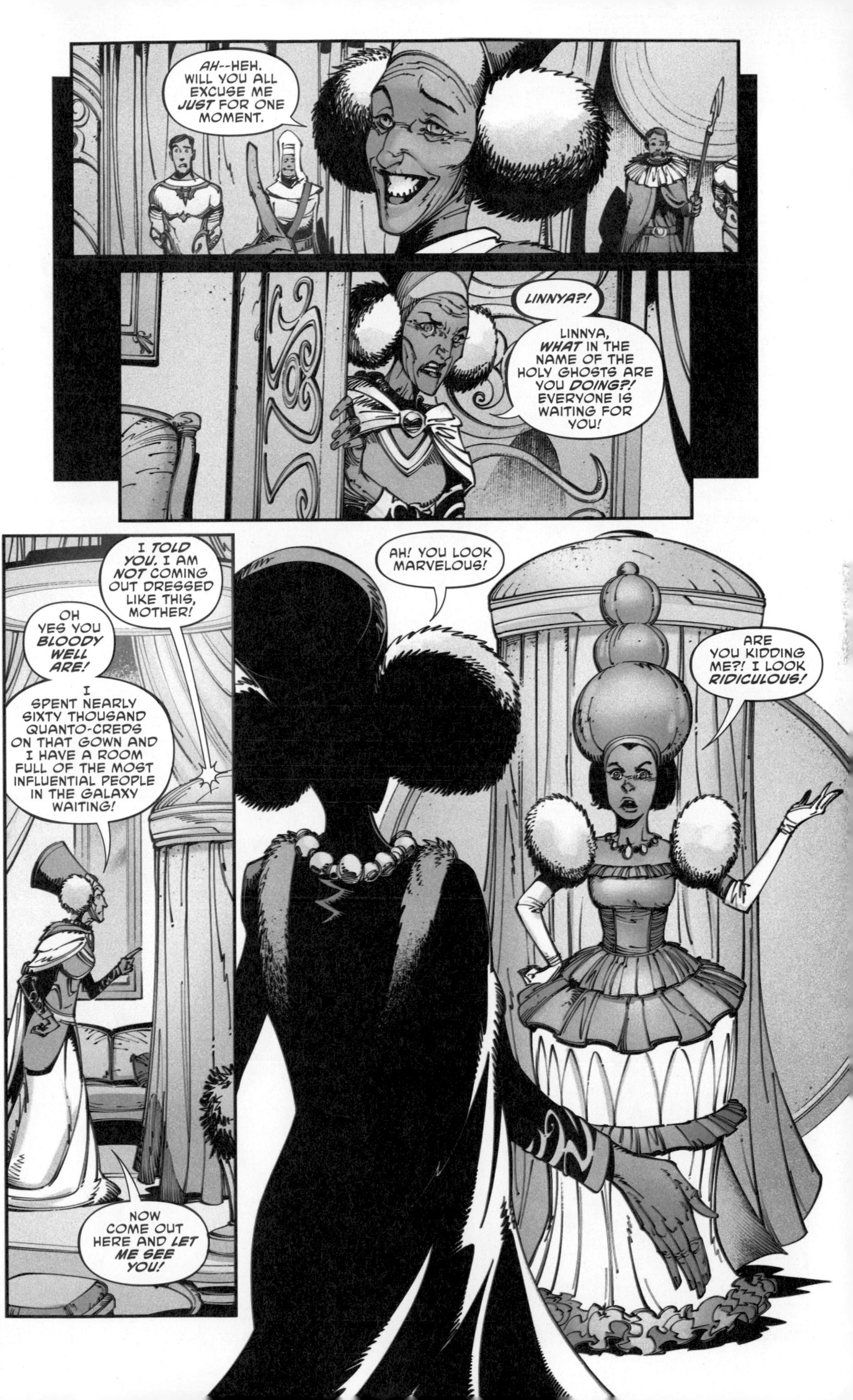
AH--HEH. WILL YOU ALL EXCUSE ME JUST FOR ONE MOMENT.
LINNYA?!
LINNYA, WHAT IN THE NAME OF THE HOLY GHOSTS ARE YOU DOING?! EVERYONE IS WAITING FOR YOU!
I TOLD YOU. I AM NOT COMING OUT DRESSED LIKE THIS, MOTHER!
OH YES YOU BLOODY WELL ARE!
I SPENT NEARLY SIXTY THOUSAND QUANTO-CREDS ON THAT GOWN AND I HAVE A ROOM FULL OF THE MOST INFLUENTIAL PEOPLE IN THE GALAXY WAITING!
NOW COME OUT HERE AND LET ME SEE YOU!
AH! YOU LOOK MARVELOUS!
ARE YOU KIDDING ME?! I LOOK RIDICULOUS!

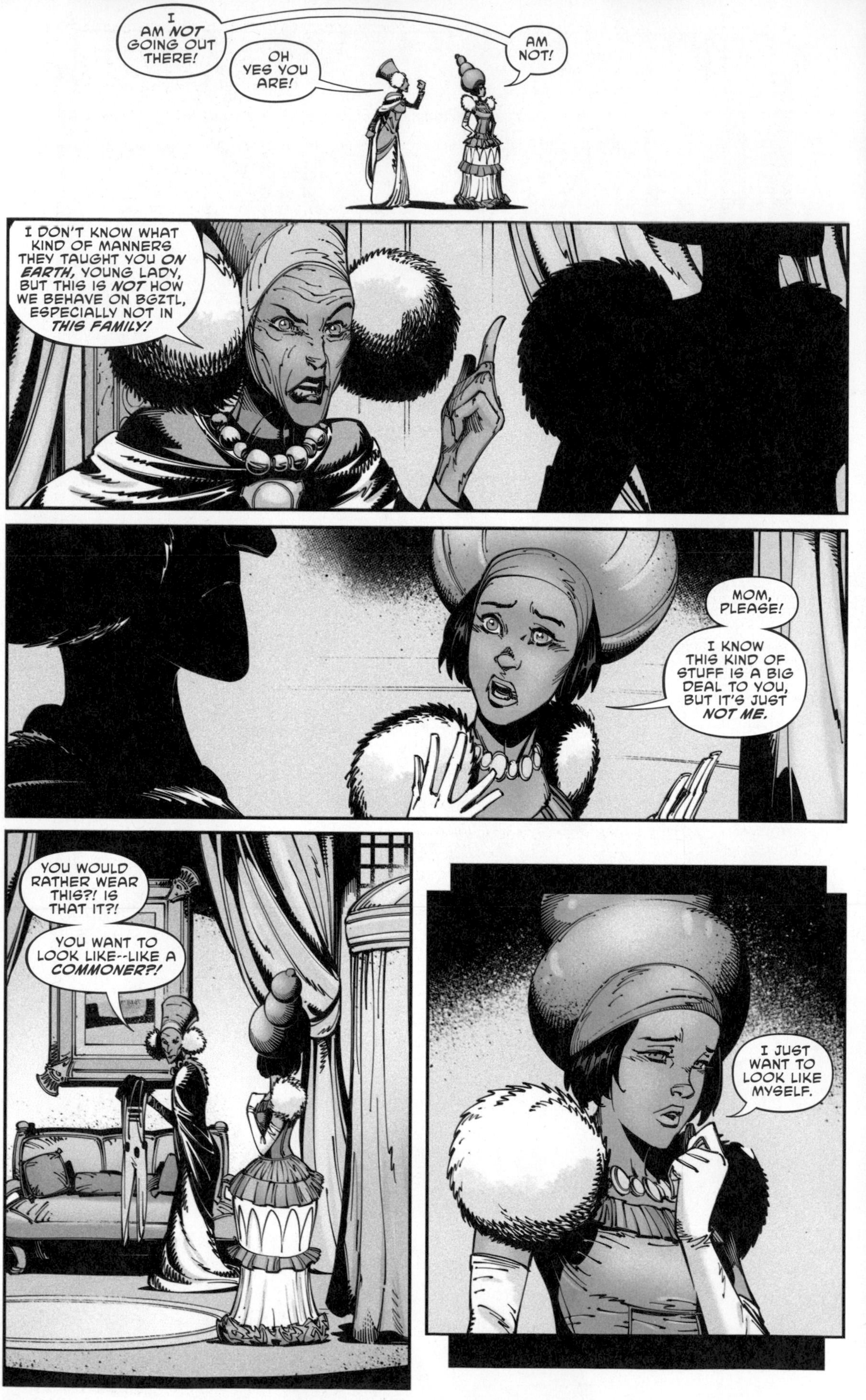
I AM NOT GOING OUT THERE!
OH YES YOU ARE!
AM NOT!
I DON'T KNOW WHAT KIND OF MANNERS THEY TAUGHT YOU ON EARTH, YOUNG LADY, BUT THIS IS NOT HOW WE BEHAVE ON BGZTL, ESPECIALLY NOT IN THIS FAMILY!
MOM, PLEASE!
I KNOW THIS KIND OF STUFF IS A BIG DEAL TO YOU, BUT IT'S JUST NOT ME.
YOU WOULD RATHER WEAR THIS?! IS THAT IT?!
YOU WANT TO LOOK LIKE--LIKE A COMMONER?!
I JUST WANT TO LOOK LIKE MYSELF.

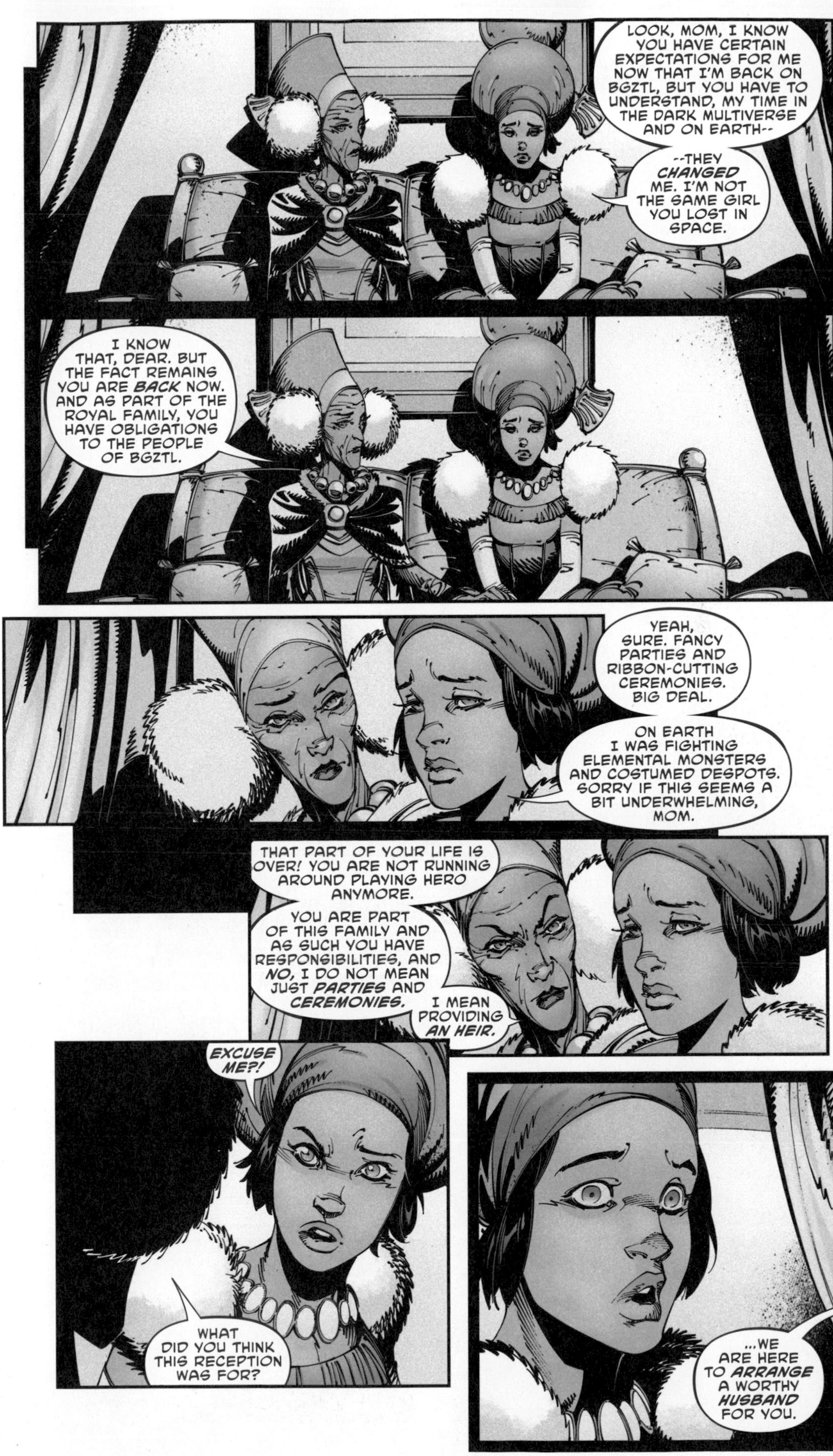
LOOK, MOM, I KNOW YOU HAVE CERTAIN EXPECTATIONS FOR ME NOW THAT I'M BACK ON BGZTL, BUT YOU HAVE TO UNDERSTAND, MY TIME IN THE DARK MULTIVERSE AND ON EARTH--
--THEY *CHANGED* ME. I'M NOT THE SAME GIRL YOU LOST IN SPACE.
I KNOW THAT, DEAR. BUT THE FACT REMAINS YOU ARE *BACK* NOW. AND AS PART OF THE ROYAL FAMILY, YOU HAVE OBLIGATIONS TO THE PEOPLE OF BGZTL.
YEAH, SURE. FANCY PARTIES AND RIBBON-CUTTING CEREMONIES. BIG DEAL.
ON EARTH I WAS FIGHTING ELEMENTAL MONSTERS AND COSTUMED DESPOTS. SORRY IF THIS SEEMS A BIT UNDERWHELMING, MOM.
THAT PART OF YOUR LIFE IS OVER! YOU ARE NOT RUNNING AROUND PLAYING HERO ANYMORE.
YOU ARE PART OF THIS FAMILY AND AS SUCH YOU HAVE RESPONSIBILITIES, AND *NO*, I DO NOT MEAN JUST *PARTIES* AND *CEREMONIES.*
I MEAN PROVIDING *AN HEIR.*
EXCUSE ME?!
WHAT DID YOU THINK THIS RECEPTION WAS FOR?
...WE ARE HERE TO *ARRANGE* A WORTHY *HUSBAND* FOR YOU.

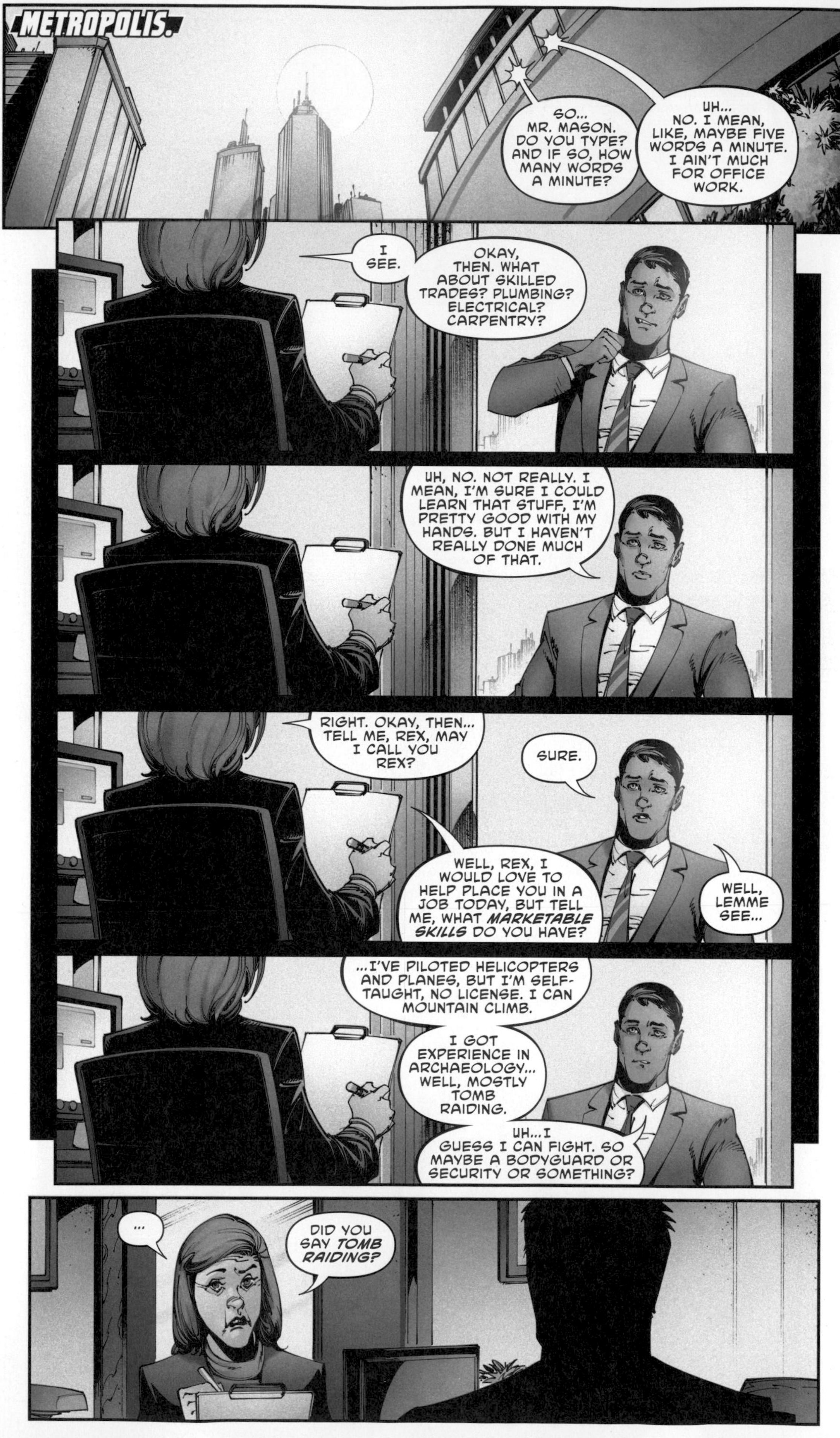
METROPOLIS.
SO... MR. MASON. DO YOU TYPE? AND IF SO, HOW MANY WORDS A MINUTE?
UH... NO. I MEAN, LIKE, MAYBE FIVE WORDS A MINUTE. I AIN'T MUCH FOR OFFICE WORK.
I SEE.
OKAY, THEN. WHAT ABOUT SKILLED TRADES? PLUMBING? ELECTRICAL? CARPENTRY?
UH, NO. NOT REALLY. I MEAN, I'M SURE I COULD LEARN THAT STUFF, I'M PRETTY GOOD WITH MY HANDS. BUT I HAVEN'T REALLY DONE MUCH OF THAT.
RIGHT. OKAY, THEN... TELL ME, REX, MAY I CALL YOU REX?
SURE.
WELL, REX, I WOULD LOVE TO HELP PLACE YOU IN A JOB TODAY, BUT TELL ME, WHAT *MARKETABLE SKILLS* DO YOU HAVE?
WELL, LEMME SEE...
...I'VE PILOTED HELICOPTERS AND PLANES, BUT I'M SELF-TAUGHT, NO LICENSE. I CAN MOUNTAIN CLIMB.
I GOT EXPERIENCE IN ARCHAEOLOGY... WELL, MOSTLY TOMB RAIDING.
UH...I GUESS I CAN FIGHT. SO MAYBE A BODYGUARD OR SECURITY OR SOMETHING?
...
DID YOU SAY *TOMB RAIDING?*

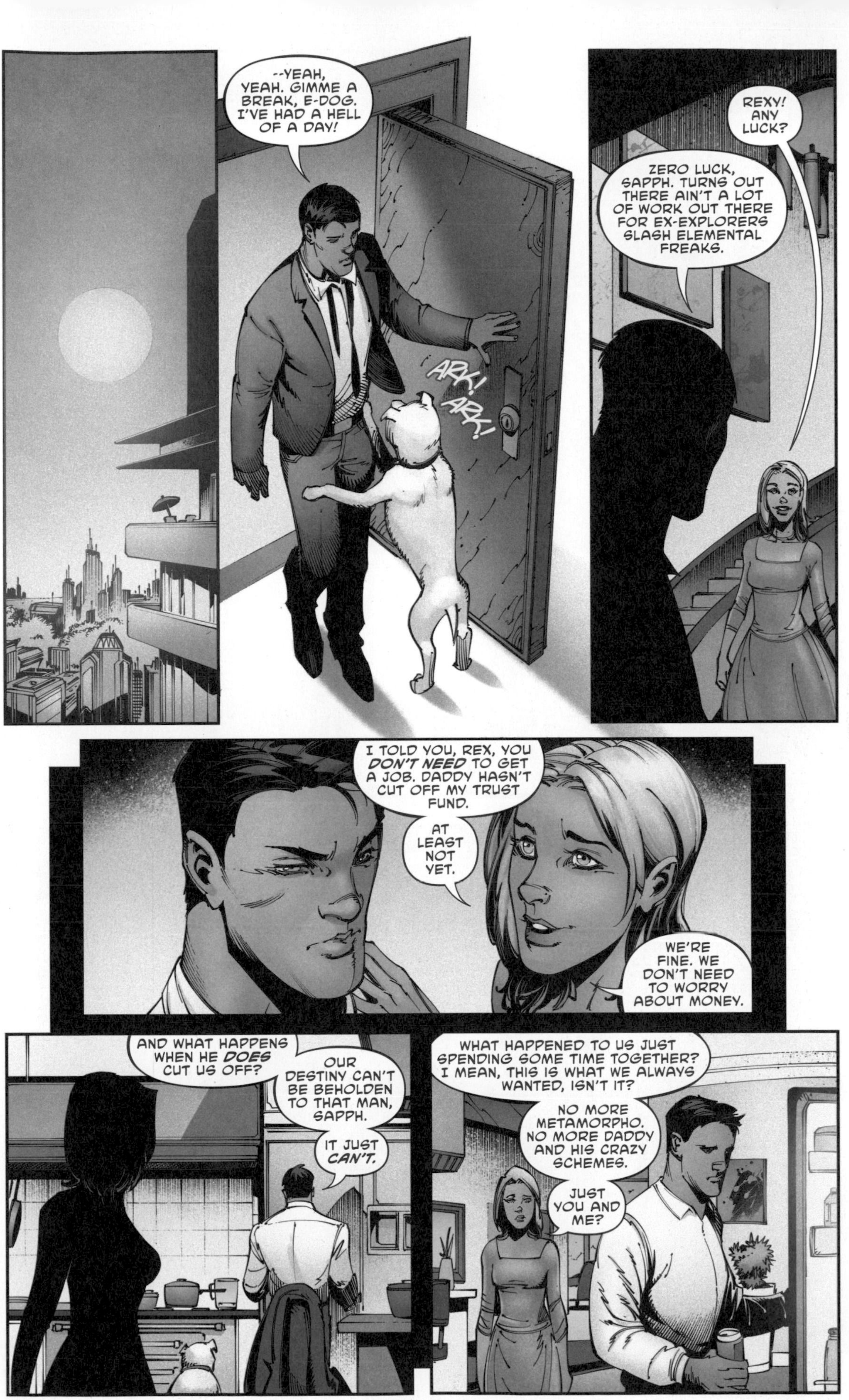
--YEAH, YEAH. GIMME A BREAK, E-DOG. I'VE HAD A HELL OF A DAY!
ARK! ARK!
REXY! ANY LUCK?
ZERO LUCK, SAPPH. TURNS OUT THERE AIN'T A LOT OF WORK OUT THERE FOR EX-EXPLORERS SLASH ELEMENTAL FREAKS.
I TOLD YOU, REX, YOU DON'T NEED TO GET A JOB. DADDY HASN'T CUT OFF MY TRUST FUND.
AT LEAST NOT YET.
WE'RE FINE. WE DON'T NEED TO WORRY ABOUT MONEY.
AND WHAT HAPPENS WHEN HE DOES CUT US OFF?
OUR DESTINY CAN'T BE BEHOLDEN TO THAT MAN, SAPPH.
IT JUST CAN'T.
WHAT HAPPENED TO US JUST SPENDING SOME TIME TOGETHER? I MEAN, THIS IS WHAT WE ALWAYS WANTED, ISN'T IT?
NO MORE METAMORPHO. NO MORE DADDY AND HIS CRAZY SCHEMES.
JUST YOU AND ME?

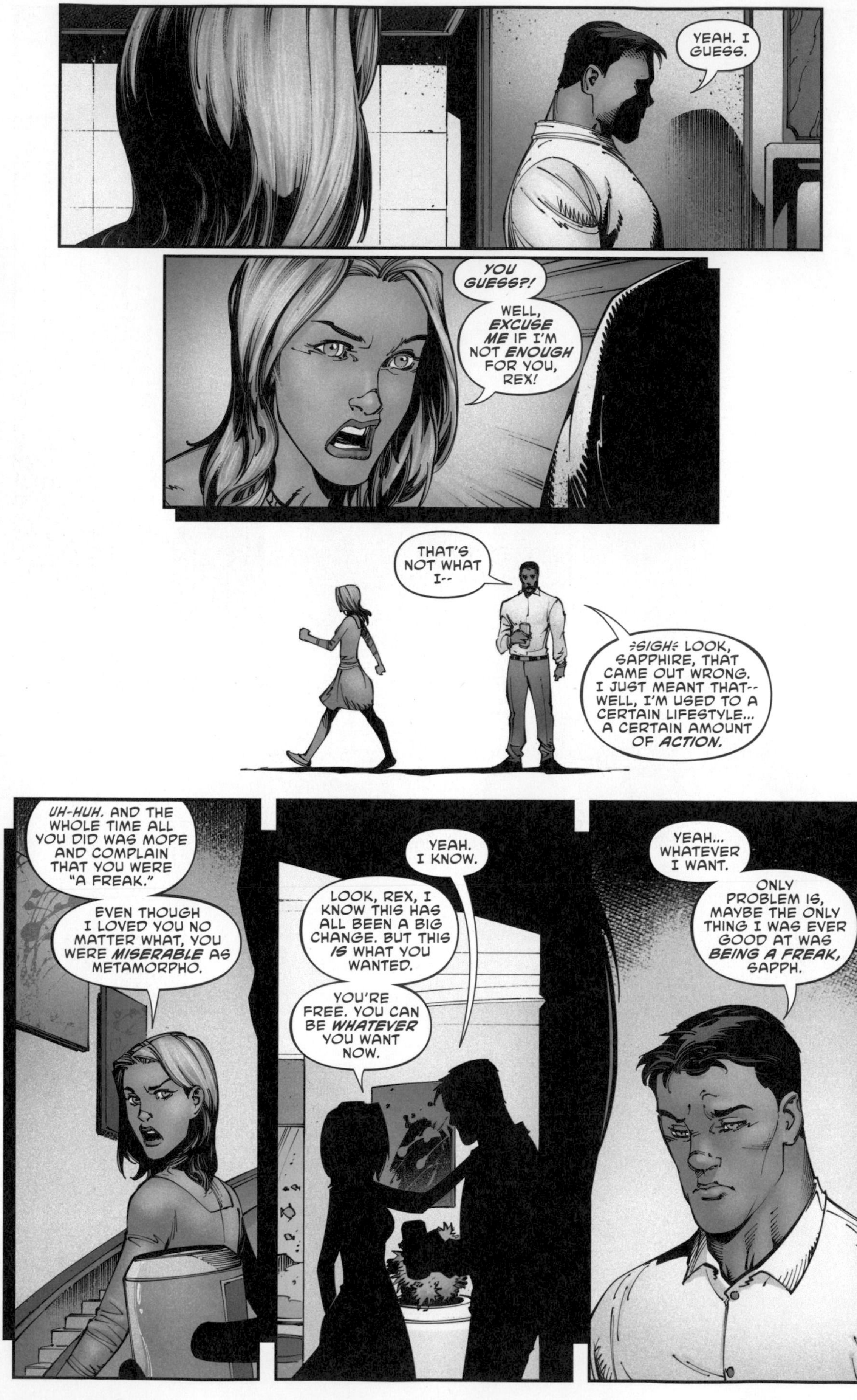
YEAH. I GUESS.
YOU GUESS?!
WELL, EXCUSE ME IF I'M NOT ENOUGH FOR YOU, REX!
THAT'S NOT WHAT I--
≈SIGH≈ LOOK, SAPPHIRE, THAT CAME OUT WRONG. I JUST MEANT THAT-- WELL, I'M USED TO A CERTAIN LIFESTYLE... A CERTAIN AMOUNT OF ACTION.
UH-HUH. AND THE WHOLE TIME ALL YOU DID WAS MOPE AND COMPLAIN THAT YOU WERE "A FREAK."
EVEN THOUGH I LOVED YOU NO MATTER WHAT, YOU WERE MISERABLE AS METAMORPHO.
YEAH. I KNOW.
LOOK, REX, I KNOW THIS HAS ALL BEEN A BIG CHANGE. BUT THIS IS WHAT YOU WANTED.
YOU'RE FREE. YOU CAN BE WHATEVER YOU WANT NOW.
YEAH... WHATEVER I WANT.
ONLY PROBLEM IS, MAYBE THE ONLY THING I WAS EVER GOOD AT WAS BEING A FREAK, SAPPH.

THE BLEED.
[THE INTERDIMENSIONAL PLANE THAT FORMS THE BARRIER BETWEEN THE WORLDS OF THE MULTIVERSE.]

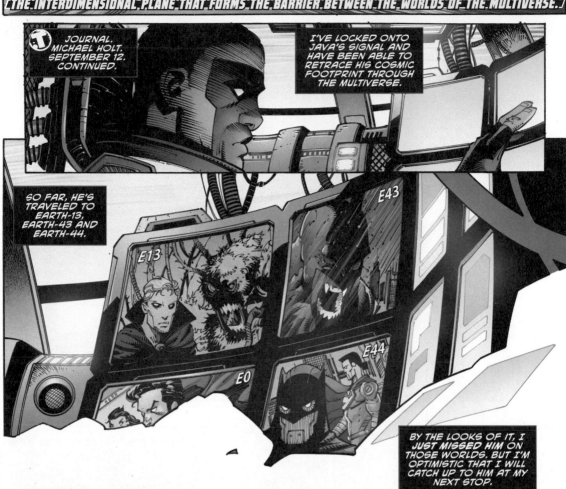

JOURNAL. MICHAEL HOLT. SEPTEMBER 12. CONTINUED.

I'VE LOCKED ONTO JAVA'S SIGNAL AND HAVE BEEN ABLE TO RETRACE HIS COSMIC FOOTPRINT THROUGH THE MULTIVERSE.

SO FAR, HE'S TRAVELED TO EARTH-13, EARTH-43 AND EARTH-44.

BY THE LOOKS OF IT, I JUST MISSED HIM ON THOSE WORLDS. BUT I'M OPTIMISTIC THAT I WILL CATCH UP TO HIM AT MY NEXT STOP.

I HAVE NO CHOICE. MY VERY LIVES DEPEND ON IT.

JAVA HAS BEEN MURDERING MY MULTIVERSAL DOPPLEGÄNGERS...

...WIPING MY ALTERNATE SELVES FROM EXISTENCE.

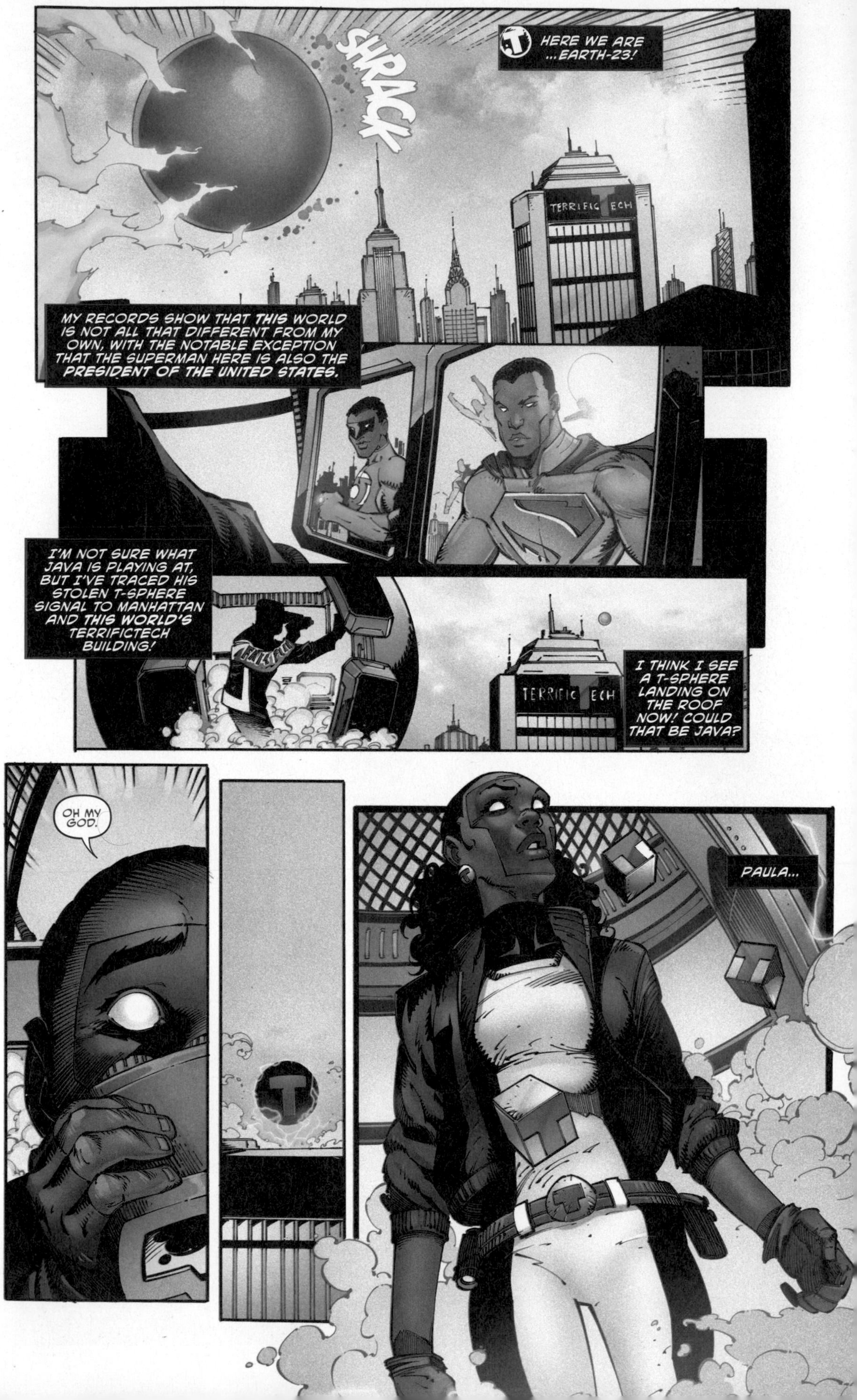
SHRACK
HERE WE ARE ...EARTH-23!
TERRIFIC TECH
MY RECORDS SHOW THAT THIS WORLD IS NOT ALL THAT DIFFERENT FROM MY OWN, WITH THE NOTABLE EXCEPTION THAT THE SUPERMAN HERE IS ALSO THE PRESIDENT OF THE UNITED STATES.
I'M NOT SURE WHAT JAVA IS PLAYING AT, BUT I'VE TRACED HIS STOLEN T-SPHERE SIGNAL TO MANHATTAN AND THIS WORLD'S TERRIFICTECH BUILDING!
TERRIFIC TECH
I THINK I SEE A T-SPHERE LANDING ON THE ROOF NOW! COULD THAT BE JAVA?
OH MY GOD!
PAULA...

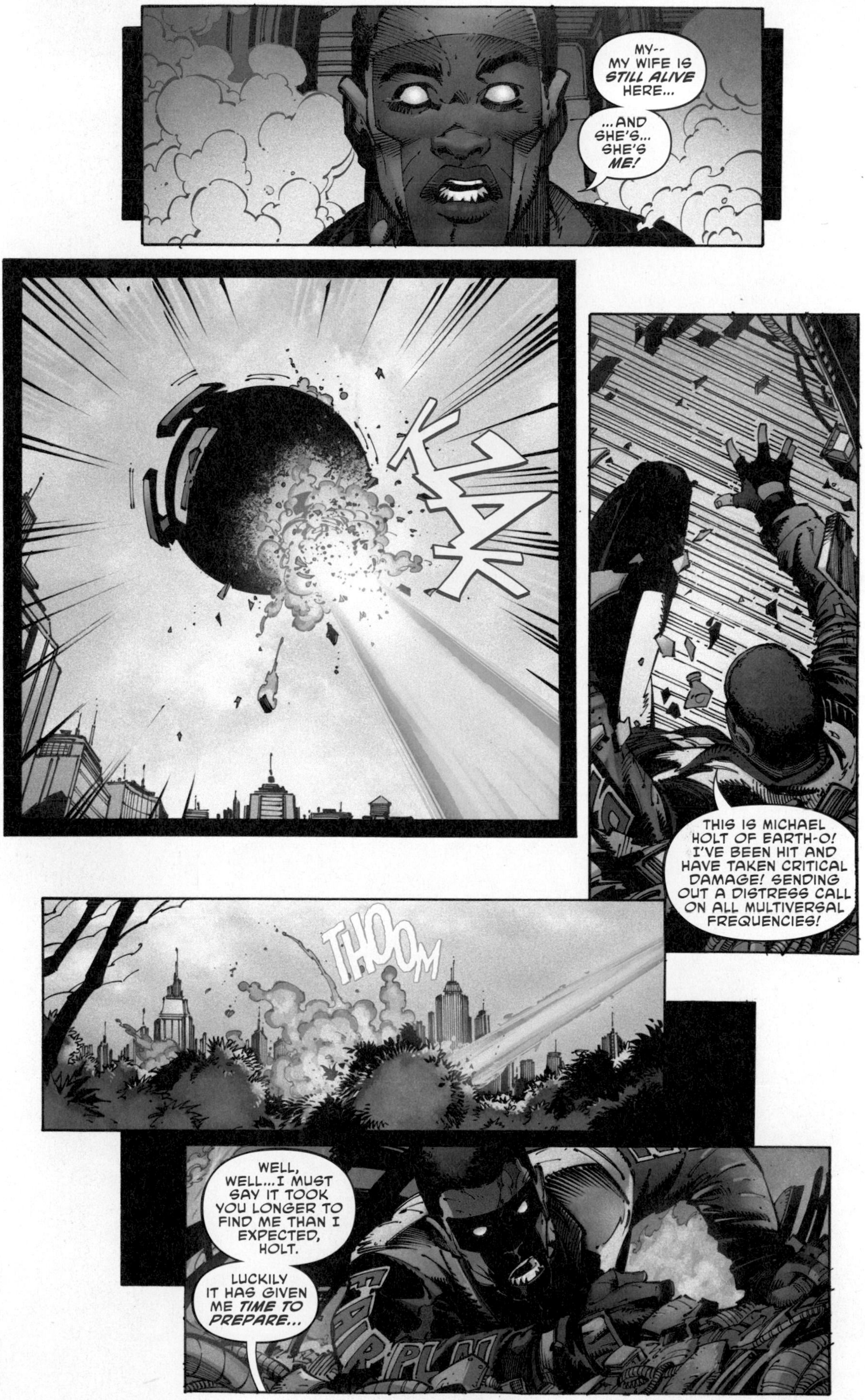
MY-- MY WIFE IS STILL ALIVE HERE...
...AND SHE'S... SHE'S ME!
KLAK
THIS IS MICHAEL HOLT OF EARTH-0! I'VE BEEN HIT AND HAVE TAKEN CRITICAL DAMAGE! SENDING OUT A DISTRESS CALL ON ALL MULTIVERSAL FREQUENCIES!
THOOM
WELL, WELL...I MUST SAY IT TOOK YOU LONGER TO FIND ME THAN I EXPECTED, HOLT.
LUCKILY IT HAS GIVEN ME TIME TO PREPARE...

MEET THE DREADFULS!

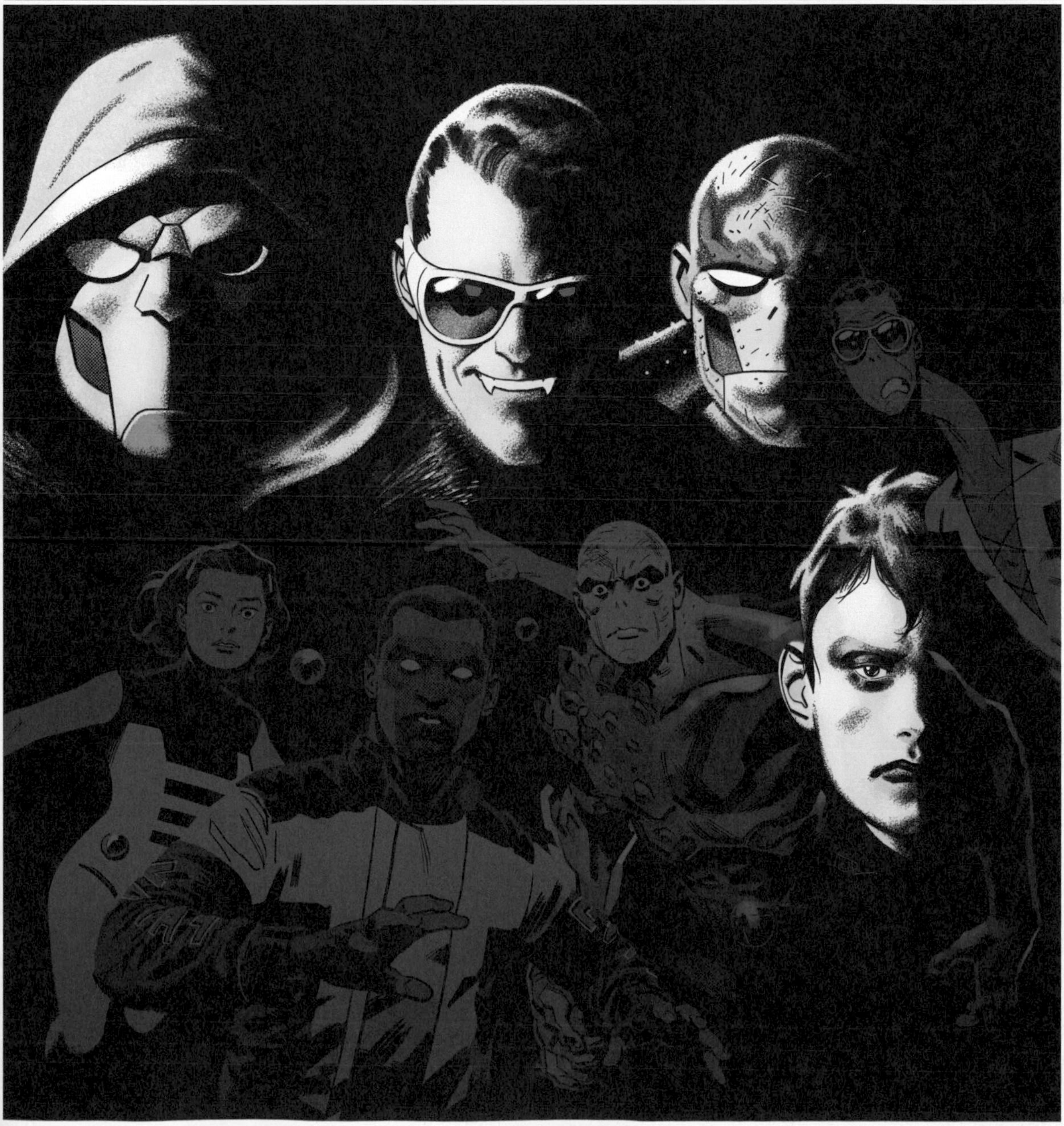

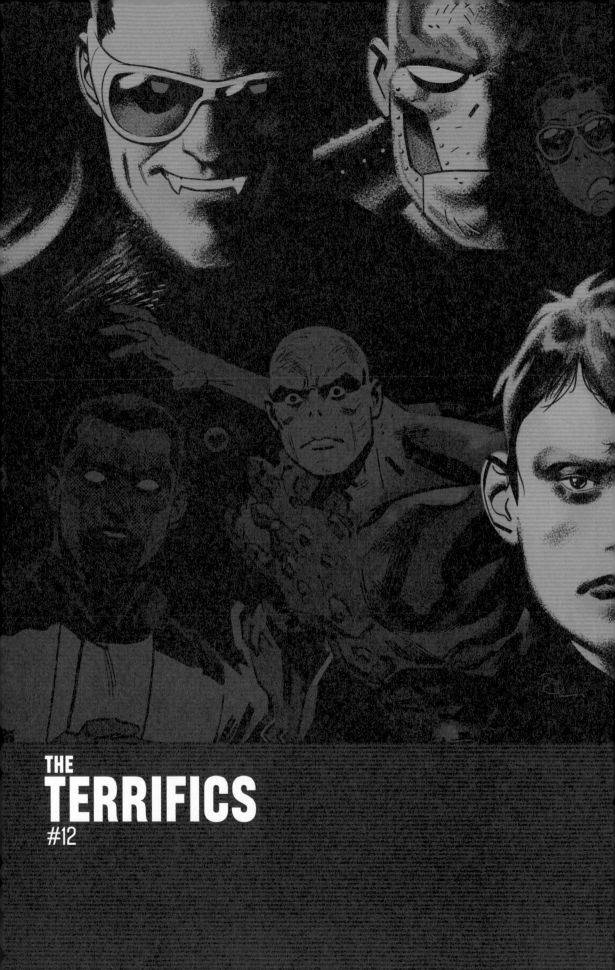

THE
TERRIFICS
#12

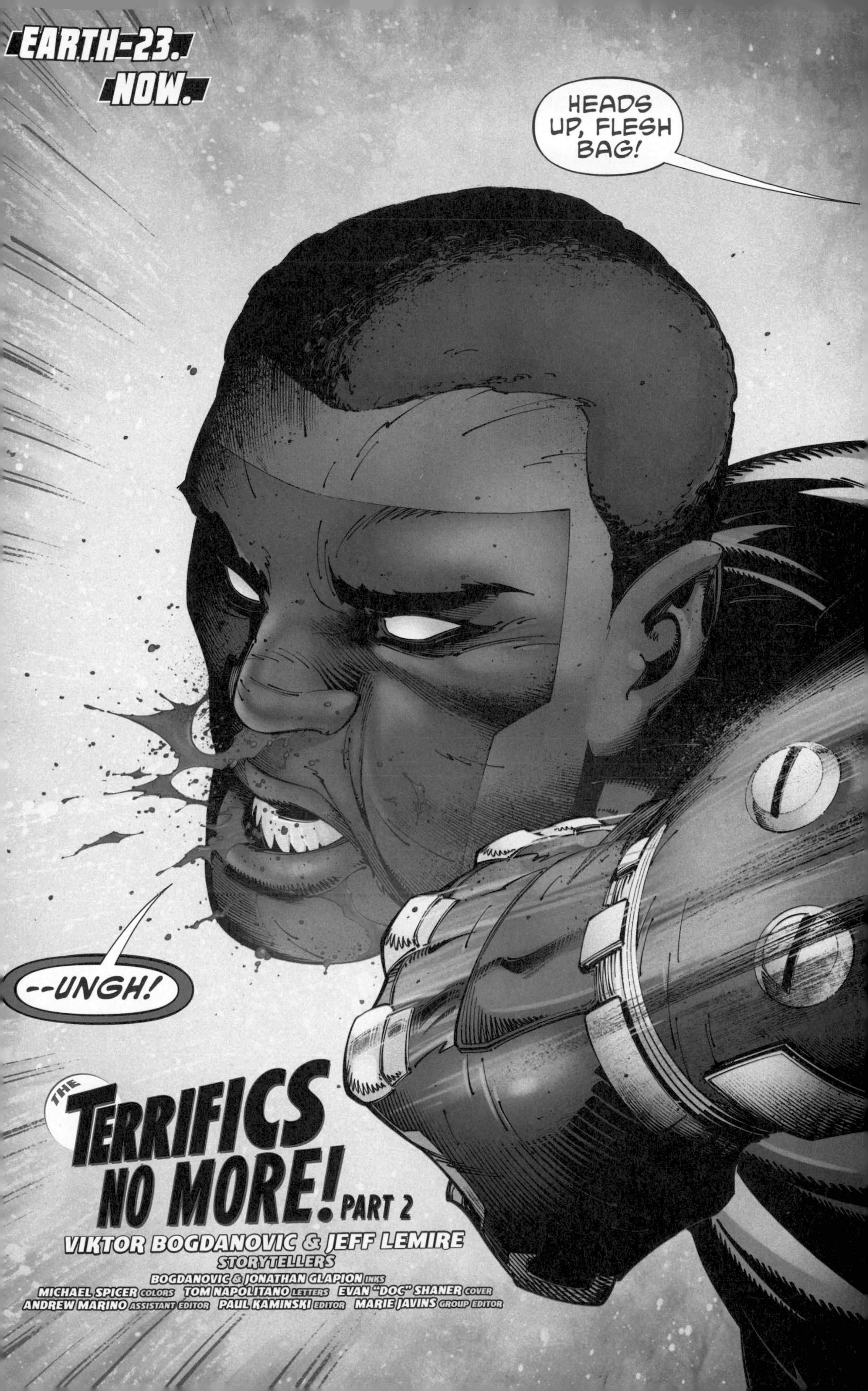
EARTH-23. NOW.
HEADS UP, FLESH BAG!
--UNGH!
THE TERRIFICS NO MORE! PART 2
VIKTOR BOGDANOVIC & JEFF LEMIRE STORYTELLERS
BOGDANOVIC & JONATHAN GLAPION INKS
MICHAEL SPICER COLORS TOM NAPOLITANO LETTERS EVAN "DOC" SHANER COVER
ANDREW MARINO ASSISTANT EDITOR PAUL KAMINSKI EDITOR MARIE JAVINS GROUP EDITOR

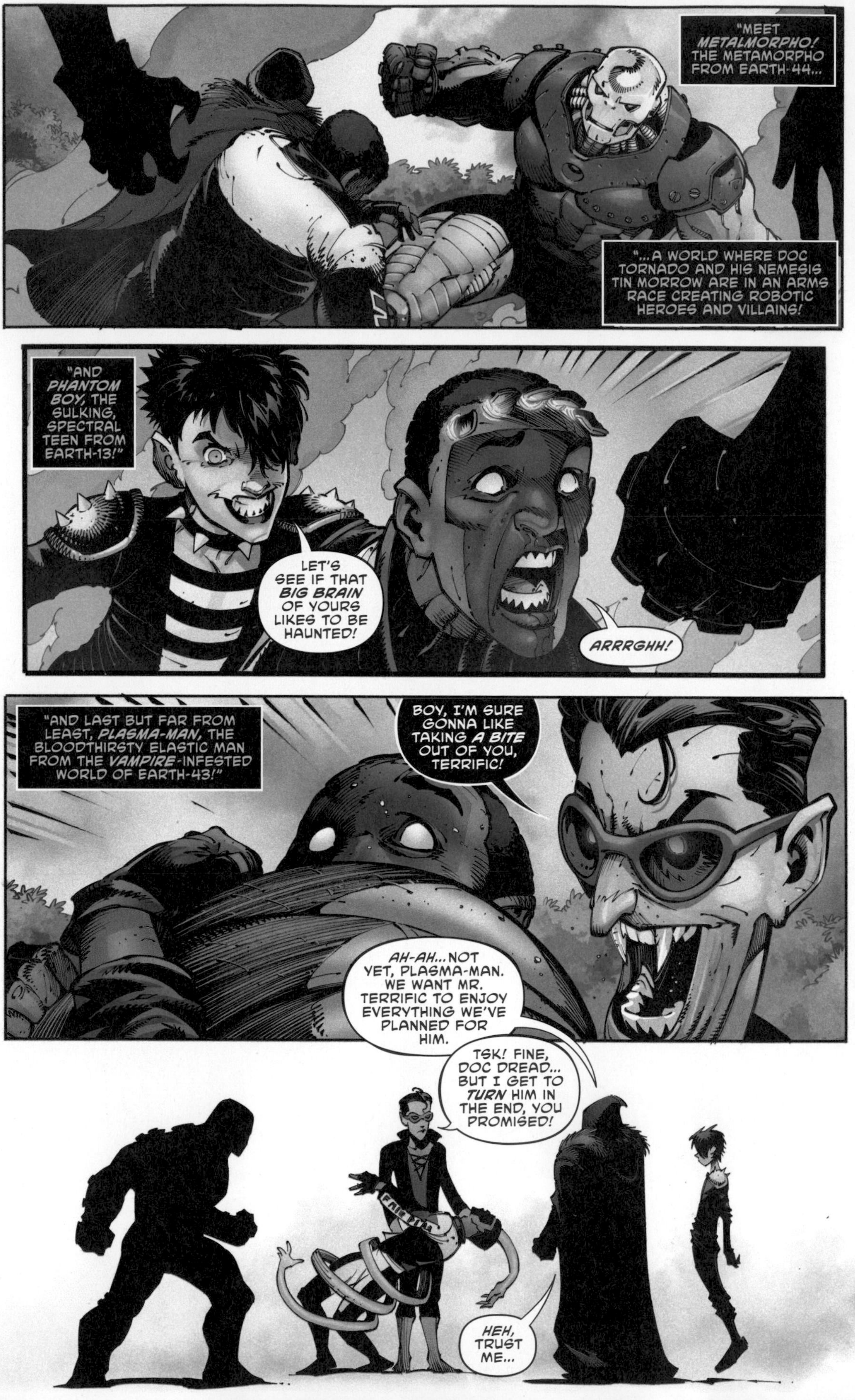
"MEET METALMORPHO! THE METAMORPHO FROM EARTH-44...
"...A WORLD WHERE DOC TORNADO AND HIS NEMESIS TIN MORROW ARE IN AN ARMS RACE CREATING ROBOTIC HEROES AND VILLAINS!
"AND PHANTOM BOY, THE SULKING, SPECTRAL TEEN FROM EARTH-13!"
LET'S SEE IF THAT BIG BRAIN OF YOURS LIKES TO BE HAUNTED!
ARRRGHH!
"AND LAST BUT FAR FROM LEAST, PLASMA-MAN, THE BLOODTHIRSTY ELASTIC MAN FROM THE VAMPIRE-INFESTED WORLD OF EARTH-43!"
BOY, I'M SURE GONNA LIKE TAKING A BITE OUT OF YOU, TERRIFIC!
AH-AH...NOT YET, PLASMA-MAN. WE WANT MR. TERRIFIC TO ENJOY EVERYTHING WE'VE PLANNED FOR HIM.
TSK! FINE, DOC DREAD... BUT I GET TO TURN HIM IN THE END, YOU PROMISED!
HEH, TRUST ME...

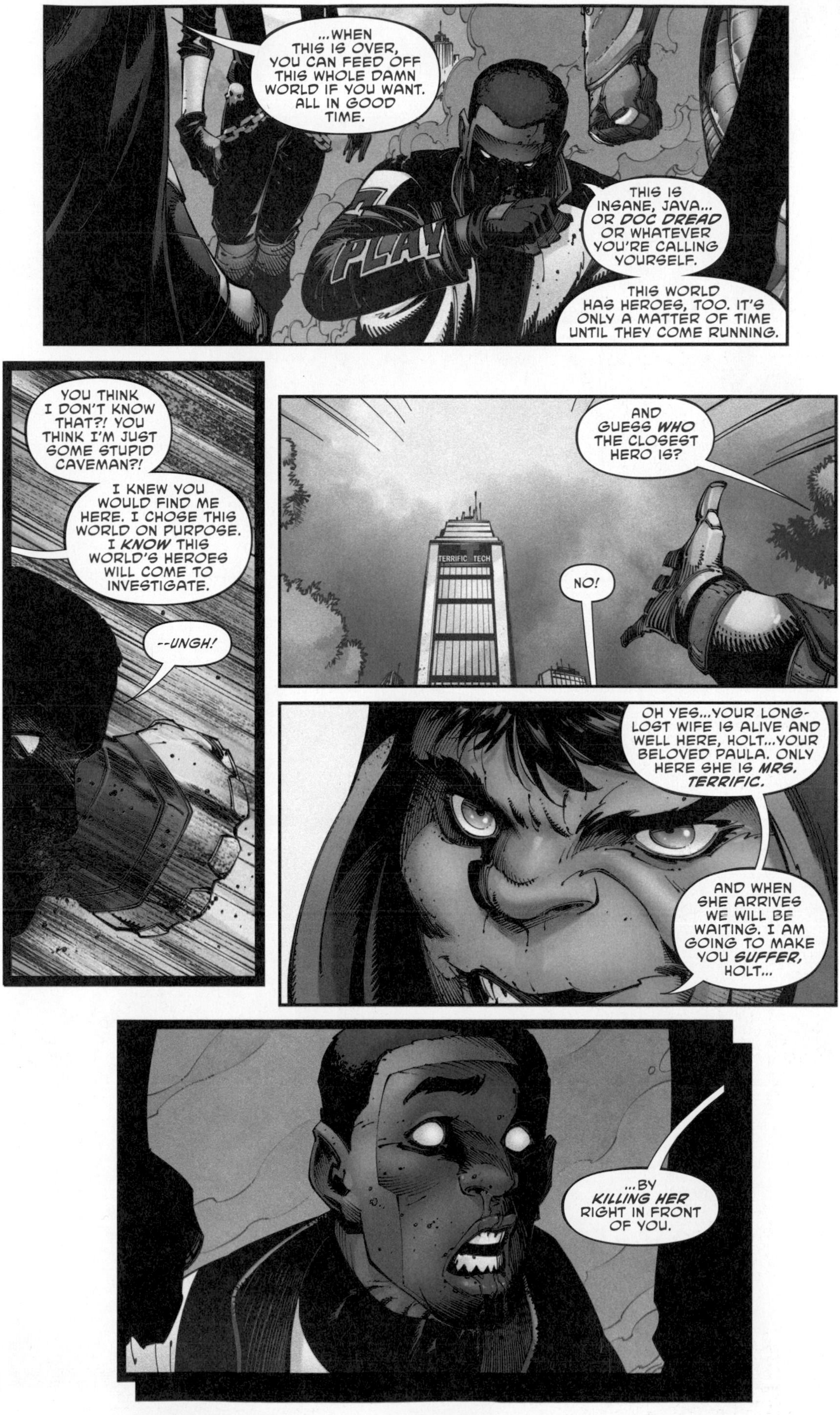
...WHEN THIS IS OVER, YOU CAN FEED OFF THIS WHOLE DAMN WORLD IF YOU WANT. ALL IN GOOD TIME.
PLAY
THIS IS INSANE, JAVA... OR DOC DREAD OR WHATEVER YOU'RE CALLING YOURSELF.
THIS WORLD HAS HEROES, TOO. IT'S ONLY A MATTER OF TIME UNTIL THEY COME RUNNING.
YOU THINK I DON'T KNOW THAT?! YOU THINK I'M JUST SOME STUPID CAVEMAN?!
I KNEW YOU WOULD FIND ME HERE. I CHOSE THIS WORLD ON PURPOSE. I KNOW THIS WORLD'S HEROES WILL COME TO INVESTIGATE.
--UNGH!
AND GUESS WHO THE CLOSEST HERO IS?
TERRIFIC TECH
NO!
OH YES...YOUR LONG-LOST WIFE IS ALIVE AND WELL HERE, HOLT...YOUR BELOVED PAULA. ONLY HERE SHE IS MRS. TERRIFIC.
AND WHEN SHE ARRIVES WE WILL BE WAITING. I AM GOING TO MAKE YOU SUFFER, HOLT...
...BY KILLING HER RIGHT IN FRONT OF YOU.

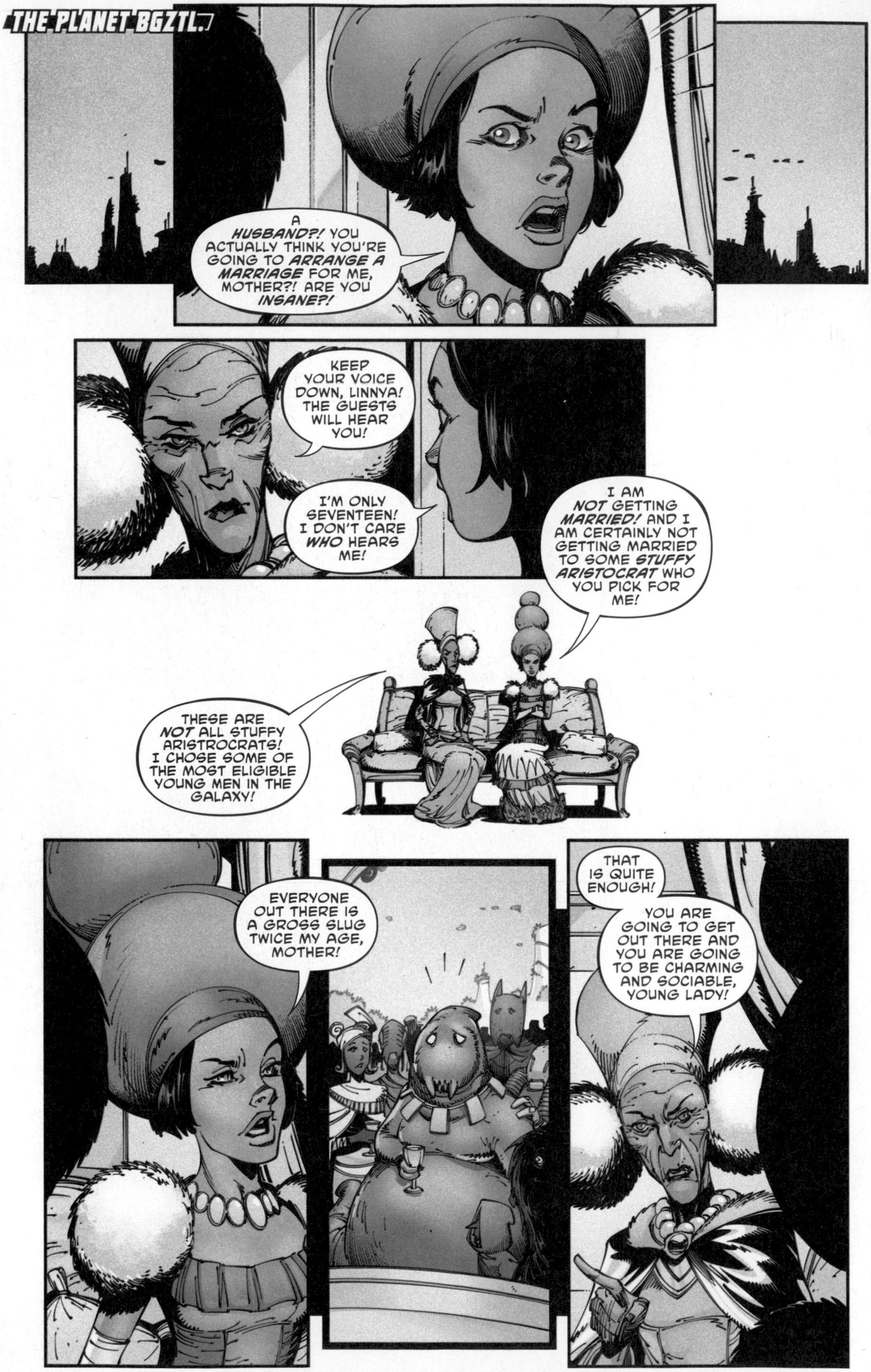
THE PLANET BGZTL.
A HUSBAND?! YOU ACTUALLY THINK YOU'RE GOING TO ARRANGE A MARRIAGE FOR ME, MOTHER?! ARE YOU INSANE?!
KEEP YOUR VOICE DOWN, LINNYA! THE GUESTS WILL HEAR YOU!
I'M ONLY SEVENTEEN! I DON'T CARE WHO HEARS ME!
I AM NOT GETTING MARRIED! AND I AM CERTAINLY NOT GETTING MARRIED TO SOME STUFFY ARISTOCRAT WHO YOU PICK FOR ME!
THESE ARE NOT ALL STUFFY ARISTOCRATS! I CHOSE SOME OF THE MOST ELIGIBLE YOUNG MEN IN THE GALAXY!
EVERYONE OUT THERE IS A GROSS SLUG TWICE MY AGE, MOTHER!
THAT IS QUITE ENOUGH!
YOU ARE GOING TO GET OUT THERE AND YOU ARE GOING TO BE CHARMING AND SOCIABLE, YOUNG LADY!

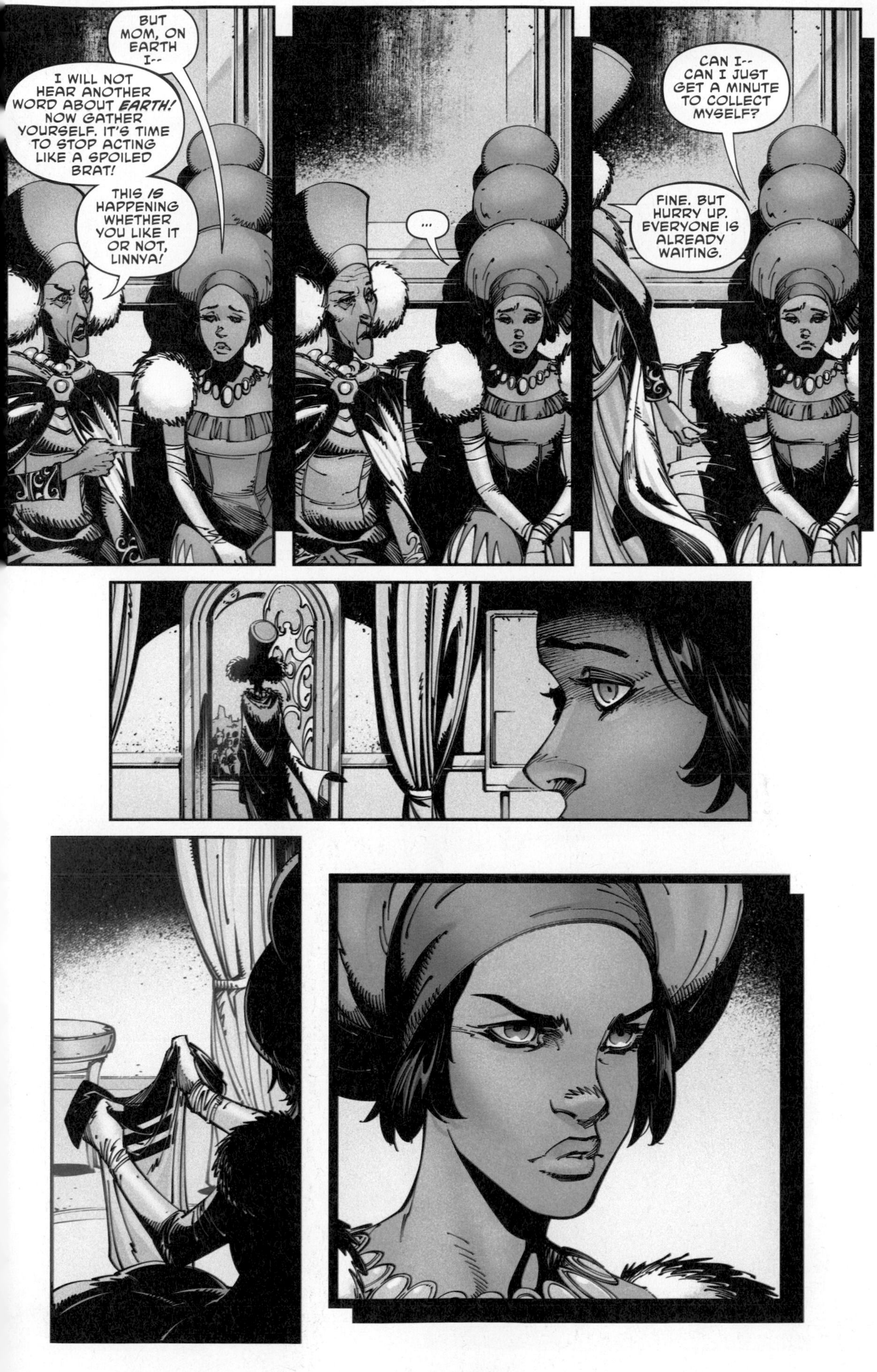
BUT MOM, ON EARTH I--
I WILL NOT HEAR ANOTHER WORD ABOUT *EARTH!* NOW GATHER YOURSELF. IT'S TIME TO STOP ACTING LIKE A SPOILED BRAT!
THIS *IS* HAPPENING WHETHER YOU LIKE IT OR NOT, LINNYA!
...
CAN I-- CAN I JUST GET A MINUTE TO COLLECT MYSELF?
FINE. BUT HURRY UP. EVERYONE IS ALREADY WAITING.

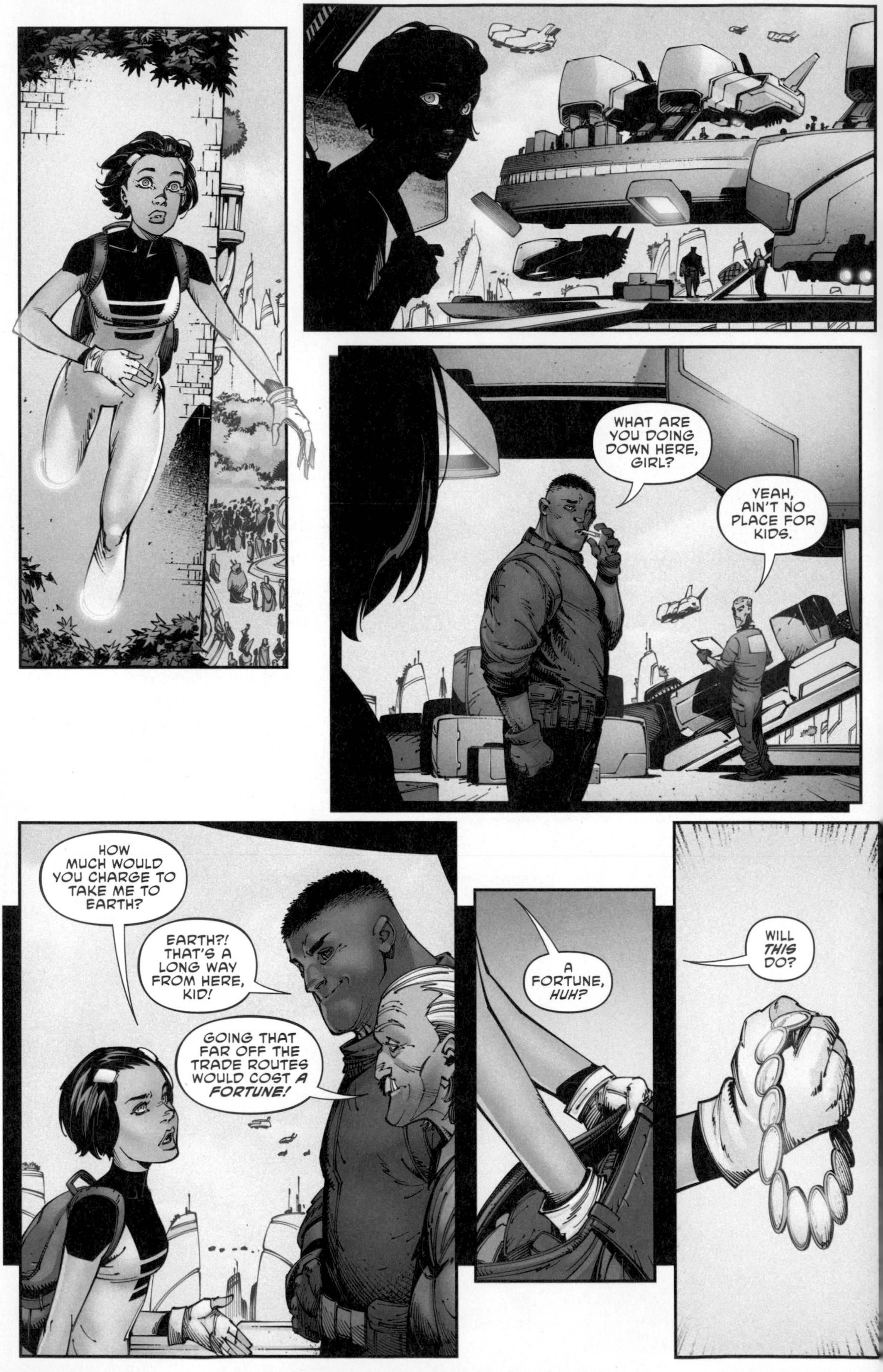
WHAT ARE YOU DOING DOWN HERE, GIRL?
YEAH, AIN'T NO PLACE FOR KIDS.
HOW MUCH WOULD YOU CHARGE TO TAKE ME TO EARTH?
EARTH?! THAT'S A LONG WAY FROM HERE, KID!
GOING THAT FAR OFF THE TRADE ROUTES WOULD COST A *FORTUNE!*
A FORTUNE, *HUH?*
WILL *THIS* DO?

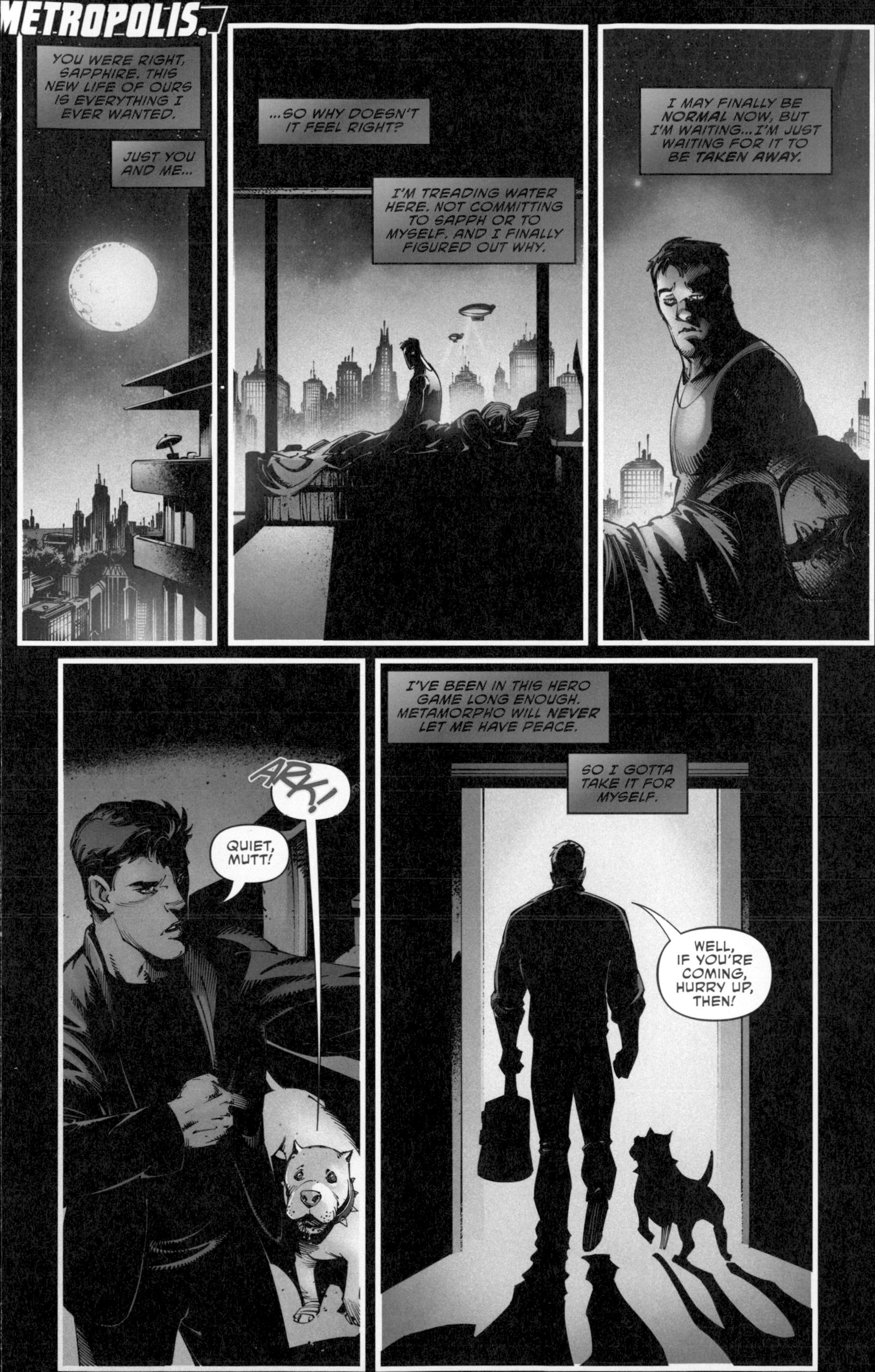
METROPOLIS.
YOU WERE RIGHT, SAPPHIRE. THIS NEW LIFE OF OURS IS EVERYTHING I EVER WANTED.
JUST YOU AND ME...
...SO WHY DOESN'T IT FEEL RIGHT?
I'M TREADING WATER HERE. NOT COMMITTING TO SAPPH OR TO MYSELF. AND I FINALLY FIGURED OUT WHY.
I MAY FINALLY BE NORMAL NOW, BUT I'M WAITING...I'M JUST WAITING FOR IT TO BE TAKEN AWAY.
ARK!
QUIET, MUTT!
I'VE BEEN IN THIS HERO GAME LONG ENOUGH. METAMORPHO WILL NEVER LET ME HAVE PEACE.
SO I GOTTA TAKE IT FOR MYSELF.
WELL, IF YOU'RE COMING, HURRY UP, THEN!

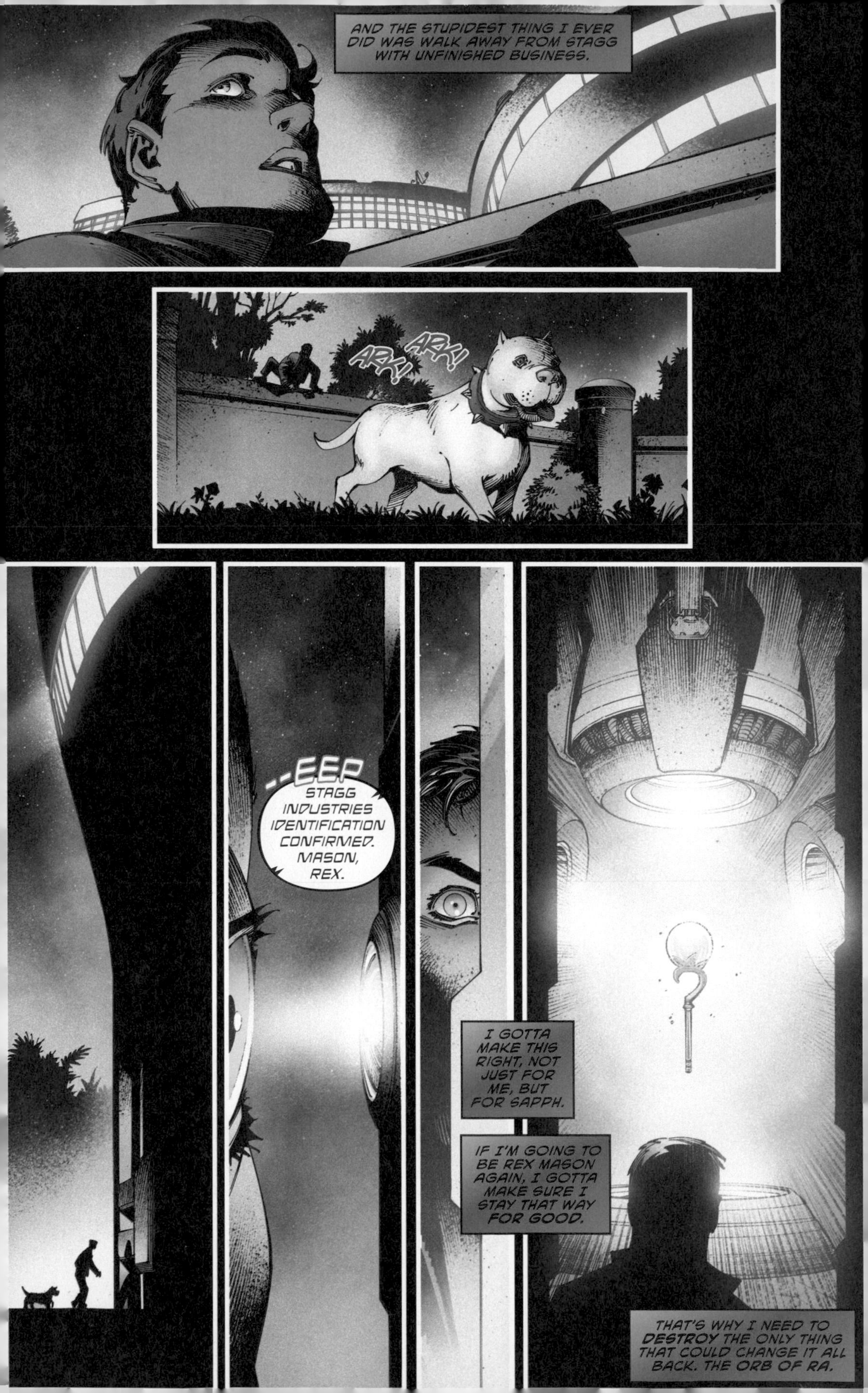
AND THE STUPIDEST THING I EVER DID WAS WALK AWAY FROM STAGG WITH UNFINISHED BUSINESS.
ARK! ARK!
--EEP
STAGG INDUSTRIES IDENTIFICATION CONFIRMED. MASON, REX.
I GOTTA MAKE THIS RIGHT, NOT JUST FOR ME, BUT FOR SAPPH.
IF I'M GOING TO BE REX MASON AGAIN, I GOTTA MAKE SURE I STAY THAT WAY FOR GOOD.
THAT'S WHY I NEED TO DESTROY THE ONLY THING THAT COULD CHANGE IT ALL BACK. THE ORB OF RA.

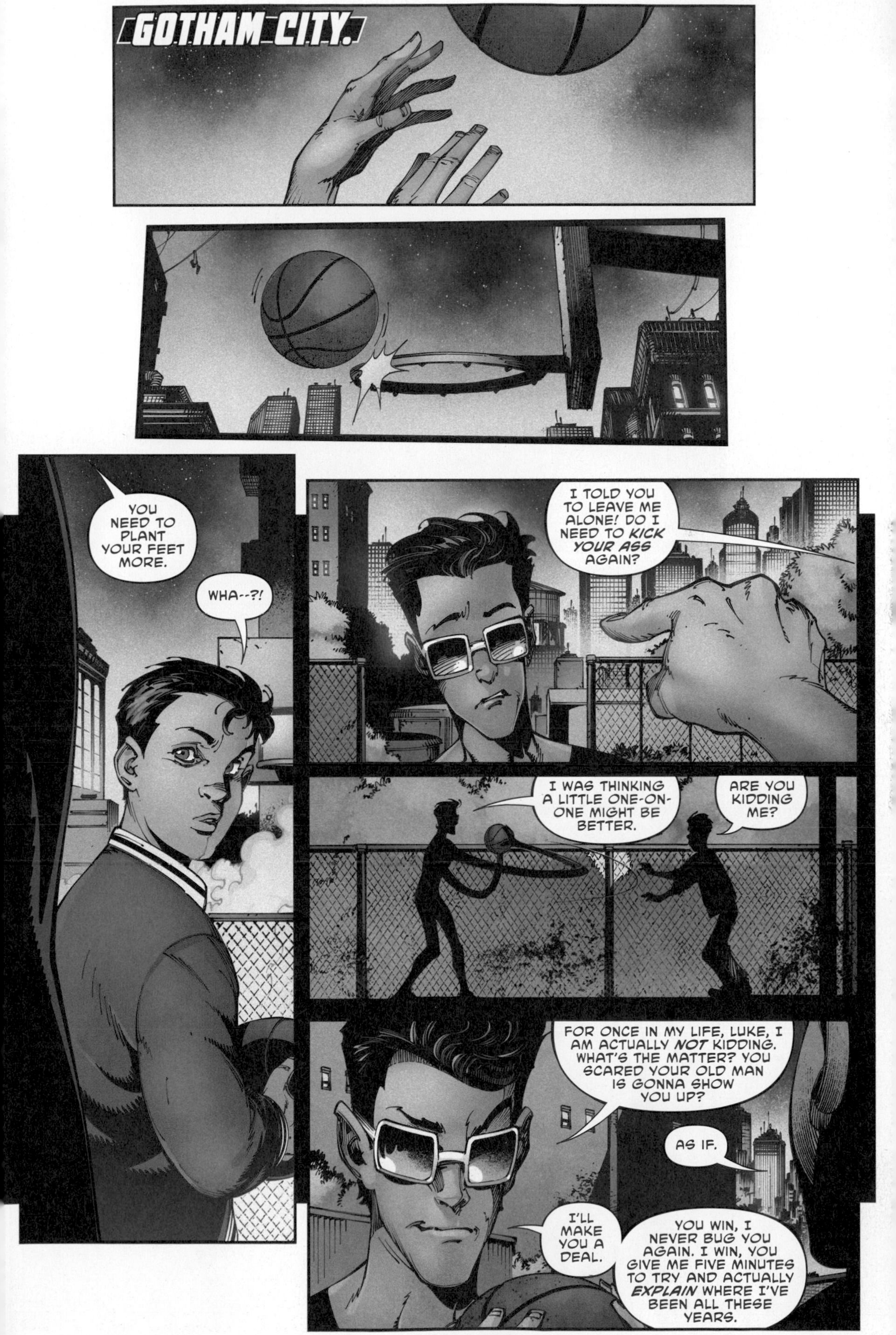
GOTHAM CITY.
YOU NEED TO PLANT YOUR FEET MORE.
WHA--?!
I TOLD YOU TO LEAVE ME ALONE! DO I NEED TO KICK YOUR ASS AGAIN?
I WAS THINKING A LITTLE ONE-ON-ONE MIGHT BE BETTER.
ARE YOU KIDDING ME?
FOR ONCE IN MY LIFE, LUKE, I AM ACTUALLY NOT KIDDING. WHAT'S THE MATTER? YOU SCARED YOUR OLD MAN IS GONNA SHOW YOU UP?
AS IF.
I'LL MAKE YOU A DEAL.
YOU WIN, I NEVER BUG YOU AGAIN. I WIN, YOU GIVE ME FIVE MINUTES TO TRY AND ACTUALLY EXPLAIN WHERE I'VE BEEN ALL THESE YEARS.

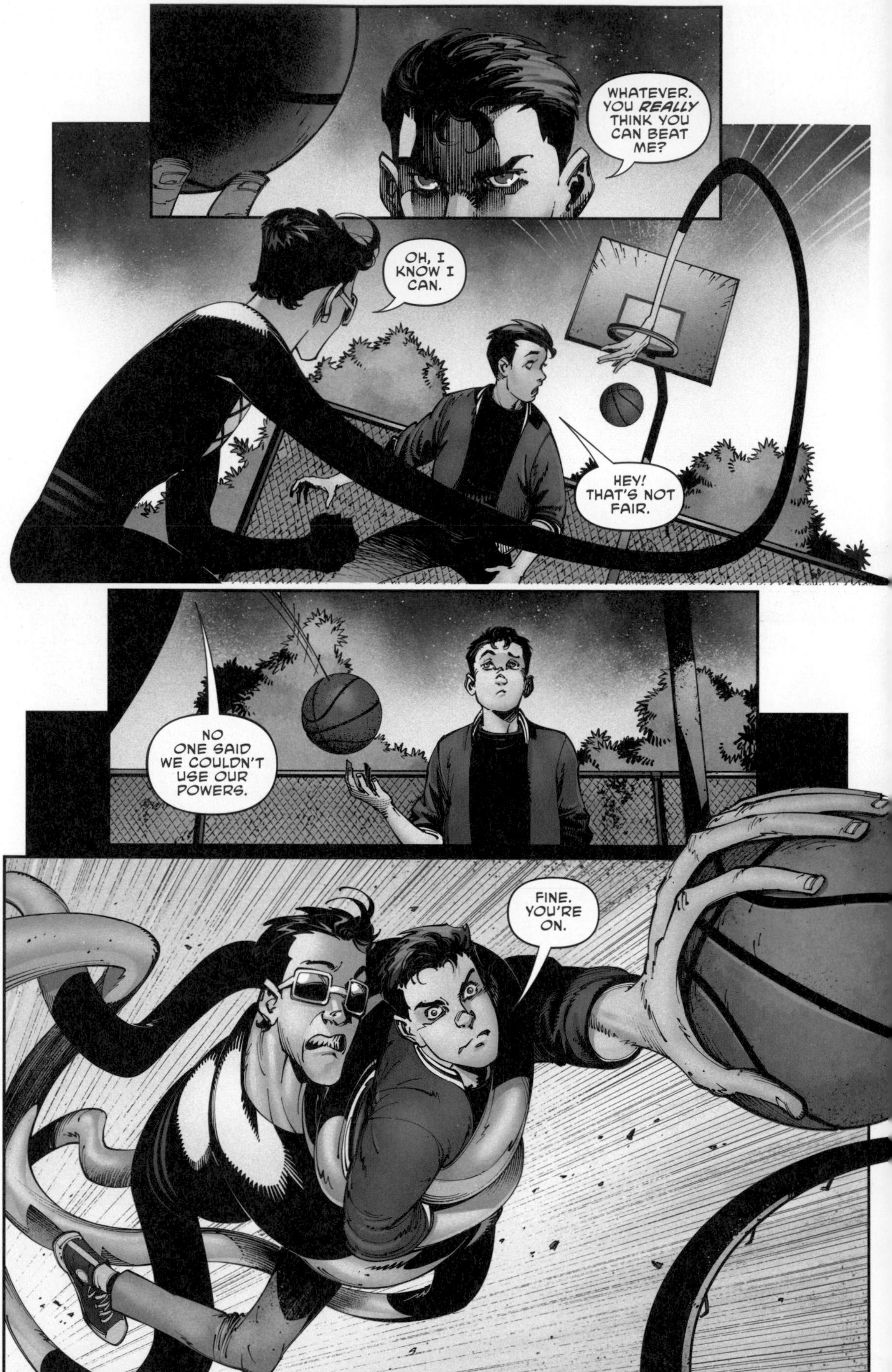
WHATEVER. YOU *REALLY* THINK YOU CAN BEAT ME?
OH, I KNOW I CAN.
HEY! THAT'S NOT FAIR.
NO ONE SAID WE COULDN'T USE OUR POWERS.
FINE. YOU'RE ON.

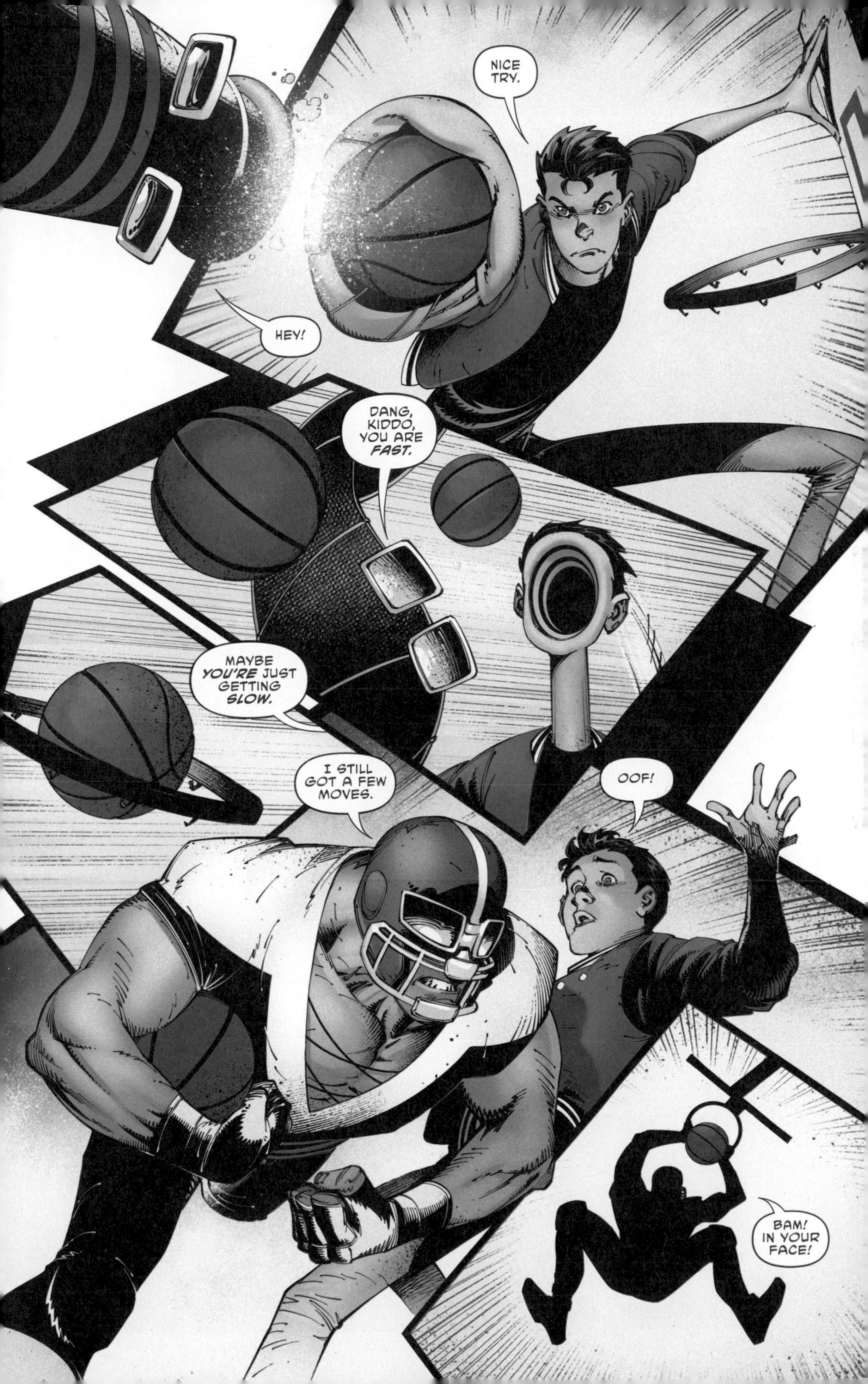
NICE TRY.
HEY!
DANG, KIDDO, YOU ARE *FAST.*
MAYBE *YOU'RE* JUST GETTING *SLOW.*
I STILL GOT A FEW MOVES.
OOF!
BAM! IN YOUR FACE!

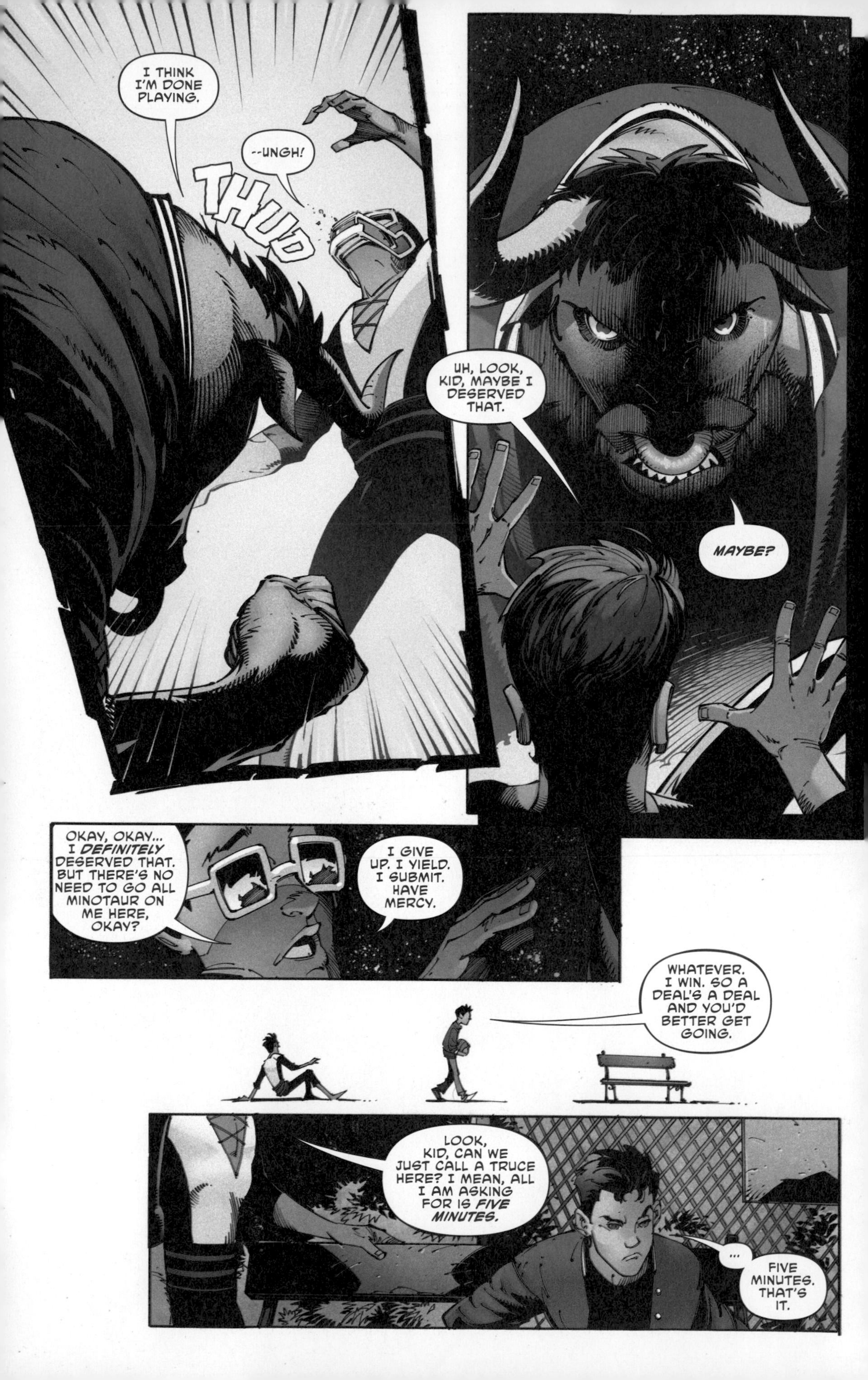
I THINK I'M DONE PLAYING.
--UNGH!
THUD
UH, LOOK, KID, MAYBE I DESERVED THAT.
MAYBE?
OKAY, OKAY... I DEFINITELY DESERVED THAT. BUT THERE'S NO NEED TO GO ALL MINOTAUR ON ME HERE, OKAY?
I GIVE UP. I YIELD. I SUBMIT. HAVE MERCY.
WHATEVER. I WIN. SO A DEAL'S A DEAL AND YOU'D BETTER GET GOING.
LOOK, KID, CAN WE JUST CALL A TRUCE HERE? I MEAN, ALL I AM ASKING FOR IS FIVE MINUTES.
...
FIVE MINUTES. THAT'S IT.

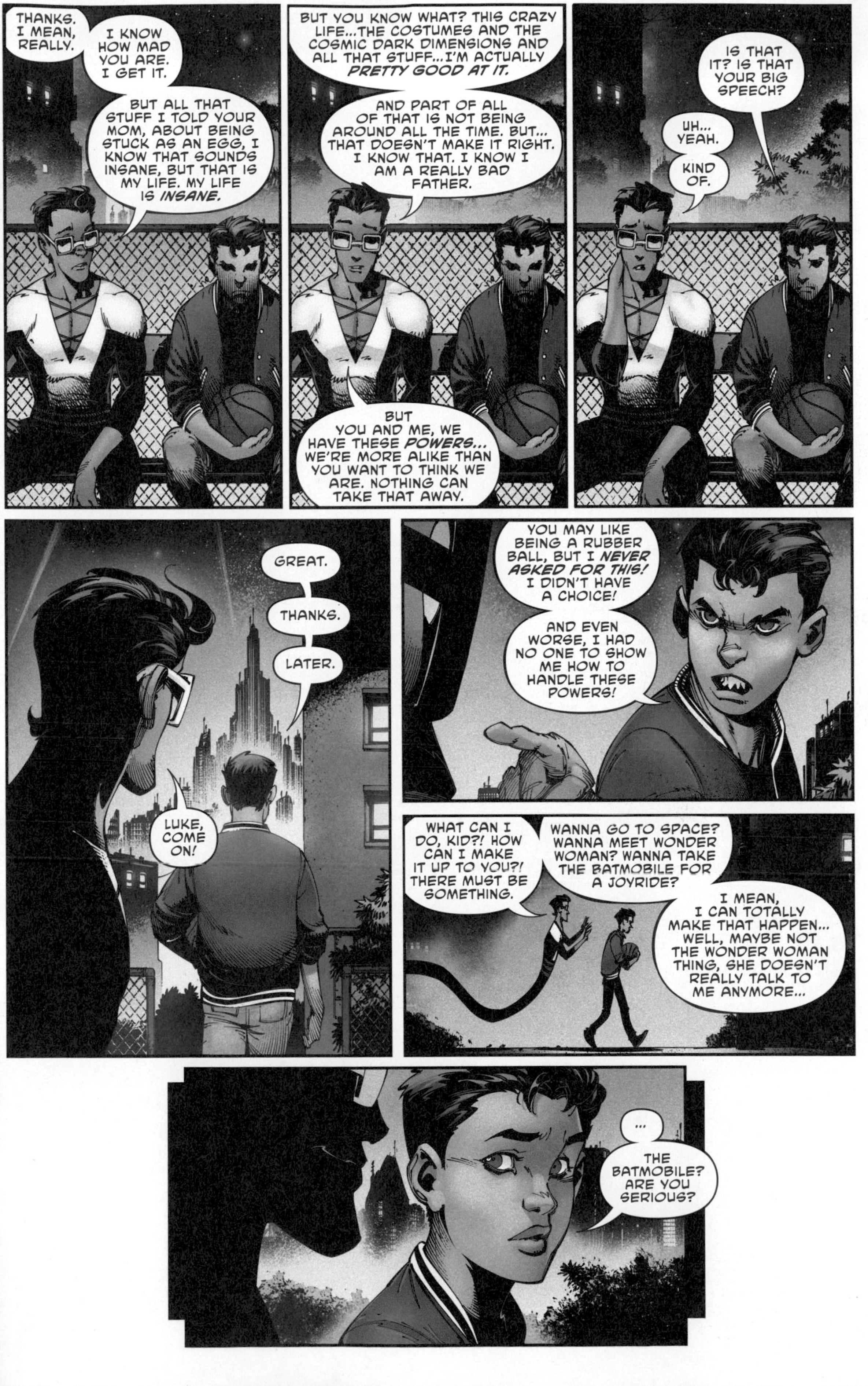
THANKS. I MEAN, REALLY.
I KNOW HOW MAD YOU ARE. I GET IT.
BUT ALL THAT STUFF I TOLD YOUR MOM, ABOUT BEING STUCK AS AN EGG, I KNOW THAT SOUNDS INSANE, BUT THAT IS MY LIFE. MY LIFE IS *INSANE.*
BUT YOU KNOW WHAT? THIS CRAZY LIFE...THE COSTUMES AND THE COSMIC DARK DIMENSIONS AND ALL THAT STUFF...I'M ACTUALLY *PRETTY GOOD AT IT.*
AND PART OF ALL OF THAT IS NOT BEING AROUND ALL THE TIME. BUT... THAT DOESN'T MAKE IT RIGHT. I KNOW THAT. I KNOW I AM A REALLY BAD FATHER.
BUT YOU AND ME, WE HAVE THESE *POWERS...* WE'RE MORE ALIKE THAN YOU WANT TO THINK WE ARE. NOTHING CAN TAKE THAT AWAY.
IS THAT IT? IS THAT YOUR BIG SPEECH?
UH... YEAH.
KIND OF.
GREAT.
THANKS.
LATER.
LUKE, COME ON!
YOU MAY LIKE BEING A RUBBER BALL, BUT I *NEVER ASKED FOR THIS!* I DIDN'T HAVE A CHOICE!
AND EVEN WORSE, I HAD NO ONE TO SHOW ME HOW TO HANDLE THESE POWERS!
WHAT CAN I DO, KID?! HOW CAN I MAKE IT UP TO YOU?! THERE MUST BE SOMETHING.
WANNA GO TO SPACE? WANNA MEET WONDER WOMAN? WANNA TAKE THE BATMOBILE FOR A JOYRIDE?
I MEAN, I CAN TOTALLY MAKE THAT HAPPEN... WELL, MAYBE NOT THE WONDER WOMAN THING, SHE DOESN'T REALLY TALK TO ME ANYMORE...
...
THE BATMOBILE? ARE YOU SERIOUS?

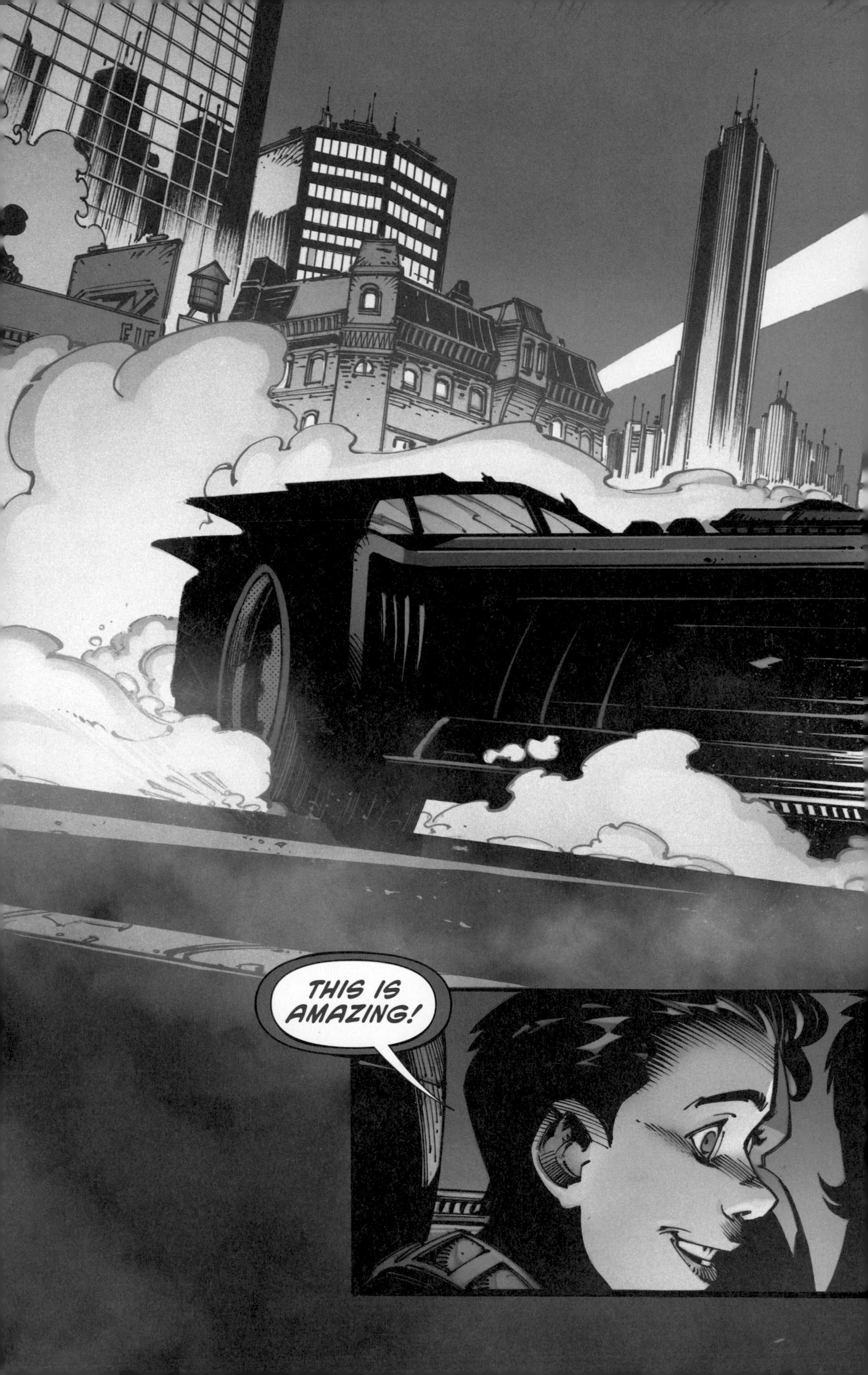
THIS IS AMAZING!

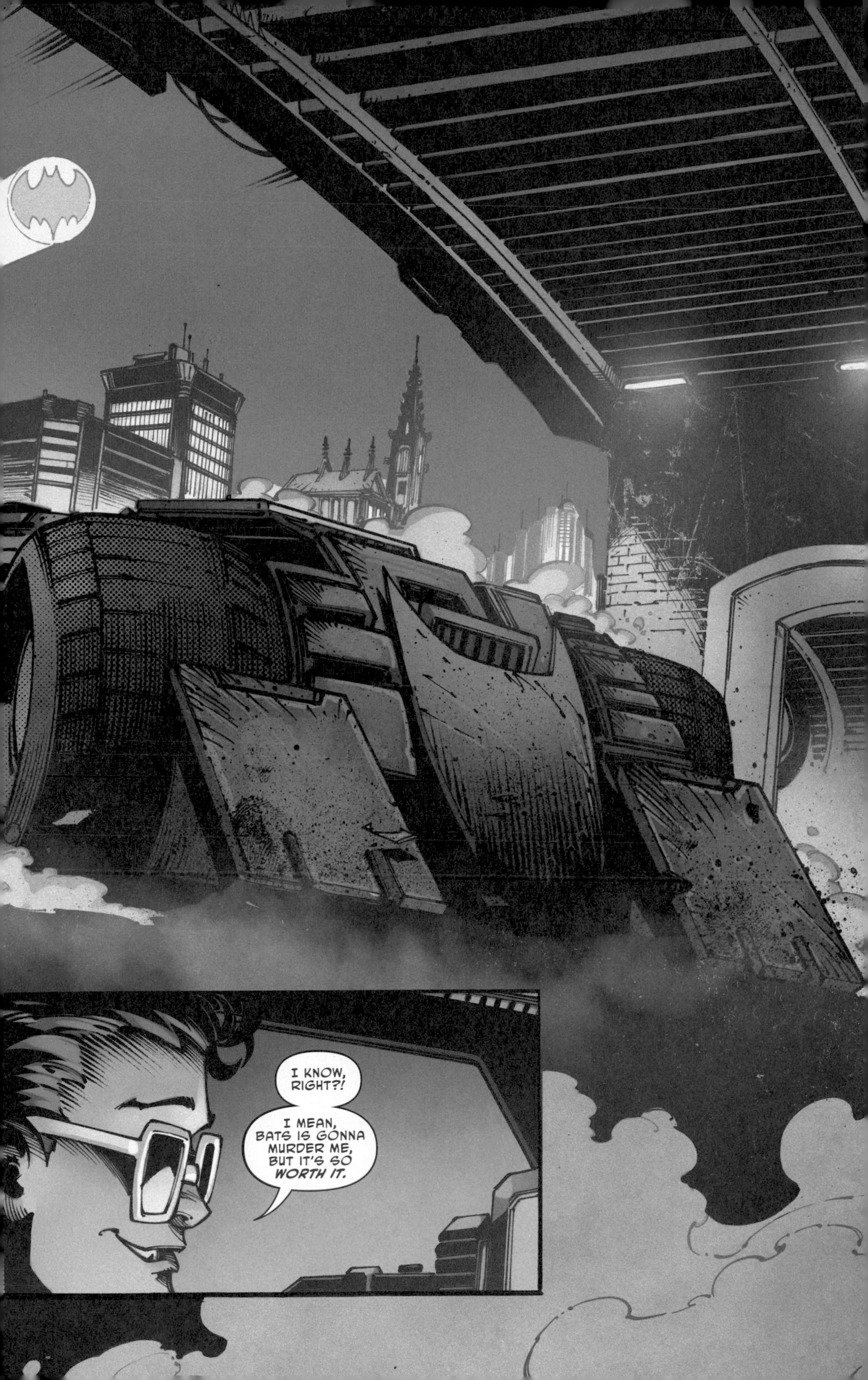
I KNOW, RIGHT?!
I MEAN, BATS IS GONNA MURDER ME, BUT IT'S SO *WORTH IT.*

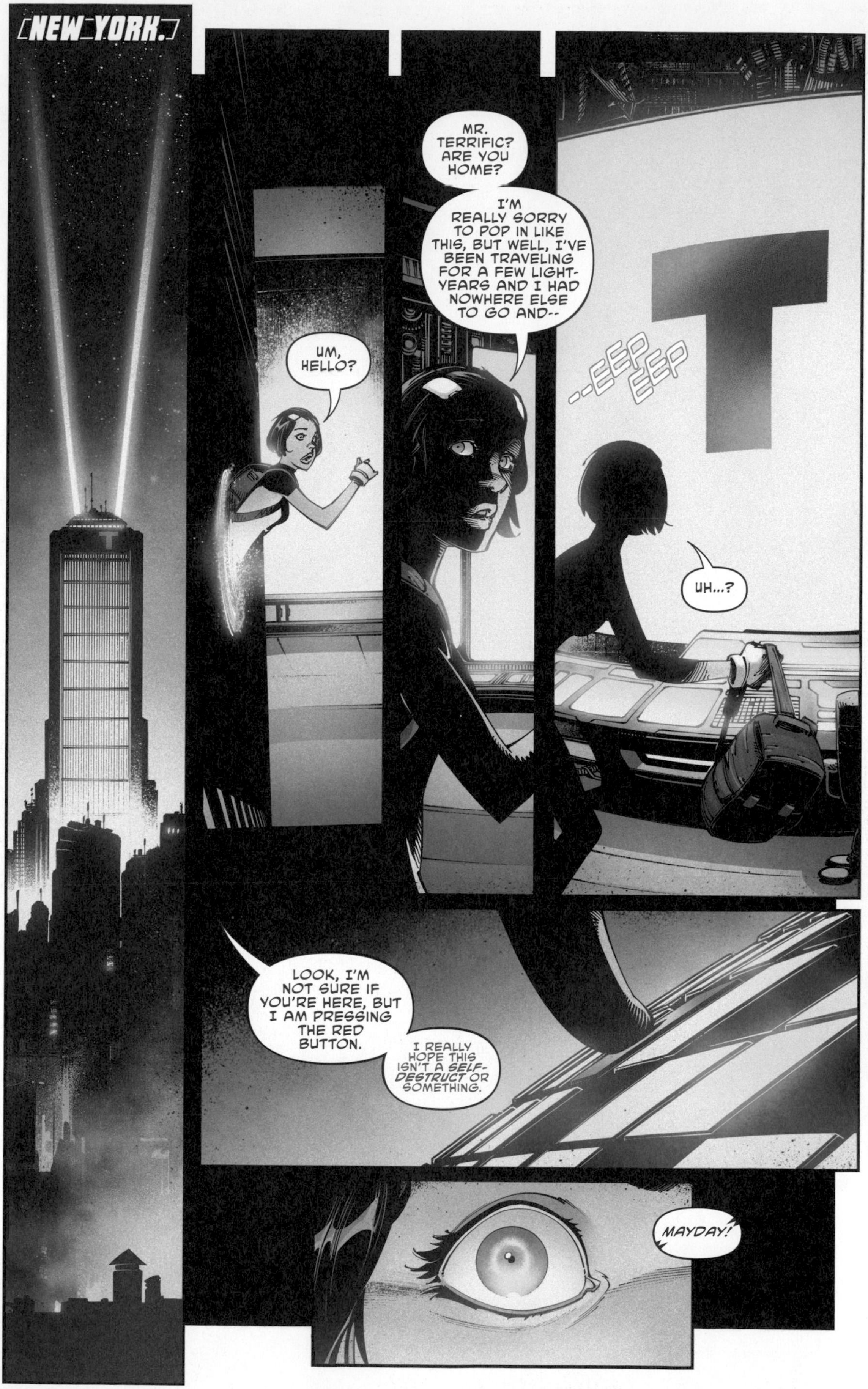
NEW YORK.
UM, HELLO?
MR. TERRIFIC? ARE YOU HOME?
I'M REALLY SORRY TO POP IN LIKE THIS, BUT WELL, I'VE BEEN TRAVELING FOR A FEW LIGHT-YEARS AND I HAD NOWHERE ELSE TO GO AND--
--EEP EEP
UH...?
LOOK, I'M NOT SURE IF YOU'RE HERE, BUT I AM PRESSING THE RED BUTTON.
I REALLY HOPE THIS ISN'T A SELF-DESTRUCT OR SOMETHING.
MAYDAY!

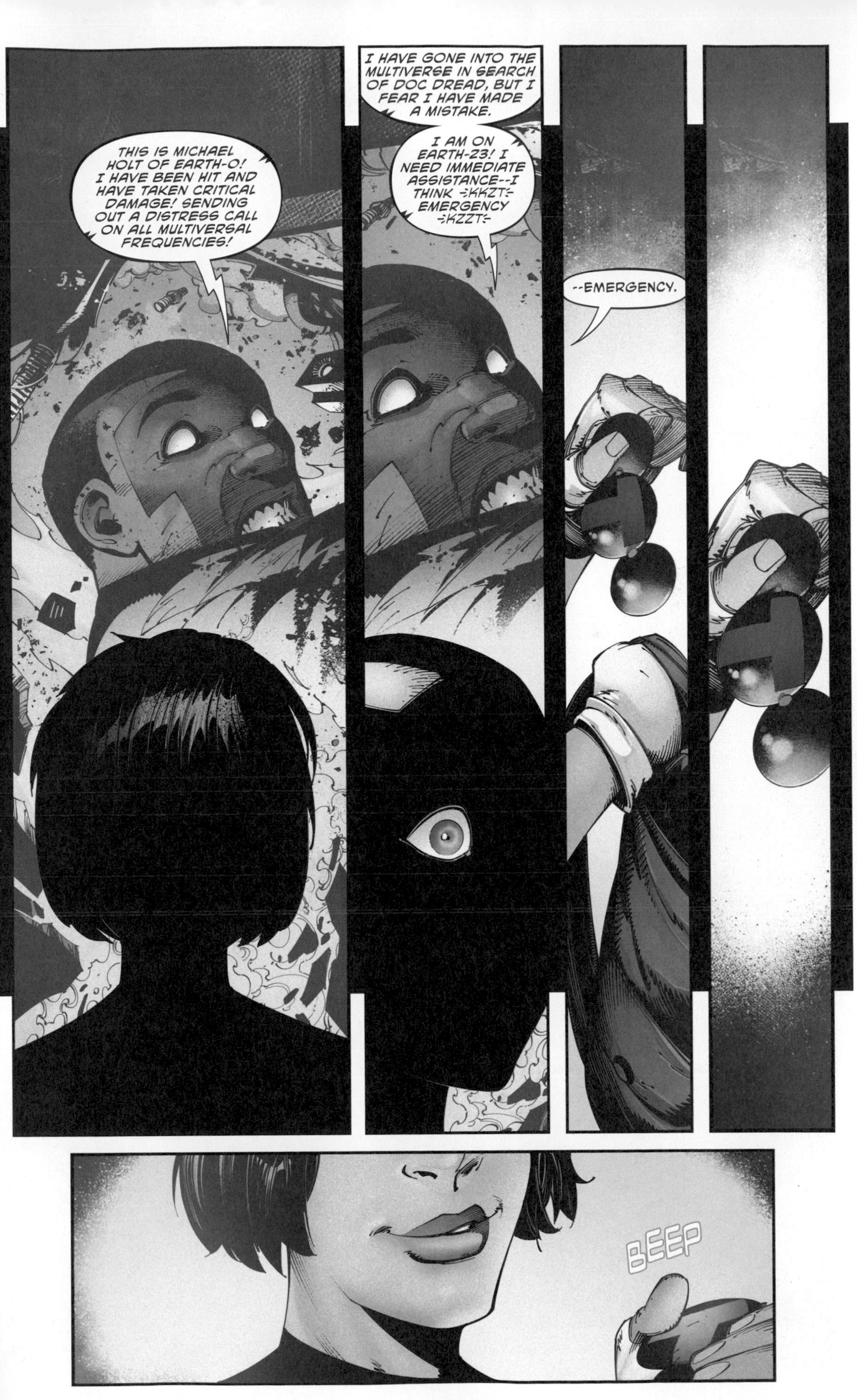
THIS IS MICHAEL HOLT OF EARTH-O! I HAVE BEEN HIT AND HAVE TAKEN CRITICAL DAMAGE! SENDING OUT A DISTRESS CALL ON ALL MULTIVERSAL FREQUENCIES!
I HAVE GONE INTO THE MULTIVERSE IN SEARCH OF DOC DREAD, BUT I FEAR I HAVE MADE A MISTAKE.
I AM ON EARTH-23! I NEED IMMEDIATE ASSISTANCE--I THINK -KKZT- EMERGENCY -KZZT-
--EMERGENCY.
BEEP

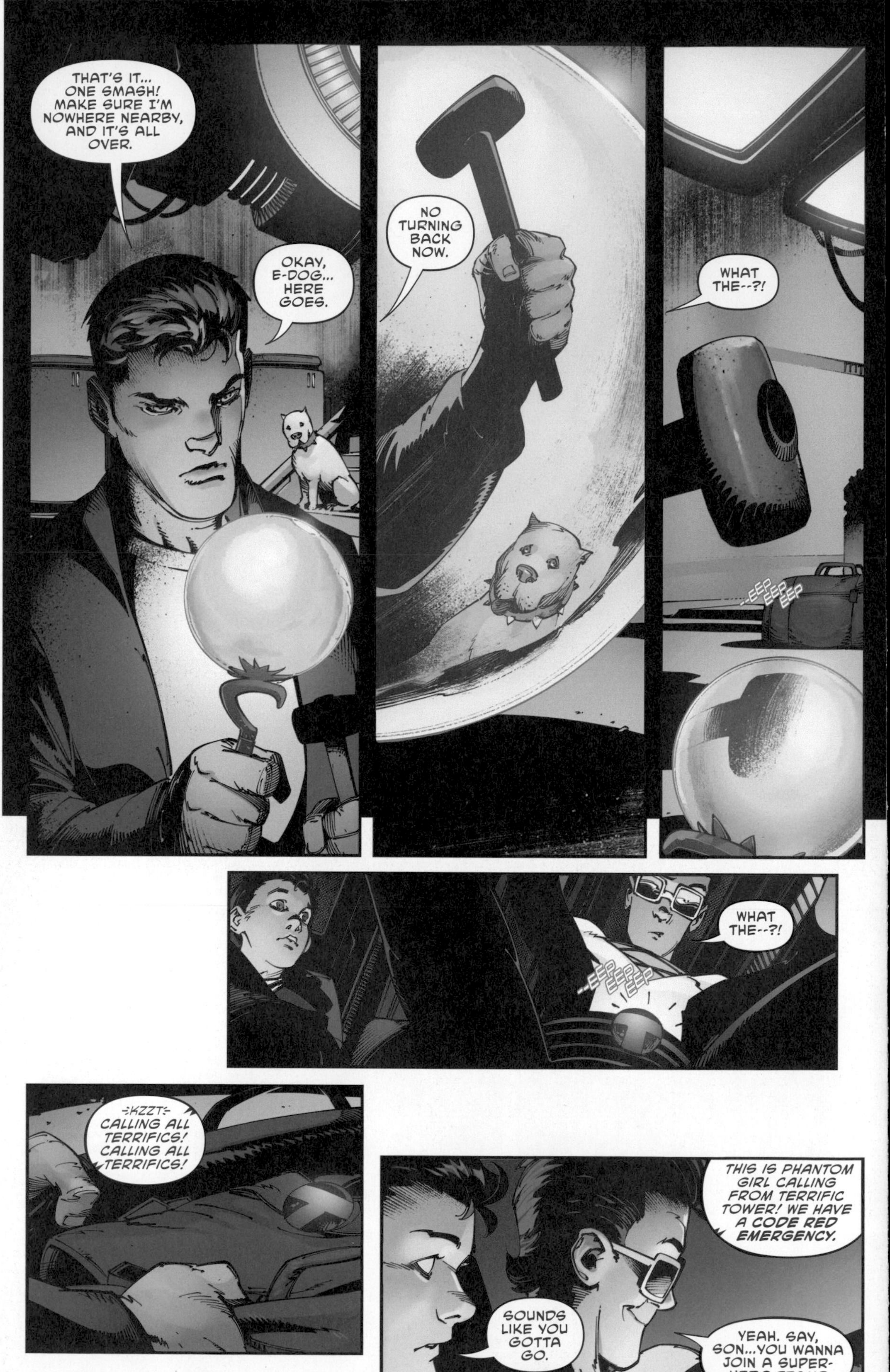
THAT'S IT... ONE SMASH! MAKE SURE I'M NOWHERE NEARBY, AND IT'S ALL OVER.
OKAY, E-DOG... HERE GOES.
NO TURNING BACK NOW.
WHAT THE--?!
-EEP EEP EEP
WHAT THE--?!
-EEP EEP EEP
-KZZT- CALLING ALL TERRIFICS! CALLING ALL TERRIFICS!
THIS IS PHANTOM GIRL CALLING FROM TERRIFIC TOWER! WE HAVE A CODE RED EMERGENCY.
SOUNDS LIKE YOU GOTTA GO.
YEAH. SAY, SON...YOU WANNA JOIN A SUPER-HERO TEAM?

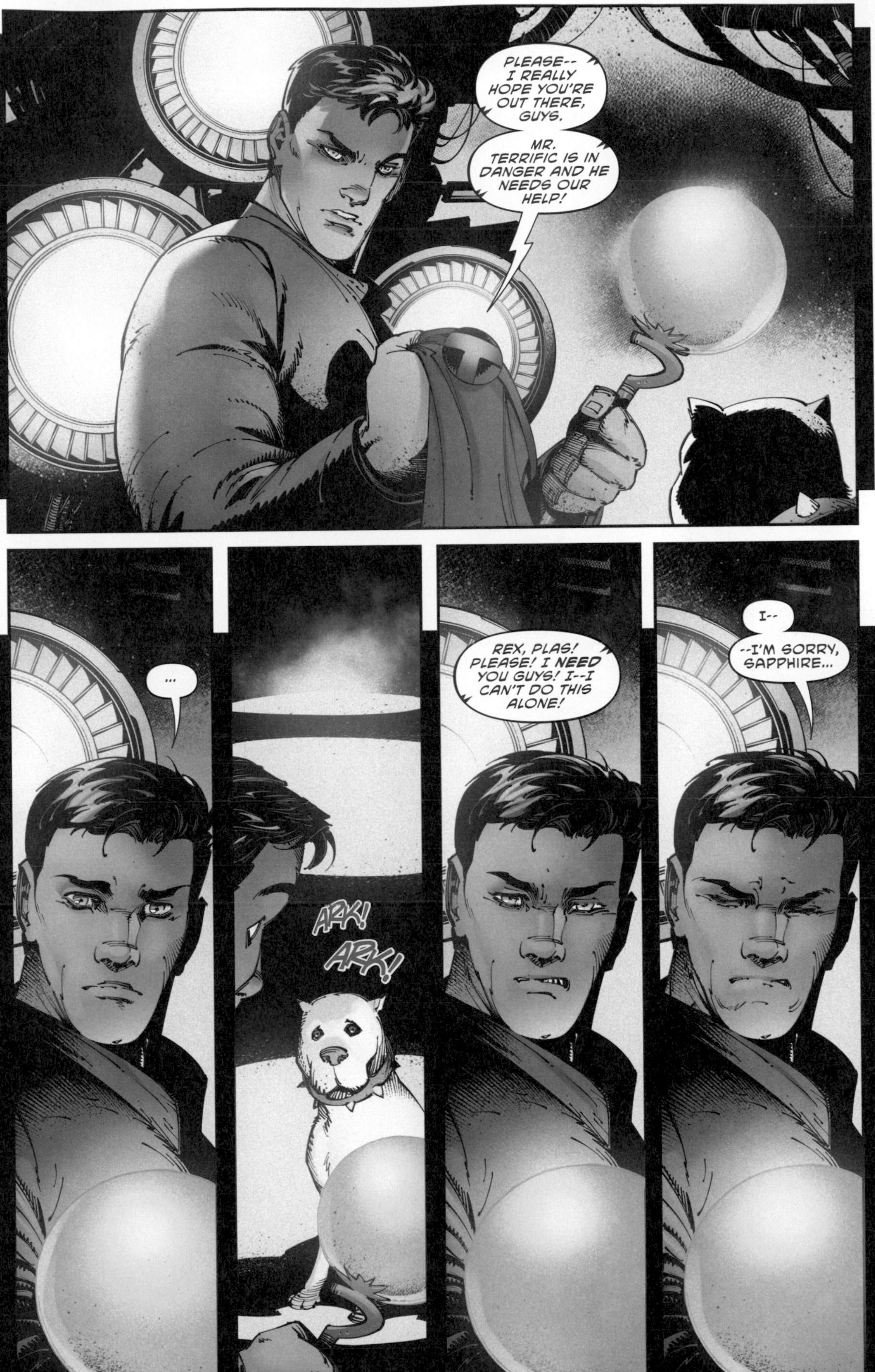
PLEASE-- I REALLY HOPE YOU'RE OUT THERE, GUYS.
MR. TERRIFIC IS IN DANGER AND HE NEEDS OUR HELP!
...
ARK!
ARK!
REX, PLAS! PLEASE! I NEED YOU GUYS! I--I CAN'T DO THIS ALONE!
I--
--I'M SORRY, SAPPHIRE...

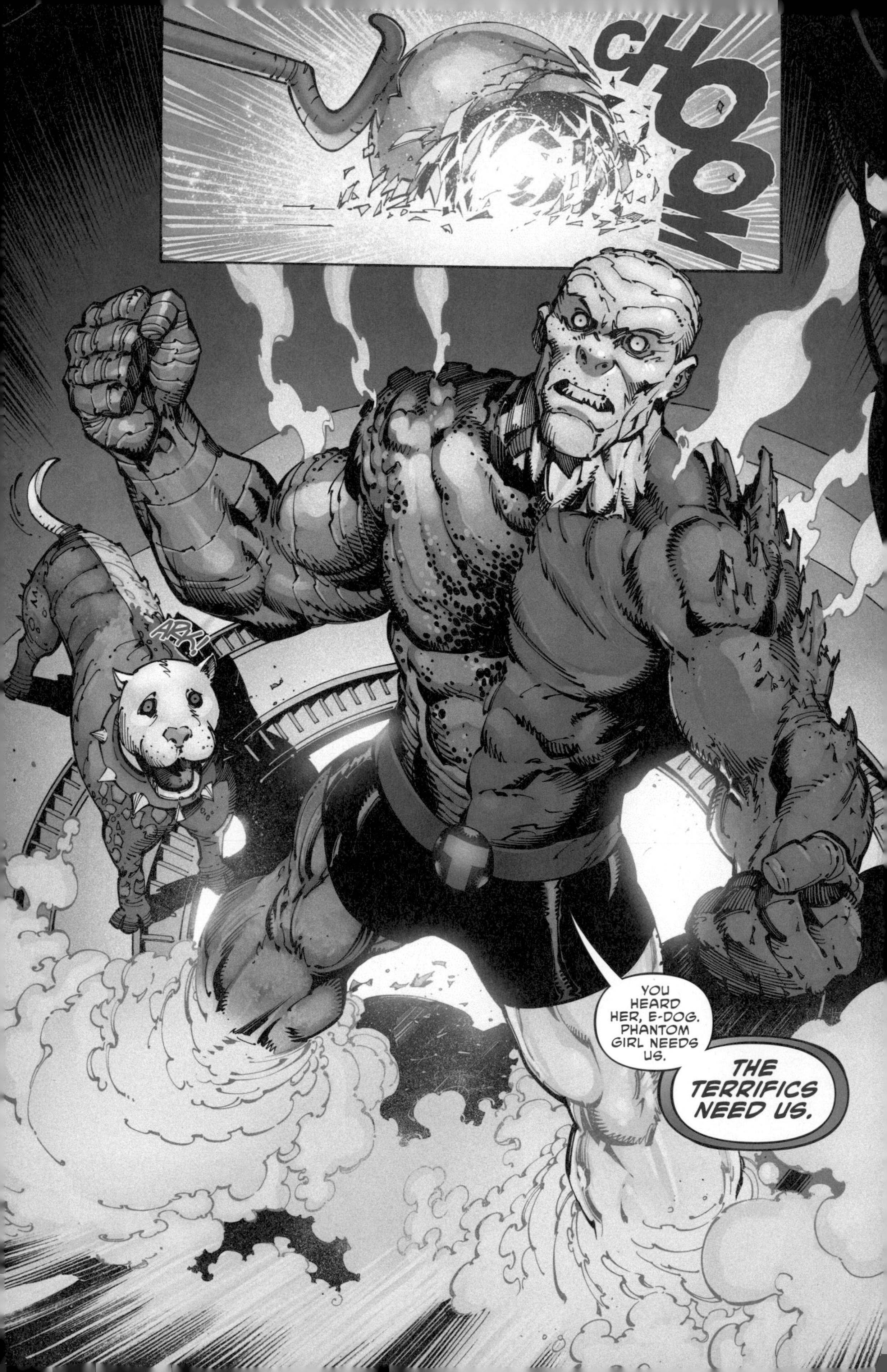
CHOOOM
ARK!
YOU HEARD HER, E-DOG. PHANTOM GIRL NEEDS US.
THE TERRIFICS NEED US.

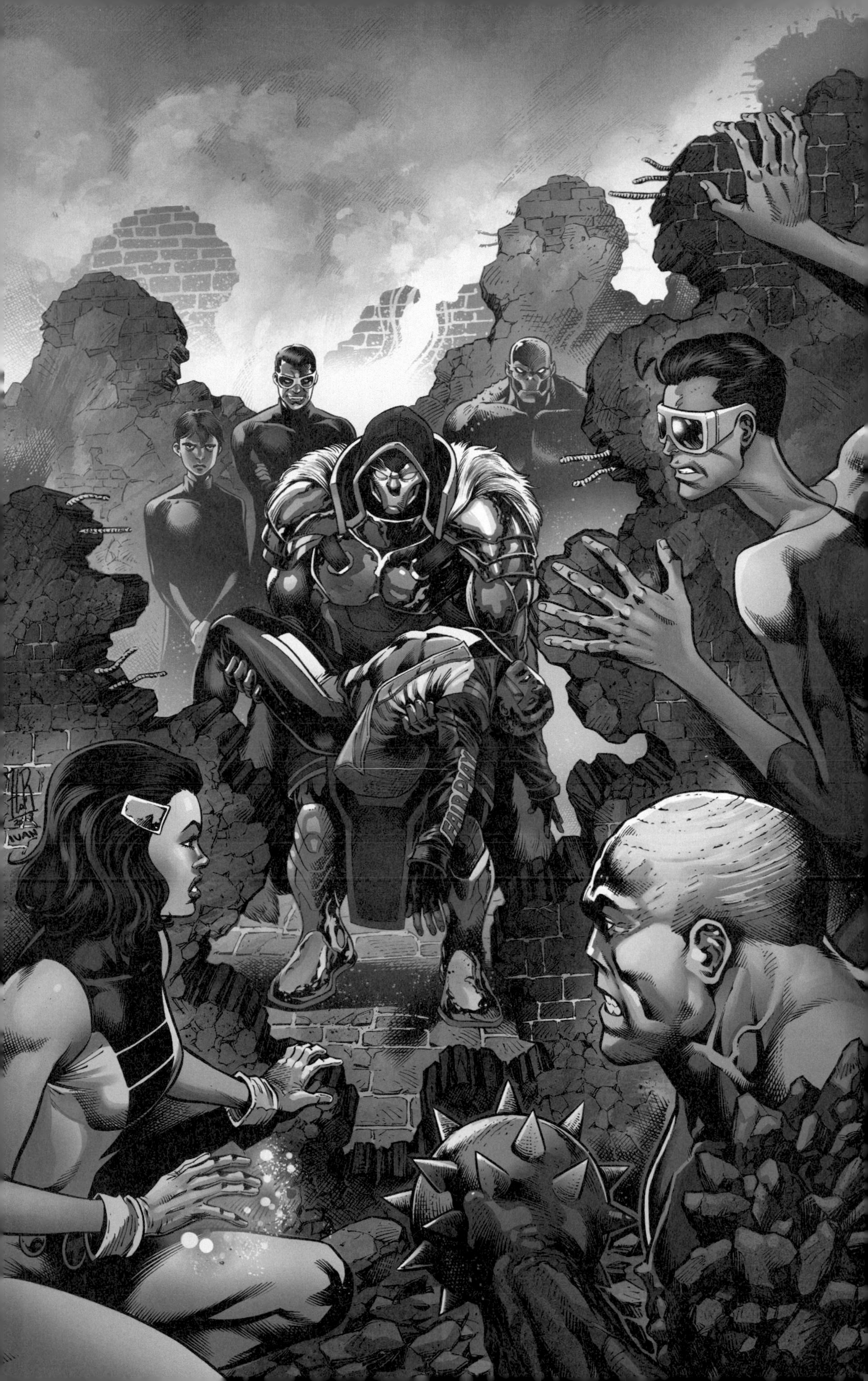
FAIRPLAY

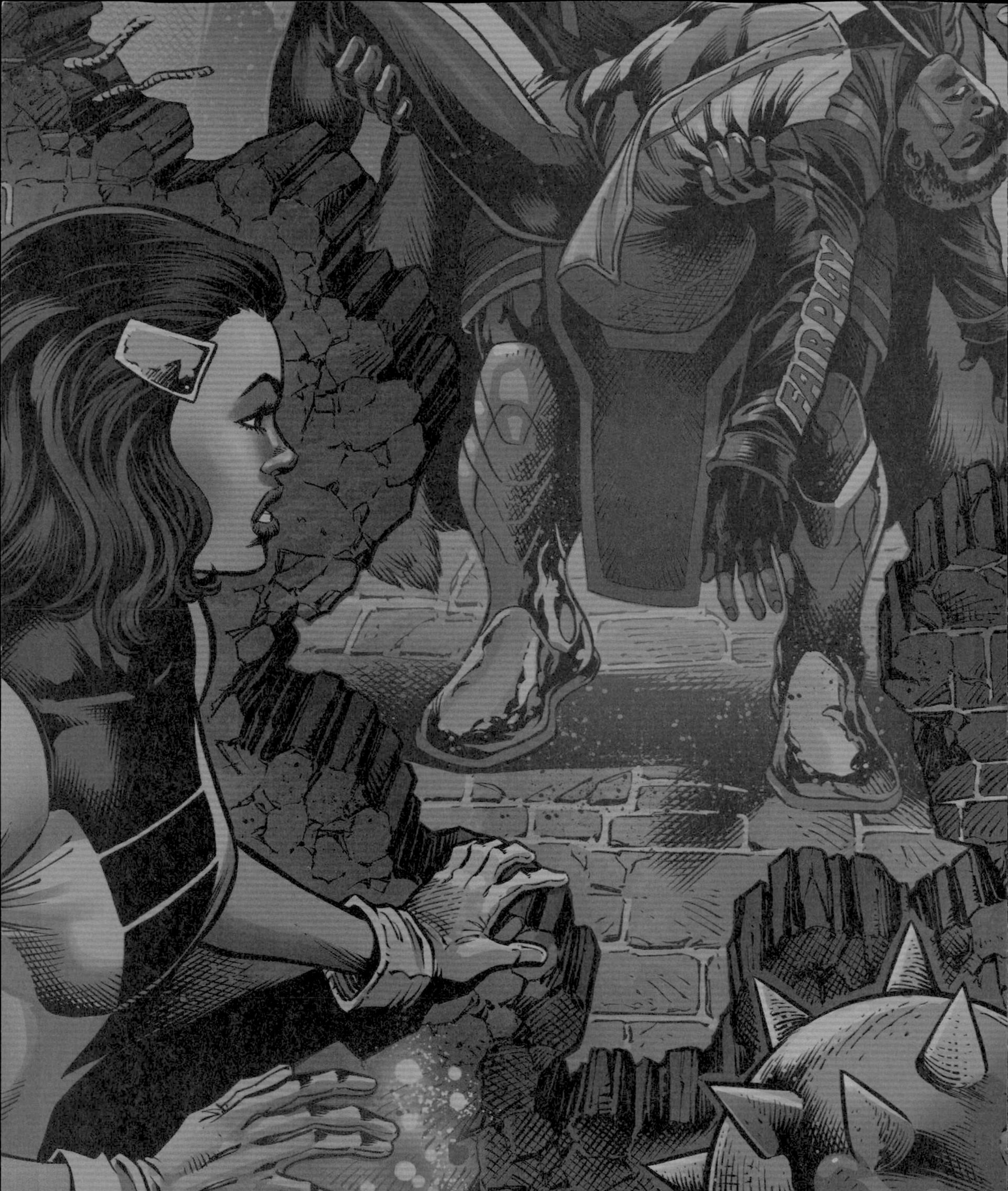
FAIRPLAY

THE TERRIFICS
#13

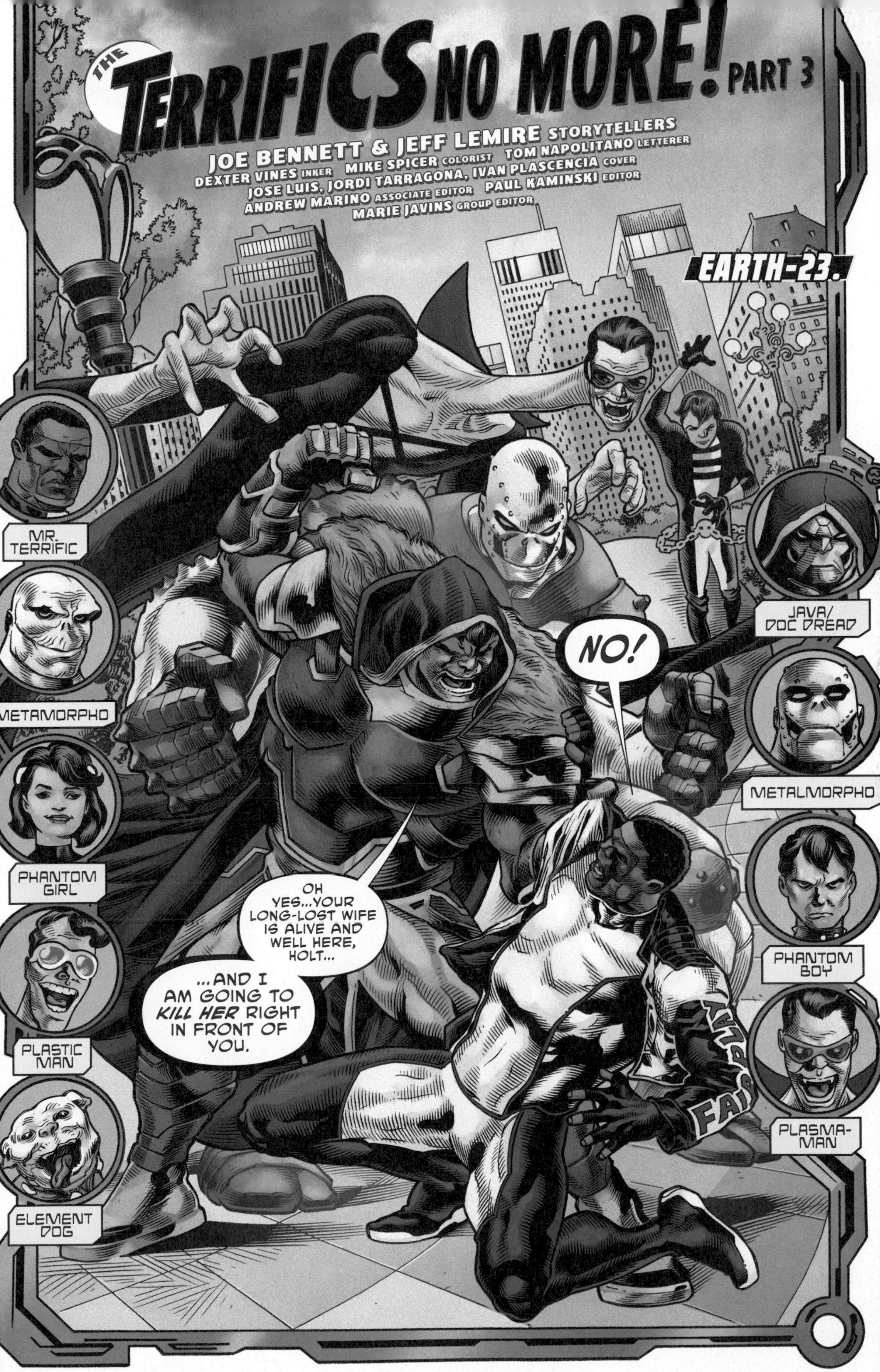
THE TERRIFICS NO MORE! PART 3
JOE BENNETT & JEFF LEMIRE STORYTELLERS
DEXTER VINES INKER MIKE SPICER COLORIST TOM NAPOLITANO LETTERER
JOSE LUIS, JORDI TARRAGONA, IVAN PLASCENCIA COVER
ANDREW MARINO ASSOCIATE EDITOR PAUL KAMINSKI EDITOR
MARIE JAVINS GROUP EDITOR
EARTH-23.
MR. TERRIFIC
METAMORPHO
PHANTOM GIRL
PLASTIC MAN
ELEMENT DOG
JAVA/ DOC DREAD
METALMORPHO
PHANTOM BOY
PLASMA-MAN
NO!
OH YES...YOUR LONG-LOST WIFE IS ALIVE AND WELL HERE, HOLT...
...AND I AM GOING TO KILL HER RIGHT IN FRONT OF YOU.

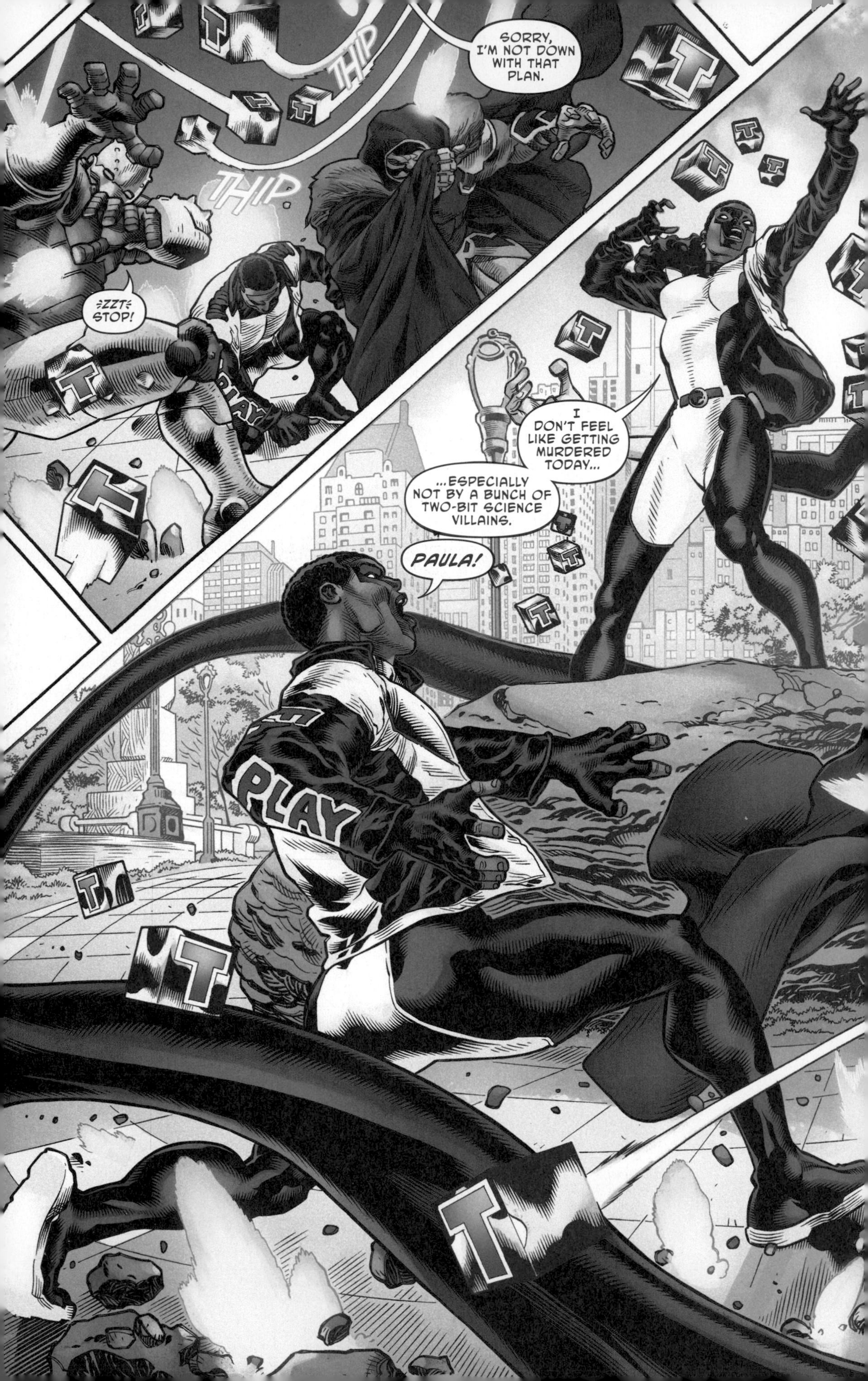
SORRY, I'M NOT DOWN WITH THAT PLAN.
THIP
THIP
ZZT STOP!
I DON'T FEEL LIKE GETTING MURDERED TODAY...
...ESPECIALLY NOT BY A BUNCH OF TWO-BIT SCIENCE VILLAINS.
PAULA!
PLAY

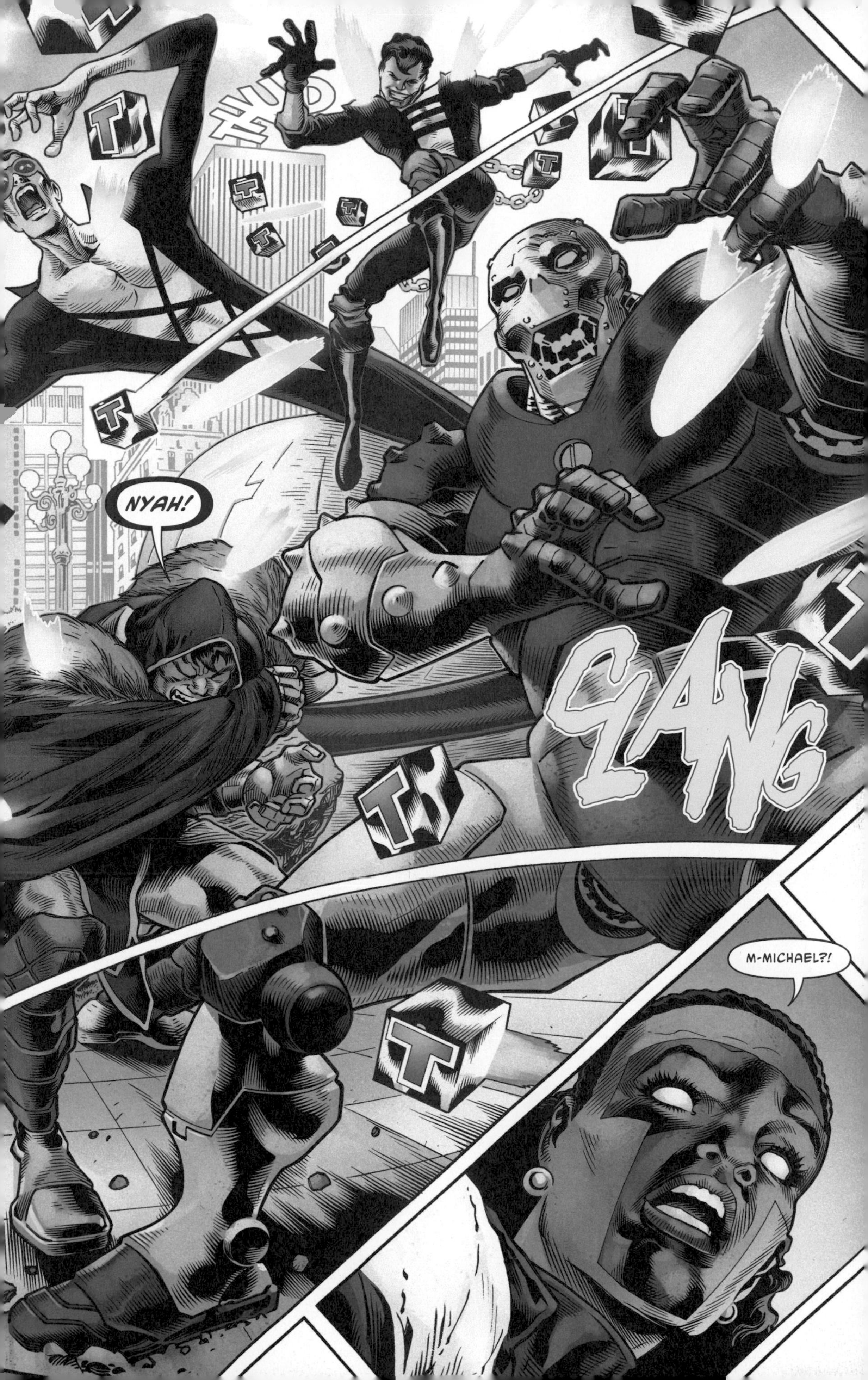
THUD
NYAH!
CLANG
M-MICHAEL?!

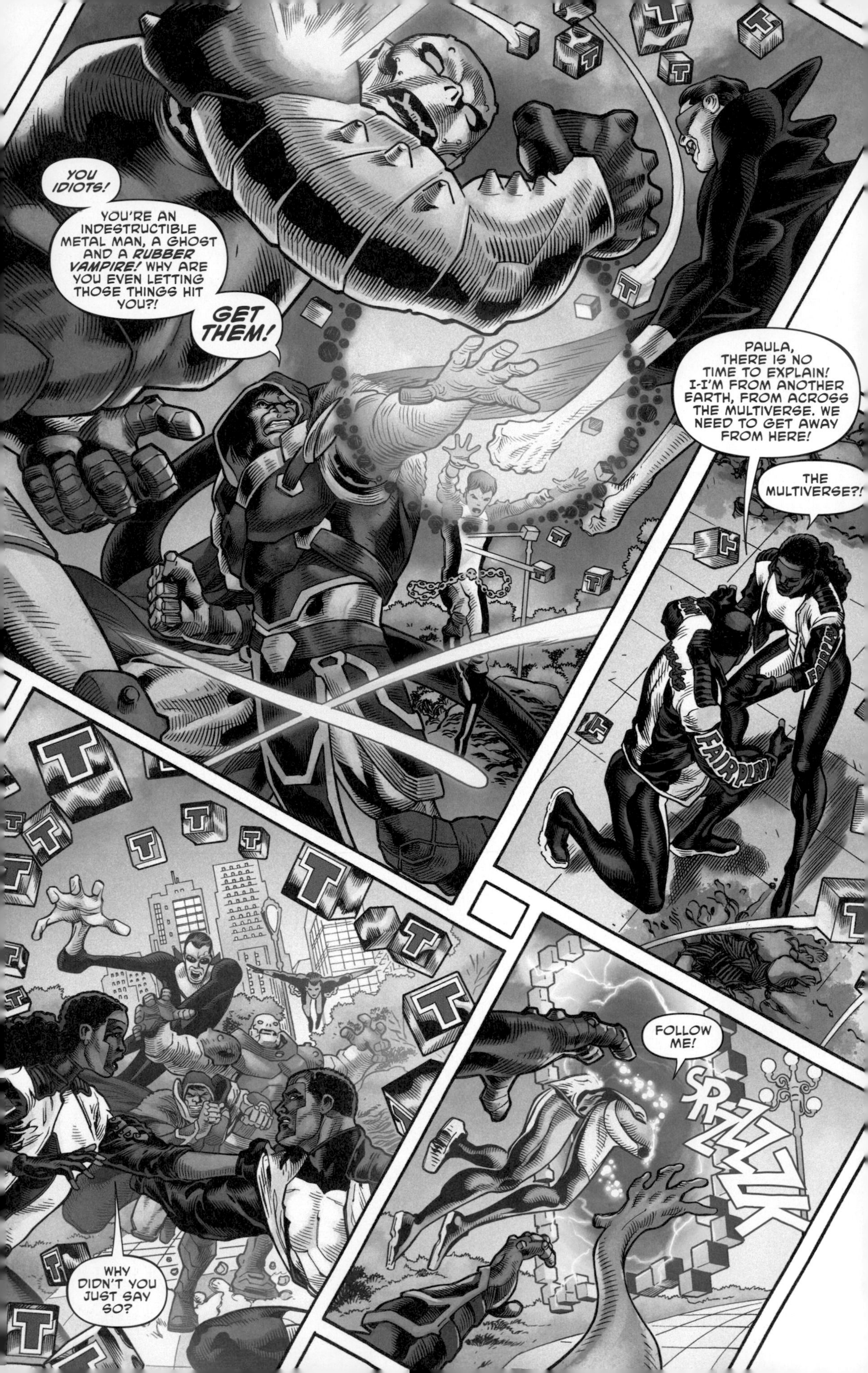
YOU IDIOTS!
YOU'RE AN INDESTRUCTIBLE METAL MAN, A GHOST AND A RUBBER VAMPIRE! WHY ARE YOU EVEN LETTING THOSE THINGS HIT YOU?!
GET THEM!
PAULA, THERE IS NO TIME TO EXPLAIN! I-I'M FROM ANOTHER EARTH, FROM ACROSS THE MULTIVERSE. WE NEED TO GET AWAY FROM HERE!
THE MULTIVERSE?!
FAIRPLAY
WHY DIDN'T YOU JUST SAY SO?
FOLLOW ME!
SRZZZK

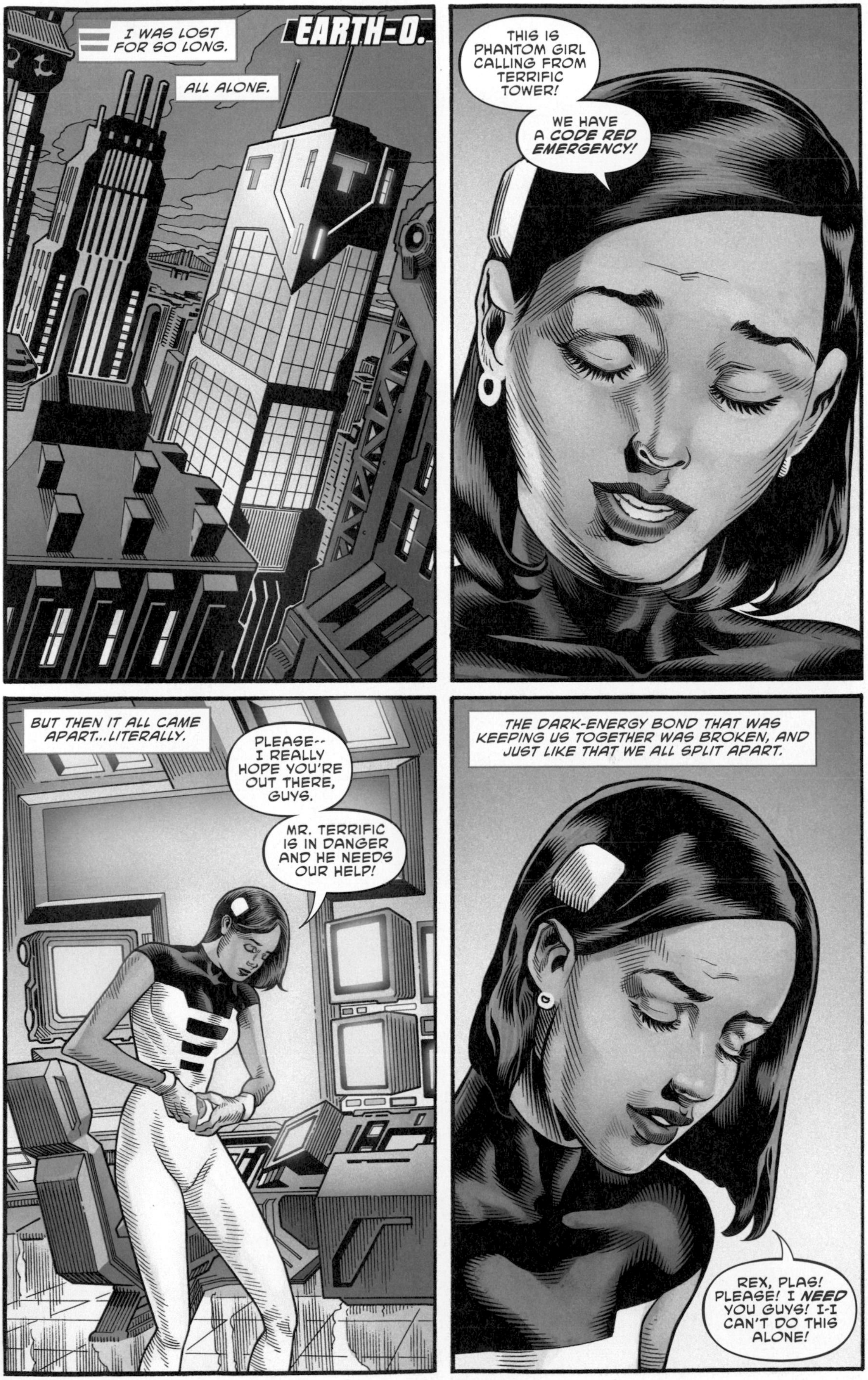
EARTH-0.
I WAS LOST FOR SO LONG.
ALL ALONE.
THIS IS PHANTOM GIRL CALLING FROM TERRIFIC TOWER!
WE HAVE A CODE RED EMERGENCY!
BUT THEN IT ALL CAME APART...LITERALLY.
PLEASE-- I REALLY HOPE YOU'RE OUT THERE, GUYS.
MR. TERRIFIC IS IN DANGER AND HE NEEDS OUR HELP!
THE DARK-ENERGY BOND THAT WAS KEEPING US TOGETHER WAS BROKEN, AND JUST LIKE THAT WE ALL SPLIT APART.
REX, PLAS! PLEASE! I NEED YOU GUYS! I-I CAN'T DO THIS ALONE!

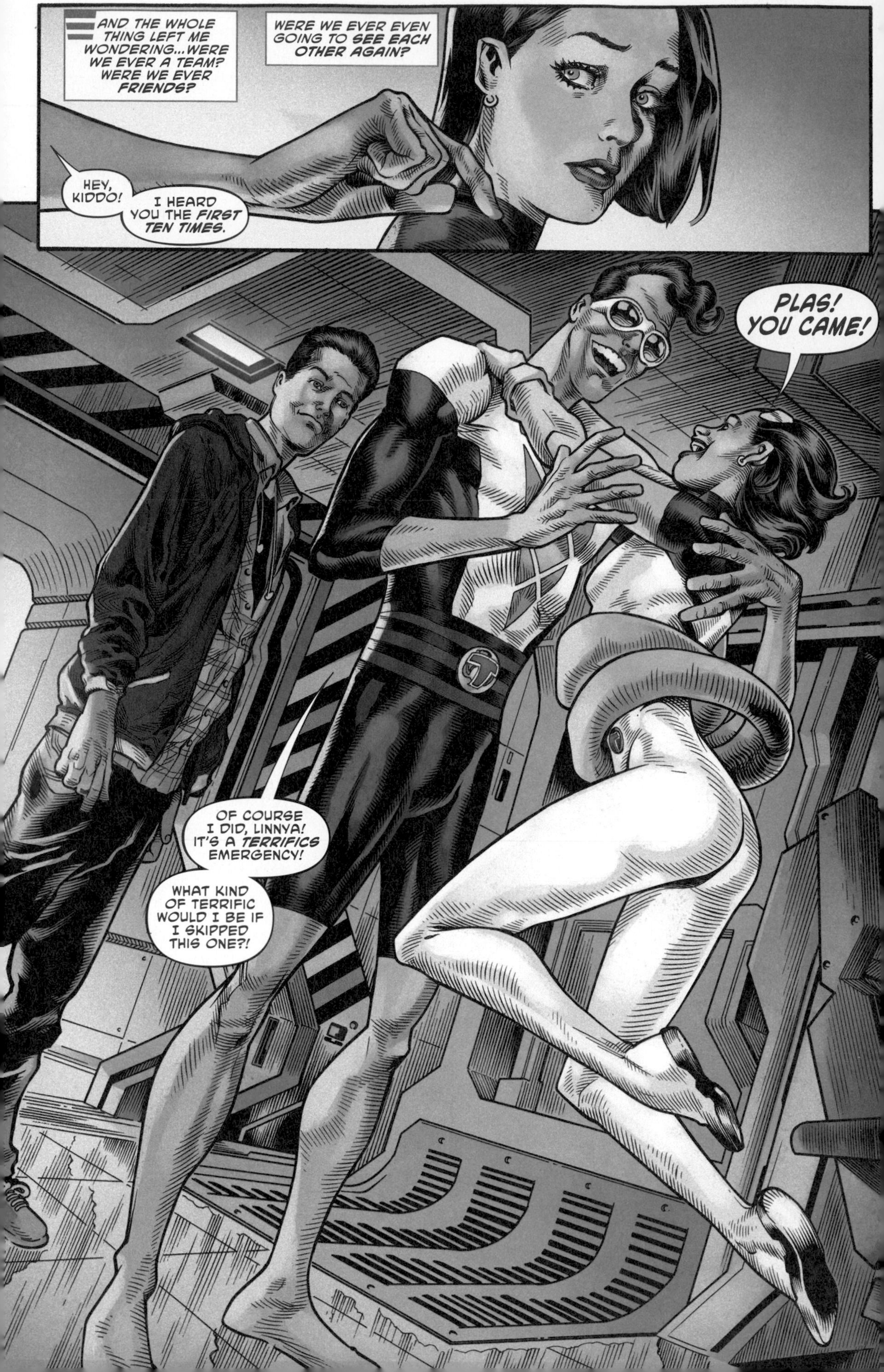
AND THE WHOLE THING LEFT ME WONDERING...WERE WE EVER A TEAM? WERE WE EVER FRIENDS?
WERE WE EVER EVEN GOING TO SEE EACH OTHER AGAIN?
HEY, KIDDO!
I HEARD YOU THE FIRST TEN TIMES.
PLAS! YOU CAME!
OF COURSE I DID, LINNYA! IT'S A TERRIFICS EMERGENCY!
WHAT KIND OF TERRIFIC WOULD I BE IF I SKIPPED THIS ONE?!

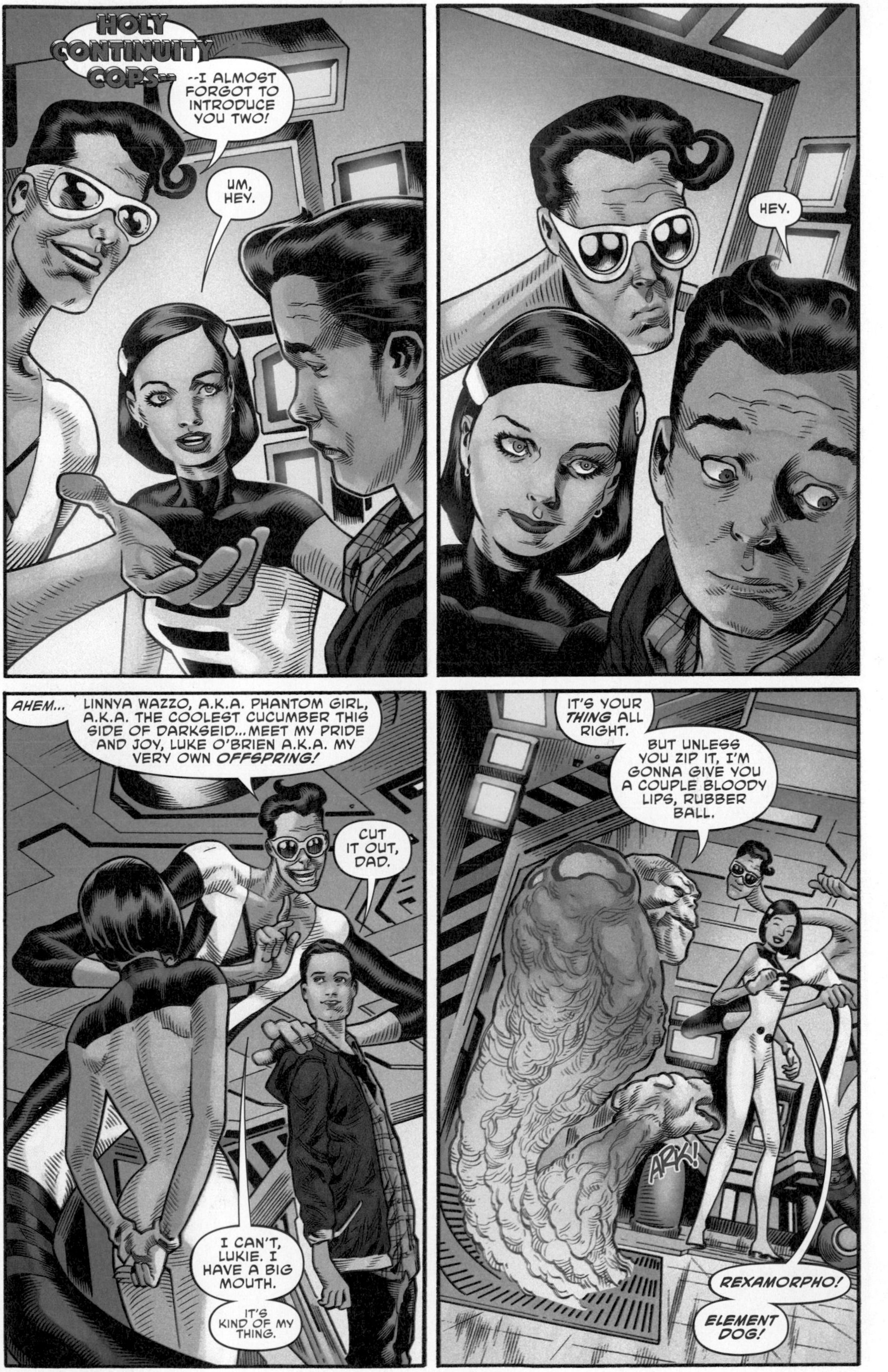
HOLY CONTINUITY COPS--
--I ALMOST FORGOT TO INTRODUCE YOU TWO!
UM, HEY.
HEY.
AHEM...
LINNYA WAZZO, A.K.A. PHANTOM GIRL, A.K.A. THE COOLEST CUCUMBER THIS SIDE OF DARKSEID...MEET MY PRIDE AND JOY, LUKE O'BRIEN A.K.A. MY VERY OWN OFFSPRING!
CUT IT OUT, DAD.
I CAN'T, LUKIE. I HAVE A BIG MOUTH.
IT'S KIND OF MY THING.
IT'S YOUR THING ALL RIGHT.
BUT UNLESS YOU ZIP IT, I'M GONNA GIVE YOU A COUPLE BLOODY LIPS, RUBBER BALL.
ARK!
REXAMORPHO!
ELEMENT DOG!

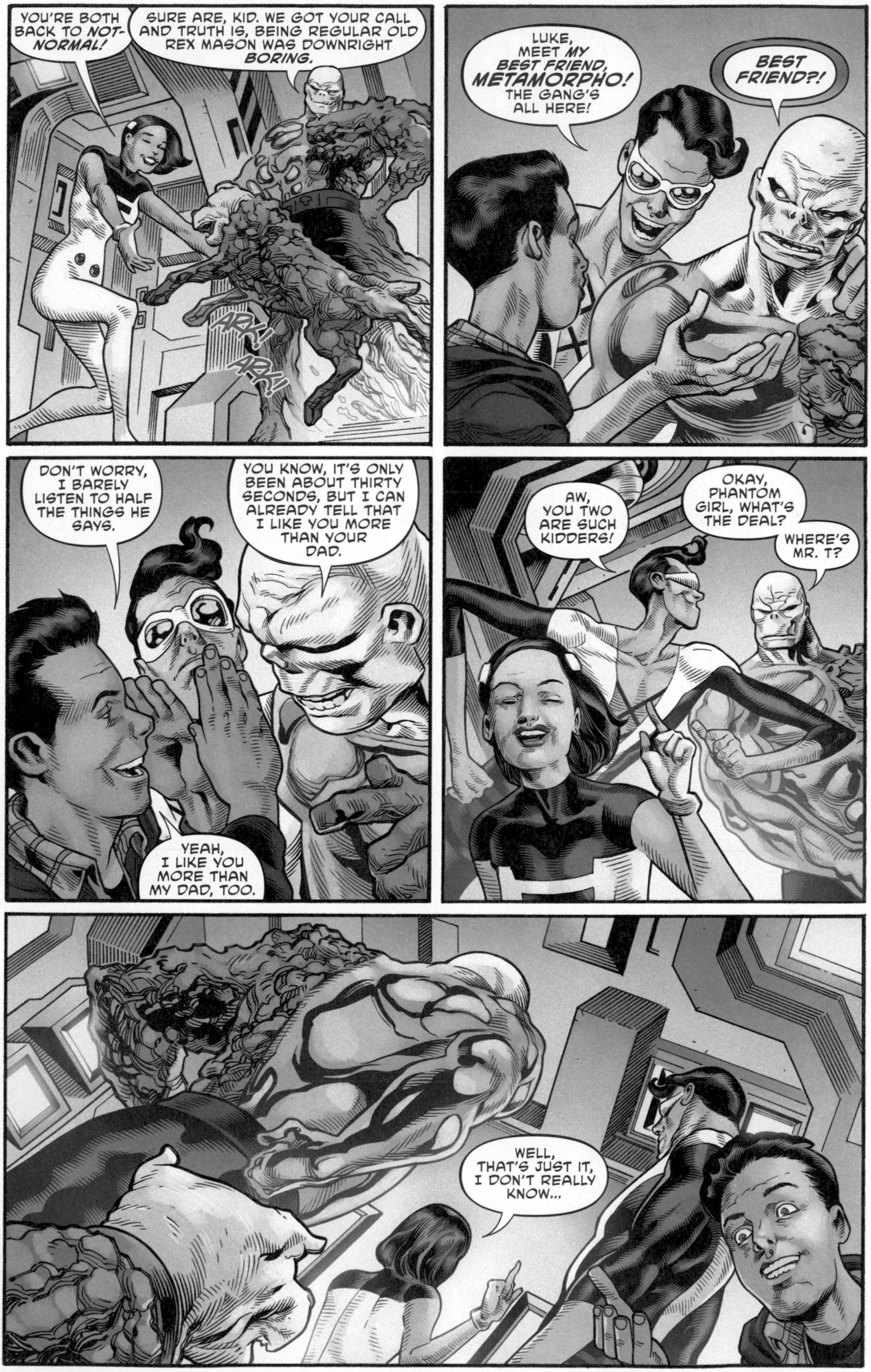
YOU'RE BOTH BACK TO NOT-NORMAL!
SURE ARE, KID. WE GOT YOUR CALL AND TRUTH IS, BEING REGULAR OLD REX MASON WAS DOWNRIGHT BORING.
ARK! ARK!
LUKE, MEET MY BEST FRIEND, METAMORPHO! THE GANG'S ALL HERE!
BEST FRIEND?!
DON'T WORRY, I BARELY LISTEN TO HALF THE THINGS HE SAYS.
YOU KNOW, IT'S ONLY BEEN ABOUT THIRTY SECONDS, BUT I CAN ALREADY TELL THAT I LIKE YOU MORE THAN YOUR DAD.
YEAH, I LIKE YOU MORE THAN MY DAD, TOO.
AW, YOU TWO ARE SUCH KIDDERS!
OKAY, PHANTOM GIRL, WHAT'S THE DEAL?
WHERE'S MR. T?
WELL, THAT'S JUST IT, I DON'T REALLY KNOW...

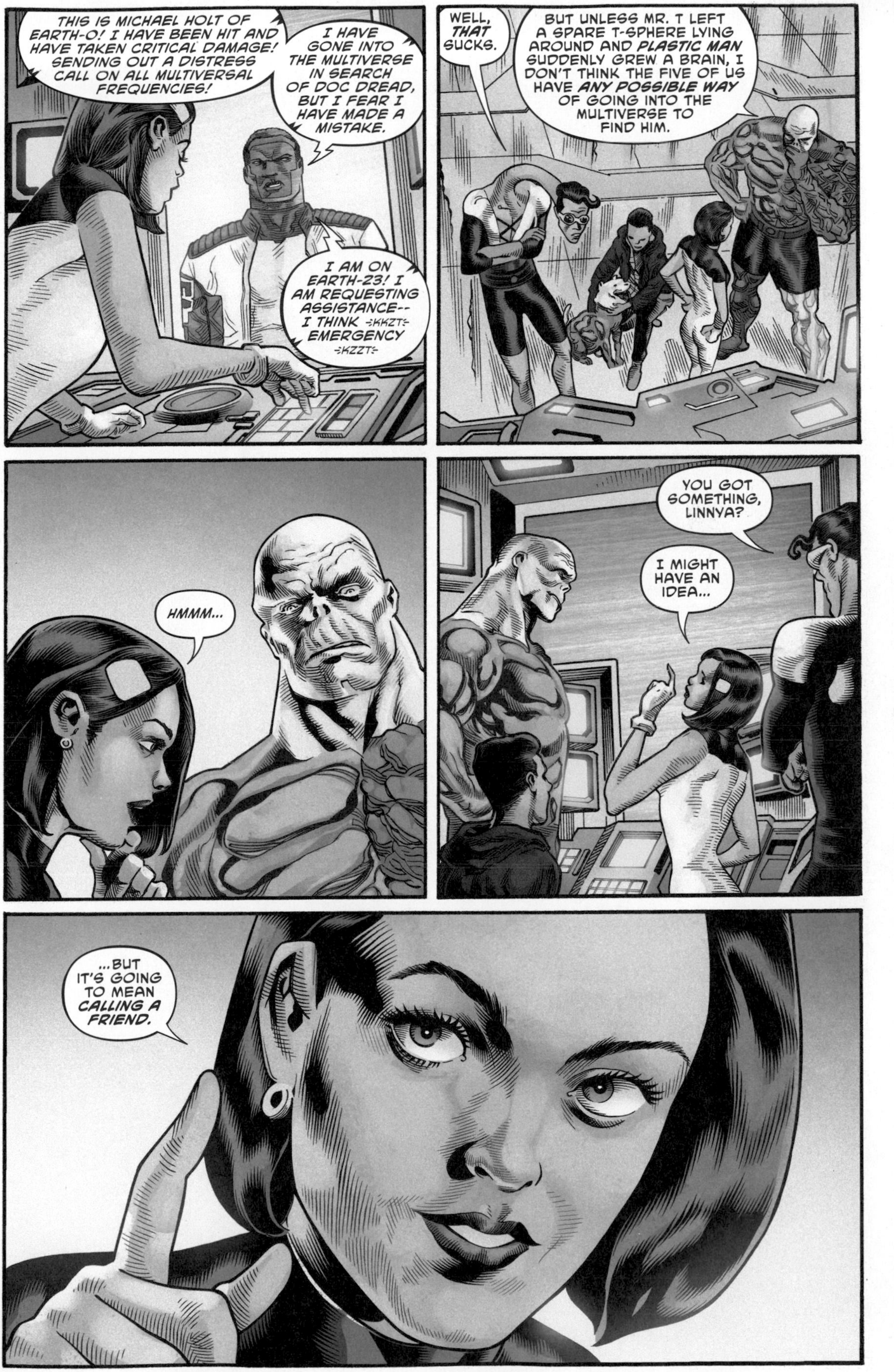
THIS IS MICHAEL HOLT OF EARTH-O! I HAVE BEEN HIT AND HAVE TAKEN CRITICAL DAMAGE! SENDING OUT A DISTRESS CALL ON ALL MULTIVERSAL FREQUENCIES!
I HAVE GONE INTO THE MULTIVERSE IN SEARCH OF DOC DREAD, BUT I FEAR I HAVE MADE A MISTAKE.
I AM ON EARTH-23! I AM REQUESTING ASSISTANCE-- I THINK -KKZT- EMERGENCY -KZZT-
WELL, THAT SUCKS.
BUT UNLESS MR. T LEFT A SPARE T-SPHERE LYING AROUND AND PLASTIC MAN SUDDENLY GREW A BRAIN, I DON'T THINK THE FIVE OF US HAVE ANY POSSIBLE WAY OF GOING INTO THE MULTIVERSE TO FIND HIM.
HMMM...
YOU GOT SOMETHING, LINNYA?
I MIGHT HAVE AN IDEA...
...BUT IT'S GOING TO MEAN CALLING A FRIEND.

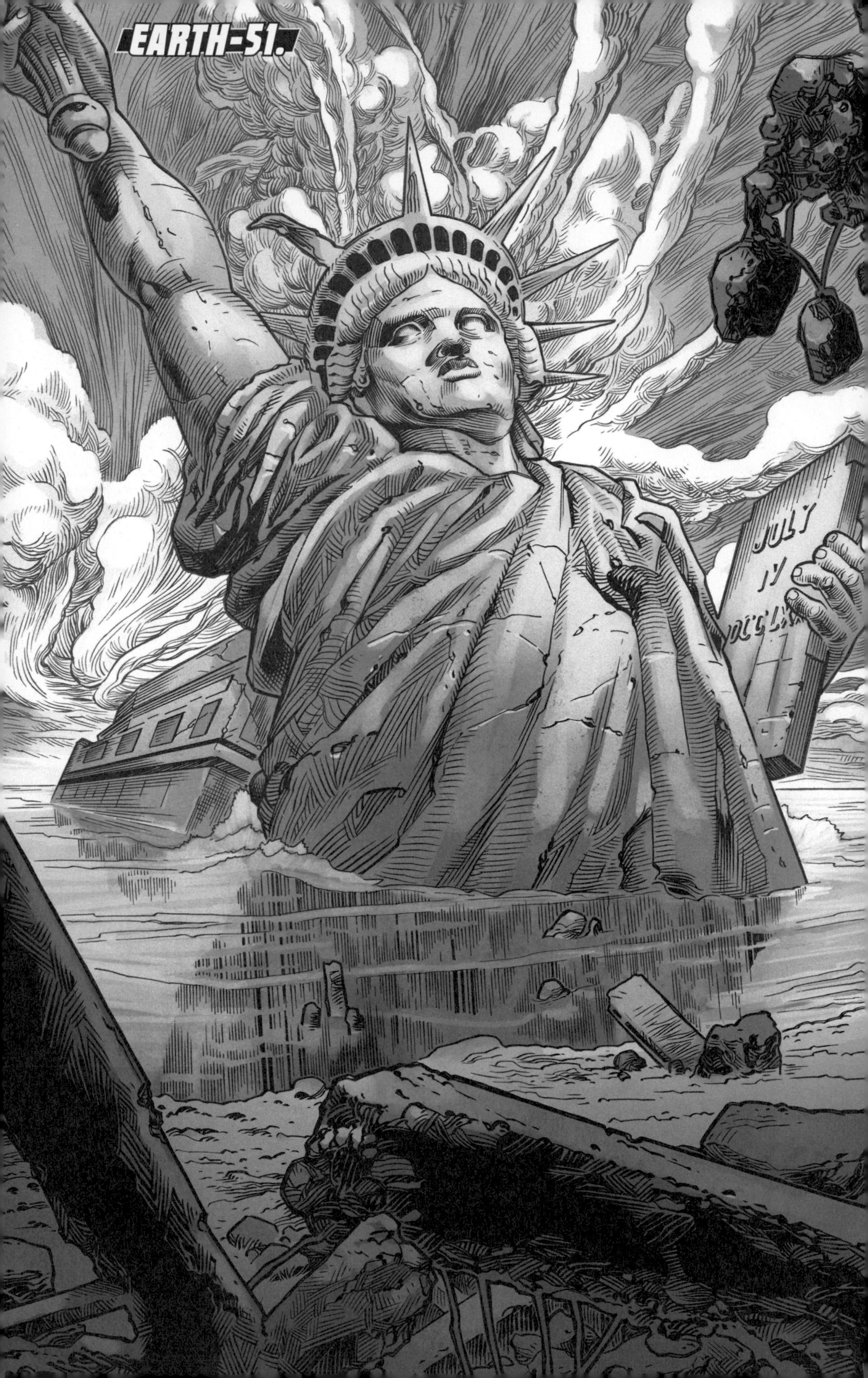
EARTH-51.
JULY
IV

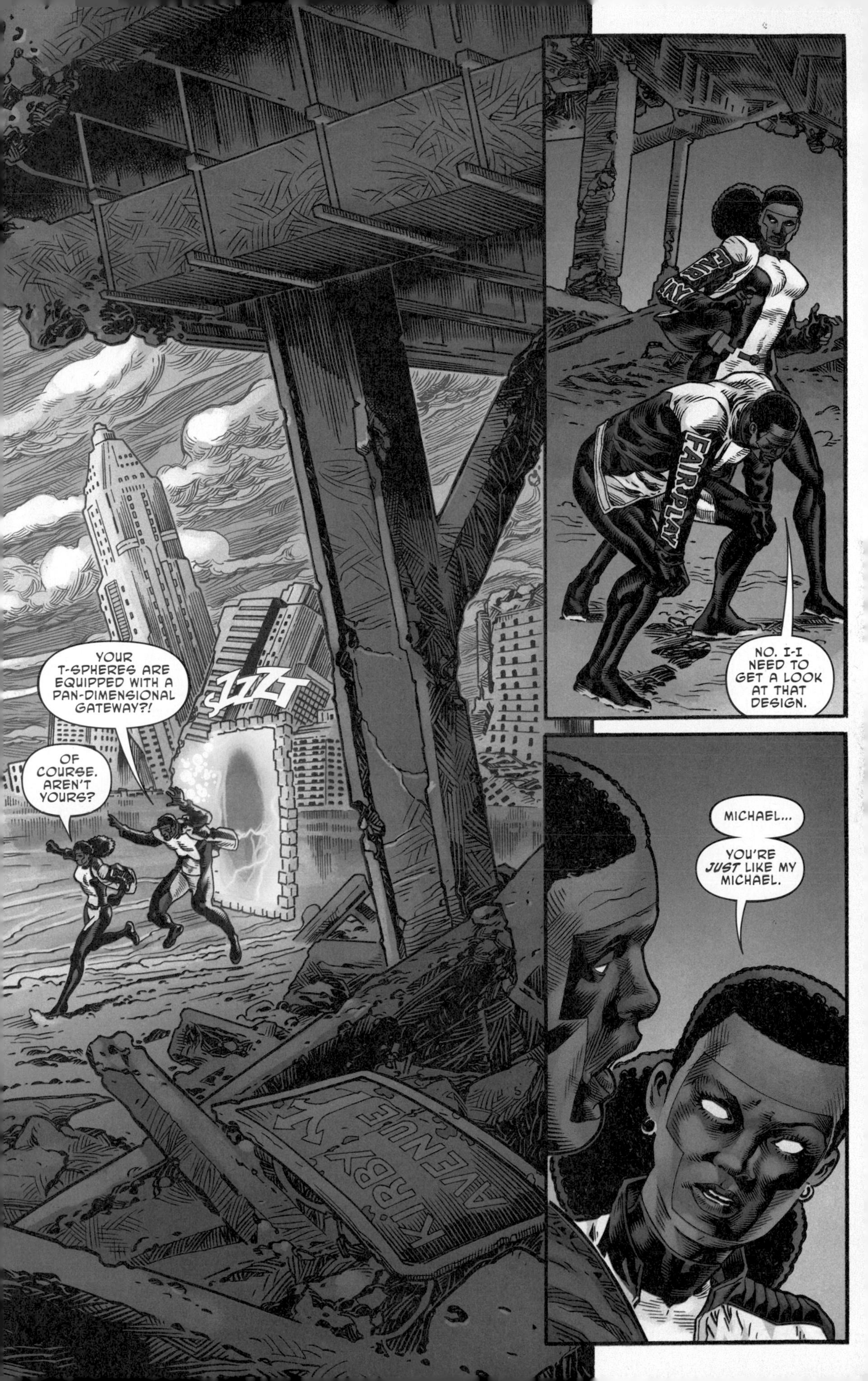
YOUR T-SPHERES ARE EQUIPPED WITH A PAN-DIMENSIONAL GATEWAY?!
SZZZT
OF COURSE. AREN'T YOURS?
KIRBY AVENUE
FAIR PLAY
NO. I-I NEED TO GET A LOOK AT THAT DESIGN.
MICHAEL...
YOU'RE *JUST* LIKE MY MICHAEL.

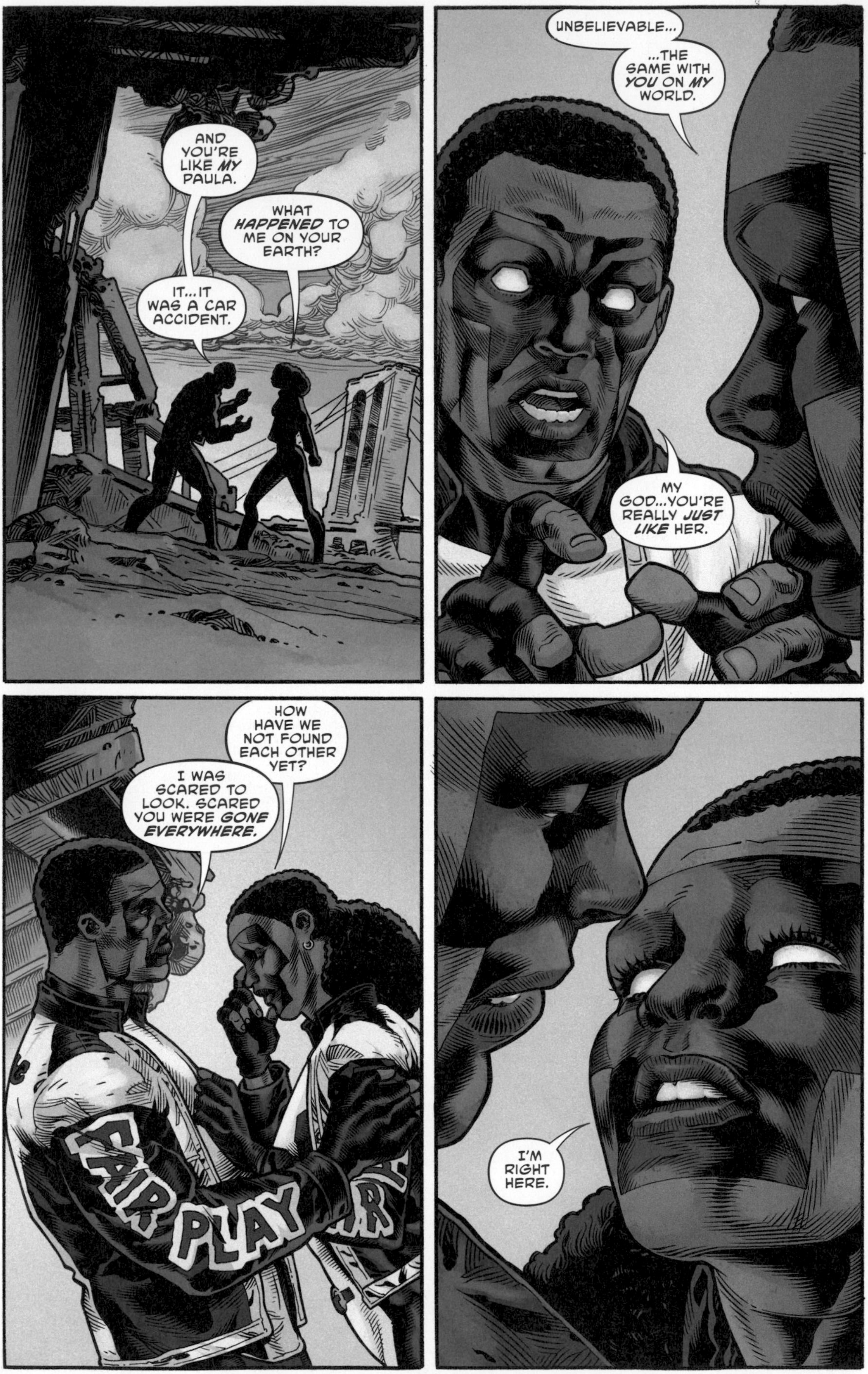
AND YOU'RE LIKE *MY* PAULA.
WHAT *HAPPENED* TO ME ON YOUR EARTH?
IT...IT WAS A CAR ACCIDENT.
UNBELIEVABLE...
...THE SAME WITH *YOU* ON *MY* WORLD.
MY GOD...YOU'RE REALLY *JUST LIKE* HER.
HOW HAVE WE NOT FOUND EACH OTHER YET?
I WAS SCARED TO LOOK. SCARED YOU WERE *GONE EVERYWHERE.*
FAIR PLAY
I'M RIGHT HERE.

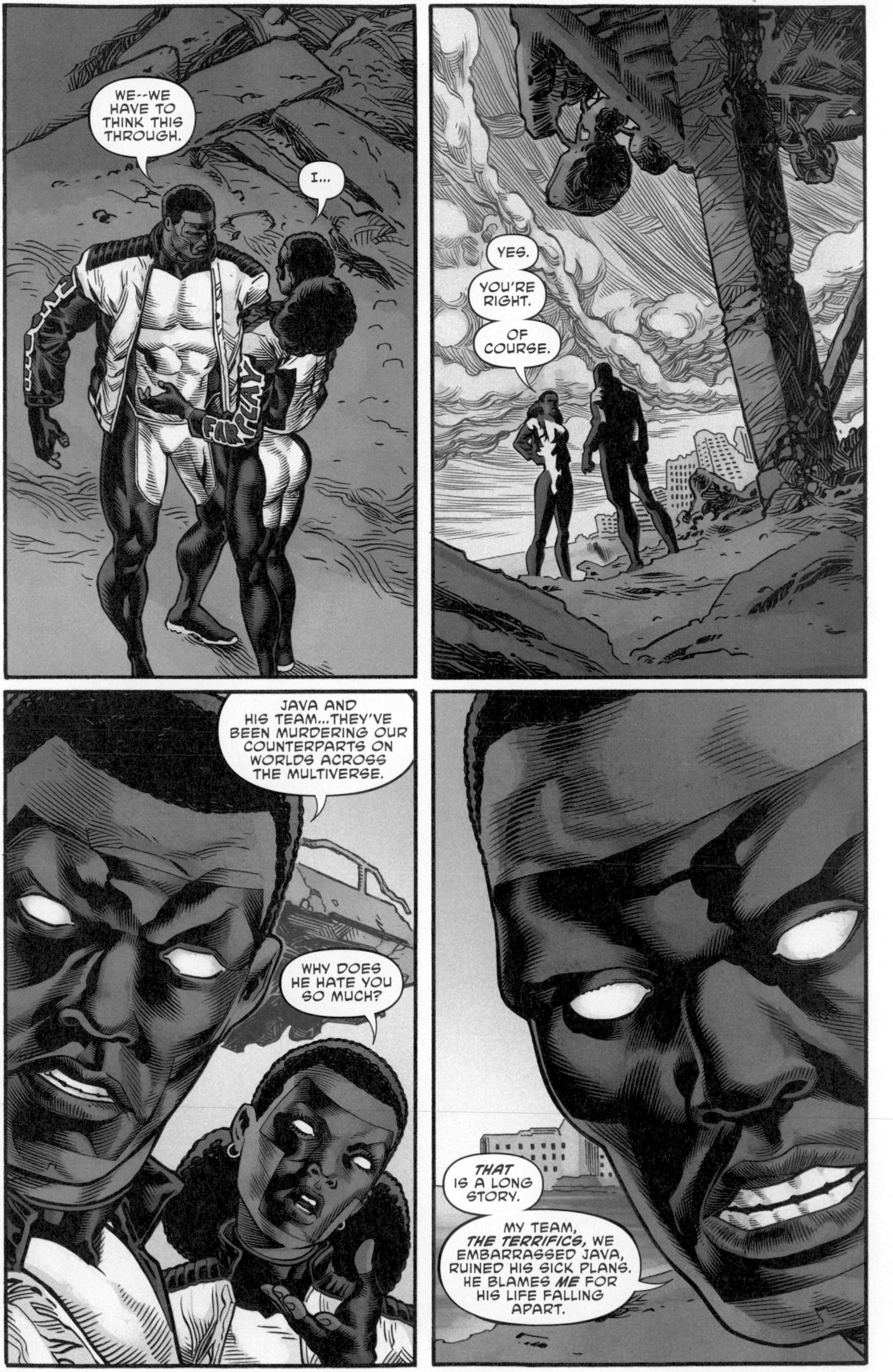
WE--WE HAVE TO THINK THIS THROUGH.
I...
FAIR PLAY
YES.
YOU'RE RIGHT.
OF COURSE.
JAVA AND HIS TEAM...THEY'VE BEEN MURDERING OUR COUNTERPARTS ON WORLDS ACROSS THE MULTIVERSE.
WHY DOES HE HATE YOU SO MUCH?
THAT IS A LONG STORY.
MY TEAM, ***THE TERRIFICS,*** WE EMBARRASSED JAVA, RUINED HIS SICK PLANS. HE BLAMES ***ME*** FOR HIS LIFE FALLING APART.

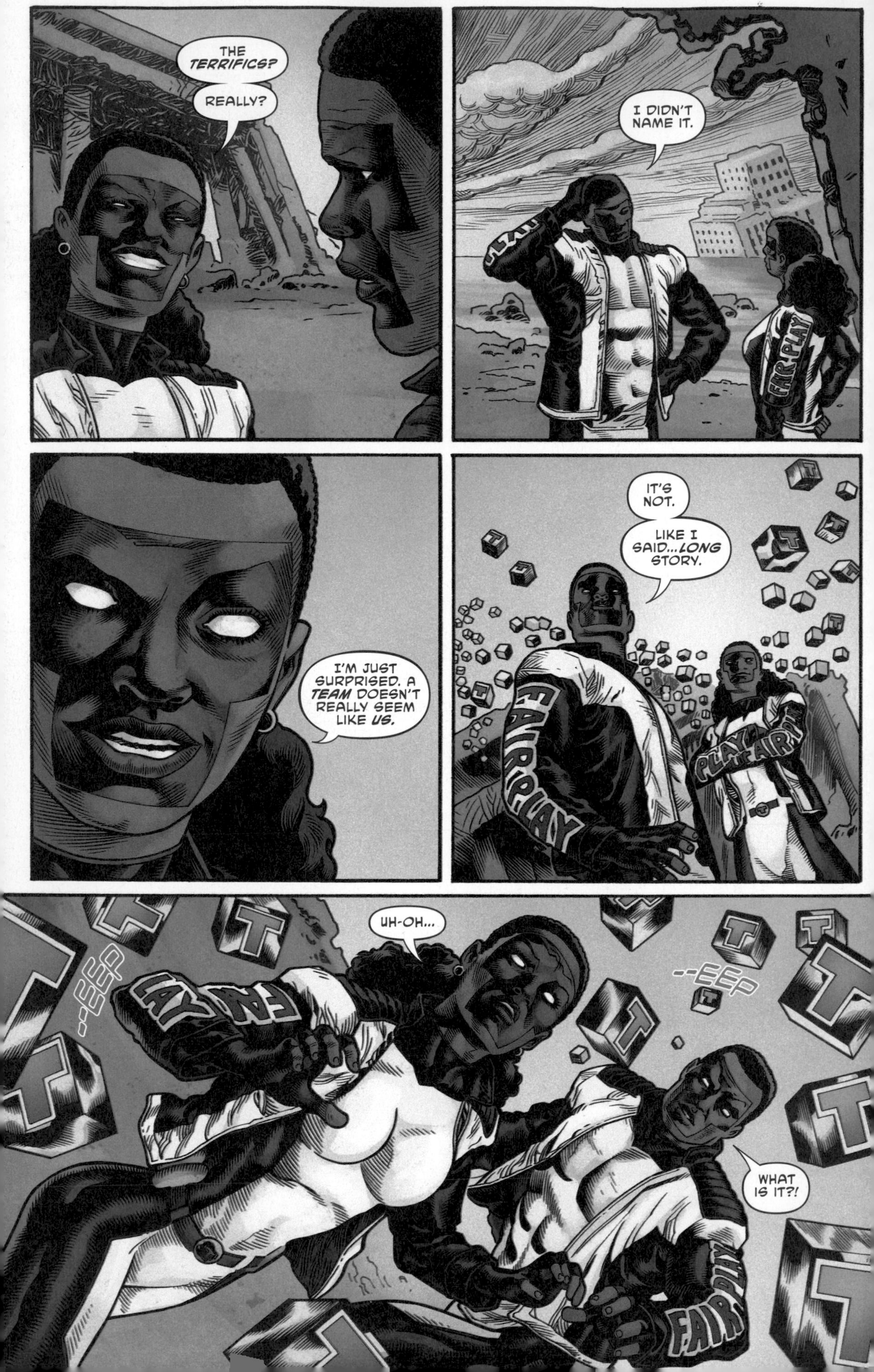
THE TERRIFICS?
REALLY?
I DIDN'T NAME IT.
I'M JUST SURPRISED. A TEAM DOESN'T REALLY SEEM LIKE US.
IT'S NOT.
LIKE I SAID...LONG STORY.
UH-OH...
--EEP
--EEP
WHAT IS IT?!

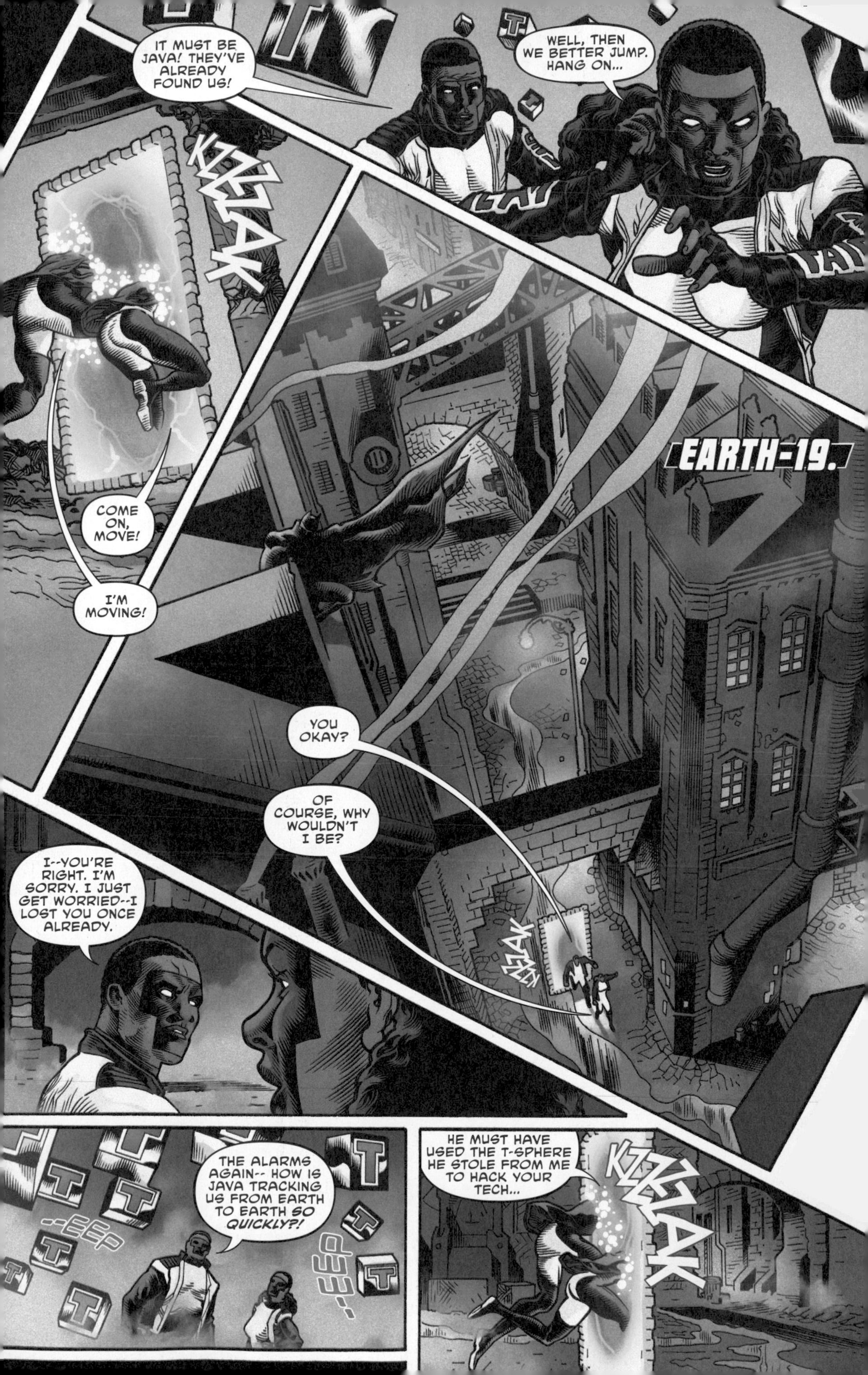
IT MUST BE JAVA! THEY'VE ALREADY FOUND US!
WELL, THEN WE BETTER JUMP. HANG ON...
KZZZAK
COME ON, MOVE!
I'M MOVING!
EARTH-19.
YOU OKAY?
OF COURSE, WHY WOULDN'T I BE?
KZZZAK
I--YOU'RE RIGHT. I'M SORRY. I JUST GET WORRIED--I LOST YOU ONCE ALREADY.
--EEP
THE ALARMS AGAIN-- HOW IS JAVA TRACKING US FROM EARTH TO EARTH SO QUICKLY?!
EEP--
HE MUST HAVE USED THE T-SPHERE HE STOLE FROM ME TO HACK YOUR TECH...
KZZZAK

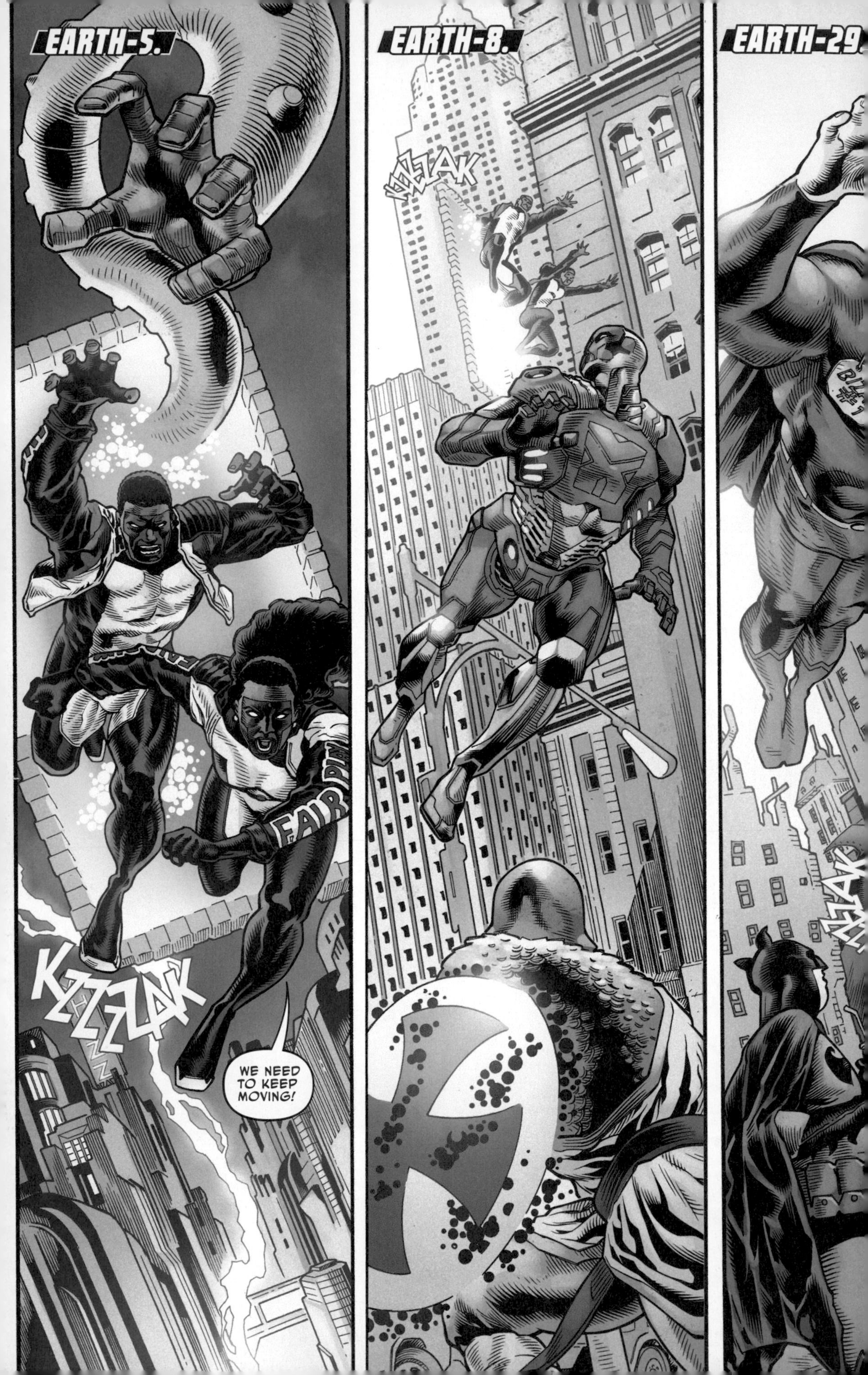
EARTH-5.
WE NEED TO KEEP MOVING!
EARTH-8.
EARTH-29.

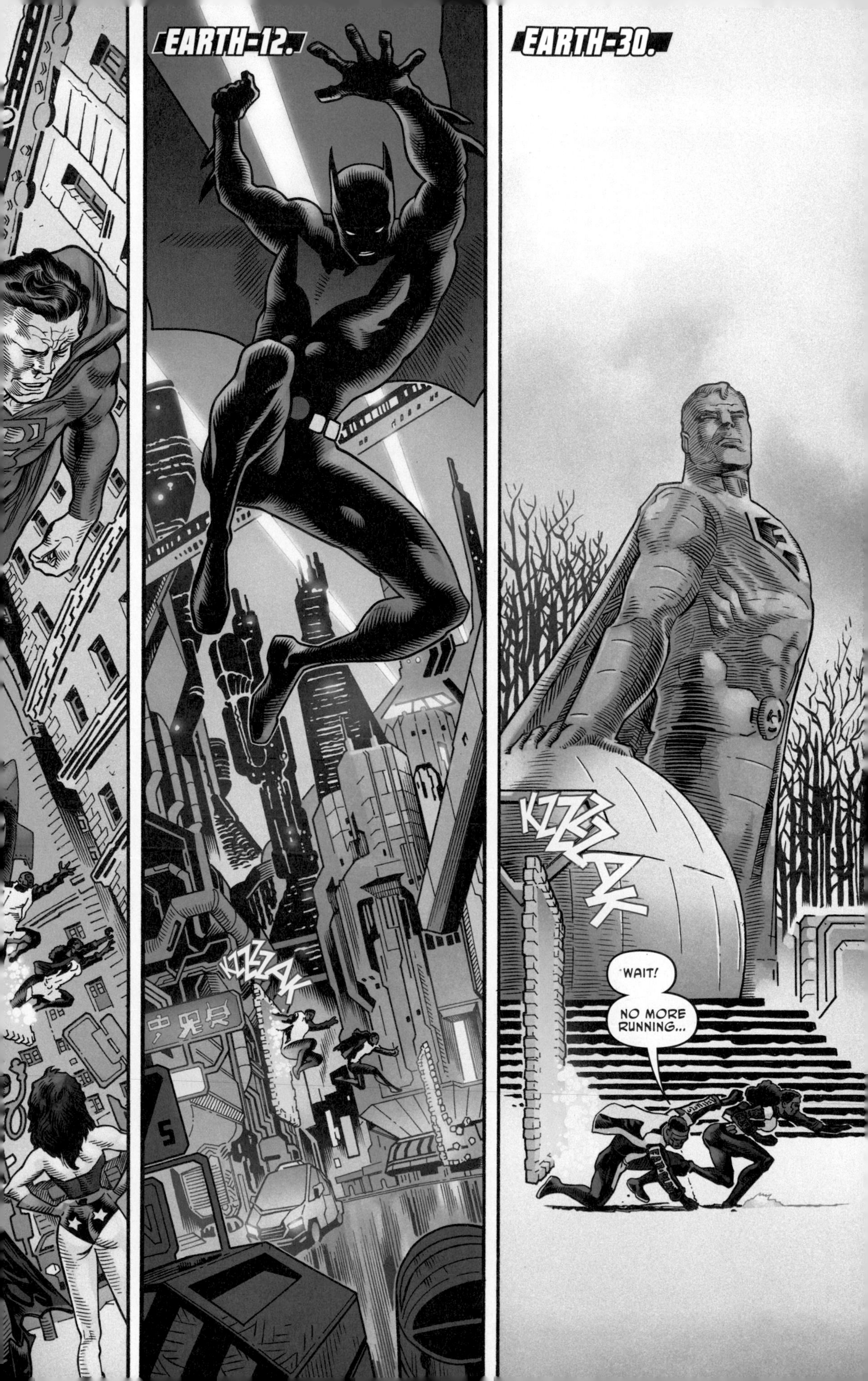
EARTH-12.
KZZZZAK
EARTH-30.
KZZZZAK
WAIT!
NO MORE RUNNING...

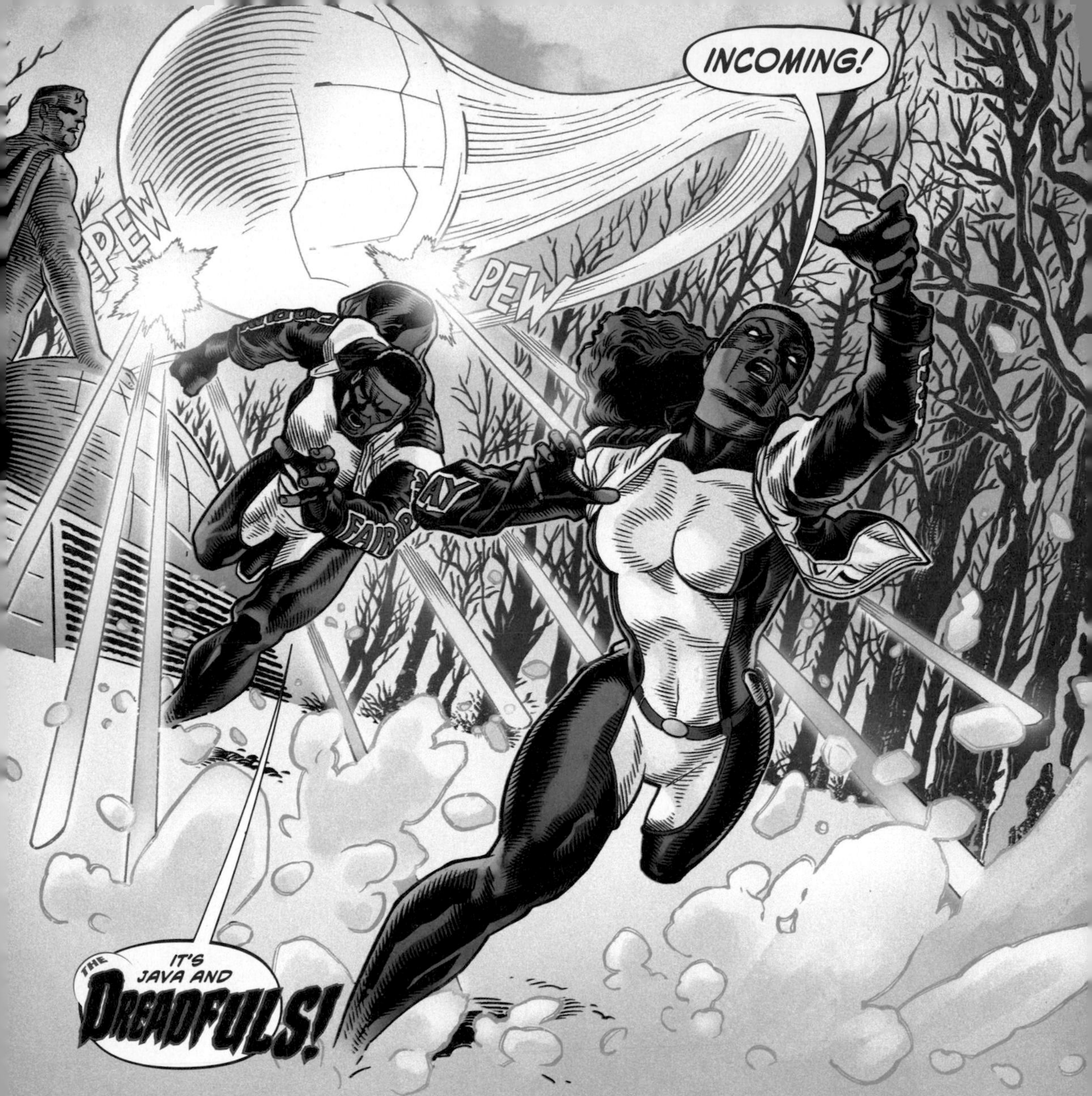
INCOMING!
PEW
PEW
THE IT'S JAVA AND DREADFULS!

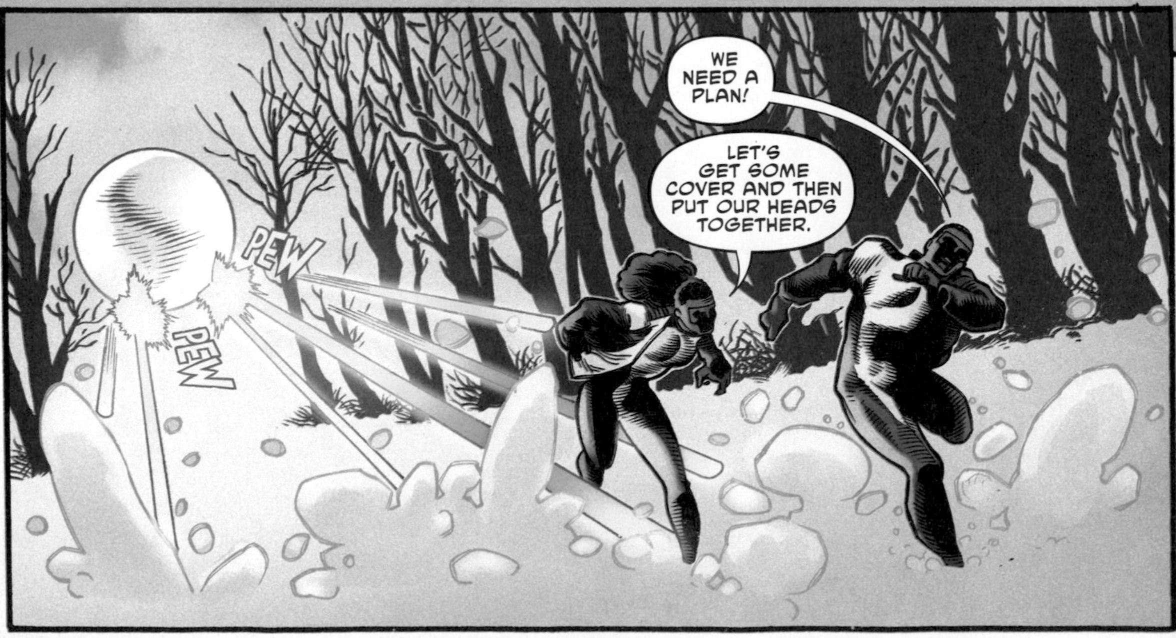
WE NEED A PLAN!
LET'S GET SOME COVER AND THEN PUT OUR HEADS TOGETHER.
PEW
PEW

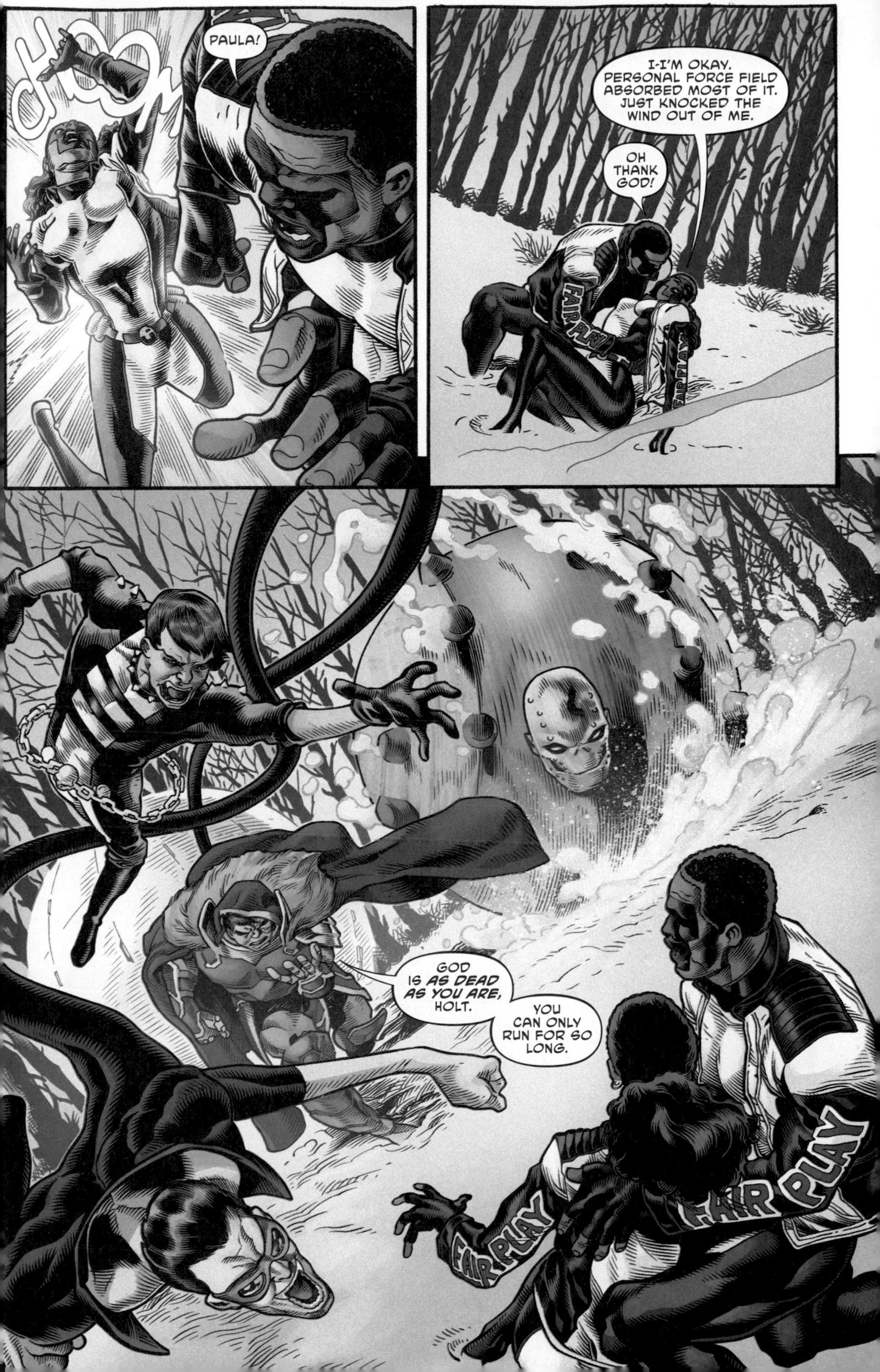CHOOM
PAULA!
I-I'M OKAY. PERSONAL FORCE FIELD ABSORBED MOST OF IT. JUST KNOCKED THE WIND OUT OF ME.
OH THANK GOD!
FAIR PLAY
GOD IS AS DEAD AS YOU ARE, HOLT.
YOU CAN ONLY RUN FOR SO LONG.
FAIR PLAY

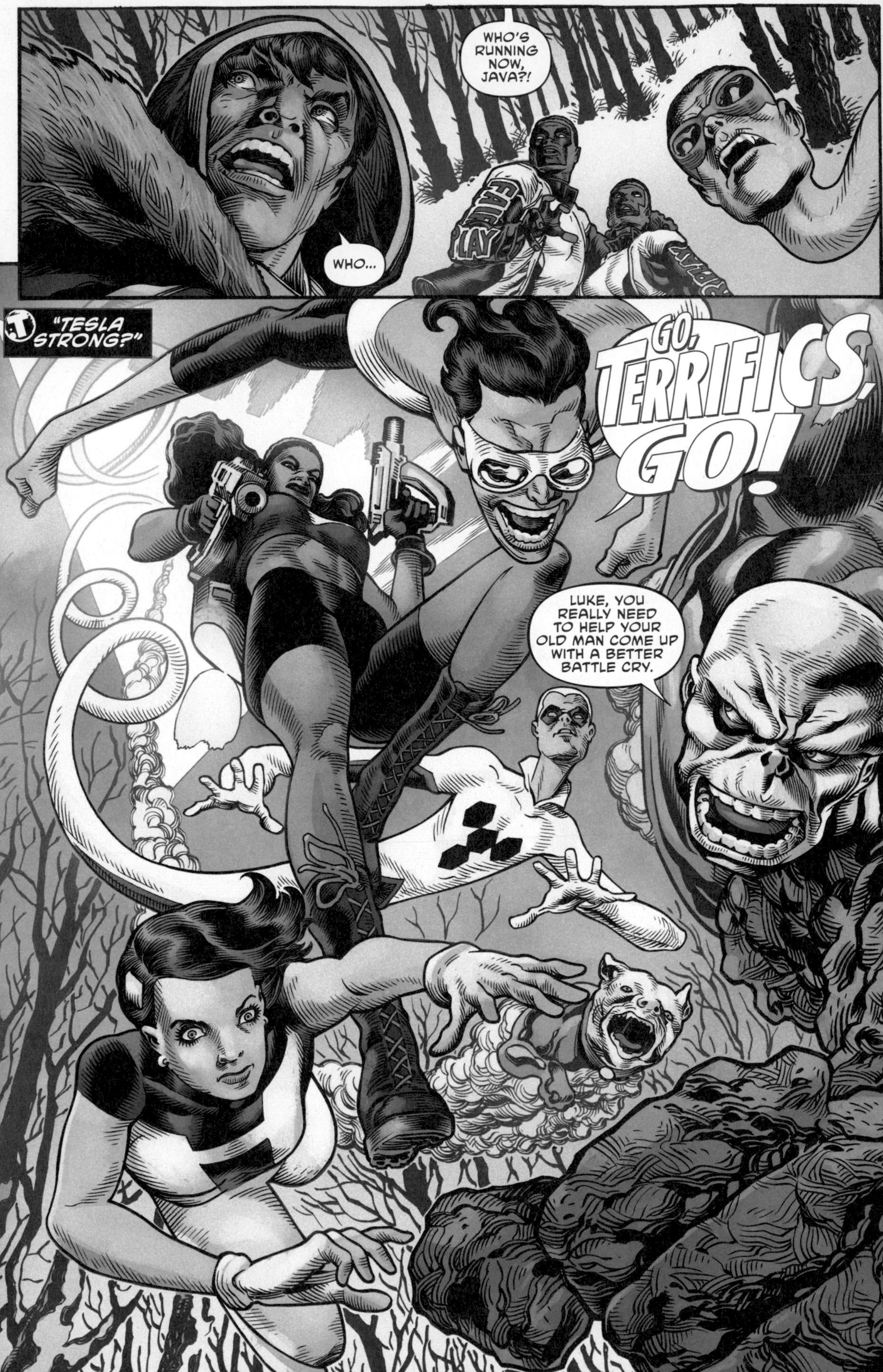
WHO'S RUNNING NOW, JAVA?!
WHO...
FAIR PLAY
"TESLA STRONG?"
GO, TERRIFICS, GO!
LUKE, YOU REALLY NEED TO HELP YOUR OLD MAN COME UP WITH A BETTER BATTLE CRY.

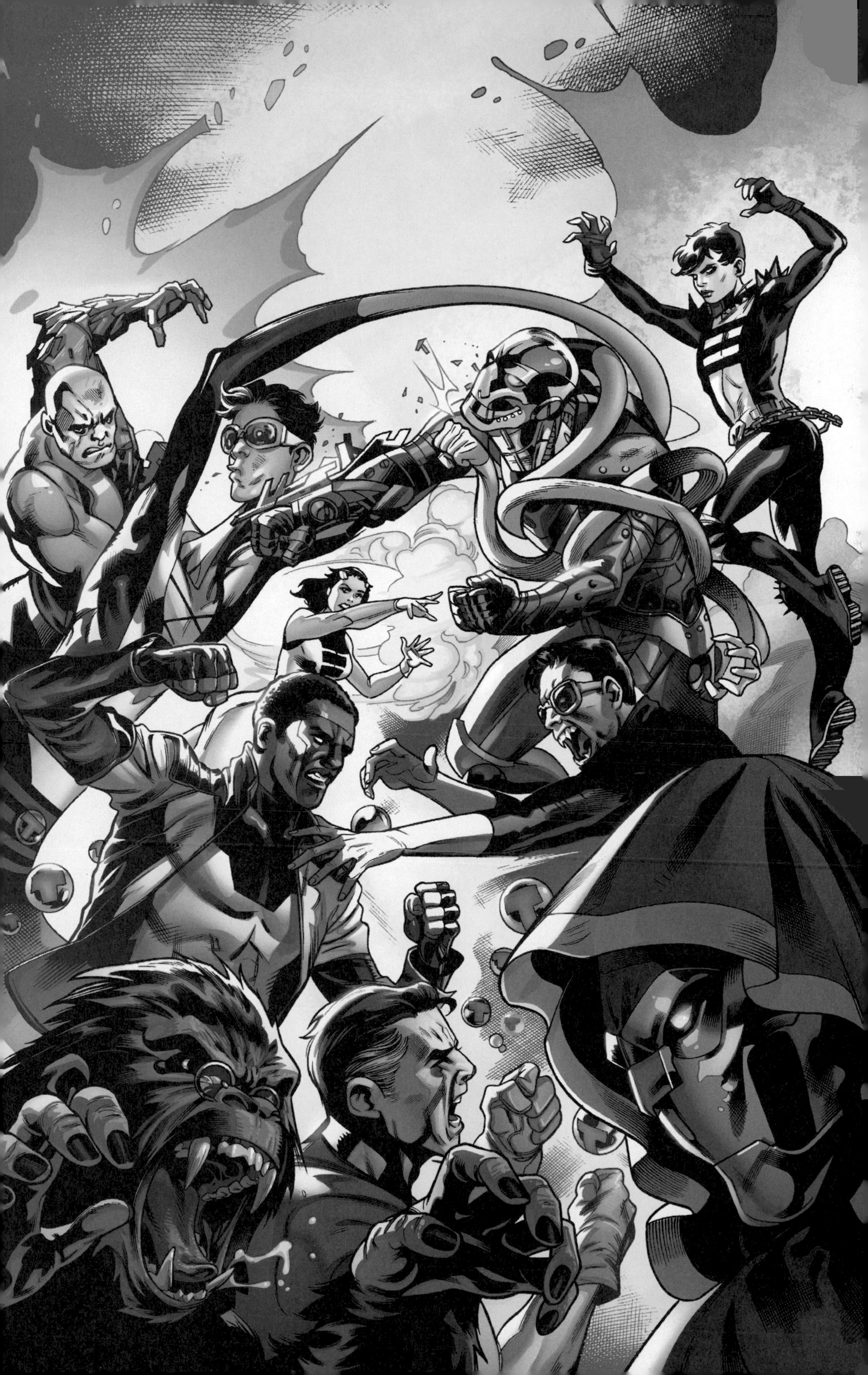

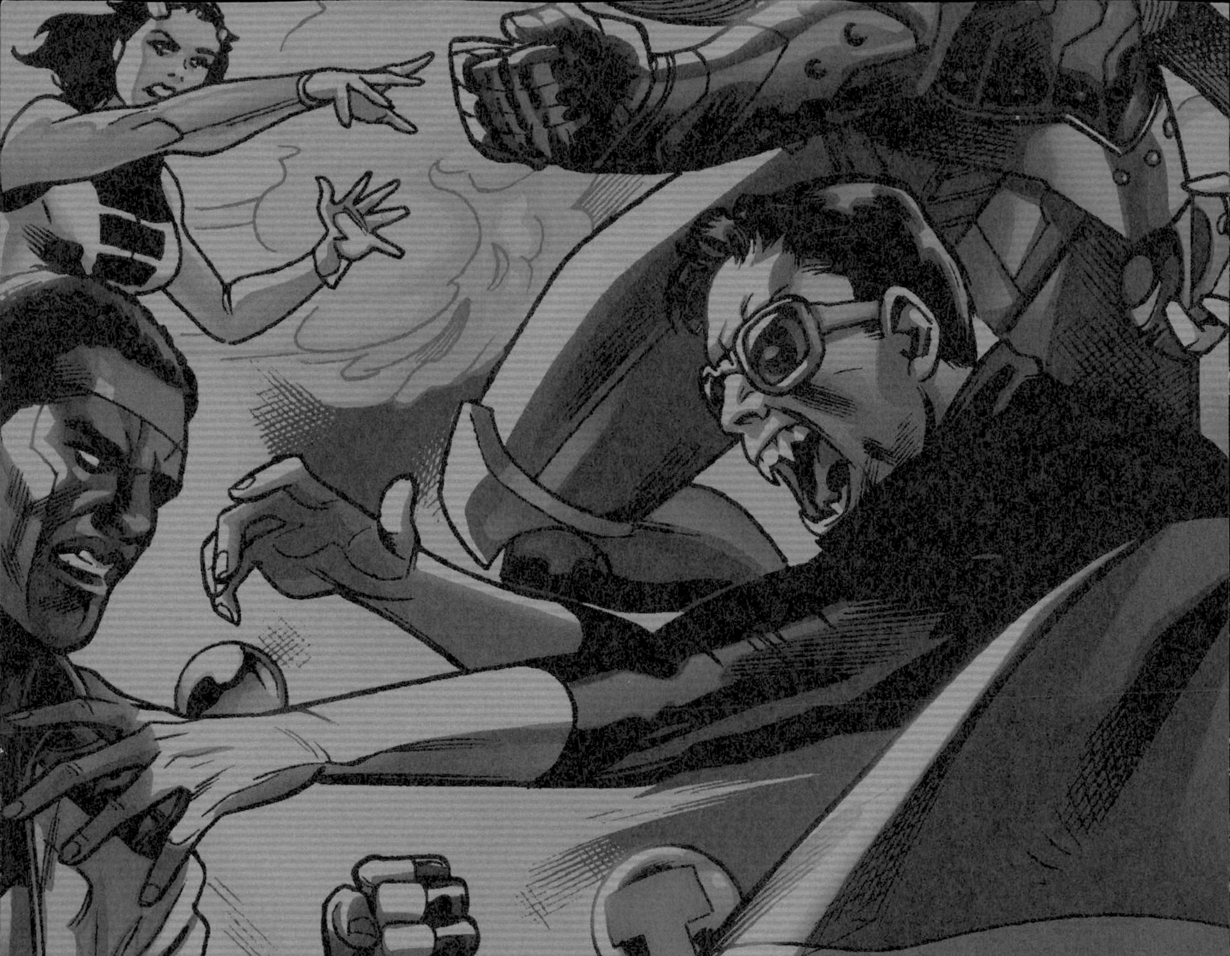

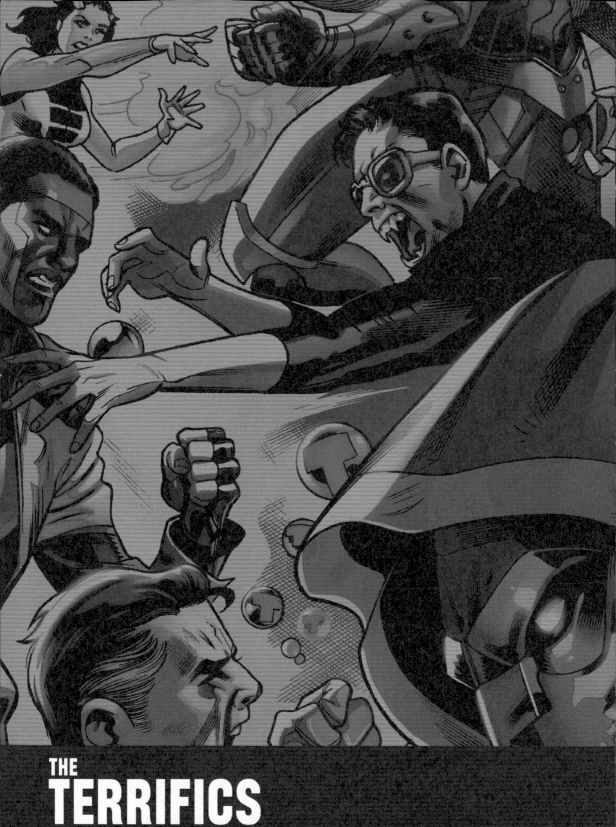

THE TERRIFICS

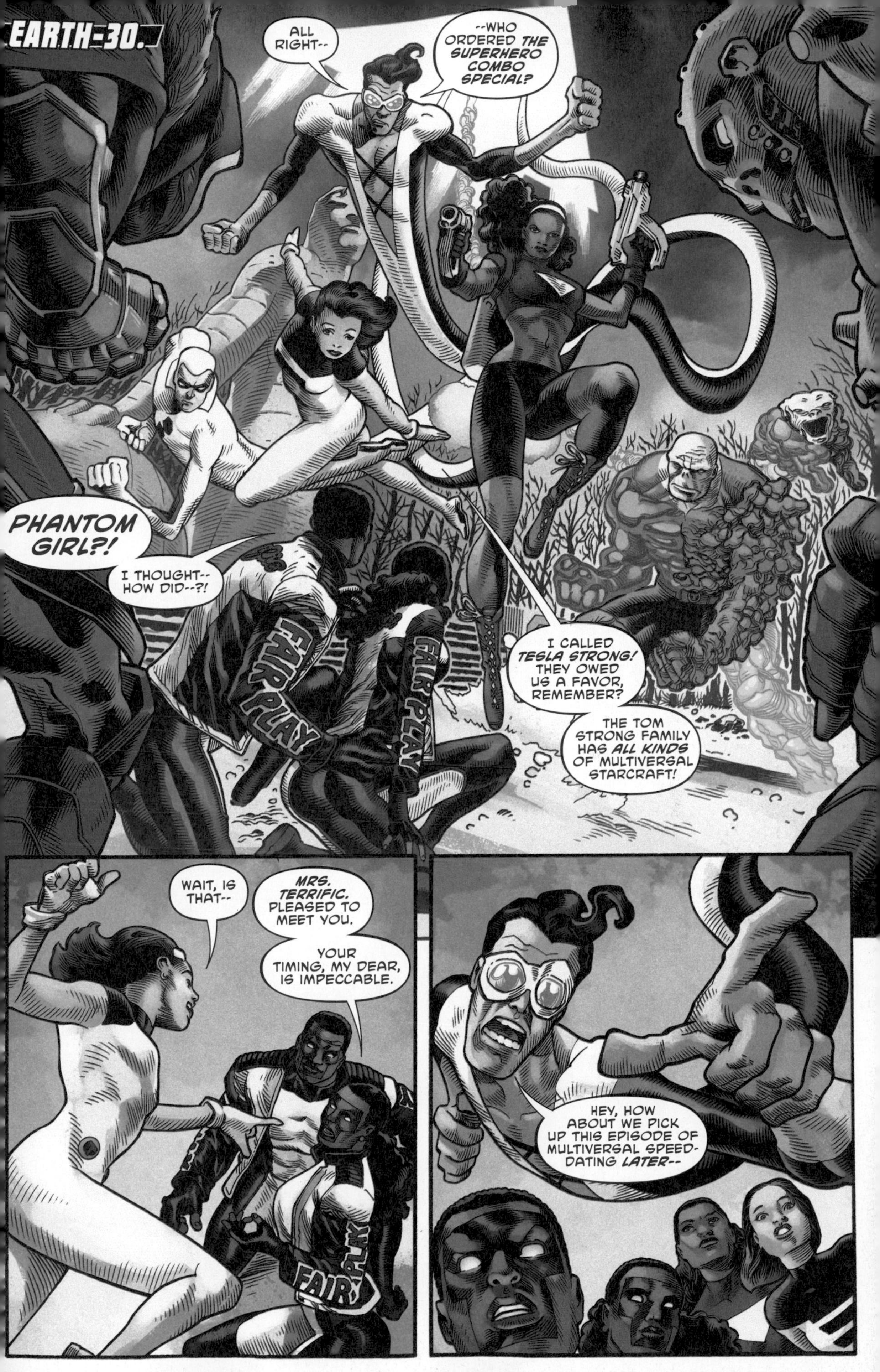
EARTH-30.
ALL RIGHT--
--WHO ORDERED THE SUPERHERO COMBO SPECIAL?
PHANTOM GIRL?!
I THOUGHT-- HOW DID--?!
I CALLED TESLA STRONG! THEY OWED US A FAVOR, REMEMBER?
THE TOM STRONG FAMILY HAS ALL KINDS OF MULTIVERSAL STARCRAFT!
FAIR PLAY
FAIR PLAY
WAIT, IS THAT--
MRS. TERRIFIC. PLEASED TO MEET YOU.
YOUR TIMING, MY DEAR, IS IMPECCABLE.
FAIR PLAY
HEY, HOW ABOUT WE PICK UP THIS EPISODE OF MULTIVERSAL SPEED-DATING LATER--

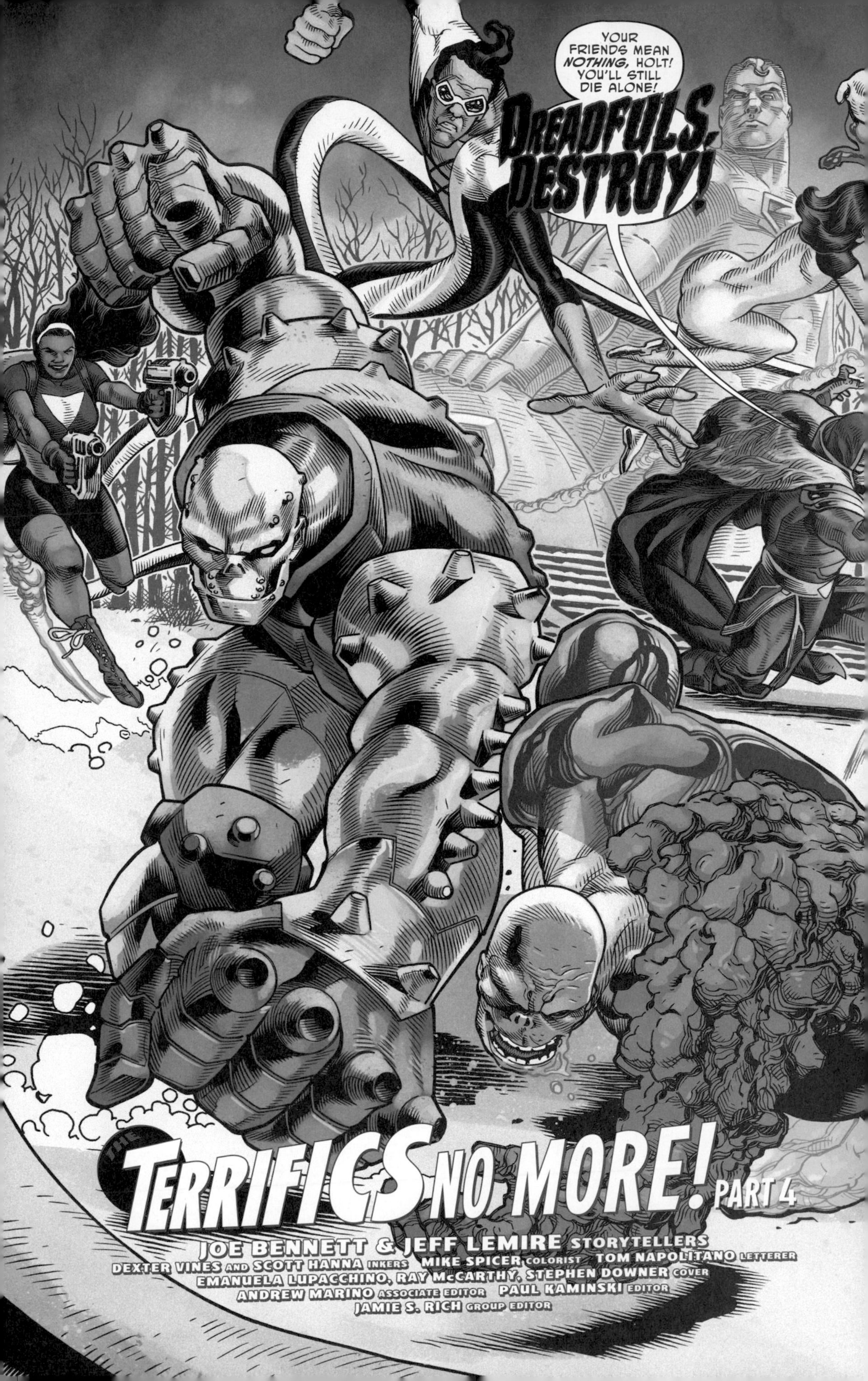

YOUR FRIENDS MEAN NOTHING, HOLT! YOU'LL STILL DIE ALONE!
DREADFULS, DESTROY!
THE TERRIFICS NO MORE! PART 4
JOE BENNETT & JEFF LEMIRE STORYTELLERS
DEXTER VINES AND SCOTT HANNA INKERS MIKE SPICER COLORIST TOM NAPOLITANO LETTERER
EMANUELA LUPACCHINO, RAY McCARTHY, STEPHEN DOWNER COVER
ANDREW MARINO ASSOCIATE EDITOR PAUL KAMINSKI EDITOR
JAMIE S. RICH GROUP EDITOR

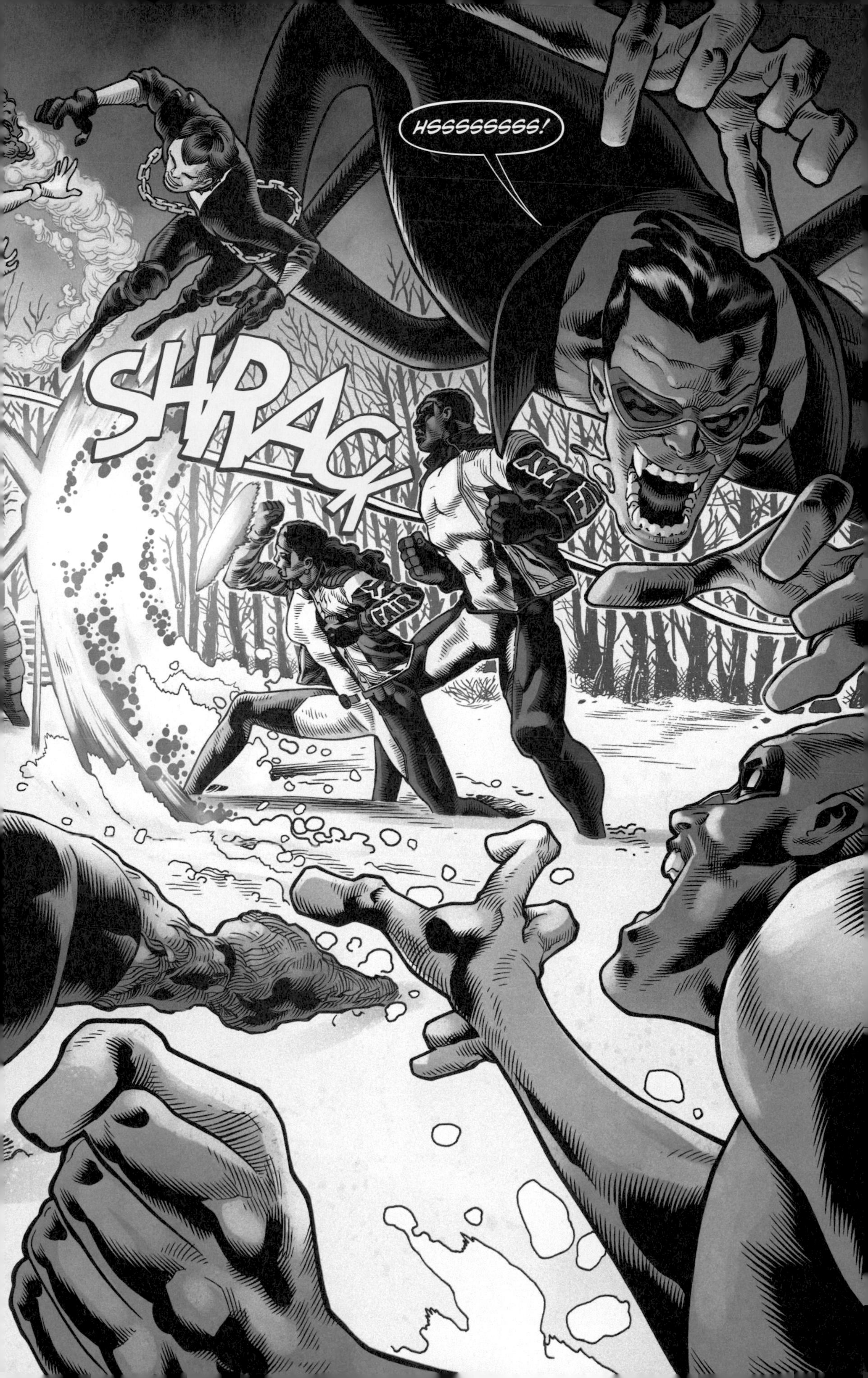
HSSSSSSSS!
SHRACK
NY FAIR
NY FAIR

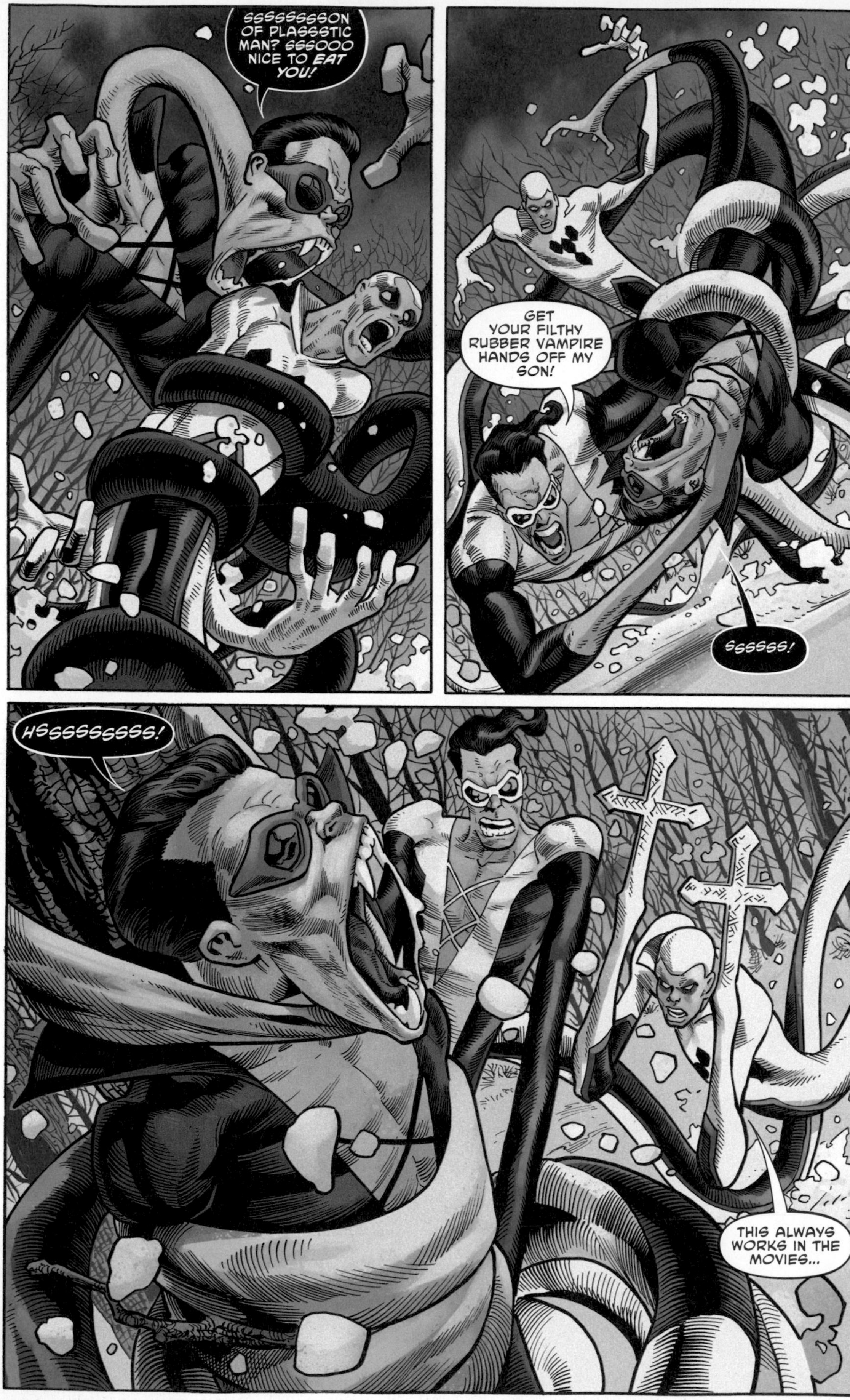
SSSSSSSSON OF PLASSSTIC MAN? SSSOOO NICE TO EAT YOU!
GET YOUR FILTHY RUBBER VAMPIRE HANDS OFF MY SON!
SSSSSS!
HSSSSSSSSS!
THIS ALWAYS WORKS IN THE MOVIES...

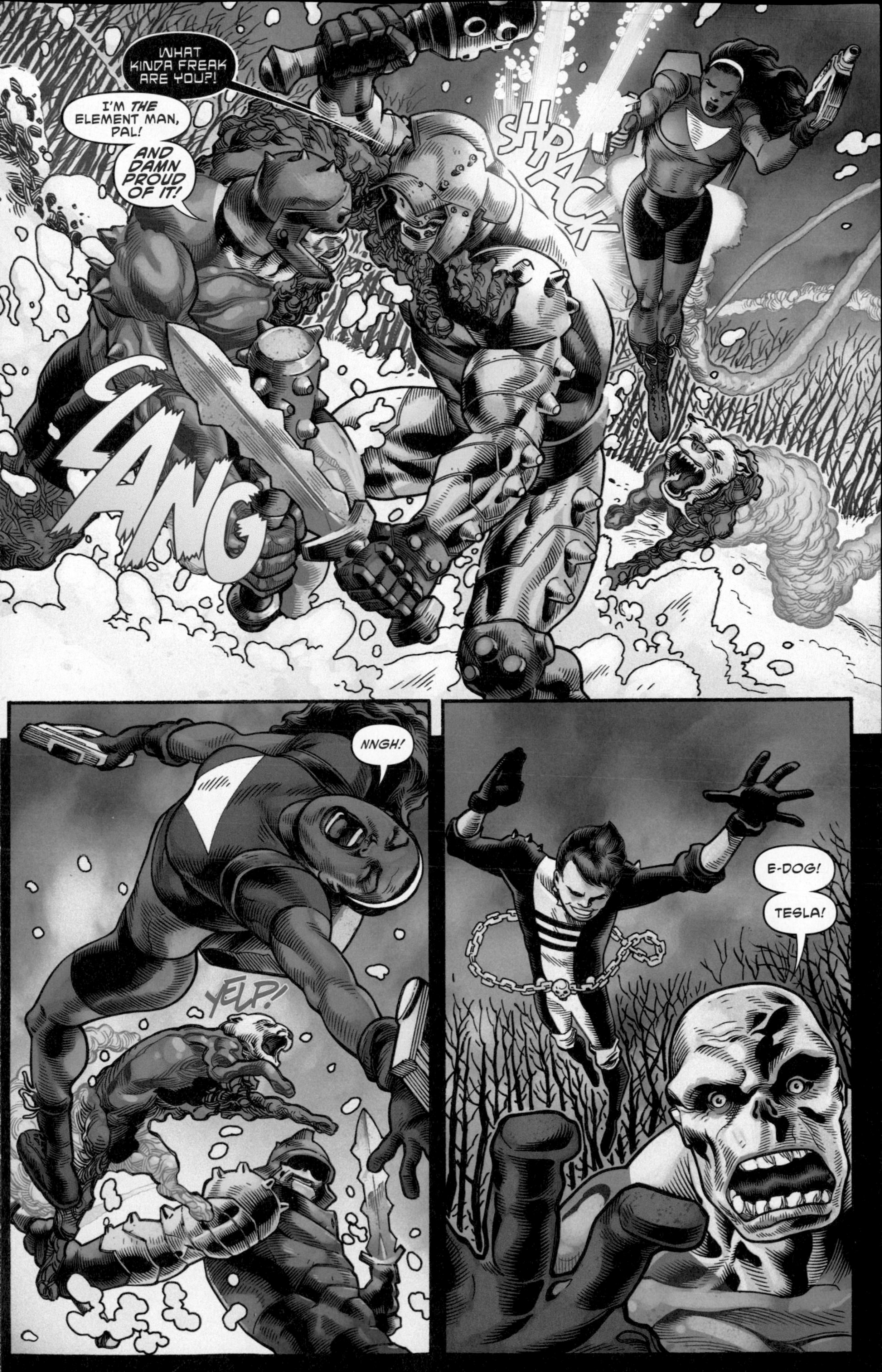
WHAT KINDA FREAK ARE YOU?!
I'M THE ELEMENT MAN, PAL!
AND DAMN PROUD OF IT!
SHRACK
CLANG
NNGH!
YELP!
E-DOG!
TESLA!

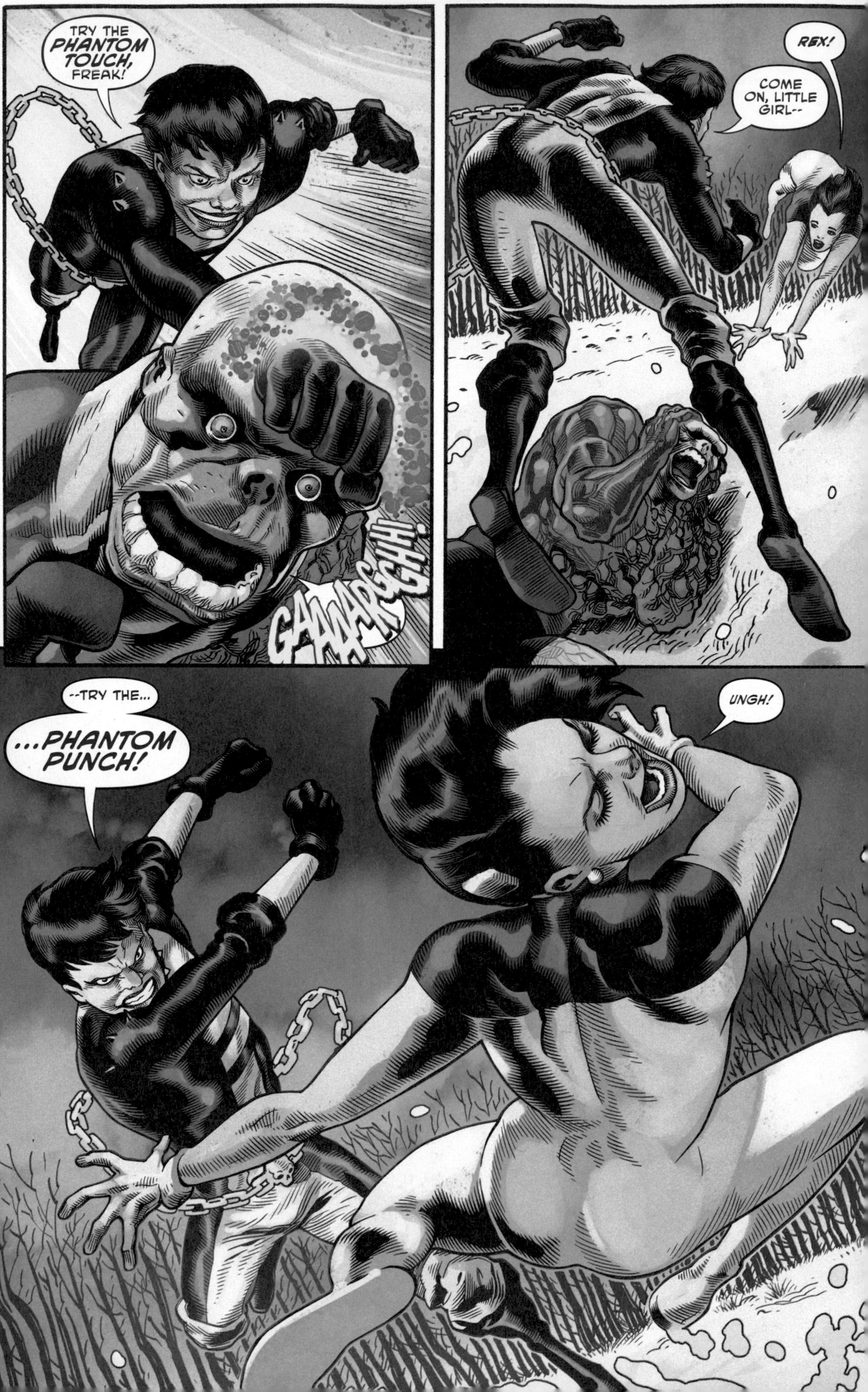
TRY THE PHANTOM TOUCH, FREAK!
GAAARGHH!
REX!
COME ON, LITTLE GIRL--
--TRY THE...
...PHANTOM PUNCH!
UNGH!

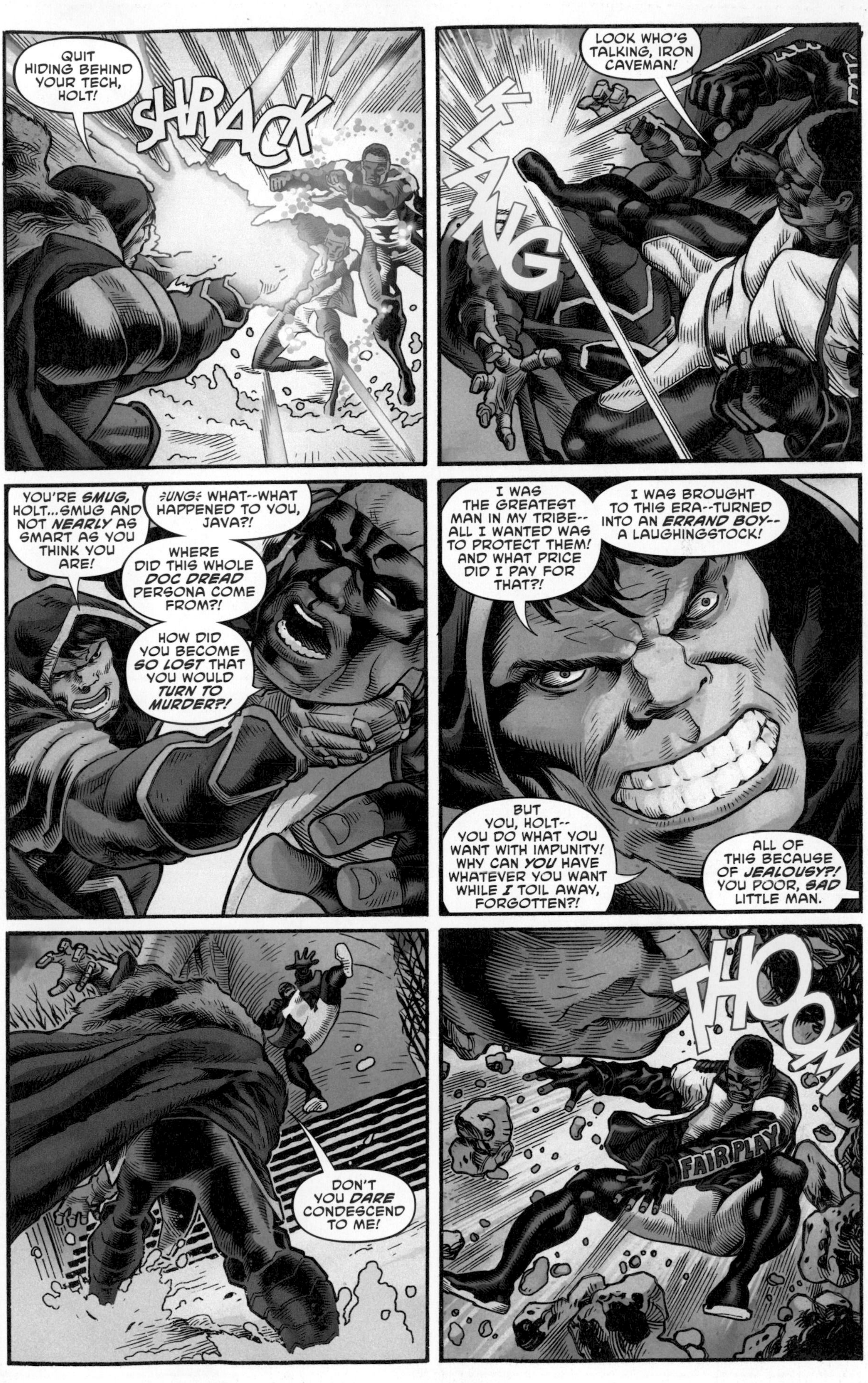
QUIT HIDING BEHIND YOUR TECH, HOLT!
SHRACK
LOOK WHO'S TALKING, IRON CAVEMAN!
KLANG
YOU'RE SMUG, HOLT...SMUG AND NOT NEARLY AS SMART AS YOU THINK YOU ARE!
UNG WHAT--WHAT HAPPENED TO YOU, JAVA?!
WHERE DID THIS WHOLE DOC DREAD PERSONA COME FROM?!
HOW DID YOU BECOME SO LOST THAT YOU WOULD TURN TO MURDER?!
I WAS THE GREATEST MAN IN MY TRIBE--ALL I WANTED WAS TO PROTECT THEM! AND WHAT PRICE DID I PAY FOR THAT?!
I WAS BROUGHT TO THIS ERA--TURNED INTO AN ERRAND BOY--A LAUGHINGSTOCK!
BUT YOU, HOLT--YOU DO WHAT YOU WANT WITH IMPUNITY! WHY CAN YOU HAVE WHATEVER YOU WANT WHILE I TOIL AWAY, FORGOTTEN?!
ALL OF THIS BECAUSE OF JEALOUSY?! YOU POOR, SAD LITTLE MAN.
DON'T YOU DARE CONDESCEND TO ME!
THOOM
FAIR PLAY

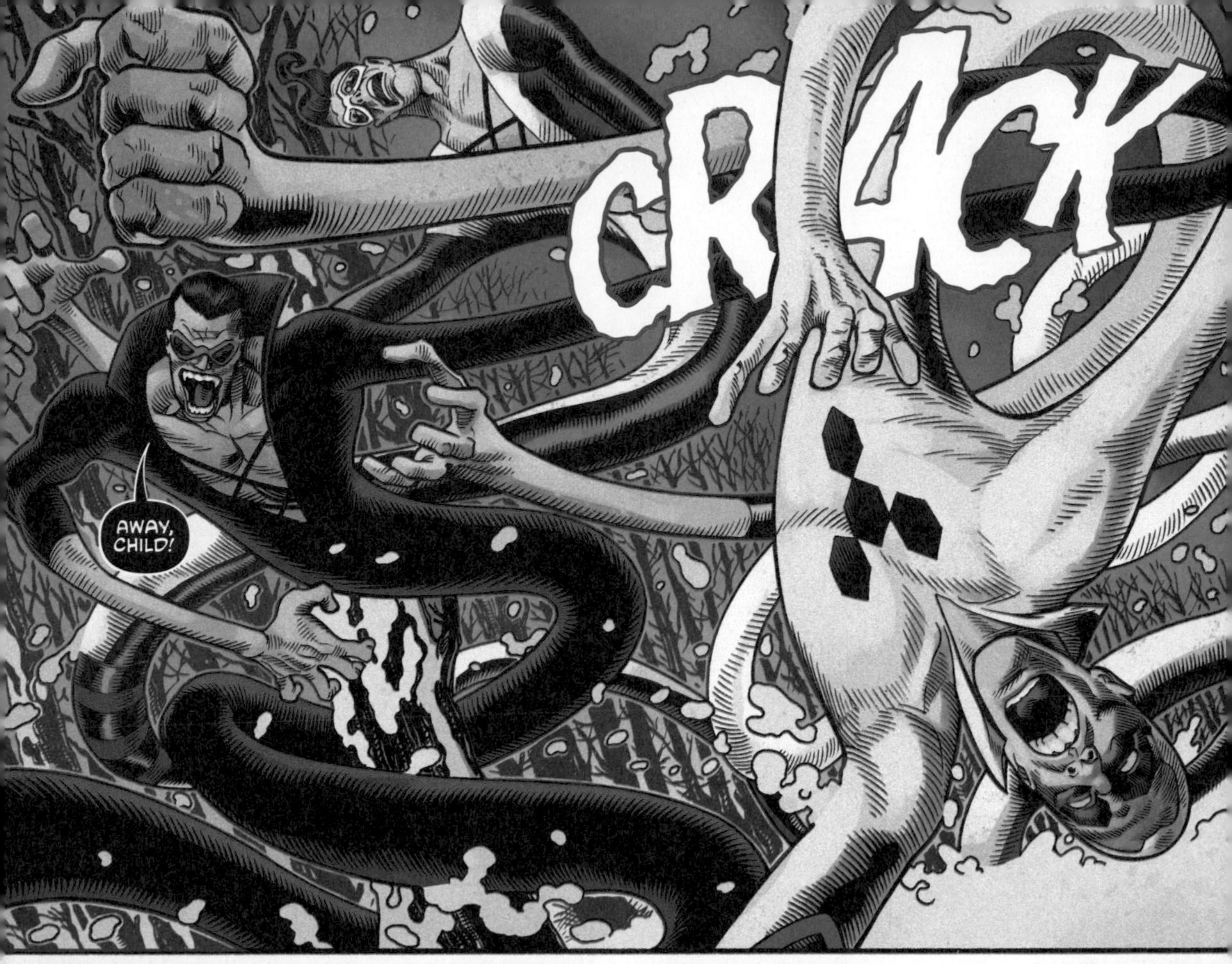
CRACK
AWAY, CHILD!

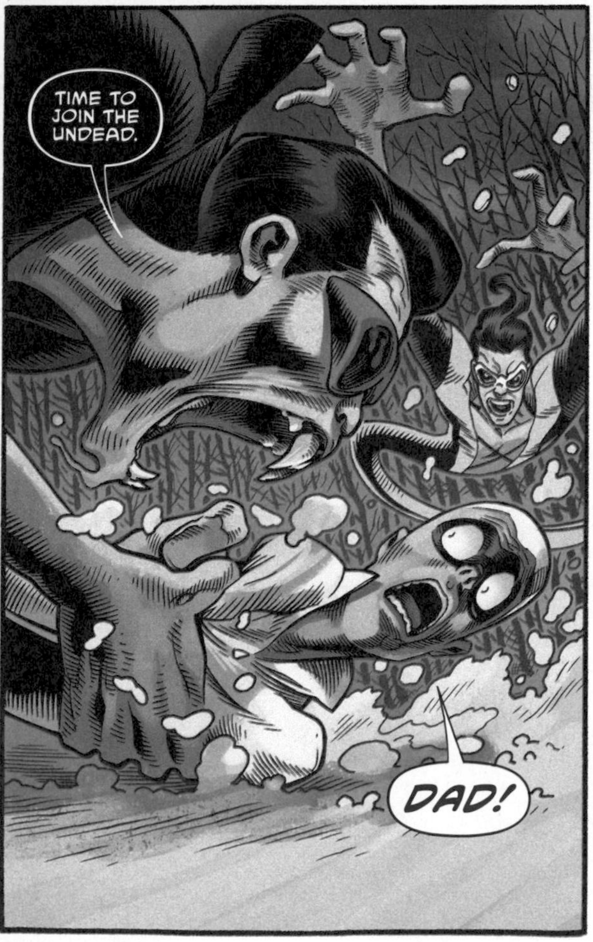
TIME TO JOIN THE UNDEAD.
DAD!

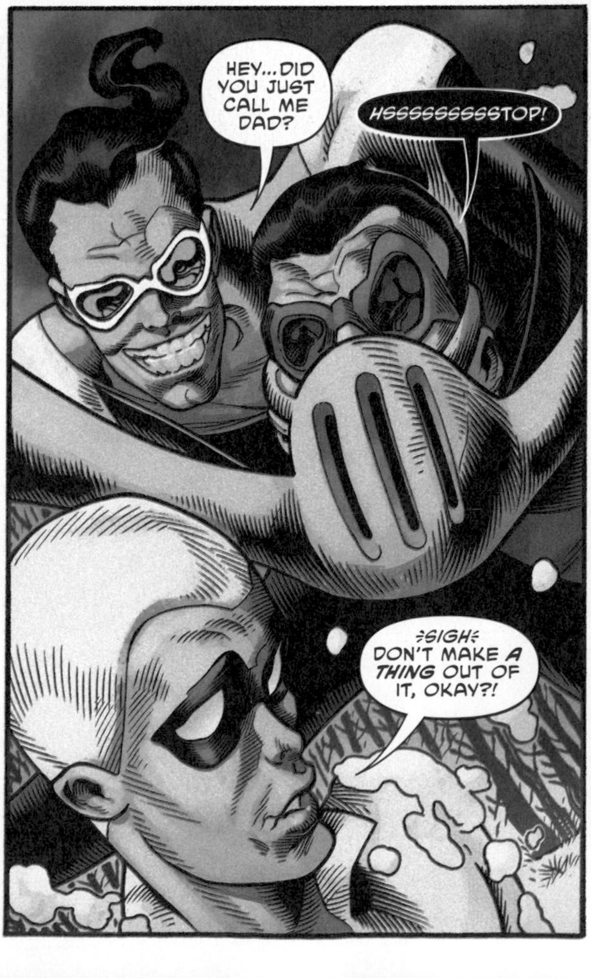
HEY...DID YOU JUST CALL ME DAD?
HSSSSSSSSSTOP!
SIGH
DON'T MAKE A THING OUT OF IT, OKAY?!

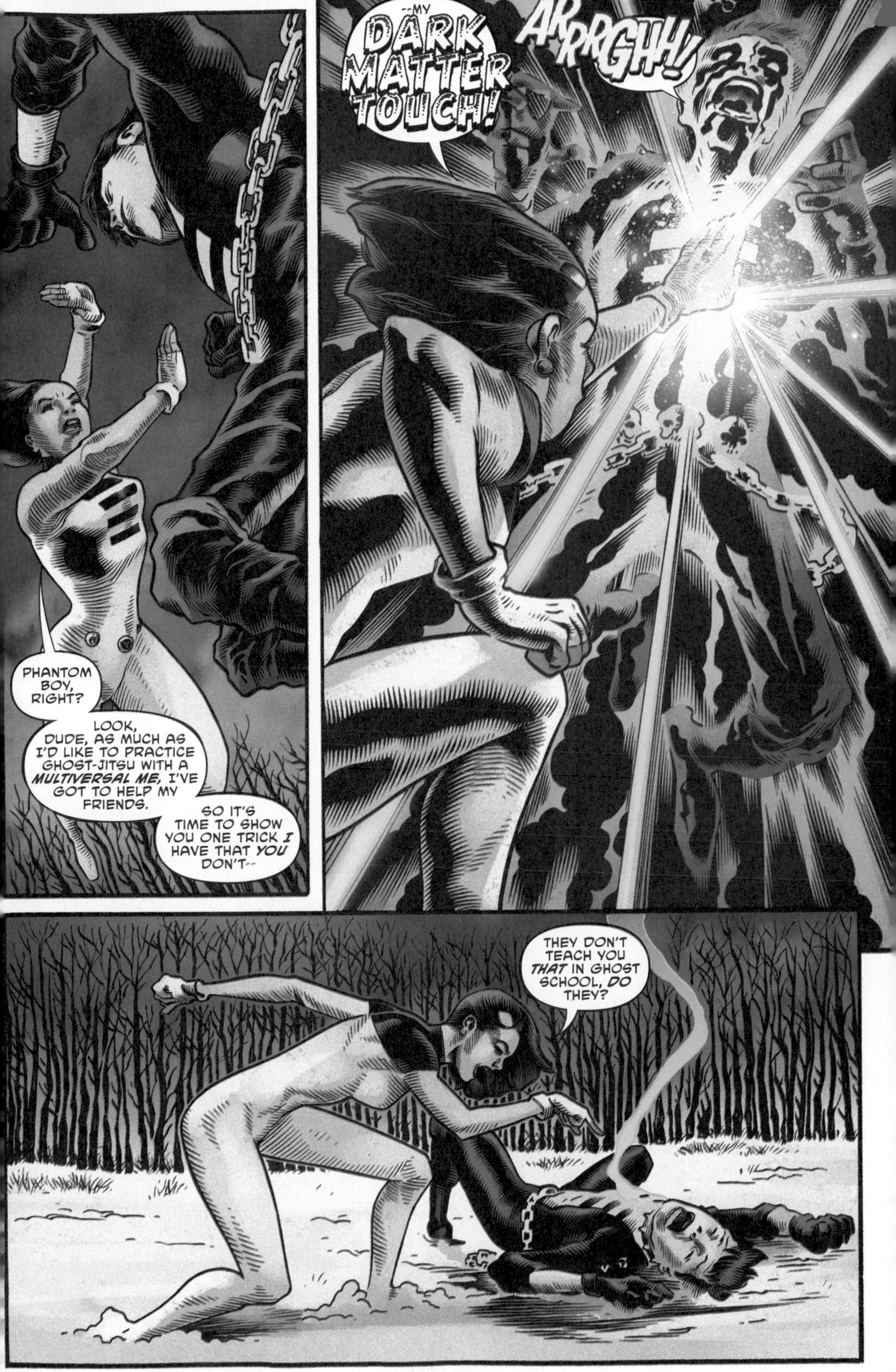
PHANTOM BOY, RIGHT?
LOOK, DUDE, AS MUCH AS I'D LIKE TO PRACTICE GHOST-JITSU WITH A MULTIVERSAL ME, I'VE GOT TO HELP MY FRIENDS.
SO IT'S TIME TO SHOW YOU ONE TRICK I HAVE THAT YOU DON'T--
--MY DARK MATTER TOUCH!
ARRRGHH!
THEY DON'T TEACH YOU THAT IN GHOST SCHOOL, DO THEY?

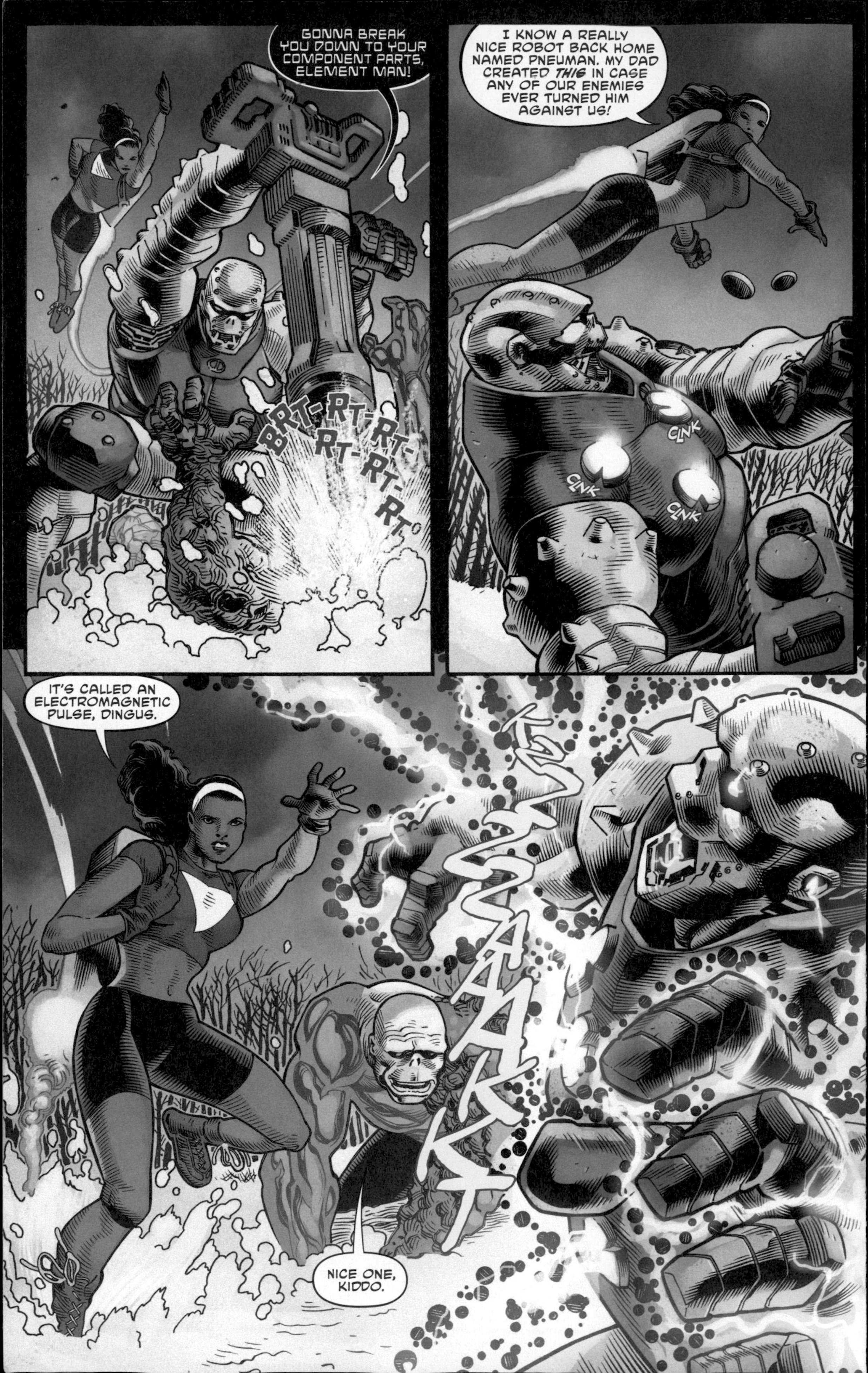
GONNA BREAK YOU DOWN TO YOUR COMPONENT PARTS, ELEMENT MAN!
BRT-RT-RT-RT-RT-RT-RT
I KNOW A REALLY NICE ROBOT BACK HOME NAMED PNEUMAN. MY DAD CREATED THIS IN CASE ANY OF OUR ENEMIES EVER TURNED HIM AGAINST US!
CLNK
CLNK
CLNK
IT'S CALLED AN ELECTROMAGNETIC PULSE, DINGUS.
NICE ONE, KIDDO.

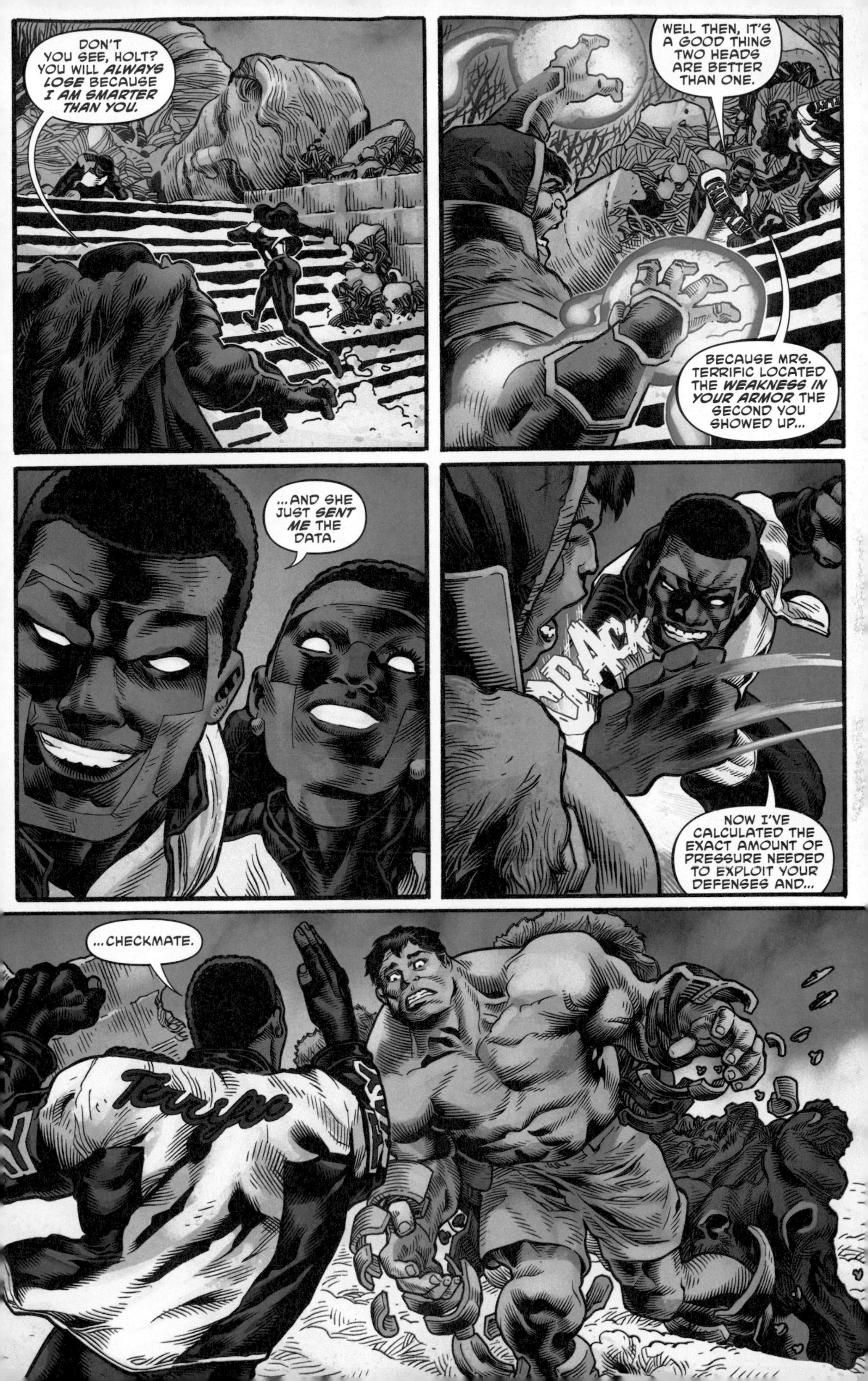
DON'T YOU SEE, HOLT? YOU WILL *ALWAYS LOSE* BECAUSE *I AM SMARTER THAN YOU.*
WELL THEN, IT'S A GOOD THING TWO HEADS ARE BETTER THAN ONE.
BECAUSE MRS. TERRIFIC LOCATED THE *WEAKNESS IN YOUR ARMOR* THE SECOND YOU SHOWED UP...
...AND SHE JUST *SENT ME* THE DATA.
CRACK
NOW I'VE CALCULATED THE EXACT AMOUNT OF PRESSURE NEEDED TO EXPLOIT YOUR DEFENSES AND...
...CHECKMATE.
Terrific

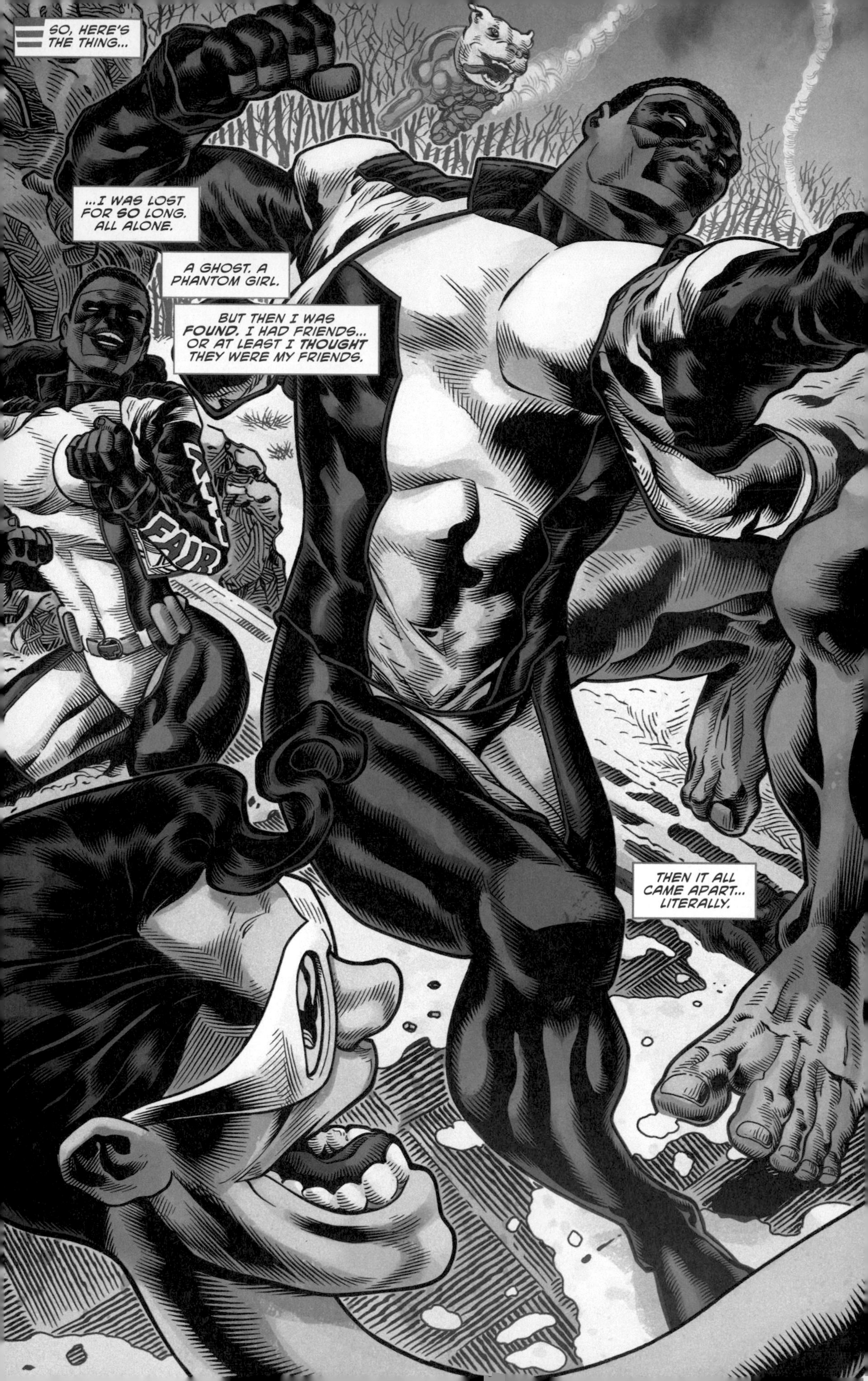
SO, HERE'S THE THING...
...I WAS LOST FOR SO LONG. ALL ALONE.
A GHOST. A PHANTOM GIRL.
BUT THEN I WAS FOUND. I HAD FRIENDS... OR AT LEAST I THOUGHT THEY WERE MY FRIENDS.
THEN IT ALL CAME APART... LITERALLY.

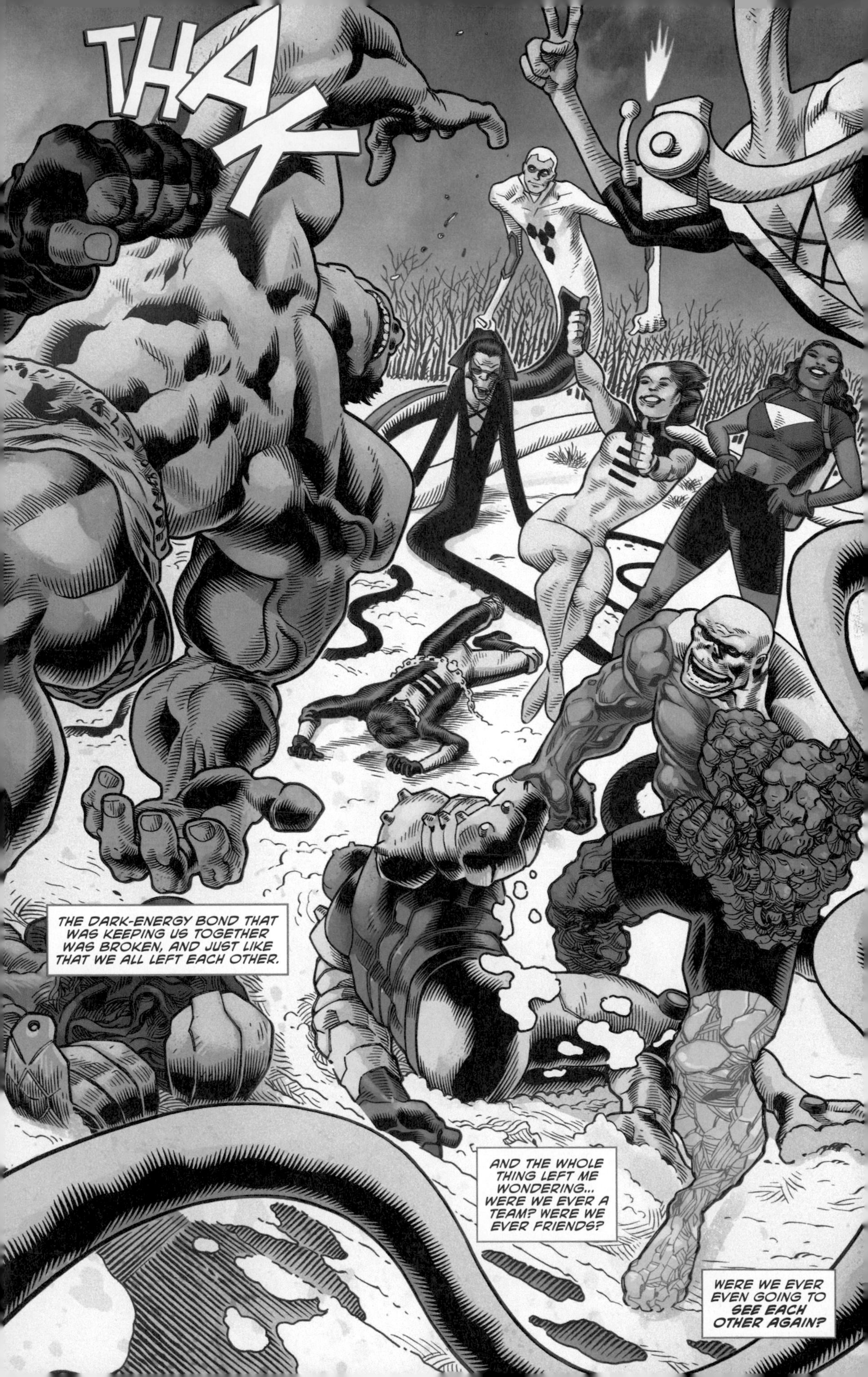
THAK
THE DARK-ENERGY BOND THAT WAS KEEPING US TOGETHER WAS BROKEN, AND JUST LIKE THAT WE ALL LEFT EACH OTHER.
AND THE WHOLE THING LEFT ME WONDERING... WERE WE EVER A TEAM? WERE WE EVER FRIENDS?
WERE WE EVER EVEN GOING TO SEE EACH OTHER AGAIN?

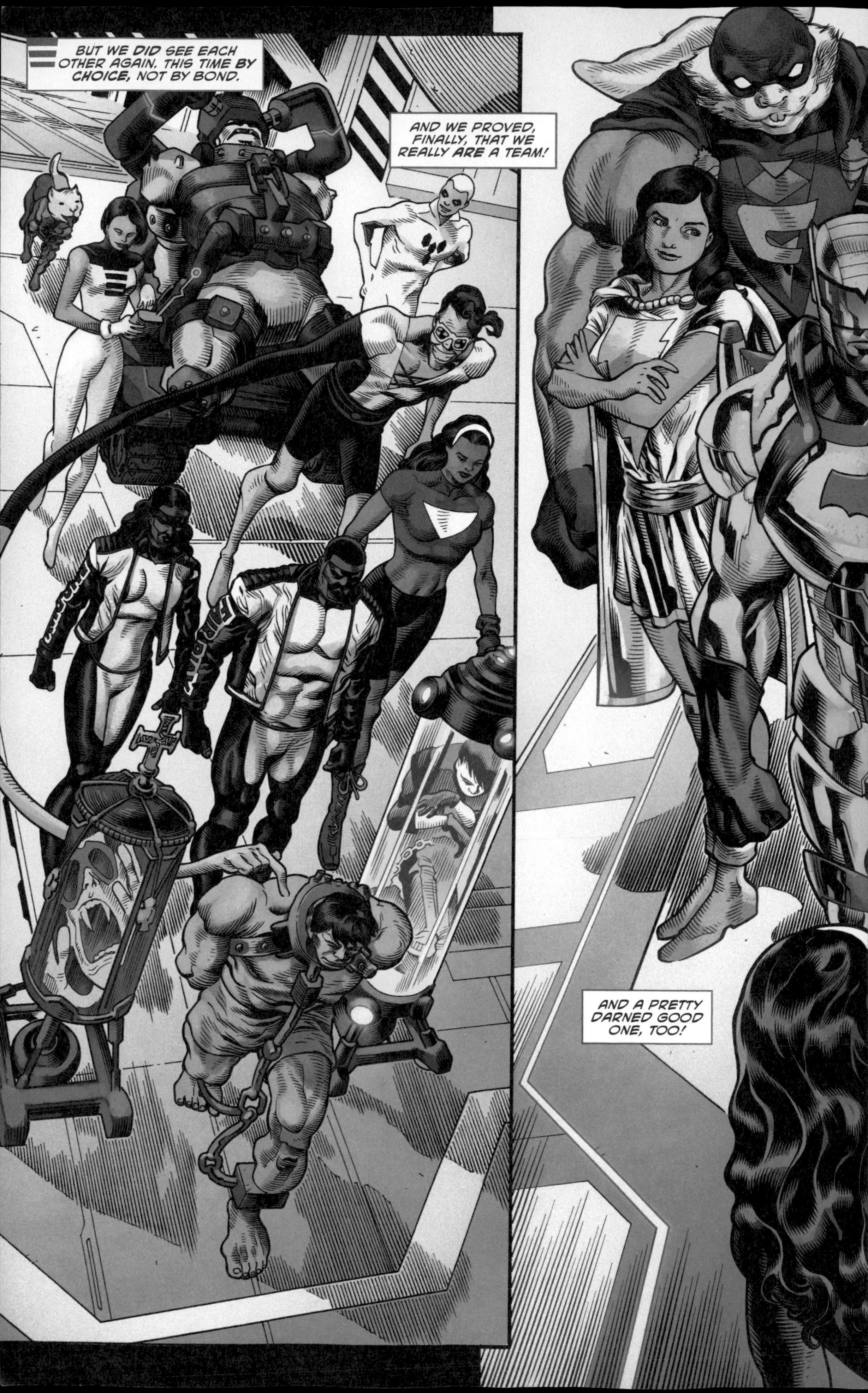
BUT WE DID SEE EACH OTHER AGAIN. THIS TIME BY CHOICE, NOT BY BOND.
AND WE PROVED, FINALLY, THAT WE REALLY ARE A TEAM!
AND A PRETTY DARNED GOOD ONE, TOO!

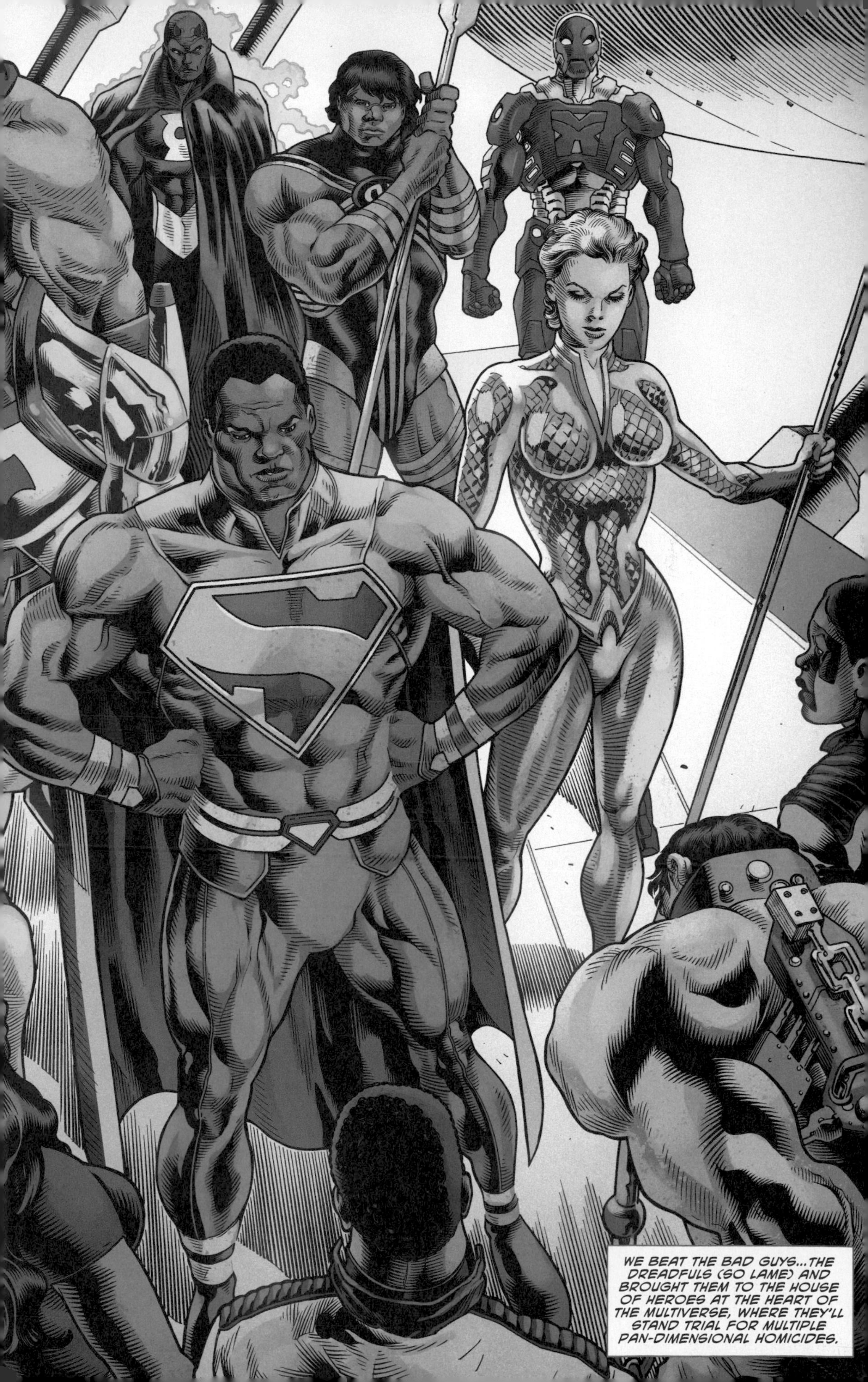
WE BEAT THE BAD GUYS...THE DREADFULS (SO LAME) AND BROUGHT THEM TO THE HOUSE OF HEROES AT THE HEART OF THE MULTIVERSE, WHERE THEY'LL STAND TRIAL FOR MULTIPLE PAN-DIMENSIONAL HOMICIDES.

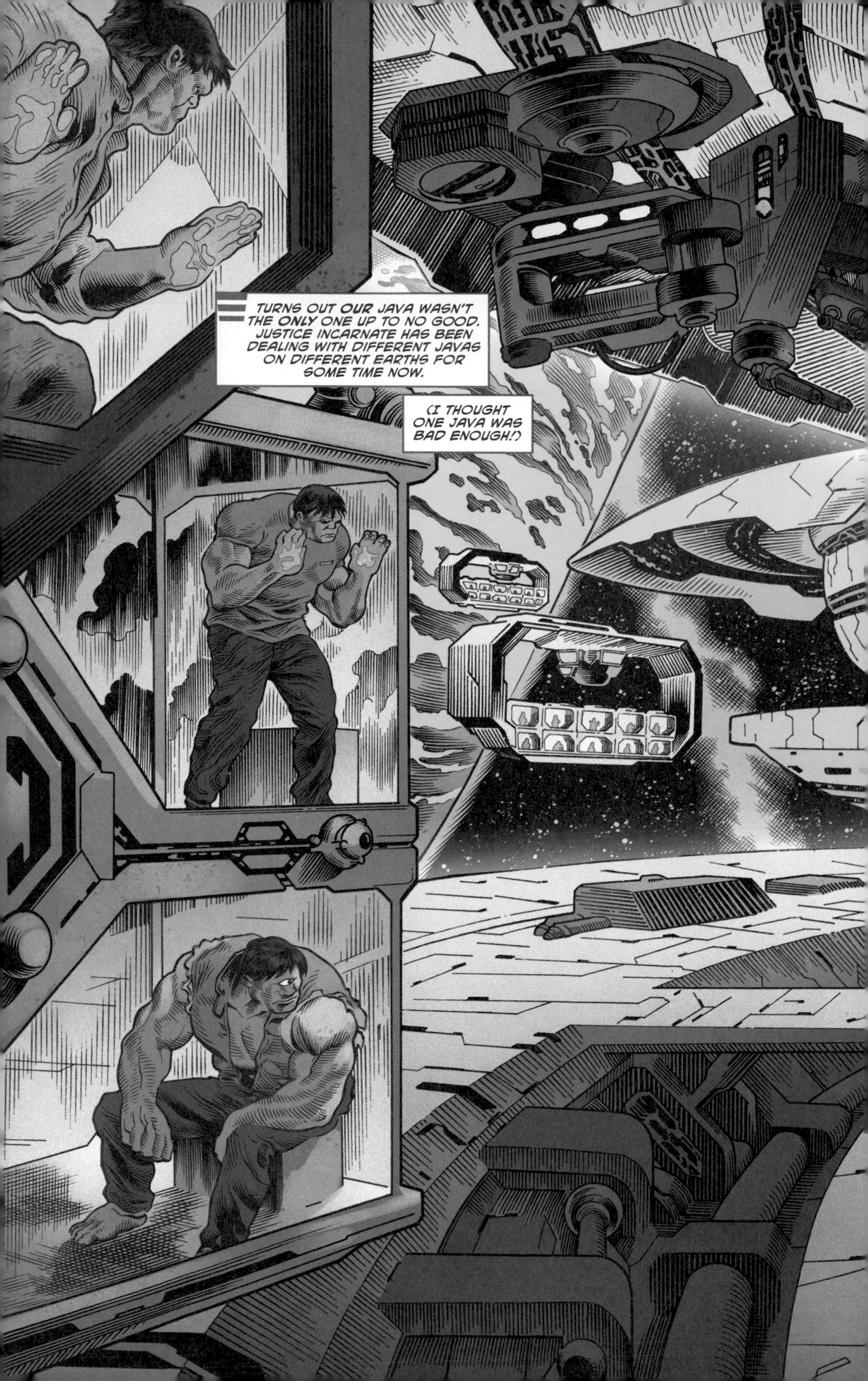
TURNS OUT OUR JAVA WASN'T THE ONLY ONE UP TO NO GOOD. JUSTICE INCARNATE HAS BEEN DEALING WITH DIFFERENT JAVAS ON DIFFERENT EARTHS FOR SOME TIME NOW.
(I THOUGHT ONE JAVA WAS BAD ENOUGH!)

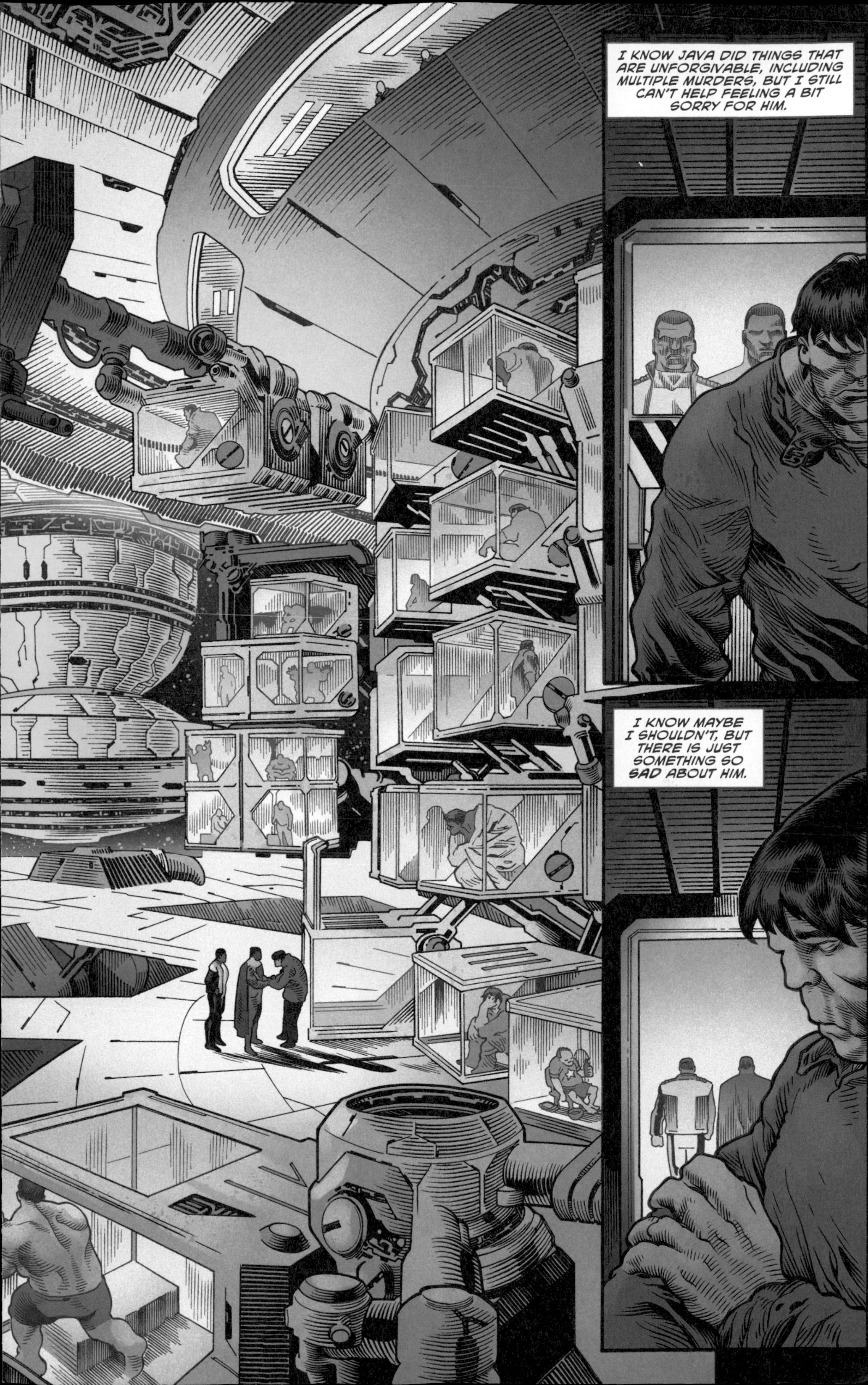
I KNOW JAVA DID THINGS THAT ARE UNFORGIVABLE, INCLUDING MULTIPLE MURDERS, BUT I STILL CAN'T HELP FEELING A BIT SORRY FOR HIM.
I KNOW MAYBE I SHOULDN'T, BUT THERE IS JUST SOMETHING SO SAD ABOUT HIM.

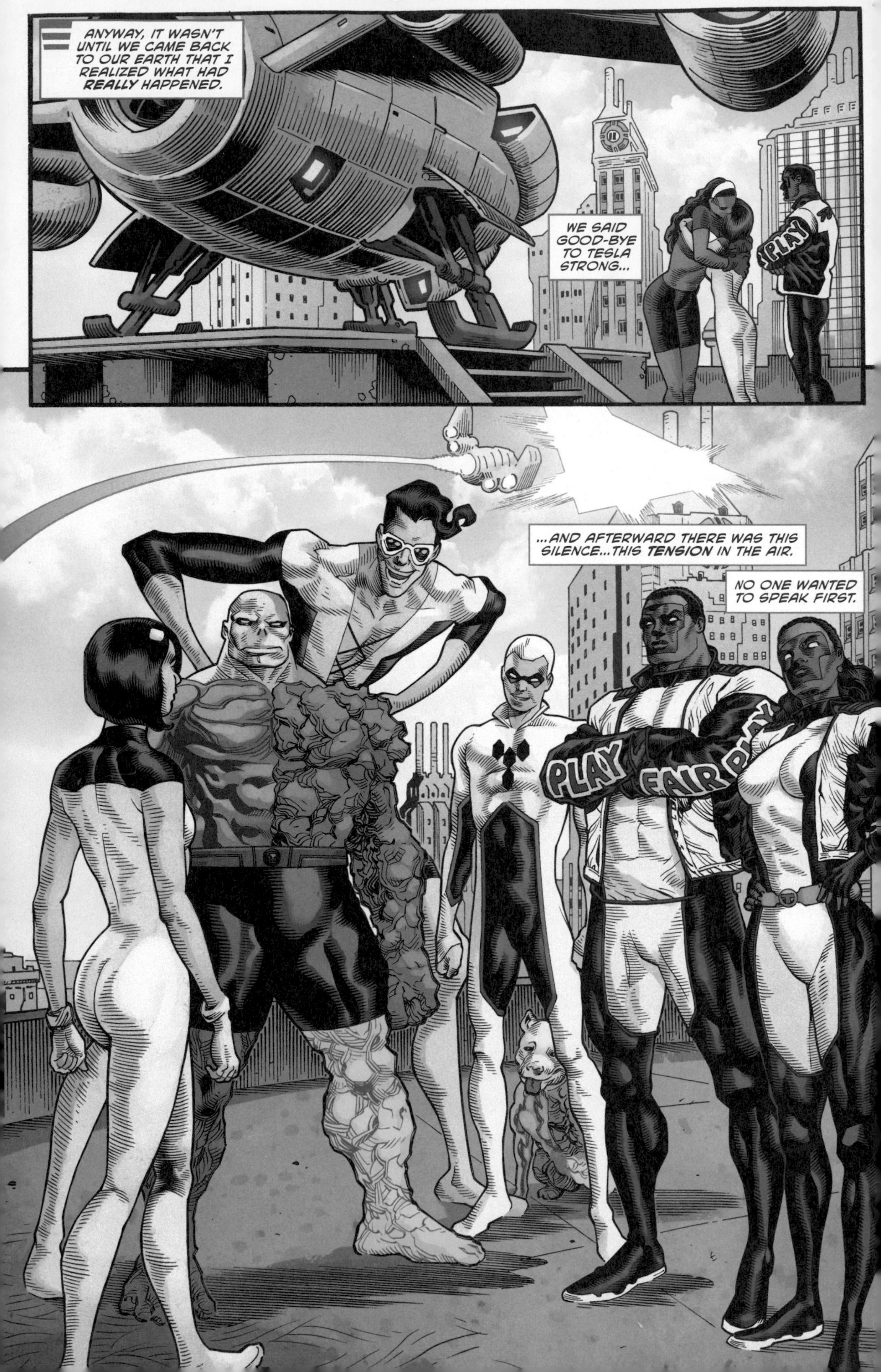
ANYWAY, IT WASN'T UNTIL WE CAME BACK TO OUR EARTH THAT I REALIZED WHAT HAD REALLY HAPPENED.
WE SAID GOOD-BYE TO TESLA STRONG...
PLAY
...AND AFTERWARD THERE WAS THIS SILENCE...THIS TENSION IN THE AIR.
NO ONE WANTED TO SPEAK FIRST.
PLAY FAIR PLAY

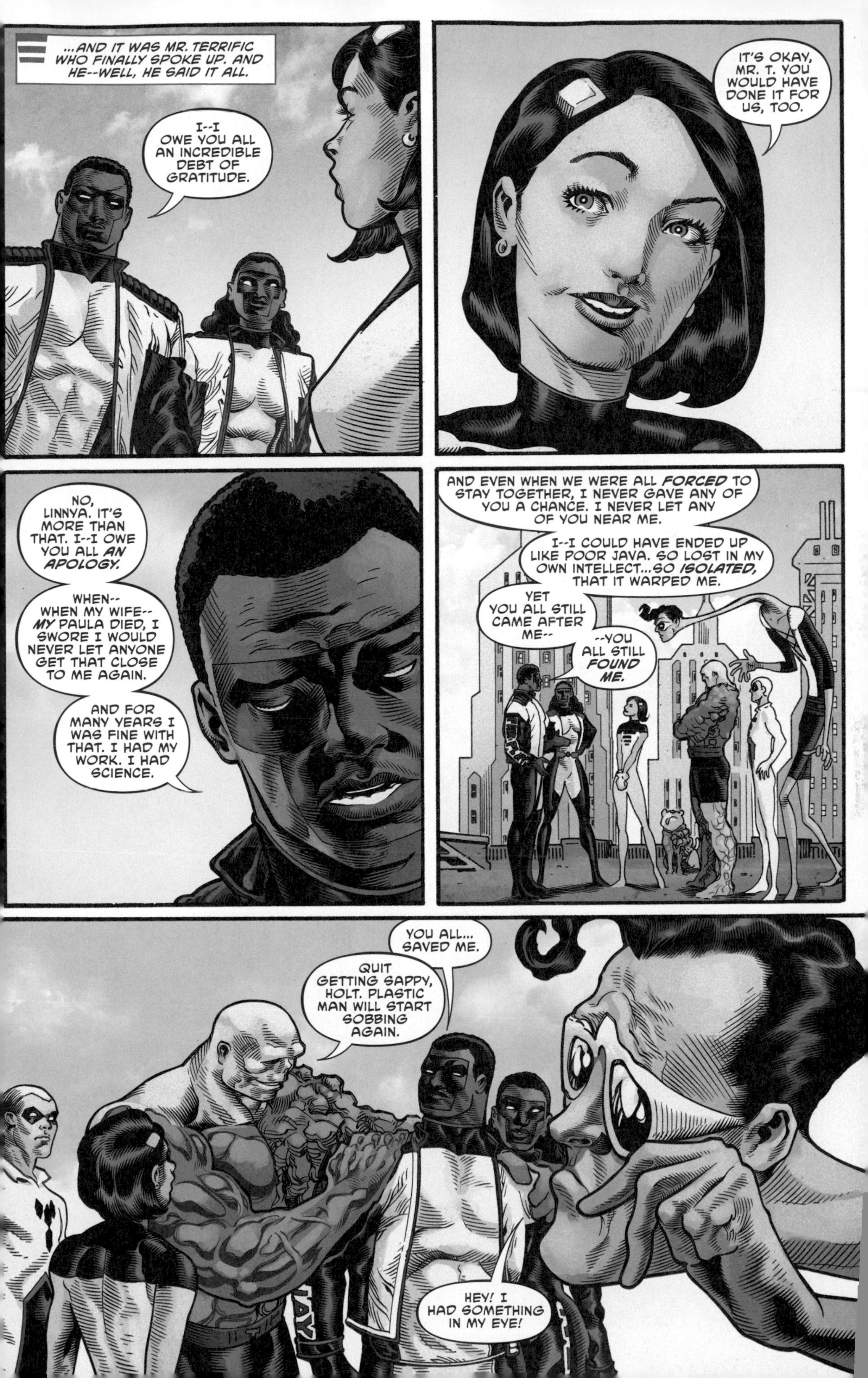
...AND IT WAS MR. TERRIFIC WHO FINALLY SPOKE UP. AND HE--WELL, HE SAID IT ALL.
I--I OWE YOU ALL AN INCREDIBLE DEBT OF GRATITUDE.
IT'S OKAY, MR. T. YOU WOULD HAVE DONE IT FOR US, TOO.
NO, LINNYA. IT'S MORE THAN THAT. I--I OWE YOU ALL AN APOLOGY.
WHEN-- WHEN MY WIFE-- MY PAULA DIED, I SWORE I WOULD NEVER LET ANYONE GET THAT CLOSE TO ME AGAIN.
AND FOR MANY YEARS I WAS FINE WITH THAT. I HAD MY WORK. I HAD SCIENCE.
AND EVEN WHEN WE WERE ALL FORCED TO STAY TOGETHER, I NEVER GAVE ANY OF YOU A CHANCE. I NEVER LET ANY OF YOU NEAR ME.
I--I COULD HAVE ENDED UP LIKE POOR JAVA. SO LOST IN MY OWN INTELLECT...SO ISOLATED, THAT IT WARPED ME.
YET YOU ALL STILL CAME AFTER ME--
--YOU ALL STILL FOUND ME.
YOU ALL... SAVED ME.
QUIT GETTING SAPPY, HOLT. PLASTIC MAN WILL START SOBBING AGAIN.
HEY! I HAD SOMETHING IN MY EYE!

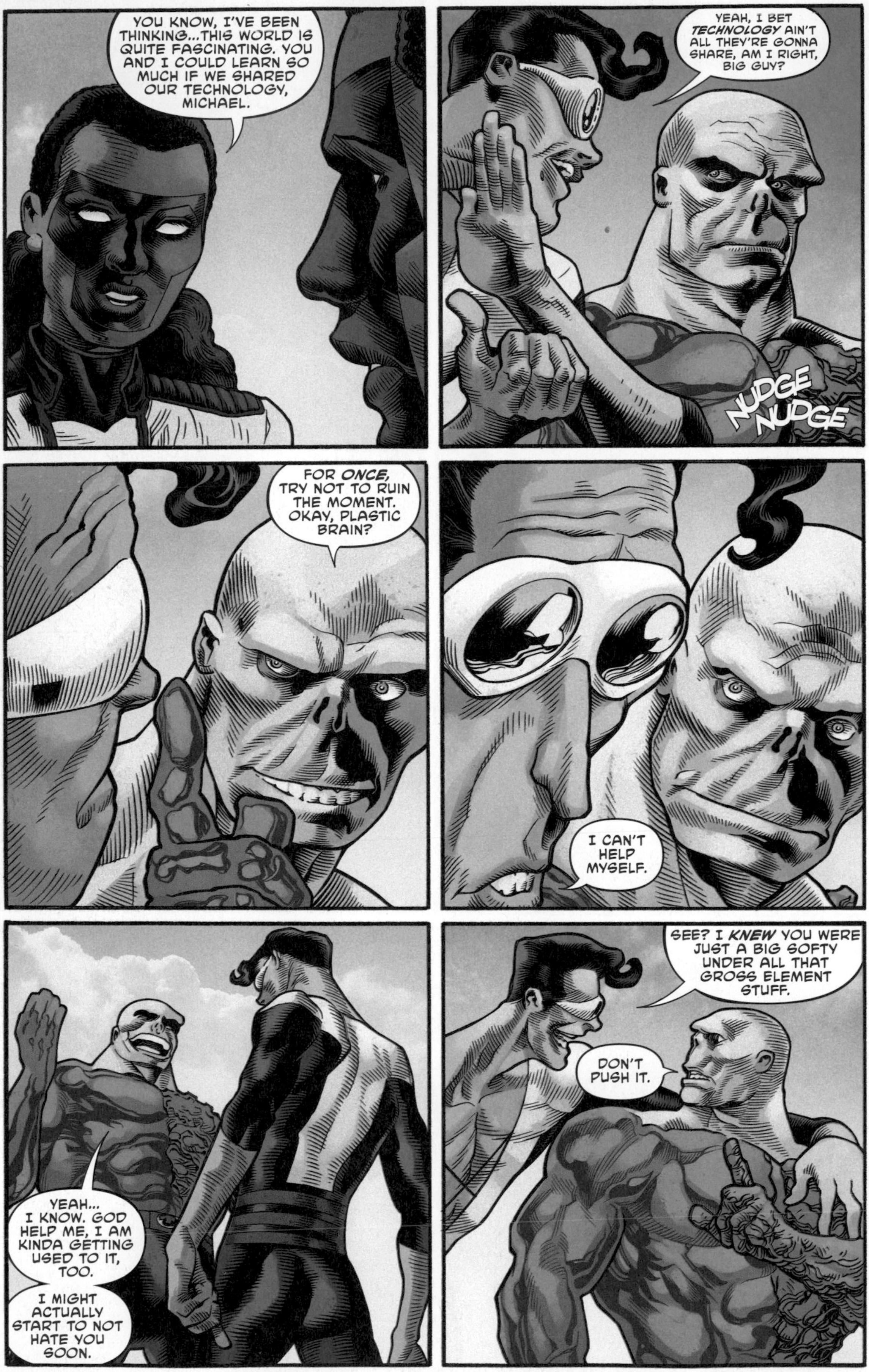

YOU KNOW, I'VE BEEN THINKING...THIS WORLD IS QUITE FASCINATING. YOU AND I COULD LEARN SO MUCH IF WE SHARED OUR TECHNOLOGY, MICHAEL.
YEAH, I BET TECHNOLOGY AIN'T ALL THEY'RE GONNA SHARE, AM I RIGHT, BIG GUY?
NUDGE NUDGE
FOR ONCE, TRY NOT TO RUIN THE MOMENT. OKAY, PLASTIC BRAIN?
I CAN'T HELP MYSELF.
YEAH... I KNOW. GOD HELP ME, I AM KINDA GETTING USED TO IT, TOO.
I MIGHT ACTUALLY START TO NOT HATE YOU SOON.
SEE? I KNEW YOU WERE JUST A BIG SOFTY UNDER ALL THAT GROSS ELEMENT STUFF.
DON'T PUSH IT.

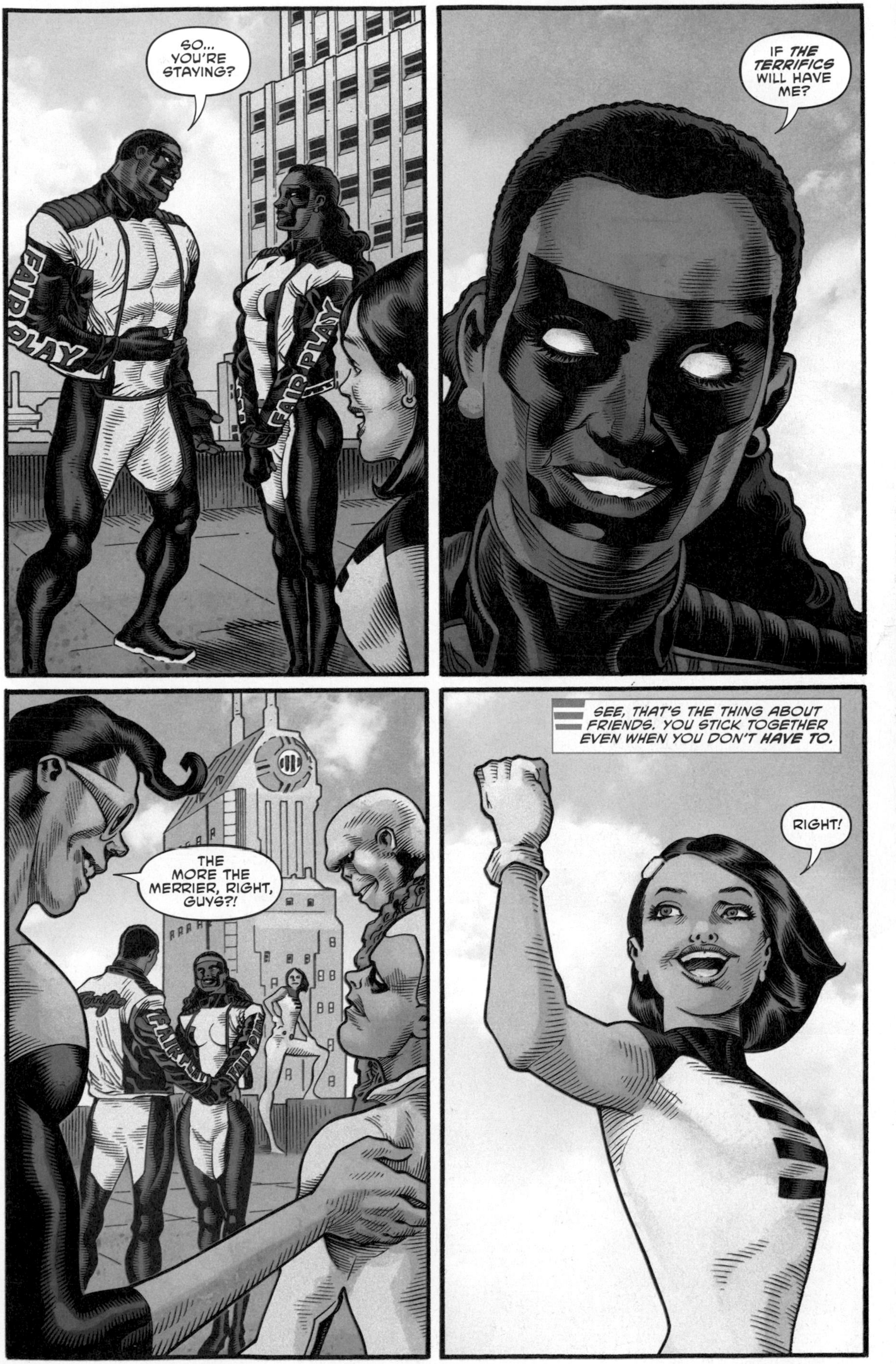
SO... YOU'RE STAYING?
IF *THE TERRIFICS* WILL HAVE ME?
THE MORE THE MERRIER, RIGHT, GUYS?!
SEE, THAT'S THE THING ABOUT FRIENDS. YOU STICK TOGETHER EVEN WHEN YOU DON'T **HAVE TO.**
RIGHT!

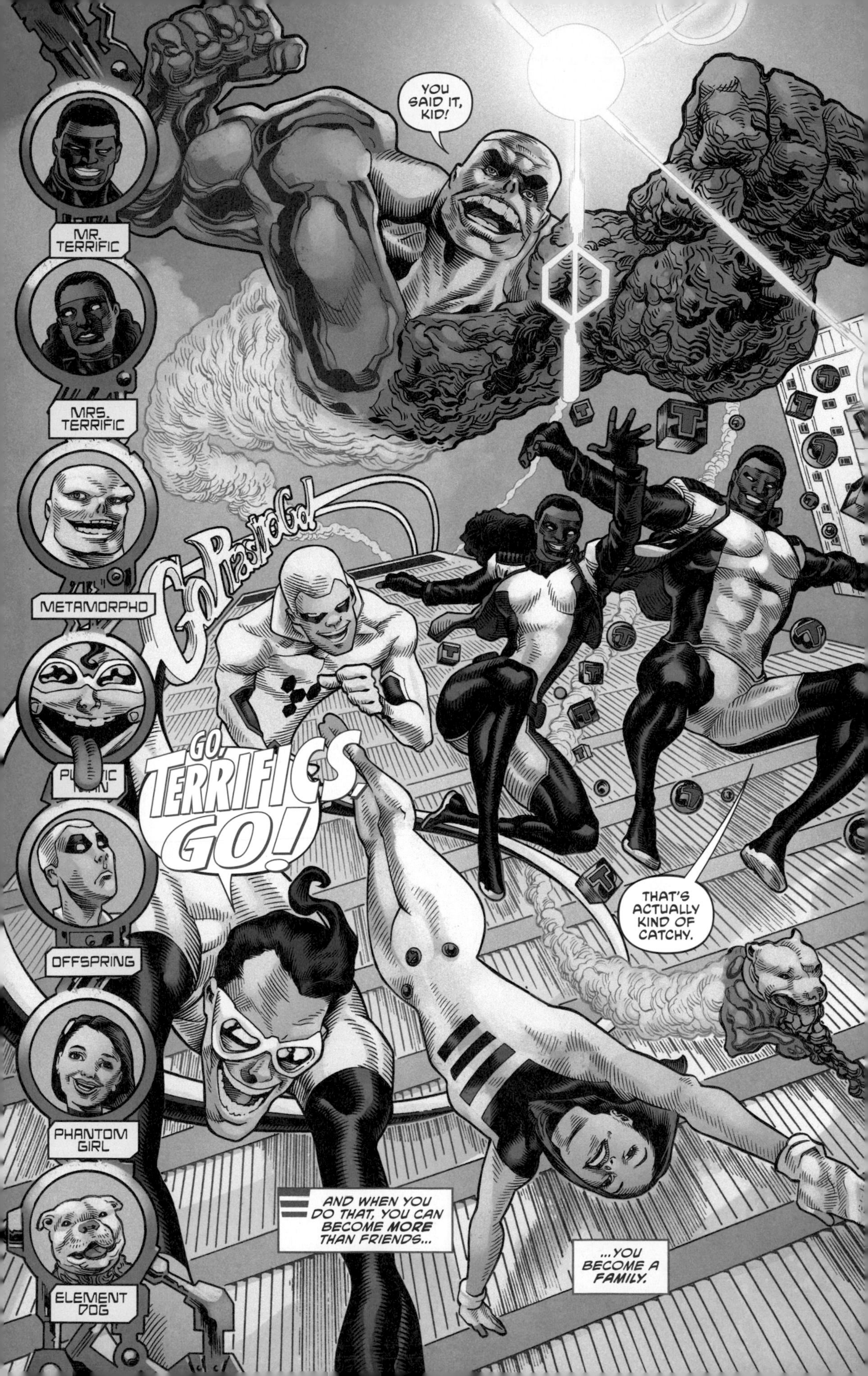

MR. TERRIFIC
MRS. TERRIFIC
METAMORPHO
OFFSPRING
PHANTOM GIRL
ELEMENT DOG
YOU SAID IT, KID!
Go Plastic Go!
GO, TERRIFICS, GO!
THAT'S ACTUALLY KIND OF CATCHY.
AND WHEN YOU DO THAT, YOU CAN BECOME MORE THAN FRIENDS...
...YOU BECOME A FAMILY.

"Great writing, awesome artwork, fun premise, and looks of cool action; GREEN ARROW's got it all."
–IGN

"Sharply written and beautiful artwork."
–CRAVE ONLINE

GREEN ARROW
VOL. 4: THE KILL MACHINE
JEFF LEMIRE with ANDREA SORRENTINO

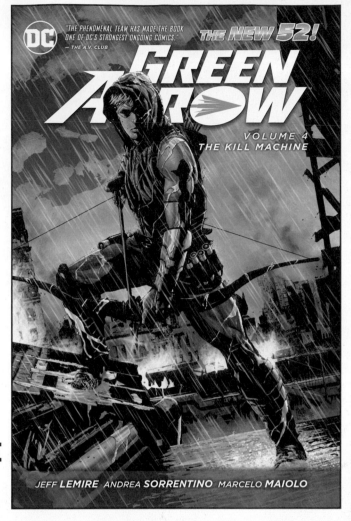

GREEN ARROW VOL. 5: THE OUTSIDERS WAR

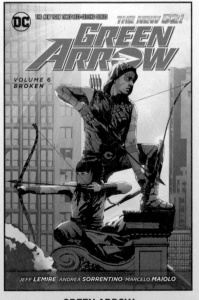

GREEN ARROW VOL. 6: BROKEN

READ THE ENTIRE EPIC!

GREEN ARROW
VOL. 1: THE MIDAS TOUCH

GREEN ARROW
VOL. 2: TRIPLE THREAT

GREEN ARROW
VOL. 3: HARROW

GREEN ARROW
VOL. 7: KINGDOM

GREEN ARROW
VOL. 8: THE NIGHTBIRDS

"This is the work of two men at the top of their games."
–THE NEW YORK TIMES

"Where nightmares and reality collide."
–THE WASHINGTON POST

"The Batman of your wildest nightmares."
–POLYGON

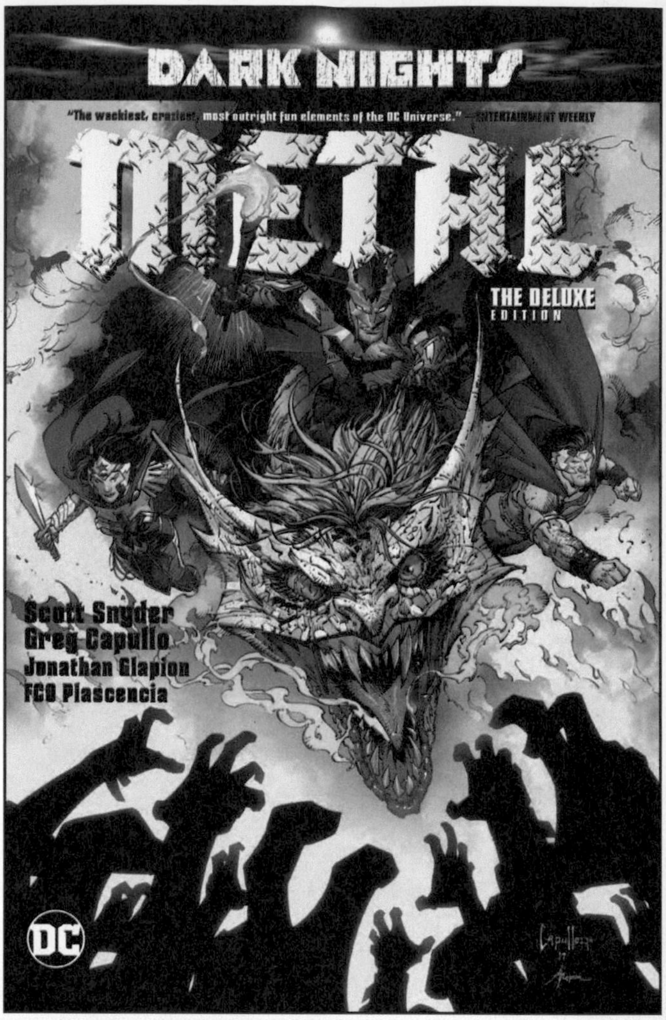
DARK NIGHTS
"The wackiest, craziest, most outright fun elements of the DC Universe." —ENTERTAINMENT WEEKLY
METAL
THE DELUXE EDITION
Scott Snyder
Greg Capullo
Jonathan Glapion
FCO Plascencia
DC

DARK NIGHTS:
METAL
SCOTT SNYDER
GREG CAPULLO

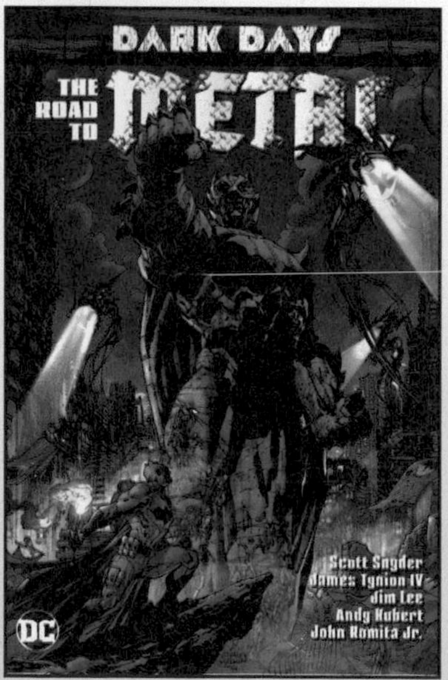
DARK DAYS
THE ROAD TO METAL
Scott Snyder
James Tynion IV
Jim Lee
Andy Kubert
John Romita Jr.
DC

DARK DAYS: THE ROAD TO METAL

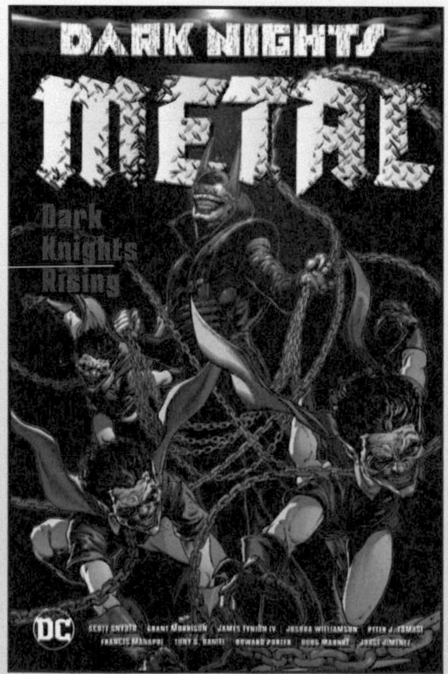
DARK NIGHTS
METAL
Dark Knights Rising
DC

DARK NIGHTS: METAL: DARK KNIGHTS RISING

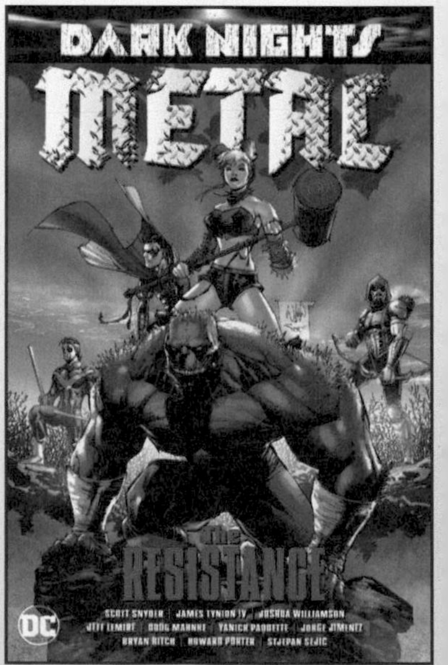
DARK NIGHTS
METAL
The RESISTANCE
DC

DARK NIGHTS: METAL: THE RESISTANCE

Get more DC graphic novels wherever comics and books are sold!

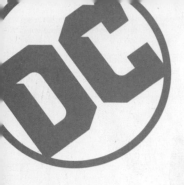